IMAGES
of America

MIDDLETOWN PACEMAKERS

THE STORY OF AN OHIO HOT ROD CLUB

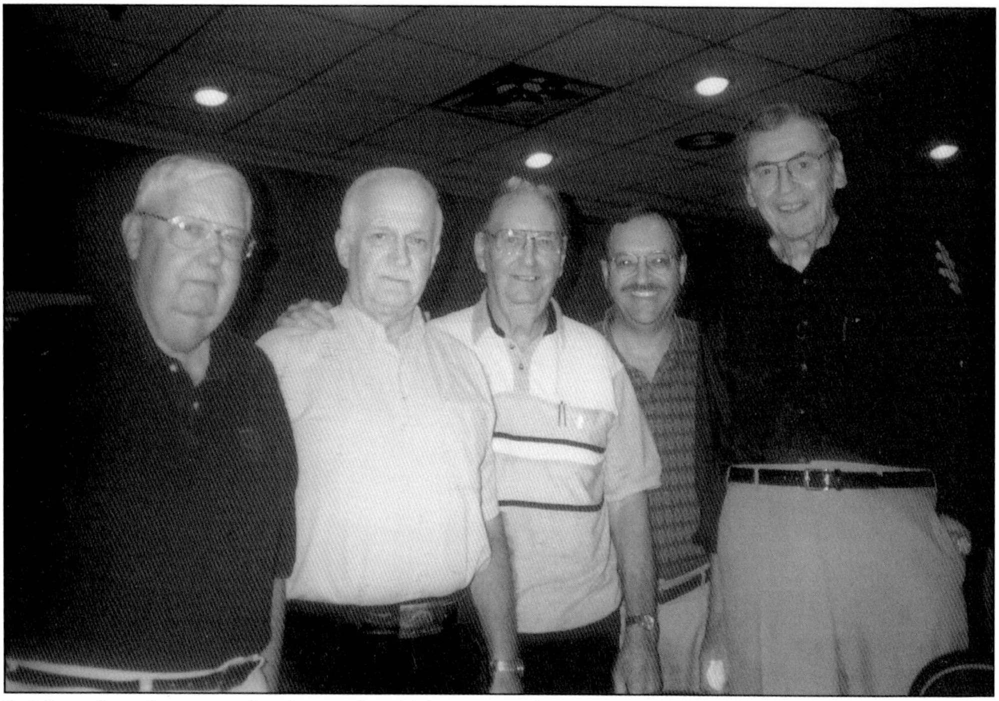

Lifelong friends pose at the September 2001 Pacemaker reunion at the Country Buffet Restaurant in Middletown. From left to right, they are Ray Palmer, Bill Burton, Wilbur "Robbie" Roberson, author Ron Roberson, and Harold "Mike" Michael. (Roberson collection, 2001.)

DEDICATION

A man must have friends or make friends; for no one ever went to heaven alone.
- John Wesley

This book is dedicated to the many men and women who wore the Pacemaker jackets and tee shirts over the club's fifteen-year run. And especially to…men like Dad, Mike, Ray, Carl, Bill, Gene, Darryl and Jim, who gave the club its heart… men like Alex, Fred, Sully, Paul and Grandpa Bill, who gave the club its soul… men like Herb, Jerry, Don, Earnie, Harold and Dick, who gave the club its character… and women like Mom, Polly, Marge, Gloria, Betty, Delores, Marcia and Kathy, who gave the club its charm and grace. To all of you this work is dedicated with love and respect.

IMAGES
of America

MIDDLETOWN PACEMAKERS

THE STORY OF AN OHIO HOT ROD CLUB

Ron Roberson

ARCADIA
PUBLISHING

ISBN 978-0-7385-1957-9

Published by Arcadia Publishing
Charleston, South Carolina

Printed in the United States of America

Library of Congress Catalog Card Number: 2002102515

For all general information contact Arcadia Publishing at:
Telephone 843-853-2070
Fax 843-853-0044
E-mail sales@arcadiapublishing.com
For customer service and orders:
Toll-Free 1-888-313-2665

Visit us on the Internet at www.arcadiapublishing.com

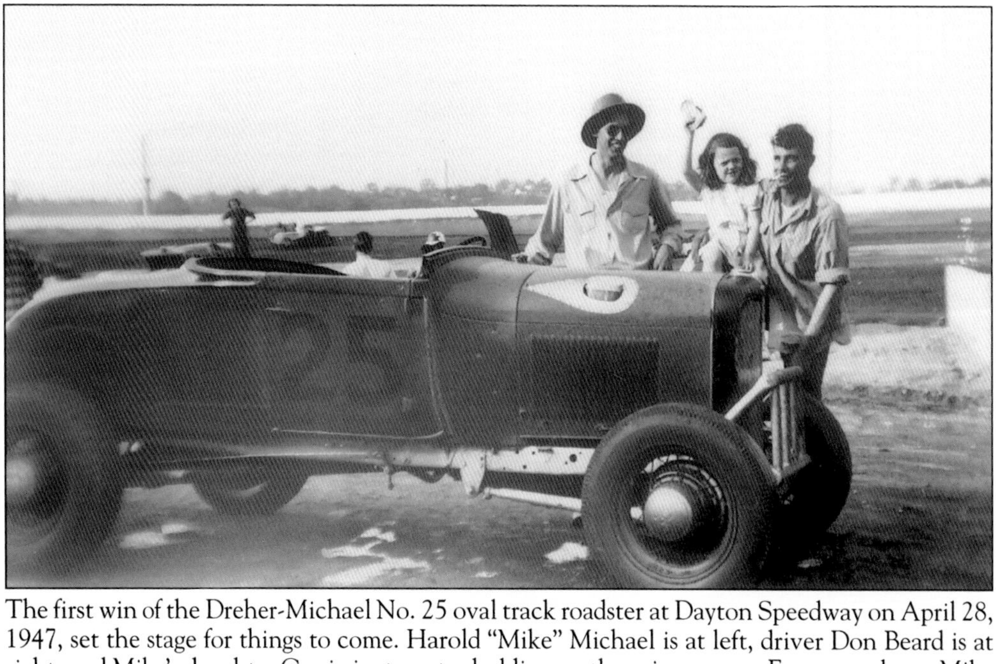

The first win of the Dreher-Michael No. 25 oval track roadster at Dayton Speedway on April 28, 1947, set the stage for things to come. Harold "Mike" Michael is at left, driver Don Beard is at right, and Mike's daughter Cassie is at center holding up the prize money. Four years later, Mike would start a hot rod club called the Middletown Pacemakers. (Michael collection, 1947.)

CONTENTS

ACKNOWLEDGMENTS

Awards become corroded, friends gather no dust.

- Jesse Owens

This history of the Middletown Pacemakers could not have been assembled or written solely by someone who was less than a year old when the club formed. I am indebted to numerous persons who helped me by supplying photographs, stories, or memorabilia. The list of contributors that have helped me with material for this book and/or its scrapbook predecessor include Wilbur "Robbie" Roberson, Arnita Roberson, Harold "Mike" Michael, Polly Michael, Bill Lovelace, Herb Sebastian, Darryl Hobbs, Kathy Hobbs, Ray Palmer, Betty Palmer, Carl Lakes, Bill Burton, Earnie Barnes, Paul Scorti, Don Klamo, Jim Neely, Fred May, Kenny Miller, Gene Wells, Delores Wells, Marge Slamka McFeeters, and former NHRA Division 3 Director Bob Daniels.

In addition to the above, a special thanks goes to my friend Ron Harmon, who processed black and white prints for me whenever contributors supplied negatives, and who helped me to locate racing periodicals over the Internet. Thanks also to my friend Bob Horton, who helped with computer scans of photos. And thanks go to my brother Marty, my sons Jason and Jeremy, my nephews Michael and Kyle and our good friend Gary Turnage, who nobly and patiently helped me search the automotive swap meets of Florida and North Carolina for period car magazines.

Special thanks go to veteran automotive writer Don Radbruch, who encouraged me to write my own book to help preserve racing history; and to Don Garlits and The Don Garlits Museum of Drag Racing, who allowed me access to museum archive materials not normally open to the public.

Very special thanks go to my parents for giving me a childhood worth remembering and especially to my wife, Sherrill, and to Jason, Jessica, and Jeremy for patience while I spent much of my time and a portion of the family budget chasing a dream.

INTRODUCTION
The Way it Was

Outside of a dog, a book is man's best friend. Inside of a dog, it's too dark to read.
- Groucho Marx

He would scour the local junkyards for usable parts, and save every spare dollar for that coveted chromed accessory. He might horse-trade a set of wire wheels for a valve job, or maybe a set of heads for a new paint job. With greasy hands, little money, and a lot of heart, the 1950s hot rodder toiled toward his dream. Working with buddies late at night in a dimly lit garage with the musty smell of motor oil, the parts would be merged into a hand-made car. They took Detroit iron, disassembled it and reassembled it into a combination never intended by the auto companies. A big, powerful, modern engine would be shoe-horned into a light weight, pre-war model car. The creation might be a shiny low-slung roadster that would hit the custom auto shows; it might be a stripped down coupe that would terrorize the local drag strip; or it might be a daily workhorse sedan that would never get beyond primer gray. In any case, it would be faster and sportier than anything Detroit offered. It was a hot rod, and its owner/driver/designer was a hot rodder. Hot rodders built dreams, and during the process lifelong friendships were forged.

Hot rodding began in southern California in the 1930s, and spread throughout the country after World War II. It came to the Midwest through the pages of *Hot Rod* and other automotive magazines, and through the efforts of the National Hot Rod Association. It survived the delinquent label of the 1950s caused by street racing and perpetuated by Hollywood "B" movies. From it spawned the sport of organized drag racing, and the Detroit muscle car era. But hot rodding had another side, an innovative side that many people do not fully realize.

The movement produced an industry of after-market products to enhance the performance level of the average automobile. Names like Edlebrock, Iskenderian, Scheiffer, Chet Herbert, Racer Brown, Hurst, Hilborn, and others started out as hot rodders trying to go faster. They developed special camshafts, high-flow heads, multi-carburetor intake manifolds, and other high-performance pieces to get a little better performance from their racecars. Soon they were providing parts and accessories to others, and a new industry was born.

Today's modern car with its electronic fuel injection starts and runs smoothly, reliably and efficiently. For this reliability we can thank the hot rodder, particularly one Stuart Hilborn, who invented fuel injection while trying to make his California dry lakes racer go faster. If you've ever witnessed a person being extricated from a wrecked and tangled car with a pneumatic device called the "Jaws of Life," you can thank the hot rodder. George Hurst, the same man who gave us the Hurst shifter, invented the device to quickly free race drivers from damaged cars. Before this invention, many highway accidents resulted in someone bleeding to death while rescuers slowly opened the car with cutting torches. If you ever enjoyed owning a GTO, 442, Super Sport, Charger, Roadrunner, Shelby Cobra, or AMX you can thank the hot rodder. These cars were Detroit's answer to the new car market created by the hot rodders and drag racers of the 1950s. And if you are a drag racer, or just a fan who likes those great John Force interviews on TV, you can again thank the hot rodder. Hot rod clubs across the country worked for a decade to get drag strips built in order to get racers off the city streets and public highways.

This book is the story of the Middletown Pacemakers, a hot rod club that operated in Middletown, Ohio, from 1951 to 1966. It was a typical hot rod club like so many others across the country, made up of guys who liked to hop up cars and have safe, legal outlets in which to enjoy them. It consisted of service station attendants, grocery store clerks, auto mechanics, steel workers, insurance salesmen, and truck drivers. They were ordinary people, but collectively they made up something special. They were my heroes, because I grew up with this car club. I was less than a year old when it formed and just shy of 16 when it dissolved. My dad, Wilbur "Robbie" Roberson, my grandfather, Bill Lovelace, and my uncle, L.G. "Larry" Meade, were all charter members. From the time I was five years old, I attended nearly every club meeting and club function. I grew up at reliability runs, car shows, and in the dusty, noisy pits of Midwestern drag strips. This book is a history of the Pacemakers club and a collection of anecdotes I either witnessed or heard told many times. It is the story of hot rodding, the story of drag racing, and the story of my childhood. No one ever grew up in a better setting.

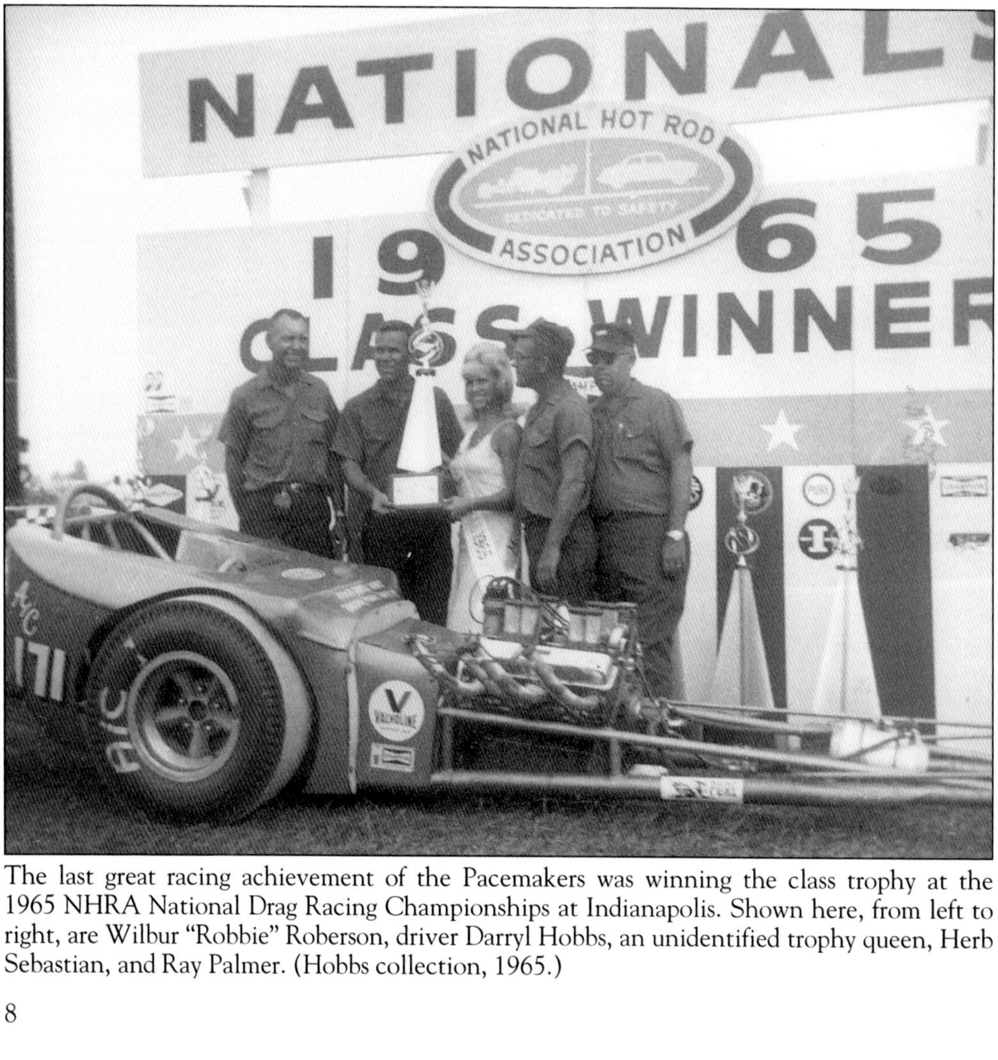

The last great racing achievement of the Pacemakers was winning the class trophy at the 1965 NHRA National Drag Racing Championships at Indianapolis. Shown here, from left to right, are Wilbur "Robbie" Roberson, driver Darryl Hobbs, an unidentified trophy queen, Herb Sebastian, and Ray Palmer. (Hobbs collection, 1965.)

One

Setting the Stage on the Oval Tracks

Few things are harder to put up with than the annoyance of a good example.
- Mark Twain

My father, Wilbur "Robbie" Roberson, was born on the family farm near Ezel, Kentucky, on November 16, 1923. He was the oldest of Loren and Addie Roberson's three children, and as such would inherit many chores and odd jobs in the family business ventures. Grandpa Loren owned the family's 162-acre farm, including a white frame house and a barn, in a rustic setting with a creek running near the house complete with a small wooden bridge and picturesque waterfall. But Grandpa Loren was not a farmer and preferred to rent out the farm acreage, save for the family garden. He pursued other vocations, which included ownership of a small country grocery store and the buying and selling of tobacco grown in the area. Toward both of these ends he owned a 3/4-ton, Chevrolet stake bed truck, which also hauled livestock between tobacco and produce runs. He was a crafty businessman, whose anything-for-a-buck ambition would lead the family ably through the country's worst depression in the 1930s.

Dad grew up in those poverty stricken times. The family farm kept them in food, and the family business maintained a meager cash flow, but there were few luxuries. By the age of 13, he was driving the family truck, the aforementioned 1935 Chevy, and the family car, a 1935 Ford sedan. He first demonstrated a natural mechanical aptitude working on these vehicles and on a bicycle he hand built from bartered parts. The Great Depression bred a wonderful self-sufficiency that has never again been seen in any generation that followed. To survive, you had to be able to do things. Women made the family's clothing and canned homegrown foods for the winter. The children were assigned chores to match their level of skill. It was a time that bred hardy people.

Dad's one luxury was an occasional trip to the movie theater in nearby West Liberty. Wide-eyed, he would watch the cowboy double features, the Flash Gordon serials, and the comedy of Laurel and Hardy. But one Saturday in 1935, he saw a newsreel that would capture his imagination and ultimately change the course of his life. The flickering black and white images of Malcolm Campbell's "Bluebird" land speed record car zipping along the sandy surface of Ormond and Daytona Beach at an average speed of 276 mph made a lasting impression on the 11-year-old Kentucky farm boy. Daytona, with its white sandy beaches, seemed so exotic. The handsome Englishman seemed so brave. The sleek racecar looked so futuristic. It was a world he had never seen before, and a fascination with speed was born. Later that year, Campbell would set another record of 301 mph, this time on the Bonneville Salt Flats in Utah. The newsreels followed Campbell's progress, and Dad eagerly watched his British hero. A high performance seed was planted that would last a lifetime.

During the course of his trucking of tobacco and livestock, Grandpa Loren made numerous trips to Mount Sterling, Kentucky, a little larger city to the west. Dad heard about a sprint car race there, and with some coaxing, he convinced Grandpa Loren to take him. (Sprint cars were called "championship cars," or "big cars," in those days). This was Dad's first encounter with racers and racecars up close. The sights, the noise, and the smells of real live racing were simply awesome. He was hooked on horsepower.

In high school, Dad played on the school basketball team, and on the local traveling fast pitch softball team. In the early spring of 1941, Grandpa Loren sold the farm and grocery store in a package deal to his partner in the tobacco business and moved the family to Columbia, Tennessee. His older brother had settled there, and Grandpa Loren liked the area. He bought another farm, located outside of Columbia, just three miles from the site of today's GM Saturn plant at Spring Hill. This time he decided to run the farm himself. Dad was still a few weeks away from his high school graduation and stayed behind with relatives in Kentucky in order to finish school. He graduated class Salutatorian in June, and then moved to Columbia to rejoin the family and begin training as a machinist at the local Columbia Vocational School.

Dad began working as a machinist at Ogelsby's Machine Shop in Columbia and purchased his first vehicle, a Harley-Davidson motorcycle. That fall he decided to pursue college, and took the entrance exams at Vanderbilt University in Nashville. He was set to begin college at Vanderbilt mid year after Christmas break, when the Japanese attack on Pearl Harbor changed his plans. The United States was suddenly plunged into World War II, and Dad knew that it would only be a matter of time before he would be drafted. He decided not to enter college, but to remain working in the machine shop for the interim. He was just 19 years old when he entered the Army in 1943. He had his basic training at Fort McClellan, Alabama, and then proceeded to march across Europe with the Infantry's 35th Division. He saw action in the famous Battle of the Bulge, where he suffered severe chest wounds when hit by shrapnel from an exploding mortar shell. He nearly froze to death before medics got to him, but he made it to the field hospital, where he was transferred to Paris and underwent surgery. After a week he was moved to England and began a lengthy hospital recovery in Cheltenham. He received the Purple Heart medal and was released from the hospital to rejoin his outfit. By this time, our forces had already crossed the Rhine River and were closing in on Berlin. Hitler's suicide prompted the surrender of Germany, and the 35th saw occupation duty, including the highly emotional liberation of a Nazi concentration camp. The Division was re-equipped for the planned Japan invasion, when news came of the Air Force's atomic bomb missions on Japan and the war's impending end. Within a few weeks, Dad was home.

During the war, the family had again relocated. In 1943, after two years of farming, Grandpa Loren decided to go back into the grocery business. He received news from his sister in Middletown, Ohio, that a local grocery store was for sale. He made a trip to Middletown and purchased the store, which was located in the Mayfield area on Plymouth Avenue near Highland Street. This time he bought property and built a house in town about half a block away from the store on Carolina Street. He had gotten good prices on the properties, since property values had dropped during the war. Realizing an opportunity, he proceeded to invest his life savings by systematically purchasing every available house in the area—about 20 houses in all. He rented them out until the post-war housing shortage increased the property values to new highs. At that point he sold the houses one by one, producing a sizable nest egg.

Dad returned from the war and settled in Middletown, a thriving industrial city that lay along the Great Miami River, half way between Cincinnati and Dayton—hence the name "middle" town. He landed a job at Inland Container Company, a manufacturer of paper and cardboard packaging. He had sold his motorcycle through an uncle during the war and needed transportation. New car production was slowly coming back after converting from wartime military production, and new '46 model cars were few and far between. He found a deal on a 1939 Ford two-door sedan, a great find for the time. It was this car that offered Dad an opportunity to learn about automotive engines. The car occasionally overheated, and one day it refused to start. He got a friend to push start the Ford with another car, and during this procedure the '39's V-8 engine let go. It seems it had a head gasket leak, which had caused the overheating and subsequently allowed one cylinder to fill with water. The attempted push starting produced a broken connecting rod in that cylinder. Dad's automotive lesson ended with the purchase of a rebuilt V-8 engine and a shade tree engine swap.

In the summer of 1946, Dad met Arnita May Lovelace, a recent graduate of Middletown High School. On March 15, 1947, they were married in a small ceremony at the Harrison Street home of the bride's grandmother, Lilly Lovelace, with the bride's Uncle Sam Lovelace, a Baptist Minister, presiding. Dad's cousin Vernon Carter and his wife, Lucy, served as best man and bride's maid, respectively. Dad's sister Edna and her husband, L.G. Meade, and a few friends were also in attendance. The couple's parents, Bill and Pauline Lovelace and Loren and Addie Roberson, rounded out the guest list. Dad was 23, and the bride, my future mom, was 18. They moved into a tiny one-bedroom house on Plymouth Avenue, just one block from Grandpa Loren's grocery store. The marriage also marked the entrance of the greatest automotive influence of Dad's life—his new father-in-law, Bill Lovelace.

Grandpa Bill had learned welding as a trade and during the Great Depression found work as a welder with the railroads in Billings, Montana. Around 1931, he went to work for Montana Welding and Radiator Company, where he learned auto radiator repair from lifelong friend John Williamson. During the war, Grandpa Bill moved the family back to Middletown, and by the war's end, he had opened Lovelace Radiator Service in a shop behind the family home on Shafor Street.

Dad was fascinated with the radiator repair shop, and he was equally fascinated with his multi-talented father-in-law. Grandpa Bill had only gone as far as the tenth grade, but as an avid reader, he was self-educated. In the mid 1950s, he would become the editor of a trade magazine called *Auto Radiator Service*, and he would earn a United States patent on radiator test equipment he had designed.

Dad was also fascinated with Grandpa Bill's hobby. He was an avid auto enthusiast and would attend the area midget races with his friend Herb Dome, a local front-end mechanic who owned a midget racer. Herb's midget No. 55 had been home built on a tight budget, making his own chassis and building the Ford V-8 60 engine himself. It ran well enough, but he longed for a first-class racing operation. So Grandpa Bill Lovelace and Herb Dome entered a partnership and purchased a new Kurtis-Kraft midget from Frank Kurtis' California shop in the summer of 1948. Herb Dome drove to California from Middletown to pick up the car, a three-day drive one way, making the round trip in one week. He was so eager to show the car to Grandpa Bill that he stopped by the radiator repair shop before going all the way home to his house on Hill Street. The car had been purchased ready to run, and it was a thing of beauty perched on the trailer as Dad and Grandpa Bill inspected every inch of the shiny new racer. It came complete with a professionally built Ford V-8 60 engine. The car was very fast and proceeded to win often throughout Ohio and Indiana. The main driver was Gene Force from Richmond, Indiana. In the 1948 midget race season Force won 27 feature races, most of which were behind the wheel of the Dome-Lovelace No. 5 Kurtis-Ford. This is a huge number of wins considering the tight competition in the Indianapolis vicinity, and the dwindling race opportunities as midget racing had begun to decline.

Midget racers raced across the country on hundreds of oval tracks, both indoors and outdoors on paved, dirt, or even board surfaces. They were very fast, light-weight cars with small powerful engines and usually no transmission other than an in-and-out box that either put you in high gear or neutral. The drivers sat upright in an open cockpit that had no roll bar (until the mid 1950s). The cars could hit 90 mph in a very short distance. A typical night of midget racing would consist of a few qualifying heat races, followed by two semi-final races and the big 25 lap feature race that would be the evening finale. The semis were used to set the starting grid for the feature race, usually placing the faster cars in the back of the field.

The success of this car in its debut 1948 season is exemplified by a series of newspaper clippings that came into my possession after my grandmother, Eura Lovelace, passed away in 1993. Seven articles survive, which follow the car through a two-week period in August of 1948, right after the car was purchased. The articles report two track records and nine feature wins in nine starts.

In those two weeks, the team won more feature races than many do in a lifetime.

Gene Force's success in this car and others would earn him a ride in the 1951 Indy 500, where he finished 11th—a fine showing for an Indy rookie. Gene would eventually make four other qualifying attempts at Indy, though he did not return until 1960. That year he finished 28th. His racing career lasted into the 1970s, still winning in midget cars some 25 years after stepping into the Dome-Lovelace No. 5 Kurtis-Ford midget.

On nights when Gene wasn't available, a talented roadster driver named Dick Frazier would drive the No. 5 midget. Frazier had driven for Herb Dome off and on since 1946 in the No. 55 midget. Dick was one of the top roadster drivers in the Midwest, and his No. 32 roadster was featured on the cover of *Hot Rod Magazine* in September of 1948. That car was faithfully restored in 1991 and displayed in the Smithsonian Institute in 1992, the first racing roadster to ever have that honor. Dick began driving midgets in 1946 and big cars in 1948. He attempted to qualify at four Indy 500s between 1949 and 1952, but never made the field.

A third driver, Jack Seither, also drove the Dome-Lovelace No. 5 midget on occasions when Gene Force was not available. Jack was a short, stocky farmer from nearby Germantown, Ohio, who had a strong desire to drive racecars. He wanted to become a race driver so badly that he had cut a dirt oval track into a vacant field on his farm, and learned to drive by tearing around it in a stripped down '37 Ford. This kind of ambition and creativity only serves to show what a person would go through in order to race in those days.

A story my parents like to tell illustrates the excitement of midget racing of the era. My great-grandmother, Lily Lovelace, was a very serious lady—quiet and reserved—from a German-English farming family. When her son, Grandpa Bill, bought the midget racer in 1948, she decided that she wanted to see it race. She would have been about 70 years old at the time, and Mom and Dad were certain that she would not enjoy auto racing. Nonetheless they made the trip over to Indiana and Great-Grandma sat quietly in the car, listening to the conversation of the others. In the stands, she insisted on sitting in the top row. Mom nervously followed her up the steps that she surprisingly floated over with the sure-footedness of a mountain goat. During the heat races she sat quietly, taking in the noise and commotion of the meet in the expected stoic fashion. For the feature race, Gene was the top qualifier and started in the back. At the drop of the flag he began to pick off the cars one at a time toward yet another feature win. The crowd responded by cheering loudly at the excitement on the track. Soon Gene was running second and closing in on the leader. Dad was engrossed in the action, but he took a quick look over at Great-Grandma to see how she was doing. To his surprise, the petite little septuagenarian was on her feet waving a clenched fist high above her head and shouting at the top of her lungs, "Go Gene Go!"

Dad's first encounter with racing equipment was with this midget. The car was kept at Herb Dome's shop and Dad would go there to help prepare the car for the next race. Herb Dome was a talented front-end mechanic, but he also knew how to build racing engines. He was one of the area's earliest hot rodders, having modified a Model A Ford with a Frontenac racing head before World War II. He was driving the Fronty Ford around Middletown in 1946, when he built the No. 55 predecessor midget and its Ford V-8 engine from scratch. It was under Herb Dome's tutelage that Dad learned about racing engines.

It was during this time, probably in 1947, that Dad met another Middletown racer that would become a lifelong friend. Harold "Mike" Michael was racing a Model A Ford oval track roadster with partner Heber "Snip" Dreher, who ran a machine shop in Miamisburg. The car was driven by Don "Beardy" Beard, Benny Emerick and Doc Eshbaugh. Mike and Doc had gone to high school together in nearby Germantown. Mike frequented Grandpa Bill's radiator shop (since oval track cars are prone to damaged radiators), and he had enlisted Herb Dome to set up the front end on the track roadster. It was through these channels that Dad got to know Mike.

Mike began his racing career on water with a hydroplane in 1940, and ran against all the big names, including popular bandleader Guy Lombardo. Mike's boat had lots of power with a modified automotive Mercury V-8 engine that he had prepared, but an old style hull kept the

Merc from reaching its full potential. He had limited success, and after the war he was faced with the expense of upgrading the hull to be competitive. Instead, he sold the boat, but kept the Mercury V-8 engine.

Mike wanted to get into auto racing. He had been attending races at Dayton Speedway since he was in high school. He remembered a car No. 25 owned by Snip Dreher, which was a Model A Ford with a modified Model A four-cylinder engine. The car was no longer competitive with the four-banger, but with Mike's hot Mercury V-8 engine it could be. Mike contacted Snip and suggested a partnership. Soon the Mercury V-8 was in No. 25, and Mike and Snip were racing partners. The engine maintained the boat-style exhaust headers, which pointed straight up and gave the car a unique sound.

The team won quite often throughout the Midwest, racing mostly in southern Ohio, Indiana, and on the Hurricane Circuit run by the Granatelli Brothers at Soldier Field in Chicago. The car was basically a stripped down stock Model A roadster in 1947. For the 1948 season, the body was lowered on the car to improve cornering. For 1949, they built a new car from a Model T chassis using a lowered Model T body for improved aerodynamics. The car always ran the number 25, and it sported flames painted by Mike's talented wife Polly. Through Mike, Dad met Alex Slamka, a race fan with a flare for customizing cars; Bob Kuhn, whose family owned a trucking company in Middletown; and Danny Allen, a Middletown hot rodder who followed the racing circuit.

Around 1950, Dad became acquainted with Herb Sebastian, a Middletown High School graduate who was born in Kentucky a short distance from Dad's birthplace. Herb worked at his dad's Sohio service station on Verity Parkway and Yankee Road in the heart of Middletown. Herb was a hot rodder who drove a 1933 Ford coupe with a hopped up Mercury V-8 engine—the basic hot setup of the day. Herb drove the car to work regularly and parked it in front of the station, where it served as a beacon for hot rodders. Soon the Sohio station became a gathering place for car enthusiasts in the area.

In 1949, Dad went to work in Grandpa Bill's radiator repair shop in the alley behind Shafor Street. There he learned radiator repair, gas tank repair, and general welding skills from his amiable and talented father-in-law. These skills, along with his machine shop training, would provide the versatility necessary to one-day build hot rods and dragsters. But more important to him at the time was the satisfaction of a career that would allow him to utilize his mechanical aptitude and work on automobiles.

The following year, on August 21, 1950, I was born. This increase in the family size prompted a move to a two-bedroom house on Carolina Street, about a block away from the old Plymouth Avenue address. It also prompted Dad and Grandpa Bill to think about expanding the business, so Grandpa Bill opened a second radiator shop in 1951 in nearby Hamilton, and put Dad in charge of the Hamilton branch of Lovelace Radiator Service.

With the move to his own shop Dad was now in need of a shop pickup truck, but a new one would be too expensive. He liked the 1934 Dodge truck that Grandpa Bill had repainted in bright red with the shop logo in white letters on the doors; but Dad also wanted a hot rod, and his truck would have to serve both purposes. He found a 1945 Ford truck, tired but solid, for $75. (Ford had discontinued auto production during World War II, but continued to produce pickup trucks on a limited basis throughout the war.) He then proceeded to fit it with a 1949 Olds Rocket V-8 engine, making his own motor mounts and driveshaft. He had it painted red with white lettering to match the 1934 Dodge, and his hot rod shop truck was complete.

Several hot rods were tooling around Middletown in 1951. Besides Herb Sebastian's 1933 Ford coupe, there was Carl Lakes' Mercury powered 1934 Ford coupe, Tom Frebis's 1940 Ford sedan, and a few others. These guys were heavily influenced by the cars shown in the pages of *Hot Rod Magazine*, which was in its fourth year of publication. Editor Wally Parks was a big proponent of car clubs. Car clubs in southern California had worked with local police departments to curb the street racing that had become a serious problem there by offering safe legal outlets like reliability runs and the first organized drag races. In the spring of 1951, Parks proposed a national organization of car clubs, called the National Hot Rod Association, and he used his editorial column in the magazine to promote the idea. If hot rodding had gotten a bad name in southern California and the car clubs were the cure, the same scenario would be repeated across the country as the magazine gained readership coast to coast. If hot rodding and his magazine were to survive, car clubs would be the answer.

By 1951, Harold Michael was through with roadster racing. Roadster racing had dwindled considerably due partly to the introduction of the popular NASCAR stock cars in 1948, and partly to a general loss of paying race fans to the new free entertainment media of television. Race fans who used to attend auto races three or four nights a week were now staying home to watch Sid Caesar and Milton Berle. Races were fewer and farther apart, and the hot California cars were now touring the Midwest to find races and purses. Mike simply couldn't afford to spend the money necessary to remain competitive. He quit after the 1950 season, and by the mid 50s roadster racing would disappear altogether.

It was Mike that initiated the idea of a hot rod club in Middletown. Once he was out of the racing scene, he longed for something to fill the automotive void. He pitched the idea to Dad and a few others. They had many car enthusiast friends between their racing buddies and the guys that hung around Sebastian's Sohio station and Sully Sullivan's body shop. Everything they needed to know was laid out in the pages of *Hot Rod Magazine*, including how to start a club and how to run the events. The idea began to gel in the early months of 1951.

In August of 1951, Dad and Mom and Mike and Polly piled into our 1950 Ford sedan and headed west to attend the Bonneville Speed Trials. They saw the finest California hot rods running unbelievable speeds on the natural salt expanse. They marveled at the organization and professionalism of the meet, run by the Southern California Timing Association. Mike absorbed every detail from the example set by the SCTA and the experience served to inspire many Pacemaker automotive events that would follow.

On this trip, Dad realized a longtime dream by driving the family Ford through the flying mile course at Bonneville. His timed speed was a sedate 89 mph in the stock Ford, but it was still awesome. He was running on the same course as Malcolm Campbell did in 1935, when Campbell became the first person to break 300 mph on land. It had been 16 years since Dad watched the newsreel of Malcolm Campbell in that little movie theater in West Liberty, Kentucky. He had come a long way since then: from Kentucky, to Tennessee, to Ohio by way of Germany; and from a wide-eyed 11-year-old, to a teen-aged soldier, to a married businessman and a father. But the real automotive journey was just about to begin.

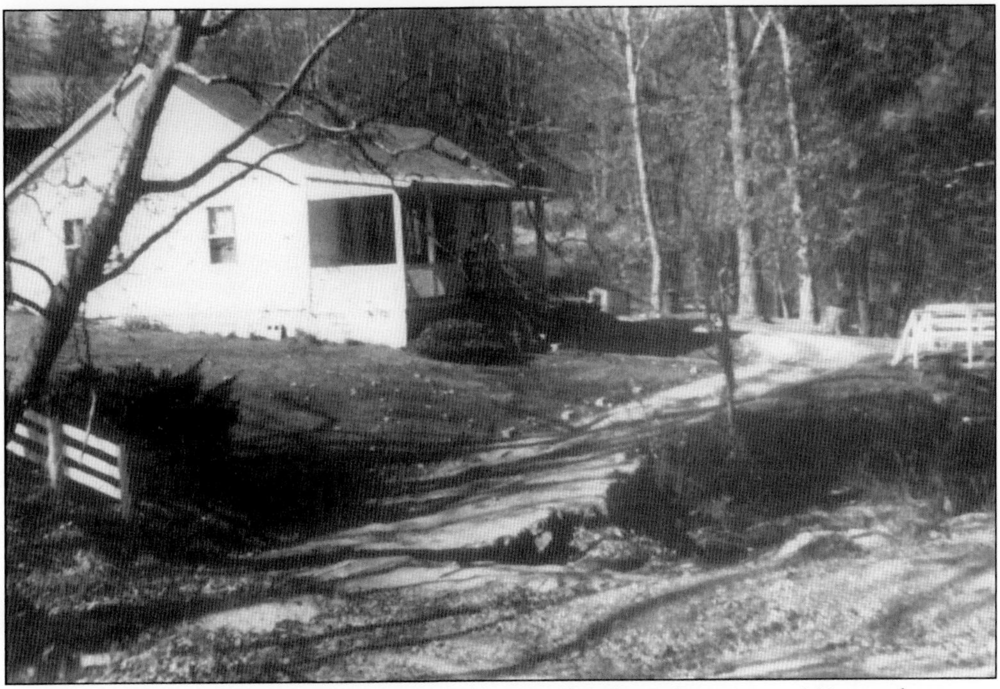

My father, Wilbur "Robbie" Roberson, was born in this frame house on a 162-acre farm near Ezel, Kentucky. Dad would spend his first 17 years, including the depression-ridden 1930s, in this picturesque setting. (Roberson collection, 1923.)

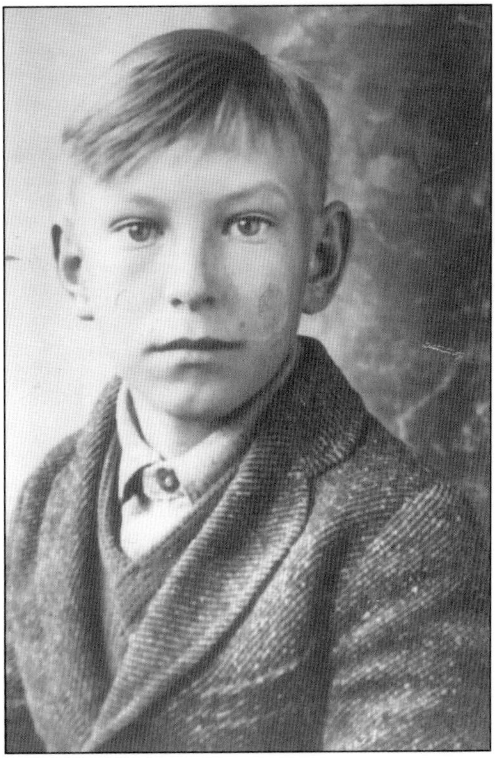

Here's Dad at about age nine. Life was not easy in rural Kentucky during the Great Depression. It was a time that bred hardy, self-reliant people. (Roberson collection, early 1930s.)

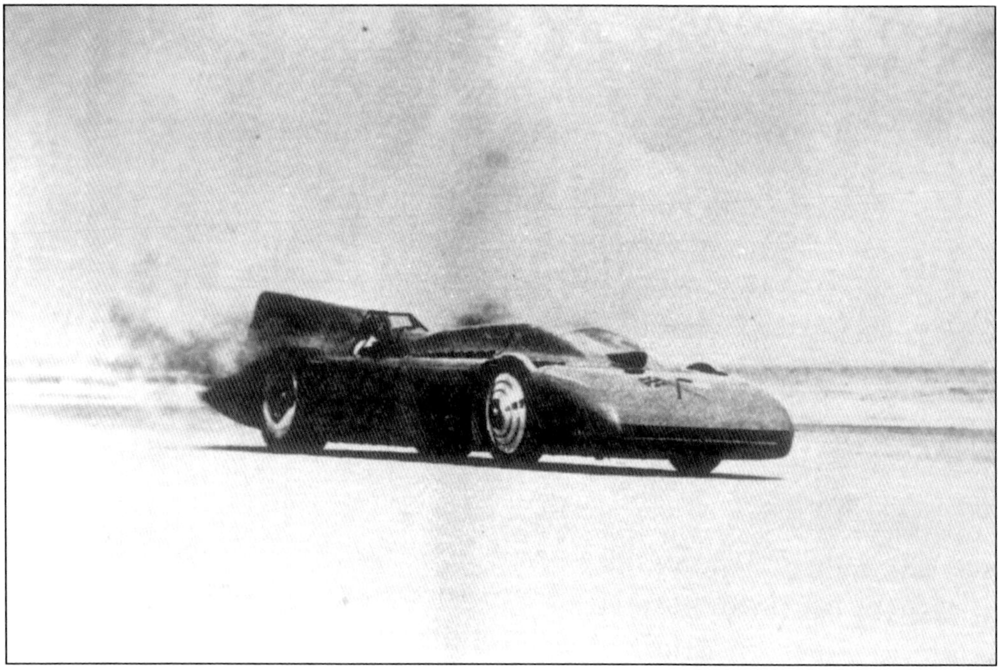

Malcolm Campbell of England set land speed records of 276 mph (Ormond/Daytona Beach) and 301 mph (Bonneville Salt Flats) in this futuristic "Bluebird" racer powered by an aircraft engine. Newsreels of this car seen by Dad at age 11 at a movie theater in Mount Sterling, Kentucky, planted a seed for speed. (Photo reprinted with permission of the Ormond Beach, Florida, Historical Society, 1935.)

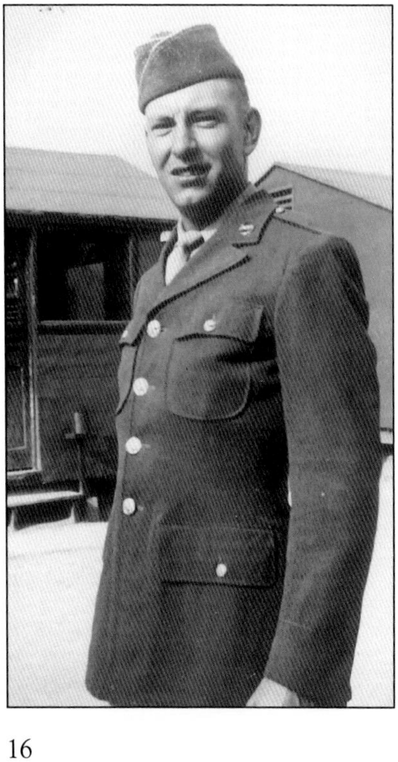

Dad entered United States Military service during World War II. This is his first military photo in his new uniform. Note the long jacket. The shorter Eisenhower jackets had not yet been issued. (Roberson collection, 1943.)

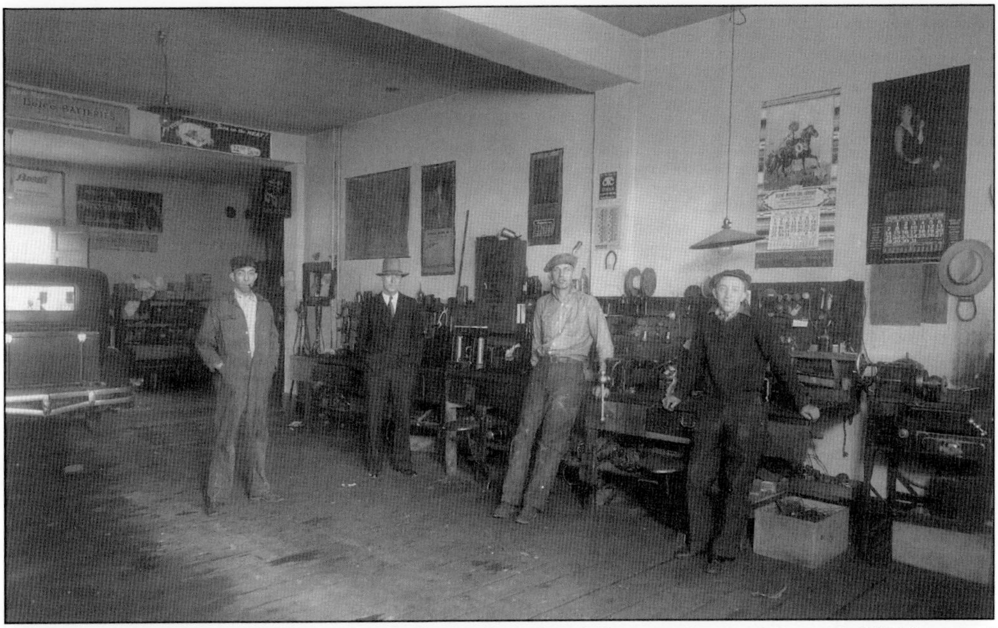

Grandpa Bill Lovelace (at left) poses with unidentified fellow workers at Montana Welding and Radiator Company of Billings, Montana. The owner, John Williamson, was a lifelong friend. (Roberson collection, 1931.)

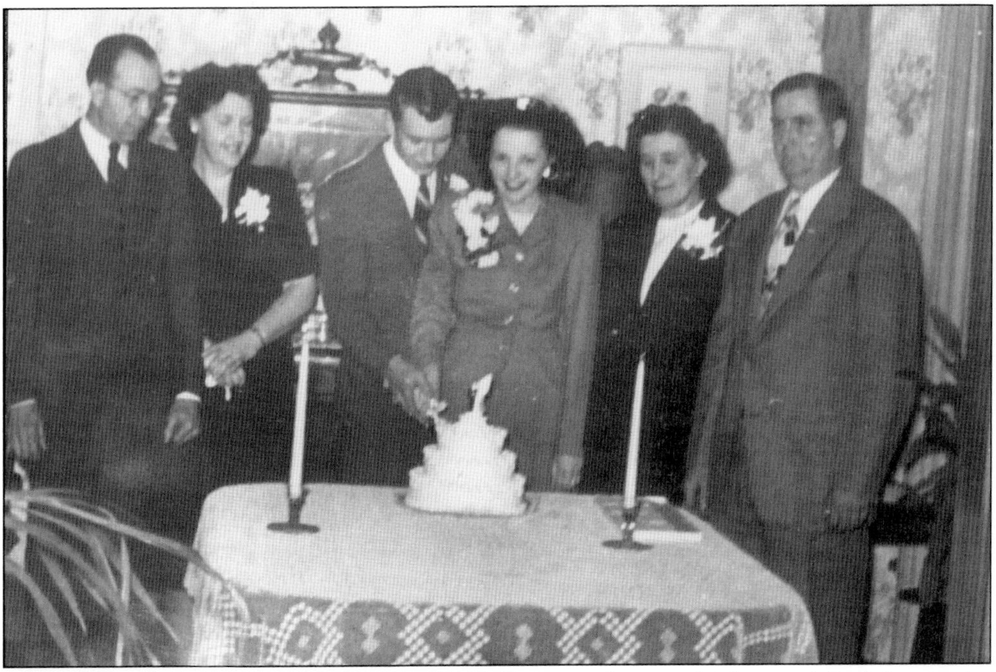

The wedding of my parents on March 15, 1947, not only united Mom and Dad, but it also brought together Dad and Grandpa Bill, two key charter Pacemakers. Without this wedding, and Dad's subsequent introduction to Harold "Mike" Michael, the Pacemakers club might never have been formed. Shown here, from left to right, are Bill and Pauline Lovelace, Dad and Mom (cutting the cake), and Addie and Loren Roberson. (Roberson collection, 1947.)

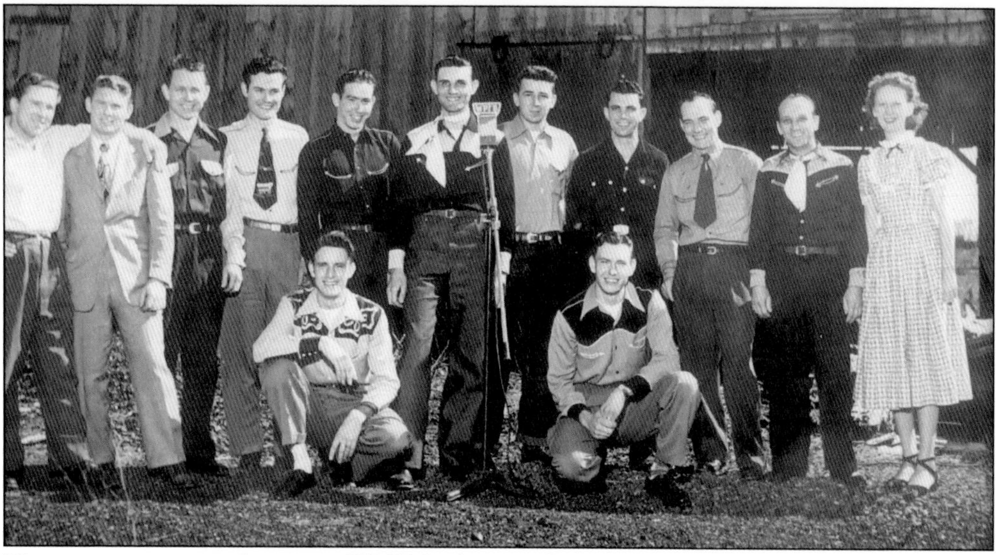

The country music performers at WPFB Radio pose for a group photograph. Standing, from left to right, are Herb ?, unidentified, unidentified, Bill Clark, unidentified, Bob Holiday, Clyde Barker Jr., fellow Pacemaker member Tug Swain, unidentified, Lou King, and Jewel Holiday. Kneeling at left is Willard Roberson, and Dad is kneeling at right. The photo is labeled "Down on the Farm Boys." (Roberson collection, early 1950s.)

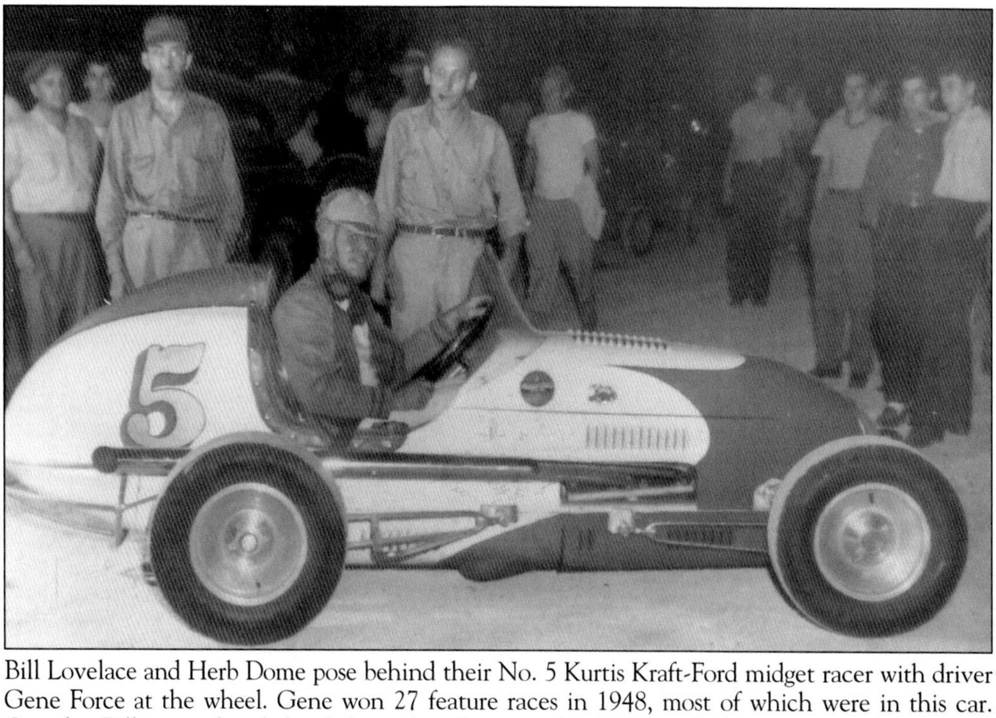

Bill Lovelace and Herb Dome pose behind their No. 5 Kurtis Kraft-Ford midget racer with driver Gene Force at the wheel. Gene won 27 feature races in 1948, most of which were in this car. Grandpa Bill is standing behind the car's tail section (with hat and glasses), and Herb Dome is standing behind the car's steering wheel (with glasses and cigar). Dad is pictured in the background, third from the right in the light-colored striped tee shirt. Dad, Grandpa Bill, and Herb Dome would all become charter club members of the Pacemakers. (Roberson collection, 1948.)

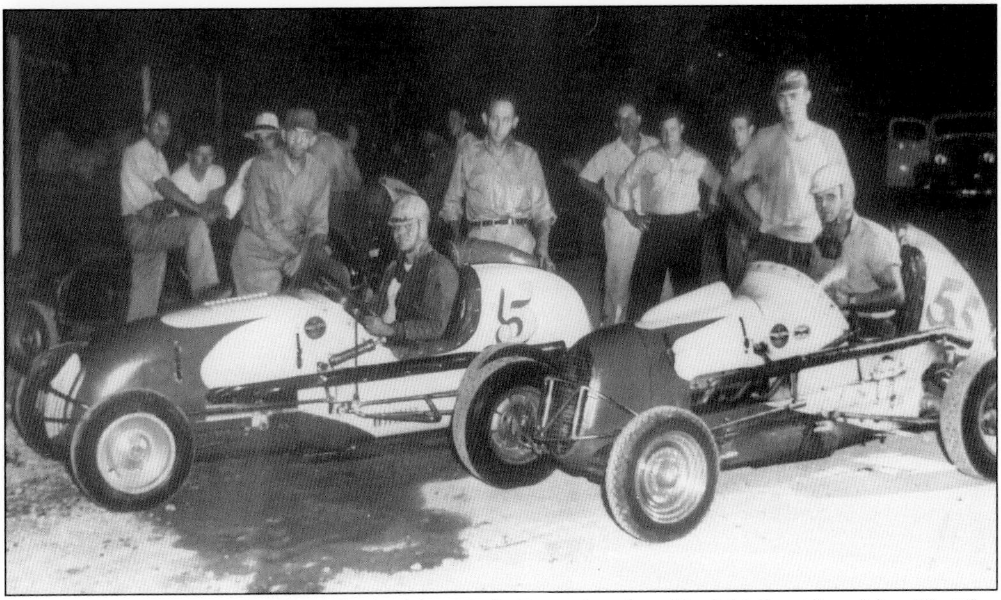

The Dome-Lovelace No. 5 is flanked by Herb Dome's other Ford V-8 midget No. 55. The team raced throughout southern Ohio and Indiana, mostly on paved tracks. Gene Force is at the wheel of No.5, with Grandpa Bill (left) and Herb Dome (right) standing to either side and several unidentified onlookers in the background. An unidentified driver sits in No. 55, with an unidentified crew member standing by. (Roberson collection, 1948.)

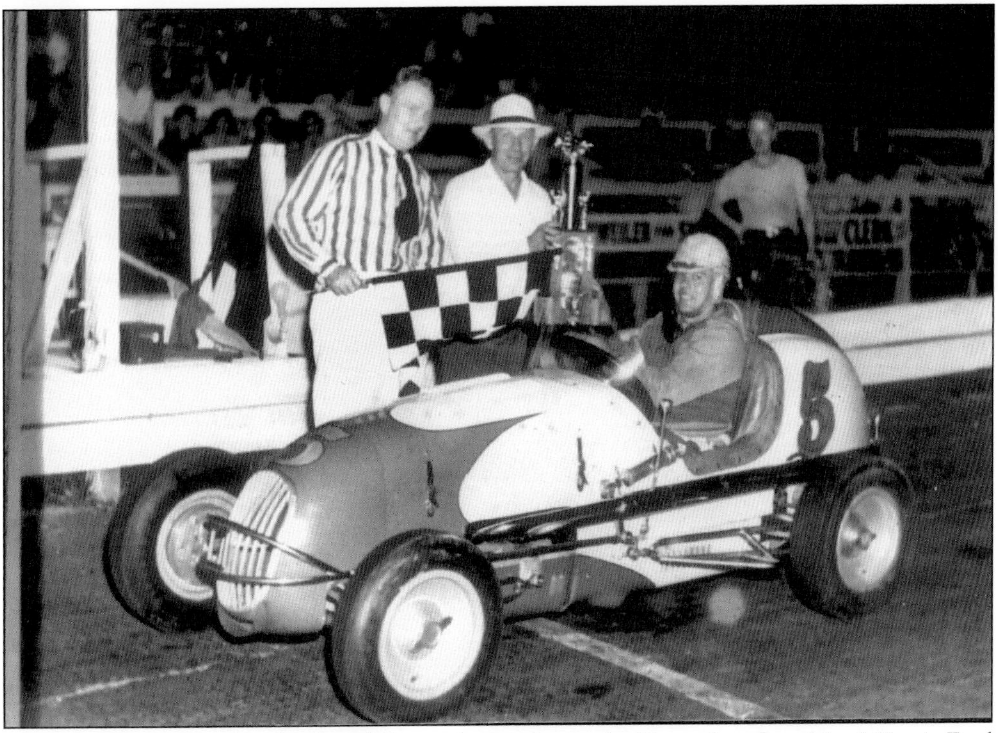

Gene Force receives the checkered flag and a trophy in the Dome-Lovelace No. 5 Kurtis-Ford at Winchester Speedway in Winchester, Indiana. (Roberson collection, 1948.)

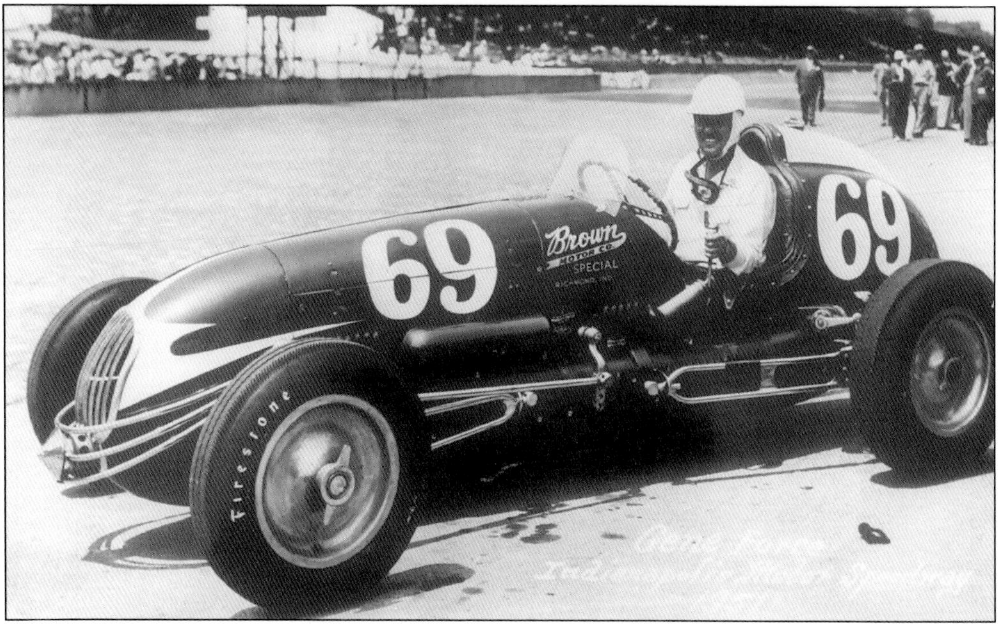

Gene Force is pictured here at the wheel of the "Brown Motor Company Special" Kurtis Offy, which he drove to a respectable 11th place in his rookie year at Indy. Despite several attempts, Gene would not make the Indy field again until 1960, when he finished 28th. (Photo courtesy of the Indianapolis Motor Speedway, 1951.)

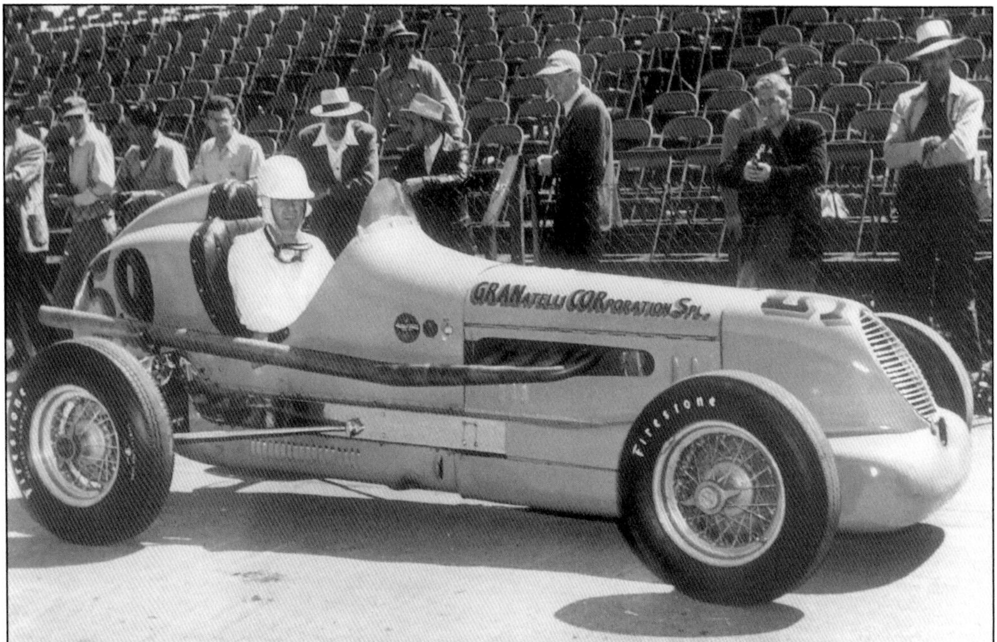

Dick Frazier, who also drove the Dome-Lovelace No. 5 midget, poses at the wheel of the No. 59 "Grancor Special" owned by the Granatelli brothers of Chicago. Dick made four attempts at Indy between 1949 and 1952 but never made the field. His best finish in the big cars was a second at Milwaukee in 1948. (Photo courtesy of the Indianapolis Motor Speedway, 1949.)

Dick Frazier poses for a studio shot at the Indianapolis Motor Speedway. Dick was a top oval-track roadster driver, but like all the roadster drivers, he had to prove himself in midgets and big cars in order to make the jump to Indy. (Photo courtesy of the Indianapolis Motor Speedway, 1949.)

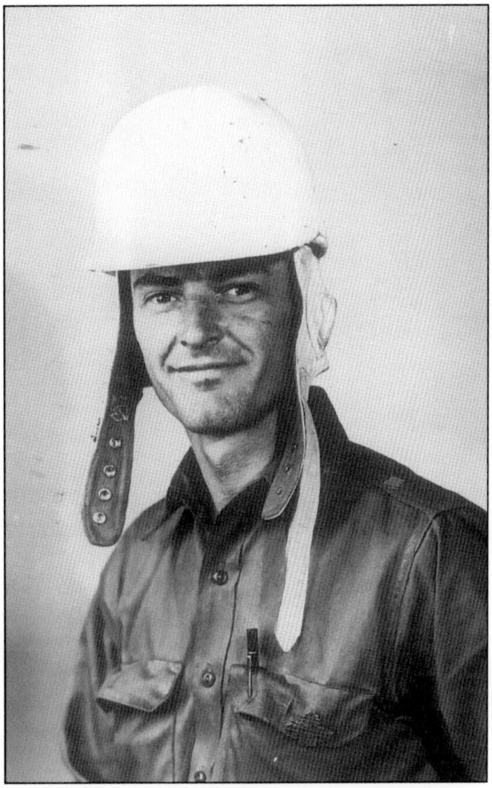

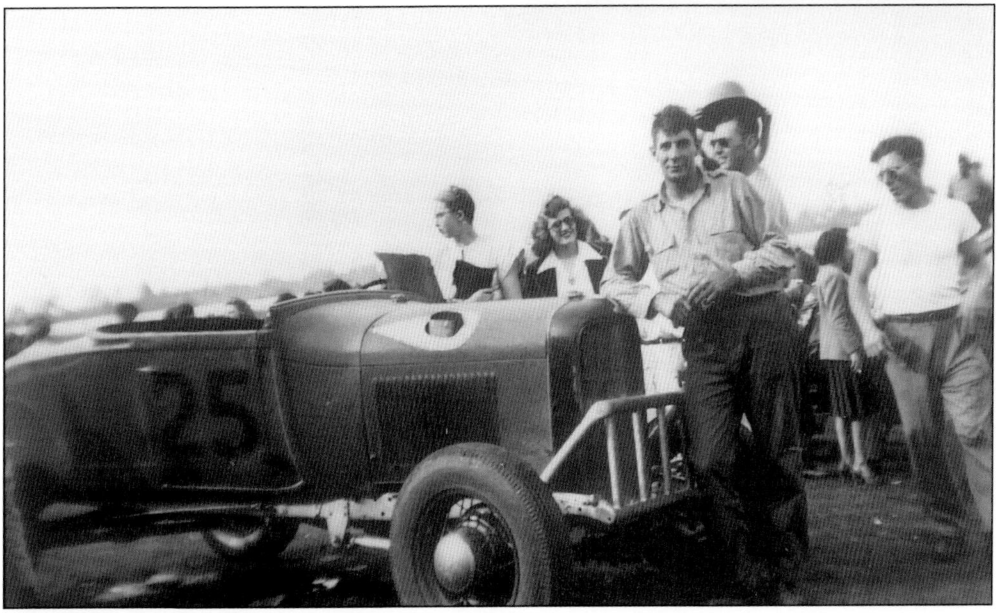

Driver Don Beard strikes a confident, relaxed pose, leaning against the Dreher-Michael No. 25 oval track roadster at Greenville Speedway in Greenville, Ohio. Benny Emerick and Mike's school friend Doc Eshbaugh also drove the car. Pictured here, from left to right, are Polly Michael, Mrs. Beard?, Don Beard, Mike Michael (tipping his hat), and an unidentified onlooker. (Michael collection, 1947.)

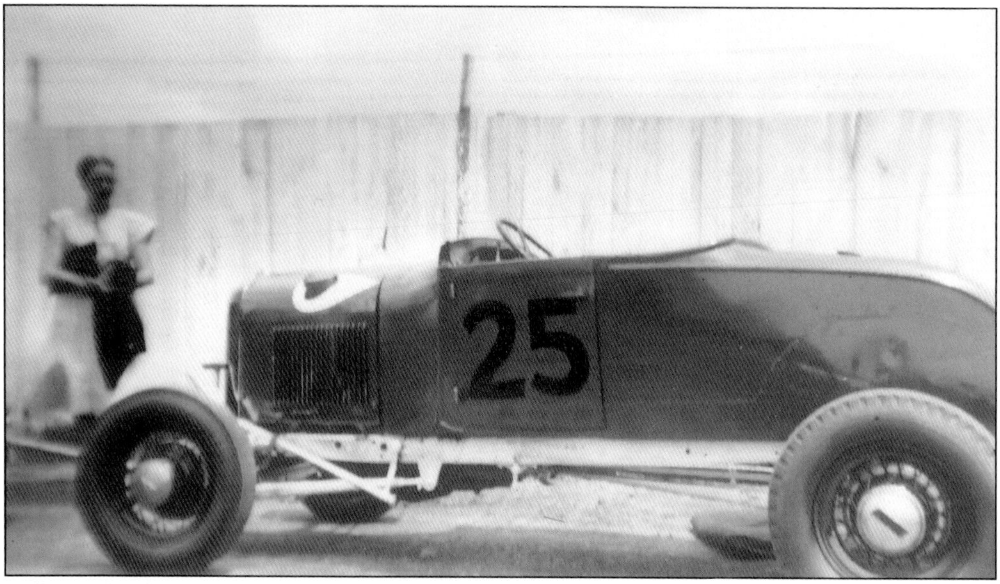

Polly Michael poses with the Dreher-Michael No 25 track roadster. Note the absence of a roll bar. Driver protection was minimal at best in post-war racing. (Michael collection, 1947.)

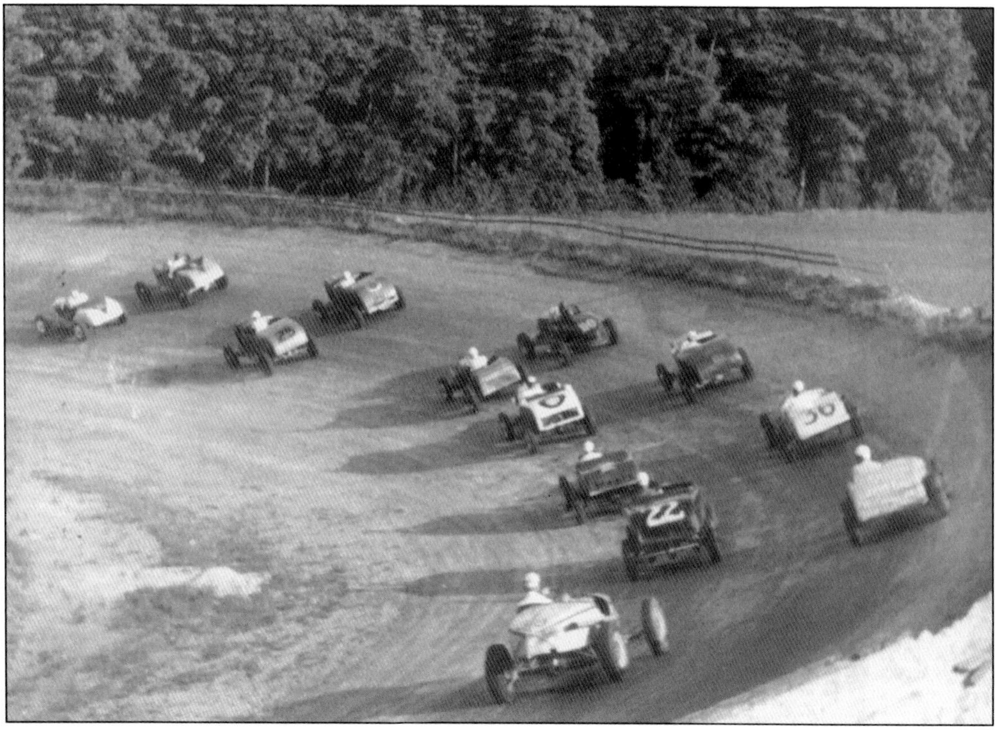

This photograph captures the start of a race at Winchester Speedway following Jimmy Morrison's flight over the wall. Relief driver Dick Frazier is at the wheel of Morrison's six-cylinder Ford powered boat-tail racer at the back of the pack. The crafty Frazier won the race from the back of the field. Don Beard in No. 25 is on the inside of the second row. (Michael collection, 1947.)

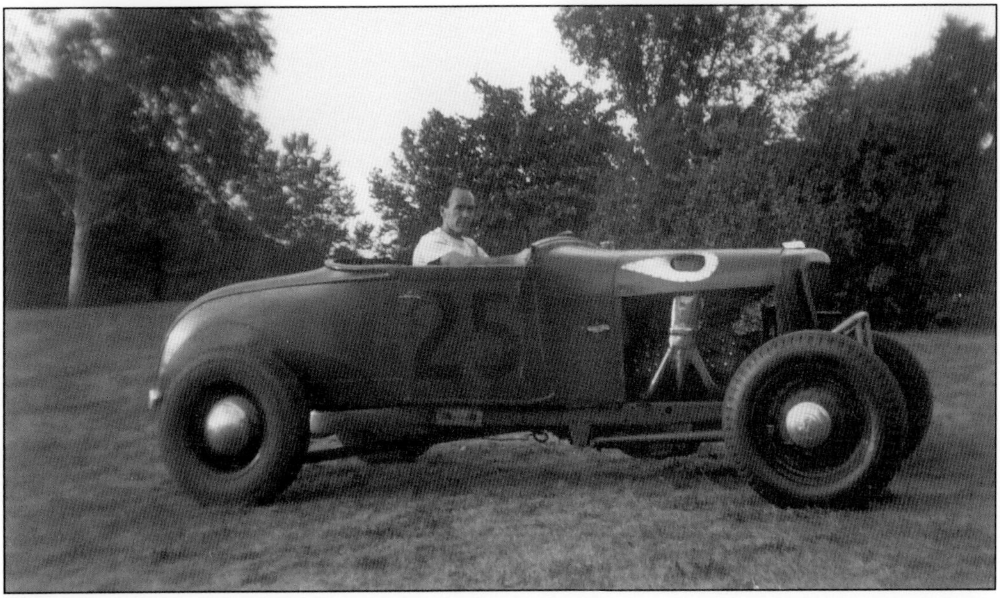

Future charter Pacemaker member Danny Allen, a Middletown machinist, poses in the No. 25 just after the car was rebuilt for the '48 race season. The car now sports a lower stance and a lighter weight "nerf bar" in front. The boat exhaust headers on the Mercury engine are in plain view in this photograph. (Michael collection, 1948.)

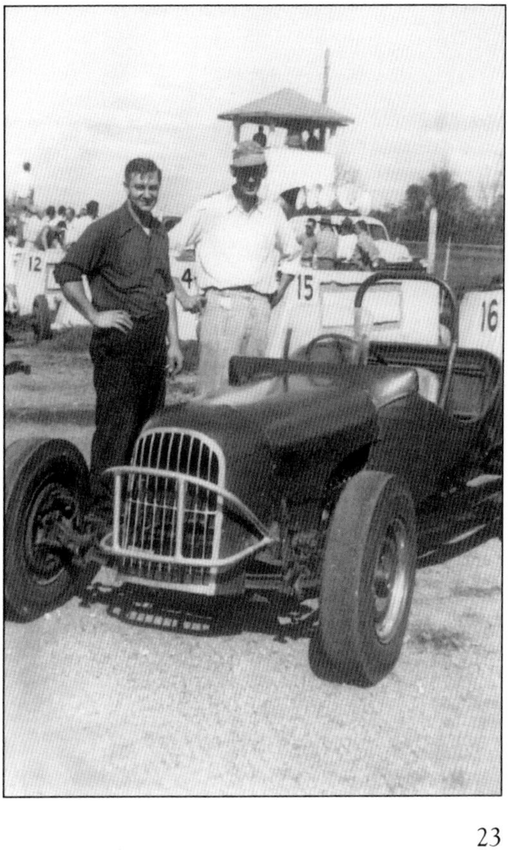

Car owners Snip Dreher and Mike pose next to the all new Model T racer with '40 Ford running gear. The Mercury V-8 was retained, but the boat exhaust headers were finally retired for a conventional exhaust system. (Michael collection, 1949.)

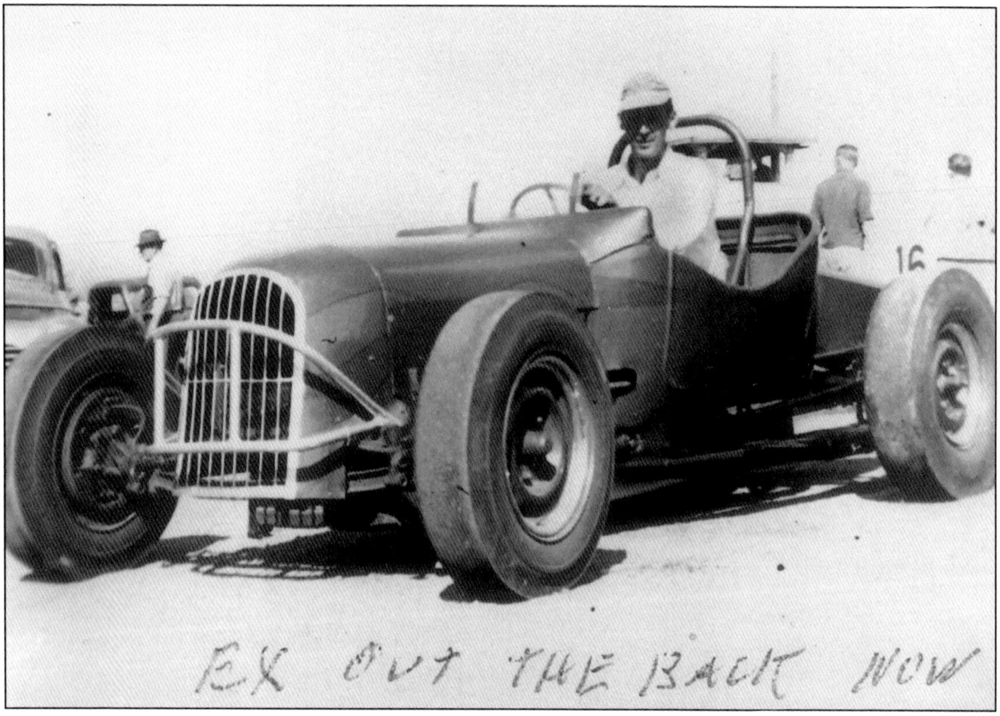

Mike poses in the new Model T racer. This angle highlights the custom nose section that Mike hand built. Note the use of a roll bar, which was rare in those days. Mike—at 6-feet 6-inches tall—towers above it. A hand written caption denotes the new exhaust system. (Michael collection, 1949.)

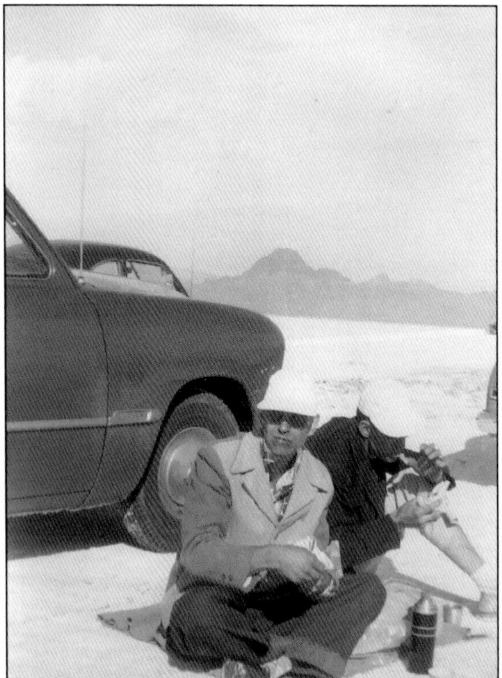

Dad and Mike share a picnic lunch at the Bonneville Salt Flats at the third annual Bonneville Speed Week in August of 1951. Dad drove the family '50 Ford through the flying mile at 89 mph. (Michael collection, 1951.)

Two

The Early Years

I don't care to belong to any social organization that would accept me as a member.
- Groucho Marx

Middletown, Ohio, was eager for a hot rod club in 1951. As in the rest of the country, the returning GIs were settled nicely into their civilian lives by 1951, but those lives were a bit different from the pre-war days. Many of the city boys and farm boys that entered the military in 1941 had no interest in returning to their old lifestyles. The population was moving to the suburbs. Shopping centers were springing up at the edge of town, along with drive-in restaurants and drive-in movie theaters. The nation, as a whole, was becoming more mobile, a nation on wheels. The GIs wanted cars, and the nation's auto makers responded with sleek new styles and powerful V-8 engines; the GIs wanted houses in the suburbs, and the industry responded with the largest housing boom in U.S. history; the GIs wanted families, and the baby boom was on.

The GIs also returned home with something new—a desire to tinker. Farm boys and city boys alike had been trained in the most modern military machine in the world. They learned to service tanks, trucks, jeeps, and aircraft. They learned to maintain modern surveillance and communications equipment. They had tapped latent mechanical skills while serving their country, and these newly honed skills demanded attention.

Harold "Mike" Michael had first gotten the idea for a hot rod club in Middletown as his round track racing operation was winding to a halt in 1950. Without a racecar, he wanted to build a hot rod for street use, and a hot rod would be a lot more fun if you were part of a club with regular club functions. Recent articles in *Hot Rod Magazine* provided guidelines for starting clubs and running club events and the magazine was laying the groundwork for the formation of a national organization of car clubs (the National Hot Rod Association) in its early 1951 issues. The timing seemed to be right. He pitched the idea to Dad and some other friends, and soon things were in motion.

By February of 1951, the word was out that a hot rod club was forming in Middletown. Mike and Dad had sold the idea first to Bill Lovelace and Herb Dome. They were older, established businessmen who would give the club credibility. Herb Sebastian was immediately interested, as was Alex Slamka, Ray Palmer Sr., Ray Jr., and a former Middletown High football star named Dick Miltenberger. Then they sold the idea to racing buddies Snip Dreher, Bob Kuhn, Danny Allen, and Dad's brother-in-law L.G. Meade. They pitched the idea to Carl Lakes, Tom Frebis and Tom's dad, Al Frebis, and all the hot rodders who hung out at Sebastian's Sohio station and Sully Sullivan's body shop. Guys who worked at the steel mill recruited fellow workers who were car buffs. Each guy in turn called everyone he knew: Fred May, Jim Tincher, Ray Boyce, Lee McGee, Jack McClanahan, Carl Bryant, Bobby Jay, Gordon Pence, Sully Sullivan, Bobby McCutchen, and Harold Agee. By word of mouth, the news spread.

The first attempt at an organizational meeting was held at Kuhn Trucking Company, but a terrible rainstorm produced a poor turnout that didn't include the older guys. The group rescheduled the meeting, and this time it was held at Grandpa Bill's radiator repair shop to assure that at least he would be there. That meeting was well attended, and the club was now in motion. This was probably in February of 1951. Other meetings followed at the radiator shop or at Kuhn Trucking Company. Racers, hot rodders, customizers, and car enthusiasts in general collected at these meetings. They elected officers, and Mike, whose organizational skills quickly became apparent, was chosen to be the club's first president. The first meeting at which dues were collected took place in March of 1951, and established the club's fiscal year from March through February.

The first order of business was to pick a name for the club. Several names were suggested, but "Pacemakers" was chosen by a vote of the members. Mike had suggested the name, which was inspired by the sporty model Hudson Pacemaker that was restyled the year before. Mike's love of oval track racing and the dominant Hudson racecars of the day led him to the idea. Herb Thomas won the NASCAR points championship in 1951 driving a Hudson Hornet. Tim Flock would win in a Hudson Hornet in 1952, and Herb Thomas would win his second championship in a Hudson in 1953.

Bylaws were written along with the club's goals. The Pacemakers would promote the sport of hot rodding with safe and legal activities for its members, work with the City of Middletown to obtain a good name in the community, and discourage street racing. It cost $5.00 to join the club, and this fee was broken down as follows: an initiation fee of $1.50, plus $2.50 for the mandatory subscription to *Hot Rod Magazine*, and $1.00 for the first month's dues. Dues were $1.00 per month payable at each monthly meeting.

Membership cards were designed to be functional and to display the club's dedication to highway safety. The business-size card had lines for the signatures of the member, secretary, and president so it could be used as a source of identification. It had the numbers 1 through 12 along the bottom edge to be punched out with each monthly dues payment. The $1.00 dues payment could only be made at the monthly business meeting so as to encourage attendance, and there was a 25¢ fee for being tardy. On the right side of the card was a prominent drawing that would demand attention each time the member pulled it out to pay dues. It was not a drawing of a hot rod, or a car in motion, but a drawing of a stoplight with the red light lit, and a superimposed foot depressing a brake pedal. This was to serve as a constant reminder that safety was a more important issue than performance.

Next came the design of the club jackets. The original club jackets from the early '50s were navy blue with the club's new insignia on the back. The insignia was designed by Fred May, who had switched his allegiance from motorcycles to cars after losing a leg in a motorcycle accident. Fred's design was a winged oval, enclosing a hot rod with the eagle-like wings spread wide. (In the early 1960s, a second-generation club jacket would be issued in red with white block lettering and a crossed checkered flags insignia). The club slogan, "Dedicated to Safety," was borrowed from the National Hot Rod Association, and it appeared on the blue jackets, as well as on special club bumper plates. The Pacemakers had the look of a real hot rod club; all they needed now were activities.

The first competitive events were small scale poker runs limited to club members. The first large scale event was a reliability run held in late March or early April of 1952. It was open to the public and covered by a local the local chapter of Dial Radio Club. A second run followed in May. In the reliability runs, contestants would be given a series of directions leading them over a planned course, at which they had to average a specific and legal speed. A typical course might be 90 miles long with an intended time of three hours or 30 mph. Contestants would check in at specified check points to make certain they had stayed on course. They would generally work in pairs, a driver and a navigator. The team that finished the course the closest to the exact allotted time, the most reliable team in the reliability run, would win the event.

Reliability runs were inspired by the early days of motorcars. At the turn of the century, automobile clubs like AAA didn't have the detailed maps of today. Instead, they would supply a set of written directions, which described the route step by step. A navigator would read the directions, which included items like, "Proceed east out of town to the Johnson farm, and turn north at the windmill. Follow the road to the first crossroads and turn east," and so forth. That was the standard format for travel in the days of sputtering runabouts and duster-clad passengers. Most roads were horse trails without names or route numbers, and few were paved outside of town. The reliability run made it into a game, where a score could be accumulated by the smallest variance from the intended time.

Some of the guys and gals became quite adept at these runs, and the competition became intense. At first, guys would compete with wives or girl friends as team partners, but many found that this led to friction, and it was better to team with someone with whom you were not so close. For example, if a team missed a turn, the navigator might say, "Uh-oh, we missed a turn back there. We need to go back a block." To which the driver might reply, "Okay, watch our time so we can make it up without breaking any laws." The same conversation between a husband and wife might be slightly different: "You missed a turn back there, Stupid!" And the driver might respond, "What do you mean I missed the turn? You've got the directions! Do you want to drive, Big Mouth?" And from there things could only go downhill.

The first club reliability run was held in March or April of 1952, and was based out of the LeSourdsville Lake amusement park parking lot. (The park was still closed for its winter off-season.) It was won by Carl Bryant and his partner, with Carl Lakes and his partner finishing second. Carl Bryant won a large trophy that was dubbed the "Sullivan Trophy," named for Sully Sullivan's son Tommy, who had passed away shortly before the event. Both Carl Bryant and Carl Lakes were quite skilled at reliability runs, and they would finish one-two in the second major run held a few weeks later.

The results of the club's second reliability run, held May 4, 1952, were reported in an article in the *Middletown Journal* newspaper. The winning drivers were listed as follows: Carl Lakes drove the winning car with a score of 995.25 out of a possible 1000 points. Carl Bryant was second with 992.50, and Bobby Jay finished third with 992.45. Fourth was George Howard with 992.30. (George Howard was Dad's uncle, and he was father to comedian G. David Howard, our cousin.) Bill Lane was fifth with 992.25, Jim Withrow sixth at 992.20, and H. Meyers seventh at 990.35. Eighth was Les Richter with 990.15, ninth was Dick Miltenberger at 990.05, and tenth was Dan Hansman at 989.10. Positions 11 through 14 were listed without scores as Lee McGee, Alex Slamka, Leon Osborn, and Clarence Pence, respectively. The article went on to state that Carl Lakes won the Lovelace Radiator Trophy, apparently donated by Grandpa Bill, and that Carl had improved from a second place finish at the club's first reliability run earlier in the year. The first 14 places all received trophies.

Another version of the runs had contestants stopping at designated points to obtain a playing card, and the team with the best poker hand at the end would win. Poker runs and reliability runs were common events for the club in the first few years, but dwindled later with the advent of drag racing and club sponsored car shows. The runs took a lot of time to prepare and quite a bit of man power to execute, so they looked for other types of events to offer in order to provide variety and prevent member burn out. As new events entered the scene, the club's attention was drawn away from these events, but the reliability runs and poker runs of the early years were important club events that made the members work together and helped the club gel.

The civic acceptance program was very important in the early days of the Pacemakers. The club made it very clear to the City of Middletown that they were there to help. Several programs were initiated toward that end. First, the city asked the club for a favor. The city's air raid siren needed to be refurbished. (The club started less than six years after World War II, and air raid sirens were still commonplace.) Middletown's siren was powered by its own generator, so as to work even if the electrical power was shut off to the area. The generator was powered by a Chevrolet six-cylinder engine, which needed attention, and this was right down the club's alley.

The club went to work on the project with unbridled enthusiasm. They decided that the siren and generator could be mounted in a pickup truck and thereby driven around town so everyone would be able to hear it. They secured an early '30s Chevy pickup that belonged to one of Herb Sebastian's brothers. He was hardly using the old truck and it had little resale value, so he was glad donate it to the cause. The club members gave the truck a tune up and delivered it to the city. Shortly after, the city decided to scrap the air raid siren project, but a good working relationship between the club and the city had been established. Things were off to a good start.

Next, the Pacemakers assisted the city police in running annual vehicle safety inspections. An inspection station would be set up somewhere in town and manned by club members. People would pull in on a volunteer basis to run their car through a series of checks on safety items like brake lights, turn signals, and parking brake, etc. The Pacemakers ran these inspections annually throughout the '50s and early '60s and received many awards from the city for this program. But the nicest gesture the city could have possibly made came as a complete surprise. In appreciation for the vehicle inspection program, the city offered a large meeting room free of charge for club meetings at the gas and electric building. The Pacemakers took advantage of this offer, since the club had outgrown the limited space and seating capacity of both Grandpa Bill's radiator repair shop and the Kuhn Trucking Company. The gas and electric building meeting room served as the club's headquarters for several years before the meetings moved to the Armco Steel Research Laboratory. In 1959, the club purchased its own building.

The other important piece of the club's image program was aimed at public acceptance. Hot rodding originated in southern California and had earned a bad name through street racers in that area. This was bad enough, but because of the location of hot rodding's birth the problem was multiplied by the Hollywood movie studios. An abundance of local hot rods were readily available, and a movie with a hot rod story line could be made quickly and on a low budget. So Hollywood cranked them out during the 1950s, with the hot rodders typically portrayed as juvenile delinquents. Titles like *Hot Rod Rumble*, *Teen Age Thunder*, *Drag Strip Girl*, and *Hot Rods to Hell* filled movie marquees from the Atlantic to the Pacific. Communities throughout the entire country had formed a bad opinion of hot rods and hot rodders even before they ever saw one in their area. This was an image that had to be overcome if a hot rod club were to survive in the conservative Midwest.

The public acceptance program had several parts. Business cards were made up for two specific programs. Members would cruise downtown Middletown and inspect parking meters. If a meter was expired, or nearly so, they would drop in a dime and leave a card that told the car owner that he or she had been assisted by the club. Members would also stop and help stranded motorists, sometimes jump starting cars, pouring in a gallon of gas or changing a flat tire. Always the business cards would be left behind like the Lone Ranger leaving the telltale silver bullet.

The most unique public acceptance program was the brainchild of Harold Michael. In the early '50s iron lungs were still in use to assist polio victims with breathing. Mike found out that Armco owned two mobile iron lung units as a public service to loan to area hospitals. They were fitted onto two pickup trucks, one Ford and one Dodge, both of pre-war vintage. When requested, the trucks would haul them, often at high speeds with a police escort to the hospital in need, which could be anywhere in southern Ohio, southern Indiana, or northern Kentucky. Mike saw two opportunities for the club to assist in this program. First, he offered to supply drivers, himself included since the high speed driving looked like fun. Second, he offered to solve a problem encountered when both vehicles made the run together. It seems that the Dodge with its flathead six-cylinder engine could not keep up with the Ford with its V-8 engine when running flat out. This was solved with a mild hop up for the Dodge. The club members milled the head and installed a larger carburetor that made the little Dodge six run right with the Ford V-8.

In the spring of 1954, the club set out to run the first organized drag races in the area. At that time the nearest drag races were at Akron, nearly 200 miles away. The Pacemakers worked in conjunction with the Middletown Police and obtained permission to use a small access road by the animal shelter outside of nearby Trenton. It was a nice flat surface about a half mile long located about a mile north of the present-day Miller Brewing plant. The road, called Riverside Drive, made a triangle with two main roads, Hamilton-Trenton Road and Wayne Madison Road. The access road was blocked off, and the two main roads served as the return road. This was not a problem, since the cars that ran there were all street legal, with the exception of one dragster that had been towed down from northern Indiana. Drag strips were so rare in the Midwest at that time that the guy was happy to tow over 100 miles in order to race his car.

The cars would enter the course from Wayne Madison Road, and line up (or stage) behind the starting line. They would be started by a flagman and make their quarter mile run westward on Riverside Drive with police radar used to report the top end speed. There was ample room to stop, since the fastest speeds would have seldom topped 90 mph. There were no elapsed times reported at drag races in those days, since that concept was not yet developed. In drag racing's early days, top speed was the only performance measurement. Because of the narrow course at Trenton cars ran one at a time for safety, and the various classes competed by comparing top speeds. After they completed their run, the contestants would return down Hamilton-Trenton Road to Wayne Madison to line up again.

This format was not so different from many other fledgling drag race meets across the country at that time. Flag starts and minimal timing equipment were the norm. Police departments and civic groups endorsed the events, which were invariably run by a host car club. Such was the humble beginning of organized drag racing.

The Pacemaker's drag racing operation didn't last due to complaints by the local residents who were unhappy with the noise, the crowds of onlookers, and the loss of the access road. They ran about three or four meets and had to shut down. The club looked at other avenues to bring drag racing into the area, including a short-lived merger with several other area clubs into the Southern Ohio Timing Association in March of 1956. The group was led by a Cincinnati Police Highway Safety Officer named Carl Poppe, who planned a permanent drag strip in the area. The group did obtain a tract of land near Lunken Airport for a drag strip, but they fell far short of raising the $45,000 needed to pave the track and improve the land—an awesome figure in the mid 1950s. Drag racing was not yet drawing the kind of crowds that would make a drag strip pay. Most drag strips of the day were leases on converted airfields where the pavement was already in place and such a large sum of money was not needed. In some cases, a civic organization would raise the necessary funds to build a drag strip, like the famous Lions Drag Strip in southern California that was funded by a local Lions Club. But the Southern Ohio Timing Association had no such benefactor, and the project staggered at the daunting task.

The Pacemakers left the group and began to plan a drag strip around Middletown. They looked at a tract of land along the Miami River bed near Hook Field. I remember going with Dad and Mike when they checked out the land to see how a drag race facility might fit onto it. I was about five at the time, and Dad kept telling me to be quiet. I kept talking to Mike as we walked along, not realizing that he was pacing off the land and I was causing him to lose count. The Pacemaker deal fell through, and Middletown never got its drag strip. However, the Southern Ohio timing Association continued to work with other area clubs and succeeded in building a drag strip along the Ohio River off Beechmont Avenue in Cincinnati. It took two years and the joining of a new member hot rodder with family connections to a paving company, but the track, called Beechmont Drag Strip, finally opened in 1958.

In June of 1954, the Pacemakers put on the first major custom auto show in the area at the LeSourdsville Lake Amusement Park. It was a huge success. The two-day show set a weekend attendance record for the park, including a single day attendance record on Sunday. It drew high quality cars from Ohio, Kentucky, and Indiana, and the public loved it. Car shows were the best means of selling the public on hot rodding. People could see the cars displayed up close and really appreciate the time and effort that goes into a show-quality car. The show included hot rods, customs, racecars, sports cars, and antiques—there was something for everyone. People came out in droves for the 1954 show, and it was repeated annually through 1965, the club's last active year. A modern version of the show continued at the park, later called Americana

Amusement Park, well into the 1990s. This was one of the longest running car shows in the United States.

With all these activities, the club got a lot of attention. The *Middletown Journal* covered the reliability runs and did a two-part feature of the first Pacemaker Custom Auto Show. The members always wore the club jackets and tee shirts, advertising the club wherever they went. Soon the club grew, ballooning up to 130 members at one time. It seemed everyone wanted to be a Pacemaker.

By 1955, Middletown had several reasons to be proud. The town's own McGuire Sisters had a national hit record, "Sincerely," on the charts, and native son Jerry Lucas' storied high school basketball career was just taking off. The Pacemakers were a growing force within Middletown by 1955. In just a few short years, they had made quite a name in the community. But in the mid 1950s, things were just starting to happen. The club's plunge into drag racing in the next few years would change the face of the club and make them nationally known in that arena.

There is one final note on 1955. At the end of the year I joined the club as an honorary member, the first such honor given to a five-year-old. I had been attending the monthly meetings with Dad on a regular basis, generally being the only small kid present. Several of the club members had commented that my attendance record was better than a lot of the members, and someone jokingly pointed out the fact that I also had no traffic violations. Fred May carried this a step further and nominated me to be an honorary member one night under new business. The club quickly voted me in and gave me a membership card, which I prominently displayed in my new Mickey Mouse wallet. That September I had started kindergarten, and two great new kids' television shows both debuted in October, *Captain Kangaroo* and the *Mickey Mouse Club*. Everything seemed right with the world: I was going to school, I was a member of a hot rod club, and I was in love for the first time, with Annette Funicello.

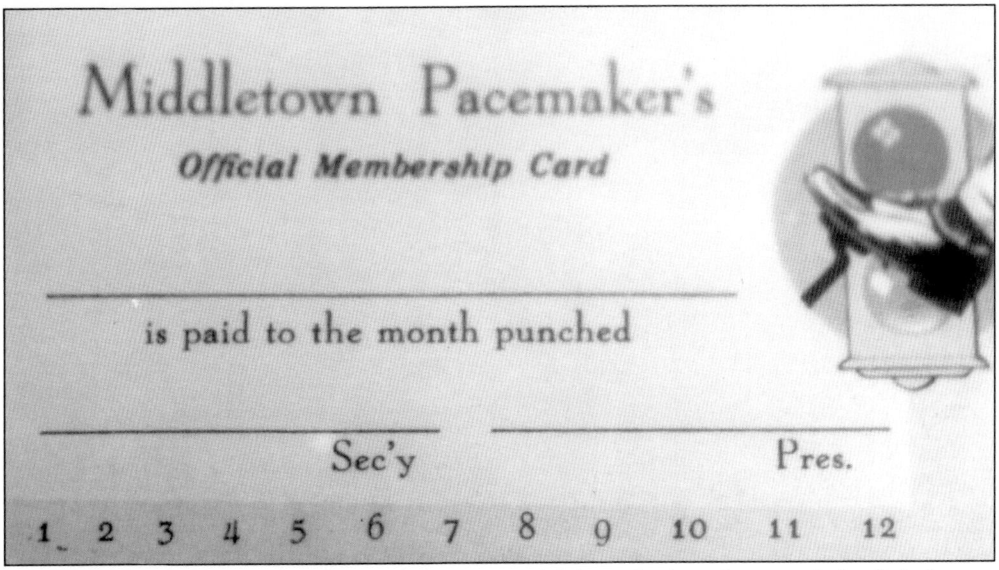

This early Pacemaker membership card shows a careful driver braking for a stoplight. Safe driving was encouraged by the club in order to help combat the nationwide delinquent reputation of hot rodders, a reputation earned by illegal street racing and perpetuated by Hollywood movies. (Roberson collection, 1951.)

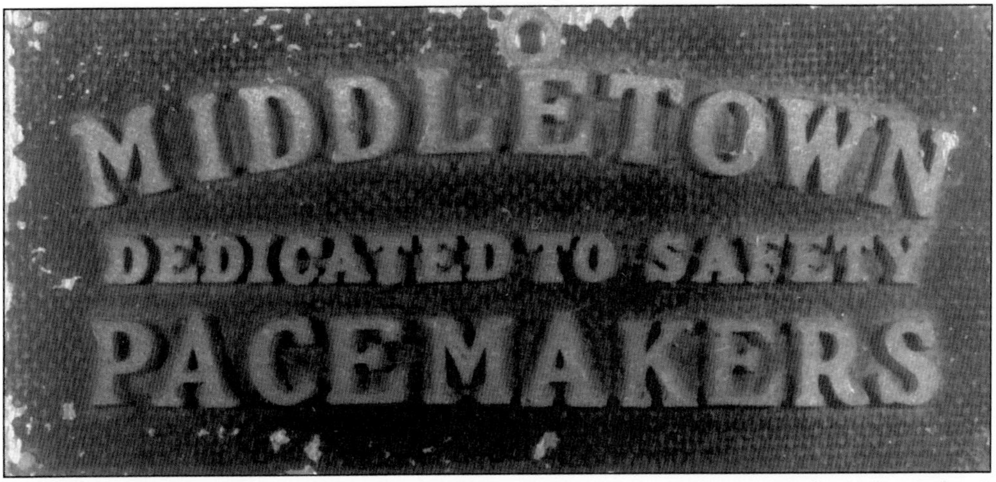

The club members' cars carried this plate with the club's name and slogan, "Dedicated to Safety," which was borrowed from the National Hot Rod Association. (Roberson collection, 1951.)

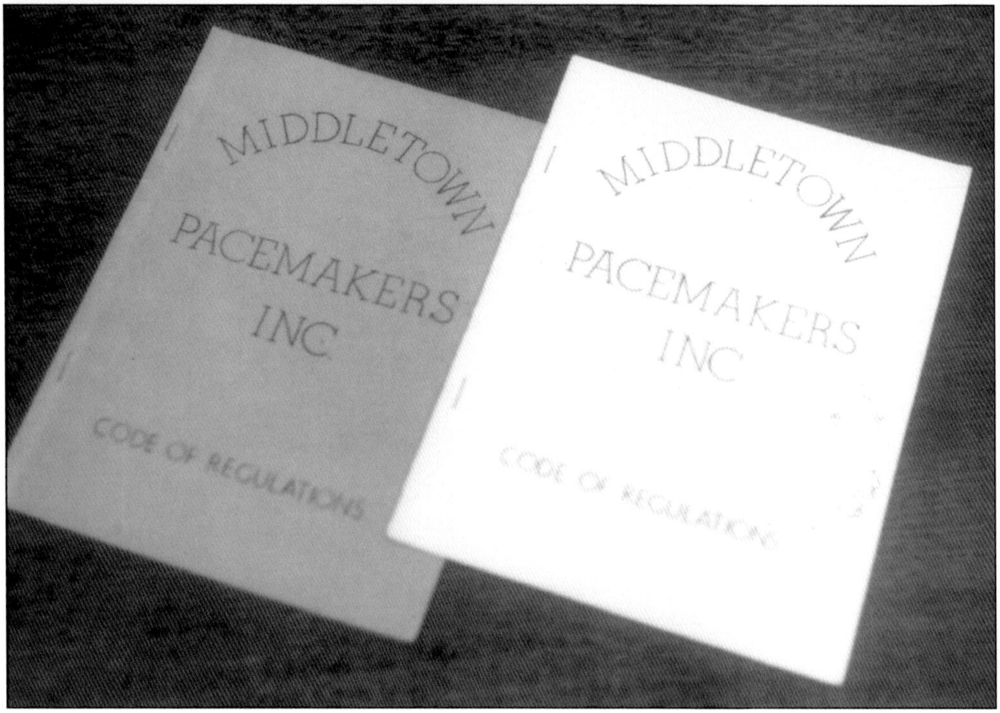

The Middletown Pacemaker Code of Regulations contained the rules and regulations of the club. It was published when the club was incorporated in 1952. (Roberson collection, 1952.)

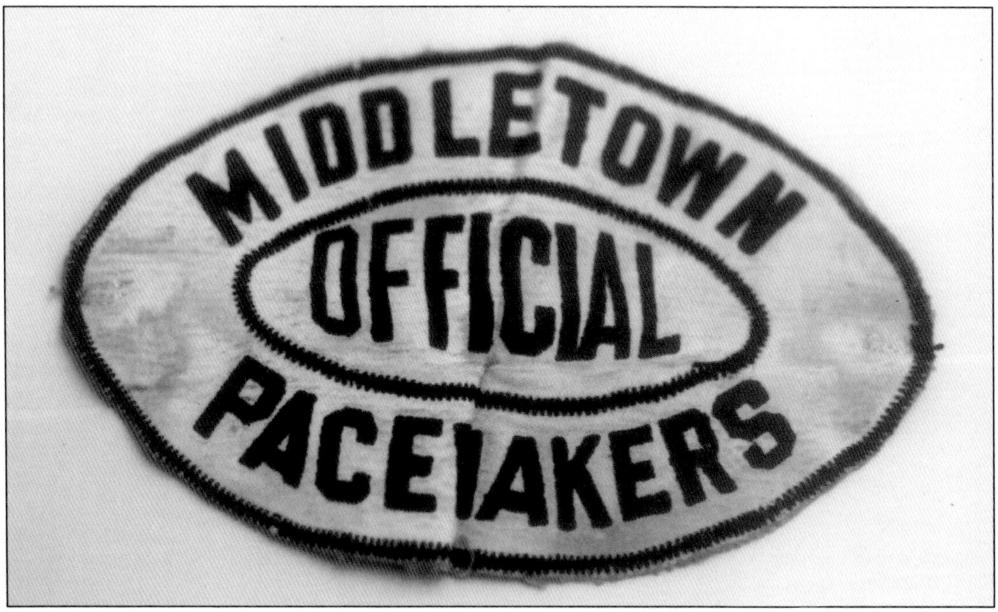

Club Members wore these armbands at reliability runs and car shows to signify which members were acting as officials at that event. The arm bands pre-dated the club jackets but were still used later. At one point the club had 130 members, and the club jackets would not necessarily signify an official at a Pacemaker event. This arm band was supplied by Harold "Mike" Michael. (Roberson collection, 1951.)

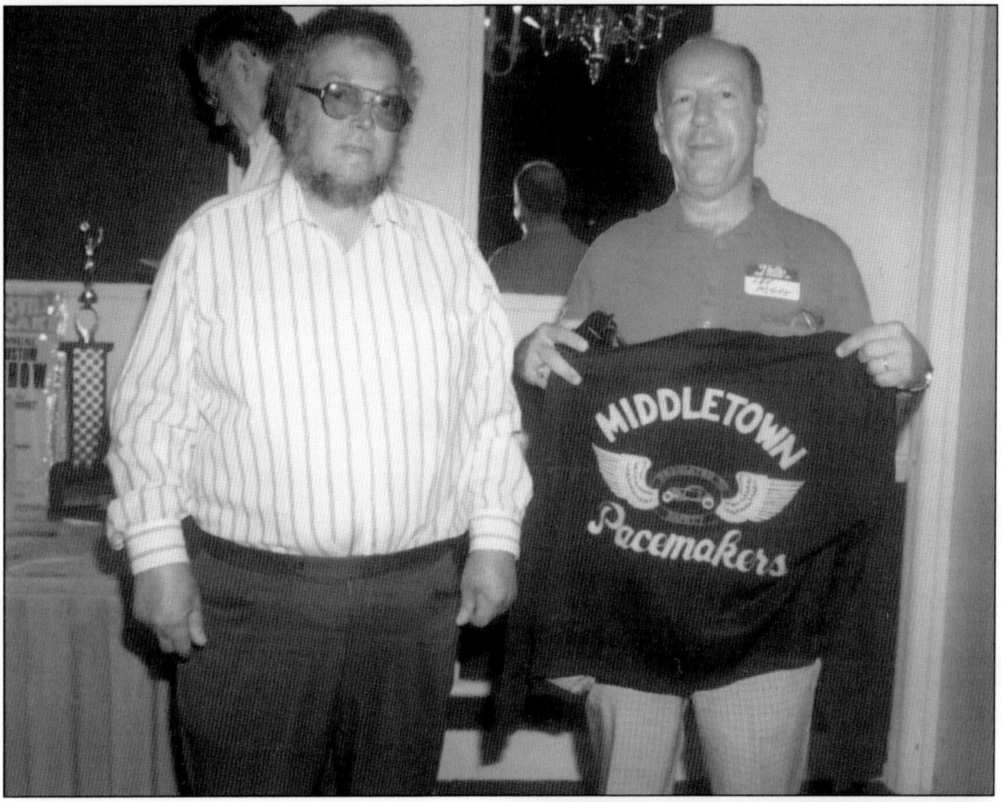

Lee McGee displays an early 1950s version club jacket at the club's first reunion in June of 1994 as Jim Tincher looks on. The winged oval logo was designed by charter member Fred May. (Lakes collection, 1994.)

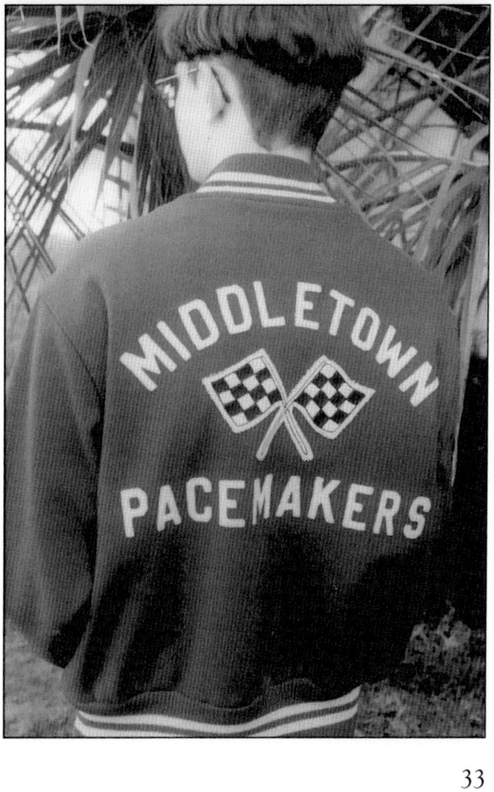

A club jacket, early 1960s era, is modeled by my son Jason. These jackets were red with white letters and carried crossed checkered flags instead of the winged oval logo that was on the earlier jackets. This particular jacket was given to me by Jim Neely, and it had belonged to his late wife Marcia. (Roberson collection.)

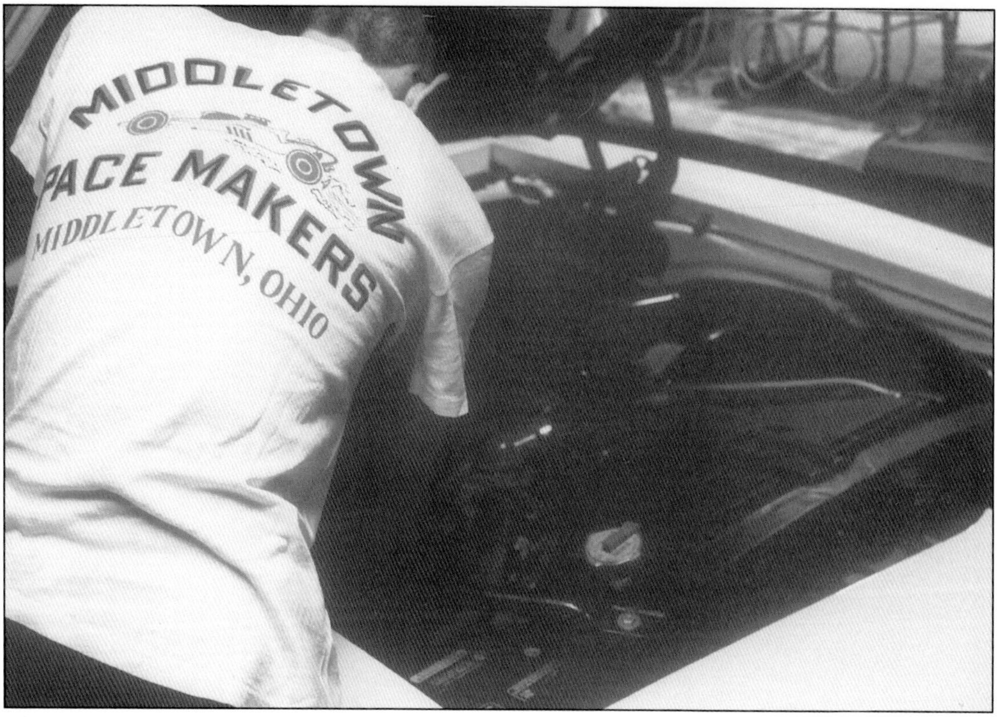

The official Pacemaker tee shirt appeared when the club began running the project dragsters and coordinating the outfits of the crew. The design by charter member Fred May graced both the front and the back of the shirt. My son Jason models a 40-year old example in this 1999 staged photo. (Roberson collection, late 1950s.)

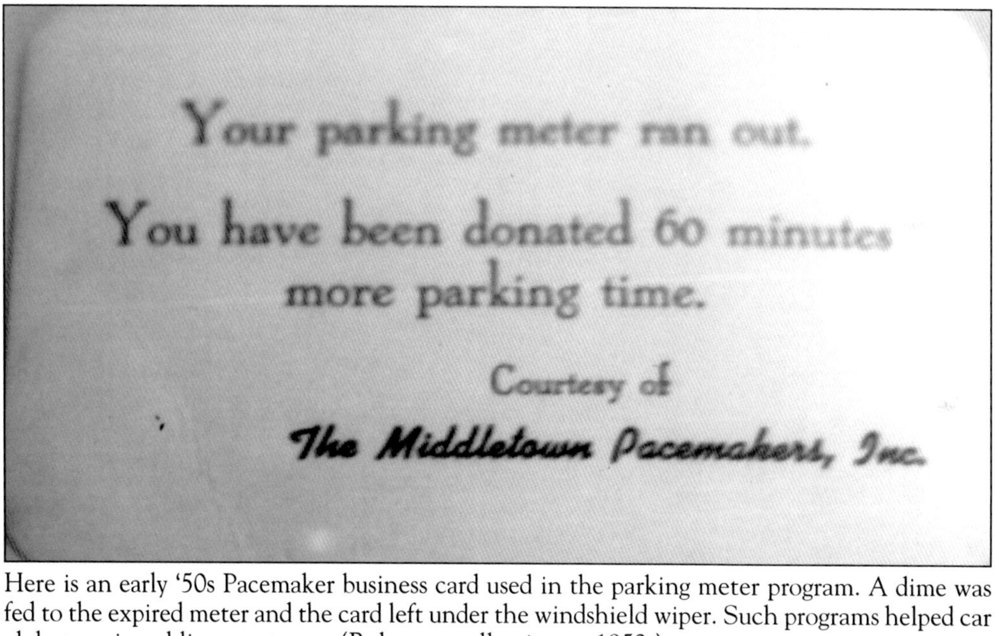

Here is an early '50s Pacemaker business card used in the parking meter program. A dime was fed to the expired meter and the card left under the windshield wiper. Such programs helped car clubs to gain public acceptance. (Roberson collection, c. 1952.)

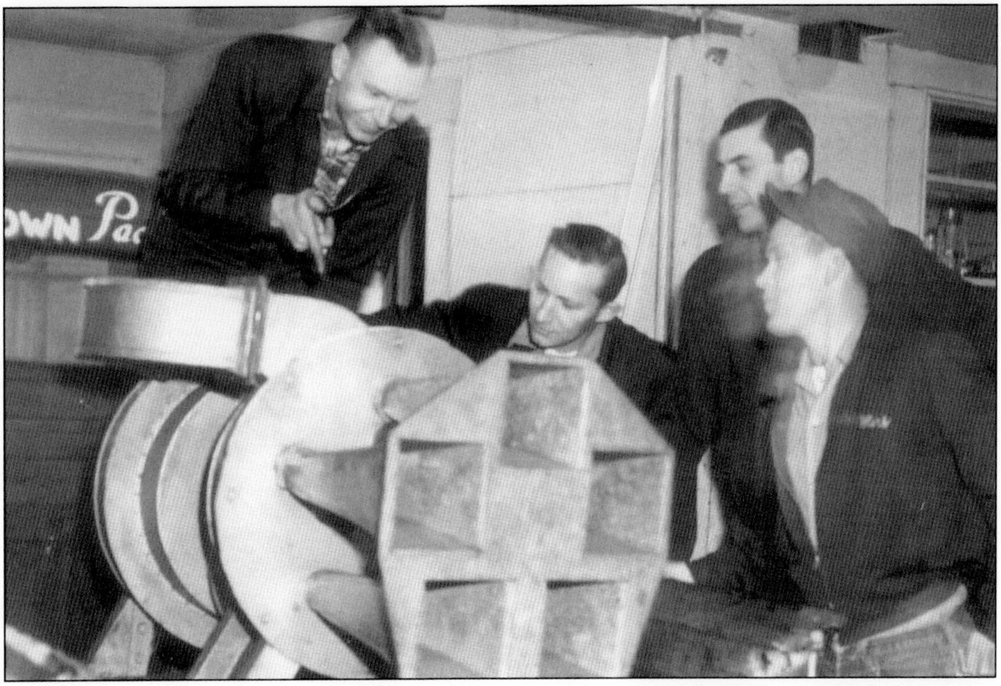

Pictured here, from left to right, are Dad, Jess Patrick, Mike Michael, and Herb Sebastian inspecting the City of Middletown's air raid siren. The Pacemakers turned it into a mobile unit by mounting in a Chevy pickup truck and running it off a portable generator. Note the club jackets. (Michael collection, 1952.)

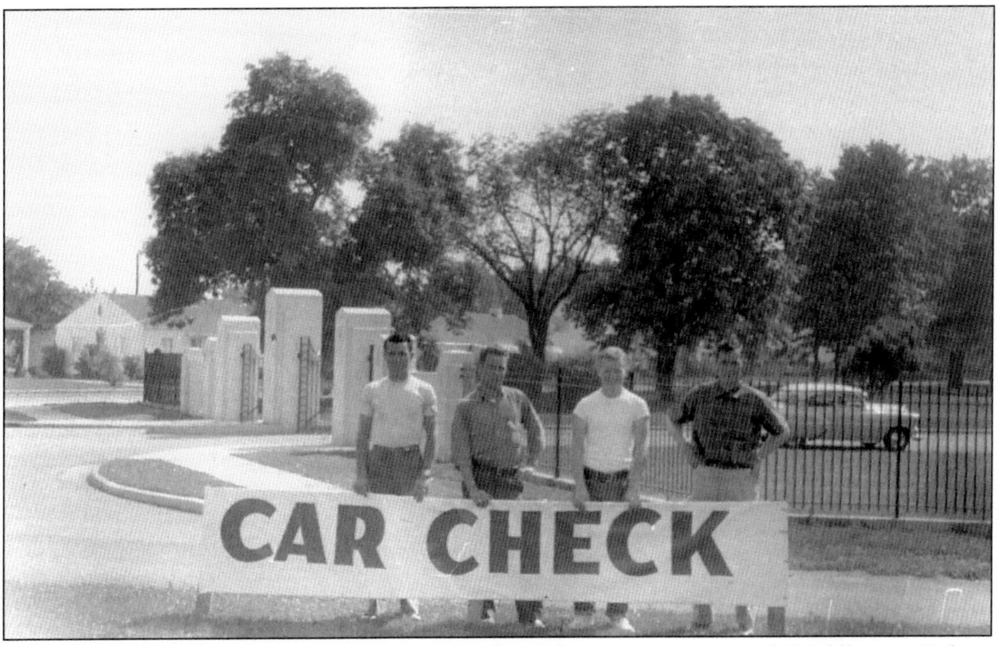

Annual vehicle safety inspections were run by the club in conjunction with Middletown Police. Shown here, from left to right, are Tug Swain, Herb Sebastian, and two unidentified members. The background is the entrance to Woodside Cemetery. (Palmer collection, Mid '50s.)

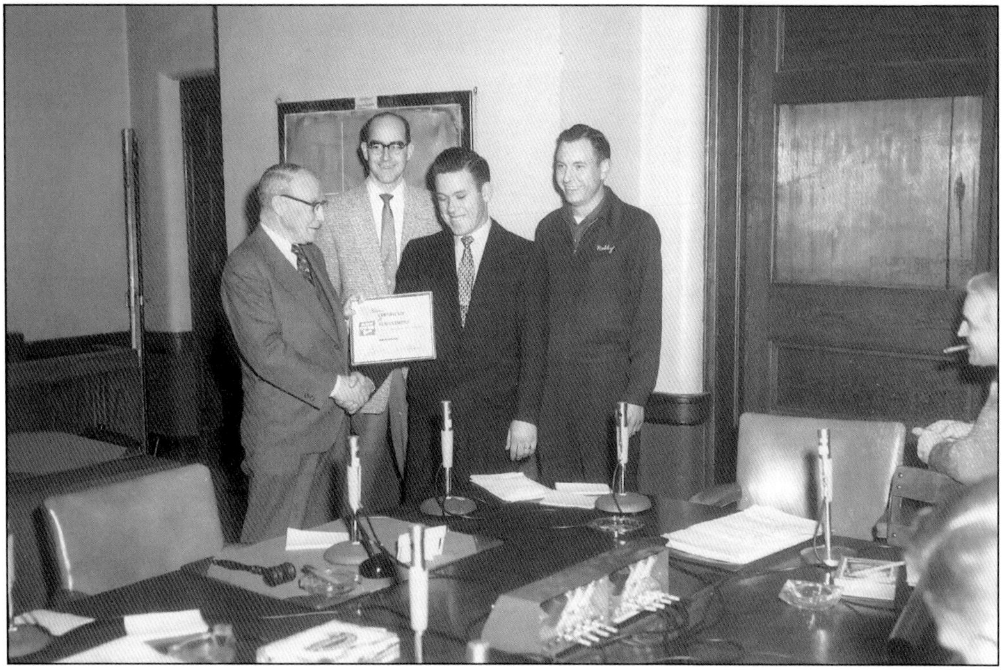

Club president Herb Sebastian accepts the city award for the club's participation in running the vehicle safety inspections. Standing, left to right, are an unidentified city official, Bob Coughlin, Herb Sebastian, and Dad. (Roberson collection, mid '50s).

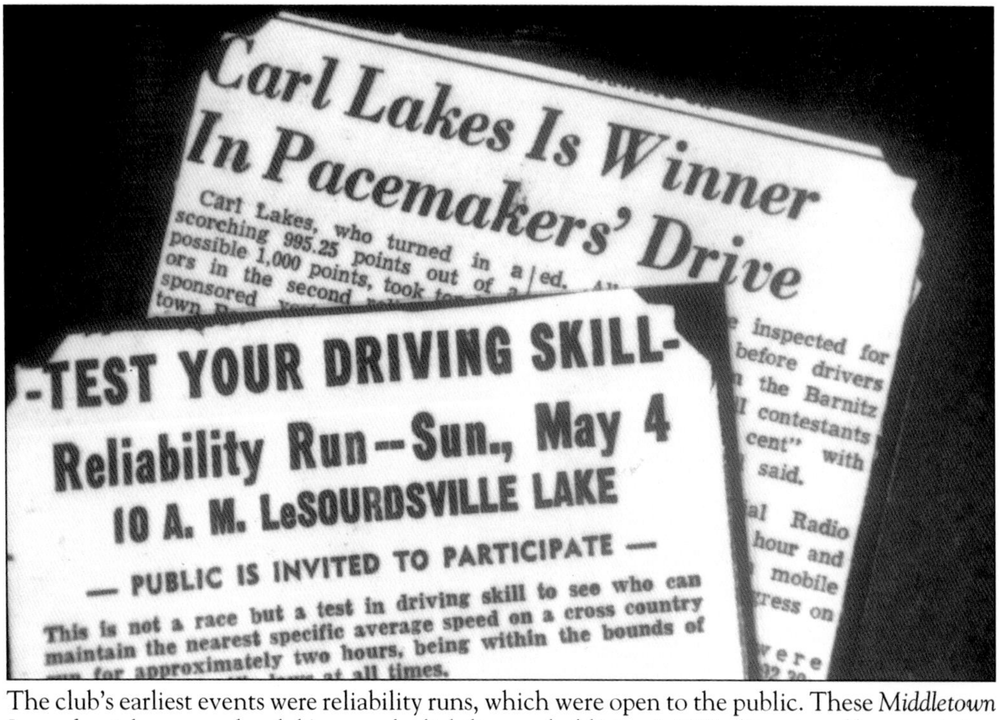

Carl Lakes Is Winner
In Pacemakers' Drive

Carl Lakes, who turned in a
scorching 995.25 points out of a
possible 1,000 points, took
ors in the second
sponsored
inspected for
before drivers
the Barnitz
contestants
cent" with
said.
al Radio
hour and
mobile
ress on

-TEST YOUR DRIVING SKILL-
Reliability Run--Sun., May 4
10 A. M. LeSOURDSVILLE LAKE
— PUBLIC IS INVITED TO PARTICIPATE —
This is not a race but a test in driving skill to see who can
maintain the nearest specific average speed on a cross country
for approximately two hours, being within the bounds of
at all times.

The club's earliest events were reliability runs, which were open to the public. These *Middletown Journal* articles report the club's second reliability run held May 4, 1952. (Reprinted by permission of the *Middletown Journal*, 1952.)

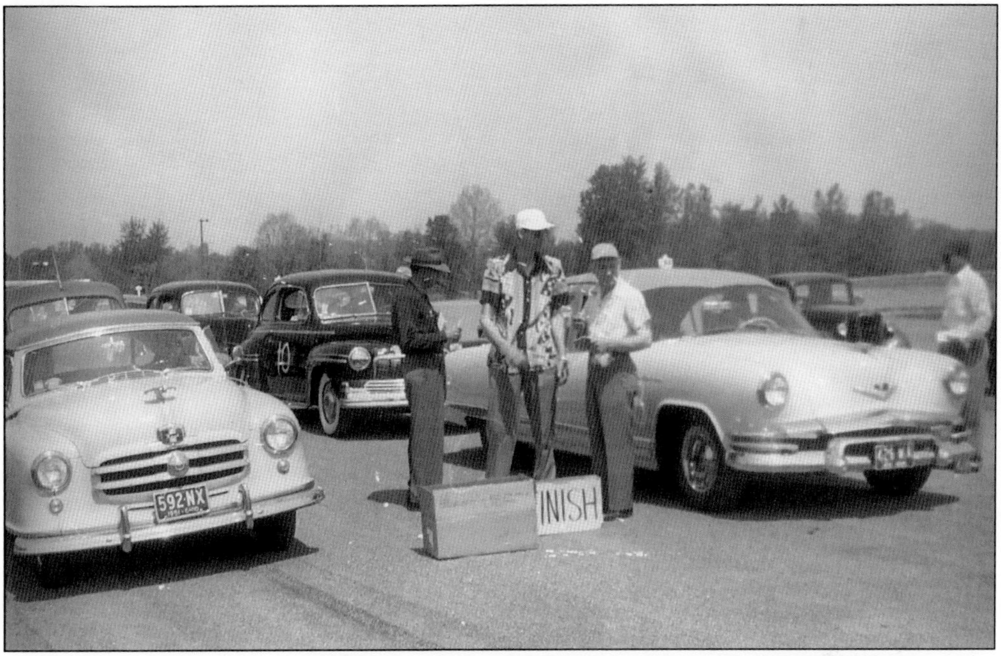

Pictured here, from left to right, Bill Lovelace, Harold Michael, and Herb Dome officiate at the club's first reliability run about March 1952. First cars in line include a Nash, a Kaiser, and a Mercury coupe. (Roberson collection, 1952.)

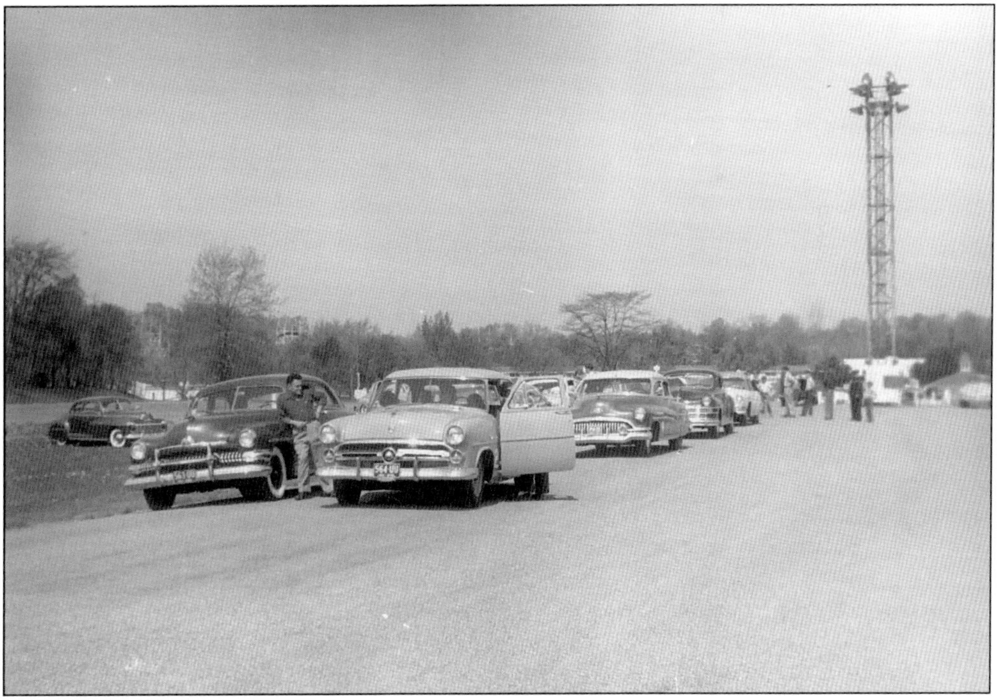

A Mercury and a new Ford head this line up of competitors at the club's first reliability run held at LeSourdsville Lake Amusement Park's vacant (off season) parking lot. Note the roller coaster peaking above the tree line just above the Mercury. (Roberson collection, 1952.)

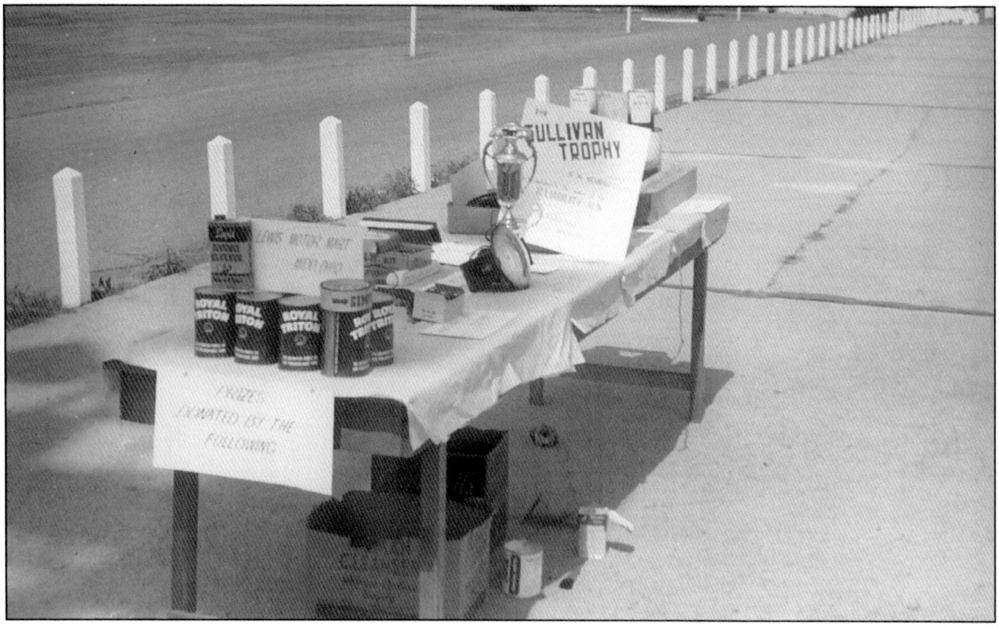

The awards table at the first Pacemaker reliability run includes the "Sullivan Trophy" named for club member Sully Sullivan's son Tommy, who had passed away just prior to the run. The event was dedicated to Tommy's memory. The trophy was won by club member Carl Bryant. (Roberson collection, 1952.)

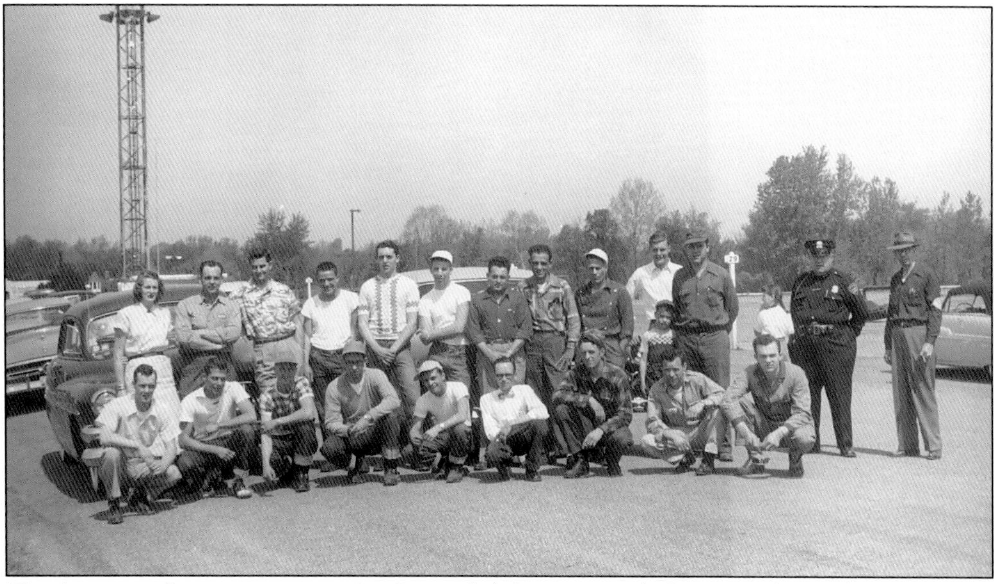

The line up of competitors at the first reliability run includes several members or future members. From left to right, they are as follows: (front row, kneeling) Ray Boyce, Tom Frebis, unidentified, Ray Palmer, unidentified, Clarence Pence, Willard Roberson, unidentified, and Bobby McCutchen; (back row, standing) Gloria Miltenberger, Jack McClanahan, unidentified, unidentified, Carl Bryant, Lee McGee, unidentified, unidentified, Fred May, unidentified, unidentified child, unidentified, Cass Michael, Officer Frank Rogers, and Bill Lovelace (with Pacemaker arm band). (Roberson collection, 1952.)

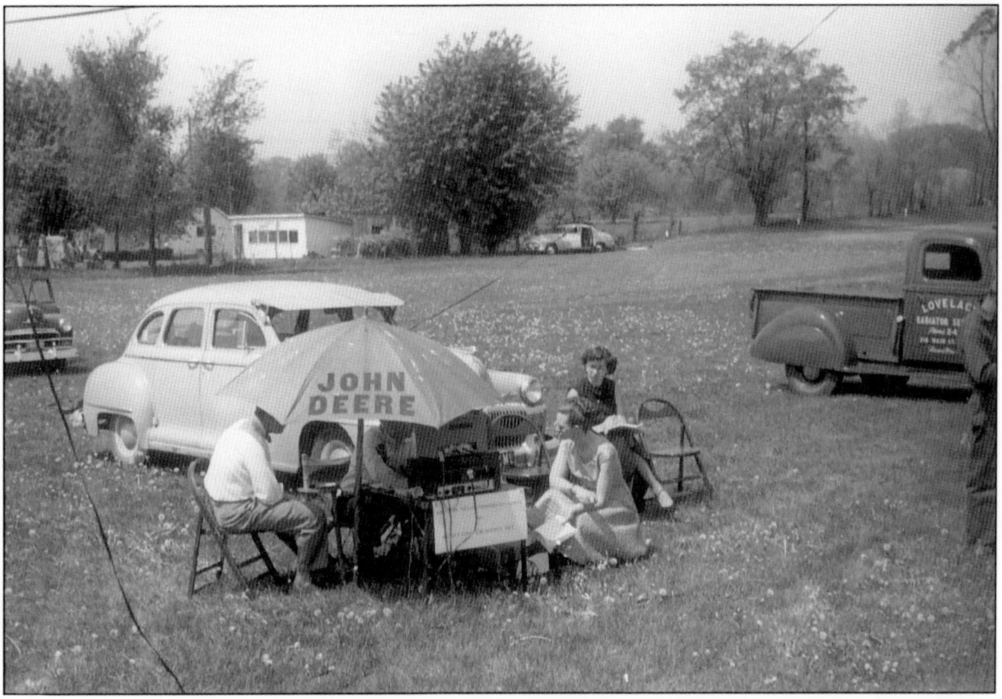

The Dial Radio Club monitors a Pacemaker's reliability run at Barnitz Field in 1952. Gloria Miltenberger kneels in the front. Others in the photo are unidentified. Dad's 1945 Ford shop truck is at right. (Roberson collection, 1952.)

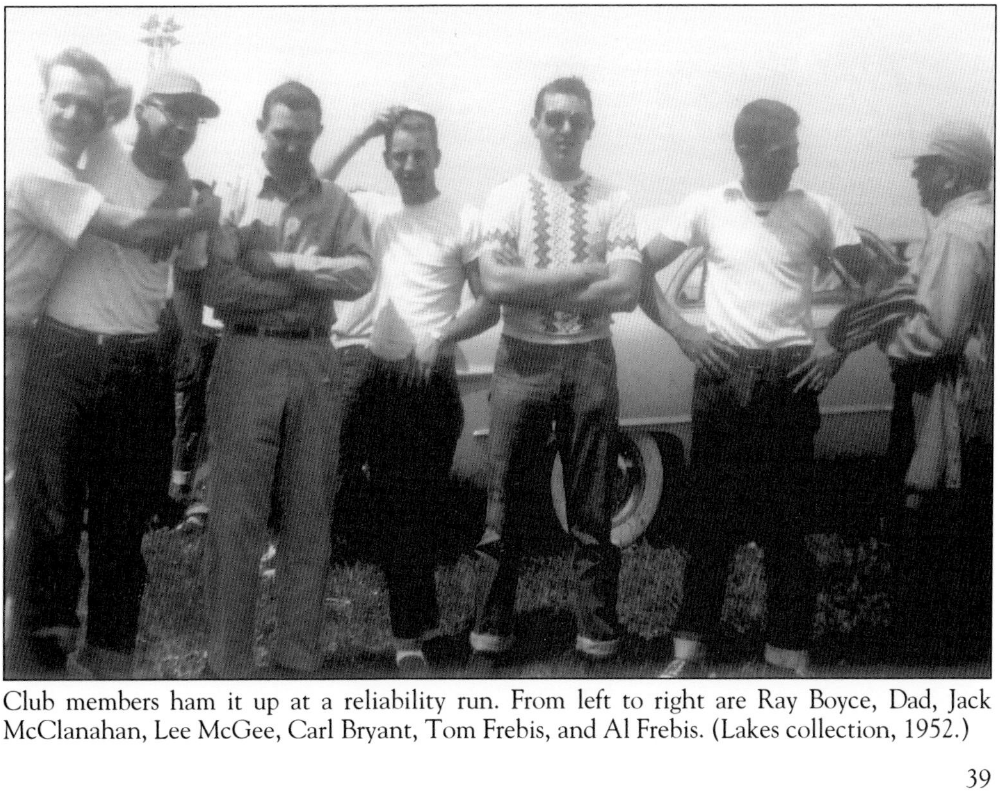

Club members ham it up at a reliability run. From left to right are Ray Boyce, Dad, Jack McClanahan, Lee McGee, Carl Bryant, Tom Frebis, and Al Frebis. (Lakes collection, 1952.)

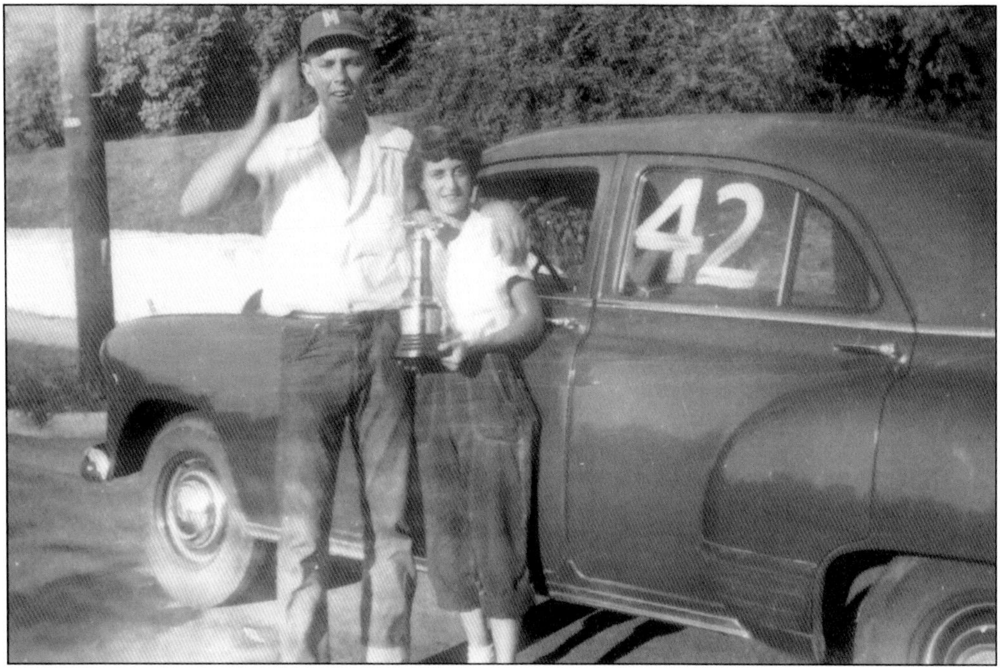

First place at the May 4, 1952 reliability run and winners of the Lovelace Radiator Trophy were driver Carl Lakes and navigator Charlotte Stein in her number 42 late model Chevy sedan. The team scored 995.25 out of a possible 1000 points, a nearly perfect score. (Lakes collection, 1952.)

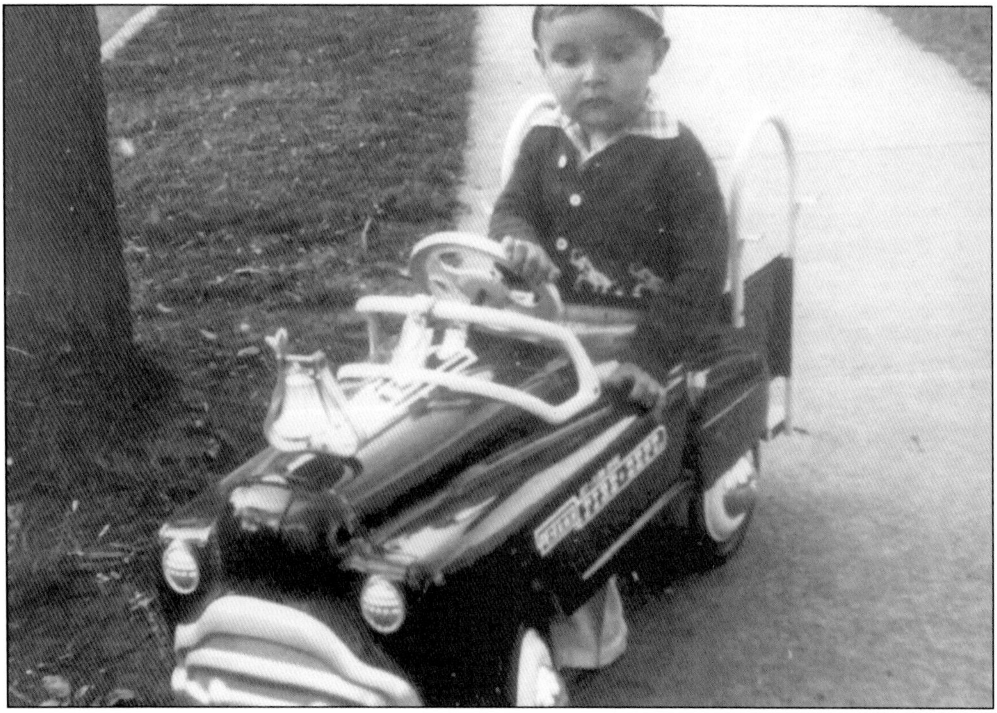

At age three I received my first set of wheels courtesy of Grandpa Bill. The color was fire engine red. (Roberson collection, 1954.)

Three

THE MEMBERS' CARS

If you think you can or you think you can't, you're right.

- Henry Ford

Hot rodding in 1951 had the same basic concepts as the sport of street rodding has today. The hot rodder would start with a '20s to '40s model car (usually a Ford) and upgrade the drive train with a more powerful engine, better brakes, and a more dependable transmission and rear end. Often they were stripped of fenders and lowered to look like racecars of the period. The car's top would be lowered in a process called chopping, and the body might be lowered over the car's frame in a process called channeling. This made them look like the wind-cheating racecars on the California dry lakes and Bonneville Salt Flats that had been lowered for improved aerodynamics. Engines were usually dressed up with chrome accessories for looks or aluminum speed equipment pieces for improved performance. Paint jobs might include pin striping or brightly colored flames like those painted on pre-war racecars. The owners sought individuality that was not available through the cookie-cutter cars coming from Detroit. Often, the hot rods were customized to the point of being one-of-a-kind vehicles.

The basic difference between the hot rodder of 1951 and the street rodder of today lies in the means for obtaining a car and the relative budget that the typical rodder in each era had available for upgrades. Today's street rods often have plush interiors and include amenities like tilt steering wheels, cruise control, air conditioning, and a paint job costing several thousand dollars. In 1951, hot rods were simple, with the vast majority of the hardware coming from junkyards. There were no fiberglass bodies or kits or specialty shops that would provide a complete turnkey car. Aftermarket parts were available, but on a more narrow scale. Build a Ford car with a flathead V-8 engine, and there were lots of parts available to make it go faster and look prettier. With any other brand or combination, the rodder was often on his own. Much horse-trading took place in order to get the parts and services needed. The clubs offered a source of various talents and an arena for information exchange. A guy who knew engines might trade a body-and-paint man an engine-rebuild for a paint job. An upholstery guy might take a set of aftermarket heads in trade for a tuck and roll job. And so the system worked.

Two speed shops in the area were popular sources of good after-market parts for the Middletown hot rodders by the mid '50s—Bob Kyle's shop in Hamilton and Brockman's in Dayton. Dick Weinle's shop in Cincinnati was a little farther drive, but it was also very popular, especially with the drag racers. Prior to those shops' existence, there were always the mail order houses like So-Cal and Racer Brown. Some of the local machinists became quite adept at hot rod pieces, and the local parts departments at the various car dealerships usually had one special counter person that all the hot rodders would ask for. The Ford garage in Middletown, for example, had Mom's cousin Dick Lovelace behind the counter, and Dick knew all the hot rodders and the parts they needed.

The Ford and Mercury flathead V-8 engines were still the engines of choice for the hot rodder in 1951. Ford had offered the same basic block since 1932, with the newer ones sporting 100 horsepower in stock form. It was relatively straightforward to build an early '30s Ford into a hot rod; start with a '32 or later Ford car, and the '48 Mercury engine would bolt right in. This change alone would increase the horsepower in a '32 Ford from 65 to 100, or about 50 percent. The '48 Mercury engine had adequate capacity for bore jobs and larger pistons that would increase the engine's displacement for additional power, and thanks to the wide use of the Ford and Mercury engines in California dry lakes racing, there were tons of aftermarket parts to add even more power. The typical hot rod Ford V-8 would sport multiple Stromberg carburetors, using intake manifolds from Edlebrock or Weiand, aluminum heads with increased compression ratios from Offenhauser, and a high performance cam from Iskenderian, Racer Brown, Chet Herbert, Clay Smith, or a host of others. These changes would push the horsepower into the 150 to 175 range, which would propel the lightweight coupes and roadsters to speeds that no Detroit iron of the day could match.

With the added power of the hopped up engines in the '30s Fords, the stock brakes and stock transmissions were substantially over matched. Both problems could be fixed by raiding the junkyards. Ford changed from cable activated brakes to hydraulic brakes with the '39 models, and upgrading to '39 brakes was relatively easy. The backing plates for the '39 would bolt into place on the older axle assemblies so all the wheel components were bolt-ons. Hot rodders needed only to run brake lines and mount the master cylinder, and the fix was in place. For the transmission, the heavier Lincoln Zephyr unit would fit nicely in place of the Ford unit and offer a considerable increase in reliability. The Zephyr unit was designed for a larger car with a V-12 engine, so it was considerably beefier internally than the little cousin Ford version.

Aircraft engine development during the war had prompted the development of higher-octane gasoline. This led to similar developments in automotive engines, beginning with Charles Kettering's work at GM. With the 1949 models, Olds started a factory hot rod trend (the term "muscle car" came later) that would last for 25 years by debuting Kettering's new high compression, overhead valve V-8 engine and placing it in a relatively light-weight sedan—the Rocket 88. The Olds sported 135 horsepower from 303 cubic inches that first year, enough to rival the hopped up Ford V-8s prior to any modifications to the Olds. Each year into the '50s the Olds engine became larger and more powerful, with 160 hp in 1953, 202 hp in 1955, and a 300-hp version available by 1957. In a few short years after its debut it would become plentiful in the junkyards and begin to challenge Ford's dominance as the rodder's choice engine. Cadillac produced a similar engine to the Olds in 1949, sporting 160 hp from 331 cubic inches, but it was used less often by the hot rodders due to the higher cost. In 1953, Chrysler would introduce the first of their hemi-head engines, which were a bit heavy but produced a lot of power. They would become the round track racer's choice in NASCAR stockcars and later in drag racing, when superchargers and nitromethane fuel would bring out the Hemi's real potential. In 1955, Chevrolet would debut a lightweight, overhead valve V-8 engine with much potential for power enhancement and optimum dimensions for hot rod applications. Its 265 cubic inches produced 162 hp, with an optional high performance 180-hp version available. Ford had bitten the bullet in 1954 with its own overhead valve V-8, and the venerable flathead was out of production. But engine swaps with these new engines were far more trouble and more expensive than the flathead swap into the plentiful '30s Ford cars. So the demise of the flathead was still a few years away in 1951.

The earliest Pacemaker members' hot rods followed the well-established Ford/Mercury formula described above. As the '50s progressed and the overhead valve engines became plentiful, the guys naturally progressed to the more complicated engine swaps to take advantage of the more powerful engines.

Herb Sebastian was the most prolific hot rod builder in the club's early years, having a long line of cars that included a Mercury-powered '33 Ford coupe, an Olds-powered '32 Ford coupe, an Olds-powered '53 Studebaker, a '32 Ford sedan similar to the famed "Orange Crate," and an

Olds-powered Model A truck, chopped and channeled for the drags, which Dad bought and completed. Herb's '33 Ford five-window coupe was his daily driver when the club formed in March of 1951. It sported a hopped up '48 Mercury engine, solid wheels, wide whitewalls, and '39 Ford taillights. This car sat out front of Sebastian's Sohio service station at Verity Parkway and Yankee Road, serving as the beacon that drew hot rodders to the site.

In 1954 or early '55, when drag racing became popular in the area, Herb set out to build a faster car. He purchased a cherry 1932 Ford five-window coupe and with the help of several club members proceeded to install a 345 cubic inch Olds V-8. The Olds featured a Chet Herbert roller cam with a four-barrel carburetor—a rather advanced induction system for the time. Herb raced the car often in the gasser classes in 1955 and '56, and it was a consistent winner. It would run 90 mph in the quarter mile, a very good speed for 1955, and eventually topped 94 in the quarter mile in 1956. It was also his daily driver in 1955, and it was my first encounter with a real hot rod, a single purpose car built strictly for fun.

My first memory of this car was when it was still under construction. My first ride in it was memorable, because the floorboards were not yet installed, and of course there were no seat belts. I remember being scared and hanging onto Dad, who told me not to look down at the rushing road surface. Easy for him to say, he could see out the windshield. I remember Herb joking about how handy it was, because if he ran over a pedestrian, he could see who it was. I was probably four years old at the time.

My kindergarten year (1955-56), we still lived in Middletown. (We would move to nearby Trenton the following summer.) I attended school with Herb's daughter, Mary Lou, who was in the first grade. Herb would pick her up after school in the coupe (now complete with floorboards), and I would always beg a ride from him. I wasn't too lazy to walk the four blocks home, I just wanted to ride in the light blue hot rod. We lived about two blocks apart, and it was out of Herb's way, but he always obliged. I remember one day, Mary Lou was already in the car and Herb was pulling away, when they saw me running toward them. "We've got no extra room today," Herb called out. I could see Mary Lou's little sister Bonnie Gem in the car along with some grocery bags, so it did look pretty crowded. "Okay," I said, but I must have looked pretty dejected. "You can ride with us tomorrow," Herb offered and began to pull away. The car went about 20 feet and stopped. Mary Lou opened the passenger door and called out, "Come on Ronnie. We'll make room." I ran to join them and crowded into the little coupe, which by then was standing room only. That was Herb. He knew how much I loved that car, and he couldn't disappoint his little buddy.

Herb began racing the car in '55, competing at the '55 Bonneville Speed Trials and at the '56 NHRA Nationals with the '32 coupe. By 1957, the club was running a dragster, and Herb's attention was drawn to it. He eventually sold the coupe. There is a lot more on this car in Chapter 5, which covers the club's early drag racing. Of all of Herb's hot rods, he was best known for the '32 coupe.

Another early club member, Carl Lakes had one of the first bona fide hot rods in the area—a 1934 Ford coupe with a bored out '48 Mercury engine. He drove the fenderless coupe around Middletown in 1951, and earned the nickname "Hot Rod Lakes" in the process. The engine was nicely detailed with twin carbs, lots of chrome accessories, and the typical chrome acorn bolt covers for the heads. In 1952, he switched to a 1940 Ford two-door sedan with a similar hopped up Mercury engine.

Tom Frebis also drove a 1940 Ford sedan in 1951 and '52. His car featured a hopped up Mercury engine and sported the fender skirts and DeSoto bumpers that were popular on hot rods of the era.

Early club member Ray Boyce had a hopped up Mercury engine in an early '30s Ford pickup truck, which was a regular in the club's early car shows. The full-fendered truck was white with Moon hubcaps. He also hot rodded a mild custom '53 Ford with a screaming hopped up Ford six for power.

Dad's bright red 1945 Ford pickup truck mentioned in Chapter 2 was another hot rod around during the 1951 formation of the club. It served the dual purpose of business vehicle and hot rod, but it was a hot rod none-the-less, sporting the basically stock 1949 Olds Rocket 88 engine that Dad had swapped for the original flathead V-8. At the time, this was the most complex engine swap among the club's cars, with Dad making his own motor mounts and drive shaft. The experience would be a valuable tool in later Olds installations in Herb Sebastian's '32 Ford and in the early club dragsters. My grandfather, Bill Lovelace's matching red shop truck, a '34 Dodge, was otherwise stock but served as his ride in 1951.

Dad's '45 Ford truck underwent some upgrades in the eight years that it was his daily driver. At first he had retained the Ford manual transmission, but it proved unreliable behind the higher horsepower Olds engine. He eventually replaced it with an Olds Hydramatic transmission, the rugged automatic that found its way into many early-1950s car brands, including independent brands like Hudson and Kaiser. That solved the breakage problems. In 1956, Dad horse-traded some engine work for a new paint job. Vaughn Patrick of Countryside Body Shop near Hamilton repainted the '45 Ford truck white with red flames, and the radiator shop logo was added in red and blue letters on the doors. The truck was usually the vehicle that towed Herb's coupe to the drags, and Herb applied a matching paint scheme to the '32. This was the striking combination that rolled into Kansas City in the fall of 1956 for the NHRA Nationals.

In 1959, Dad sold the Ford truck, and built a 1950 Studebaker truck for shop duty. It was black with gold scallops and sported a 283 Chevy V-8. In 1964, he upgraded the engine to a 327 Chevy block, which had seen one season in the club's dragster. It was balanced and blueprinted with pop-up pistons, an Iskenderian cam, and a Carter four-barrel carb. In pure street trim the light-weight truck would run 103 mph at the drags.

The '50 Studebaker truck was Dad's finest creation. Again he had made his own motor mounts and drive shaft, which linked a three speed Chevy manual transmission with overdrive to the Studebaker rear end, providing the truck with six forward speeds. This allowed the use of a 4.56:1 rear end ratio for rapid acceleration when not in overdrive. The overdrive would allow highway speeds at a reasonably low RPM. Dad hand made his own shift linkage and retained the stock column shift format. A button on the dash could deactivate the overdrive and provide a passing gear courtesy of the low 4.56 rear end. The interior featured black and gold seats stitched by Grant Upholstery in Hamilton, and a wood grain finish on the dash, applied by Bobby Hammil, a hot rodder friend in Hamilton. Fellow club member Gene Wells, a paint and body man by trade, applied the nine coats of hand rubbed black lacquer and created the gold scallops. Wide whitewalls, DeSoto bumpers, and Cadillac hubcaps gave the truck the traditional '50s look.

Also in 1959, Dad purchased a Model A Ford truck from Herb Sebastian, who had chopped the top and channeled the body before losing interest in the project. Dad dropped in an Olds V-8 and ran the truck at the drags for about a year, topping 106 mph in the B/Altered class.

Harold Michael's oval track roadster experience was over by 1951, but his love for roadsters was not. Mike's street driven hot rod was a 1932 Ford roadster, fully fendered with a hopped up Mercury V-8. The car was nicely detailed and quite fast, owing to Mike's racing experience. He would see some drag strip time in this car later on. Earlier, Mike and Bob Kuhn had owned matching 1939 Ford convertibles. Bob Kuhn would seek out and find a duplicate '39 convertible to his 1940s ride in the 1960s, and Alex Slamka would help him restore it. The beautiful maroon convertible, with tan top and interior, won trophies at many area car shows into the early '70s.

Another early '50s Ford/ Mercury rod was Alex Slamka's highly customized 1936 Ford roadster, built on a '39 Ford frame. Alex owned the car, but it was co-built by fellow club member Waldo Gray. It had the basic '48 Mercury engine and Lincoln Zephyr transmission package, but it also sported some extensive body modifications. The body was channeled to lower it onto the frame and give the car a lower profile. The rear fenders were filled to give the body a one-piece appearance. The front fenders were removed in favor of cycle fenders, and the grille was replaced with the classic '32 version. Ten coats of hand rubbed crimson lacquer paint were applied by Sully Sullivan, and tuck and roll upholstery completed a great looking show car that was possibly the most beautiful of all the Pacemaker creations. Alex drove the car for several years, showing it often in area car shows and displaying it at local car dealerships. He sold the car to the club, and it was used as a raffle car at a mid-1950s Pacemaker car show. Sadly, the guy who won the car wrecked it a few weeks later in some kind of a high-speed test outside of Middletown, and it was completely destroyed.

Alex showed the finished '36 roadster in shows as far away as Indianapolis, but the first time he entered a show the car was still in primer. The first custom car shows in the area were held at the Dayton Field House at the Montgomery County Fairgrounds. This was probably 1953 or early '54. Alex had just gotten the car on the road and really wanted to show the car, so he and Waldo Gray drove it up to Dayton and entered it. Alex was so unsure of its road dependability that he had Ray Palmer and Dick Miltenberger follow them to Dayton in Ray's '41 Ford, in case the '36 broke down. At the show, Alex wound up parked next to a beautiful 1932 Ford roadster from Detroit that had been pictured in one of the California car magazines, quite a feat for a Midwest car in 1953. Word quickly got around the show floor that the '32 was a show-only car that wouldn't even run. The word was that it had a dummy engine with no internal components and had to be trailered in and pushed onto the show floor. The guys were pretty ticked off about such a high degree of professionalism. Then the show ended, and the owner got into the immaculate pale blue '32 and fired up a very healthy sounding engine and drove the car out of the field house. The guys watched in wonder as the car disappeared out of the entrance. Then Alex got into his primered roadster—and it wouldn't start!

After the roadster, Alex bought a '56 Thunderbird and proceeded to customize it by removing the chrome and redoing the car's taillights, incorporating larger Edsel units. This gave the car a unique look in a model that was rarely chosen to customize in the first place. Alex's custom T-Bird was a regular in the Pacemaker car shows throughout the mid 1960s.

Harold and Polly Michael owned his and hers '56 T-Birds after Mike sold his street roadster. Mike had bought a new one in '56, with both tops and a continental kit. The following year they ran across a used one in an estate sale, and Polly wound up with her own T-Bird. His was red and hers was black.

Ray Palmer drove a gold colored '41 Ford business coupe with Mercury power in the mid 1950s. The engine featured two Stromberg 97 carburetors and Offenhauser aluminum heads. He raced the car at the early organized drag meets that the Pacemakers held outside of Trenton in 1954.

Bill Burton joined the club in 1955, just out of military service, and began construction of a '32 Ford five window coupe. It was built initially with a '48 Mercury V-8, highly detailed to accent the car's midnight blue paint job. It sported cycle fenders and custom nerf bars, and he often ran it without a hood. Bill began racing the car at local drag strips, and eventually replaced the Mercury engine with a hopped up Olds engine. Through a series of modifications, the car topped 89 mph with the Mercury, and ultimately 111 mph with the Olds in the altered coupe classes at Beechmont Dragway.

Dave "Skip" Swisher owned a beautiful 1940 Ford two door sedan in the mid '50s. It was powered by a Cadillac V-8 and sported a slick paint job by Bill Neal, a popular paint and body man with the rodders in the area. Skip's '40 was a regular at the early club car shows.

In the late '50s, a shy, skinny kid walked into Sebastian's Sohio station and asked Herb if he could reassemble three Stromberg carburetors for him. The carbs were going into the 1948 Ford sedan he was hopping up, and he needed help getting them back together. Herb said he would help, and the kid went back to his car. He emerged a few minutes later with a cardboard box containing the disassembled array of parts that at one time had been three complete Strombergs. Herb surveyed the mess, not expecting the parts to be inter-mixed and the disassembly to be so complete. Slowly the carbs went back together as the kid told Herb about his car, and Herb told him about the car club. Soon after, in 1959, Don Klamo joined the club, and built his second hot rod—a 1947 Ford coupe with a Buick V-8 engine. A little later, a beautifully detailed and rare 1932 Studebaker Rockne coupe with a Chevy V-8 was on the street, on the drag strip, and in local car shows. The coupe was co-built by Marion Hounshell and a Trenton paint and body man named Ronnie Wright, and it sported maroon paint with white pinstriping and wide whitewall tires. Don would go on to build and race a long line of dragsters with partner and fellow club member Marion Hounshell and a third partner, Gary Rupp, of eventual top fuel dragster fame. Don's race career would extend into the '90s, with his sons taking over the wheel of a 190-mph sportsman dragster. This long race career started with the desire for a hot rod and Herb's assistance with the Stromberg carbs.

Marion Hounshell had a beautiful '49 Ford pick up truck with a '57 Olds engine that he sometimes drag raced. The street-driven truck was entered in the B/Gas class at the NHRA Nationals at Detroit in 1959 and '60. It was jet black with unique chrome side pipes that went up through the running board and exited over the rear fenders.

Joe Patrick, brother to another early member Jess Patrick and cousin to Herb Sebastian, ran a body shop in nearby Trenton, and had a string of hot rods that transcended into the street rod era for several decades. One early '60s rod of his was quite memorable: a show quality Model A roadster pickup painted metallic green and sporting a Chevy V-8. Beautifully detailed, it featured white interior, white soft-top and tarp, and a lot of chrome.

The Pacemakers had 130 members at the club's peak, and there were many neat rods and customized cars over the club's fifteen-year history. I can't do justice to all of them for the lack of photos and details, but I will mention a few more. Dick Beckett had a hopped up GMC six in a Chevy coupe that screamed on the drag strip. Fred May drove a '53 Studebaker, and Paul Scorti built a beautiful custom Chevy that was a consistent show winner. Jerry Williams drove a powder blue '56 Ford truck that was nicely detailed, and Danny Allen had a '33 Ford truck in the mid-to-late '50s (fellow club member Dale Foreman owned the same truck for a while). Prior to the truck, Danny had a '39 Ford with a Mercury engine that he drag raced. Kenny Hall represented the minority sports car segment of the club with a diminutive Saab powered by a 37 horsepower, two-cycle engine with a transmission that free wheeled at highway speeds to enhance gas mileage. Dick Miltenberger had a sports car fling in the early '60s, with the first Jaguar XKE that I had ever seen. Herb Sebastian even tooled around in a 1960 VW Karmen Ghia for a while.

By the end of the decade, the face of the club was changing. The new members were drawn by the club's successes on the drag strip, and the street hot rods were being replaced by single purpose drag racers. Drag racing had progressed to a higher degree of sophistication, and the days of the dual-purpose street-strip car were over. Earnie and Harold Barnes raced a '61 Corvette. Jim Neely and John Buehl bought a super stock Plymouth, and John (father) and Dick (son) Kauffman bought a Ford version. Don Klamo and Marion Hounshell ran a series of dragsters, and the club ran its long line of project dragsters. The days of the club's reliability runs were over. By 1960, the focus of the Pacemakers had turned to drag racing.

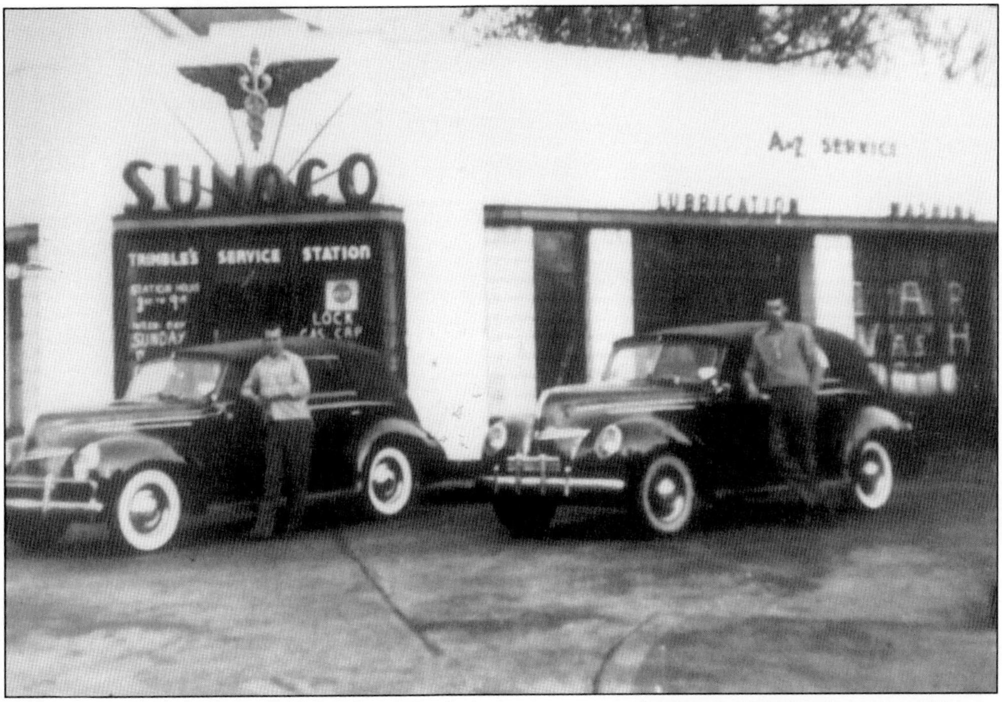

Bob Kuhn (left) and Harold Michael (right) pose next to their twin '39 Ford convertibles in front of Trimble's Sunoco station. In the late '60s Kuhn would restore another '39 to match this one. (Michael collection, 1945.)

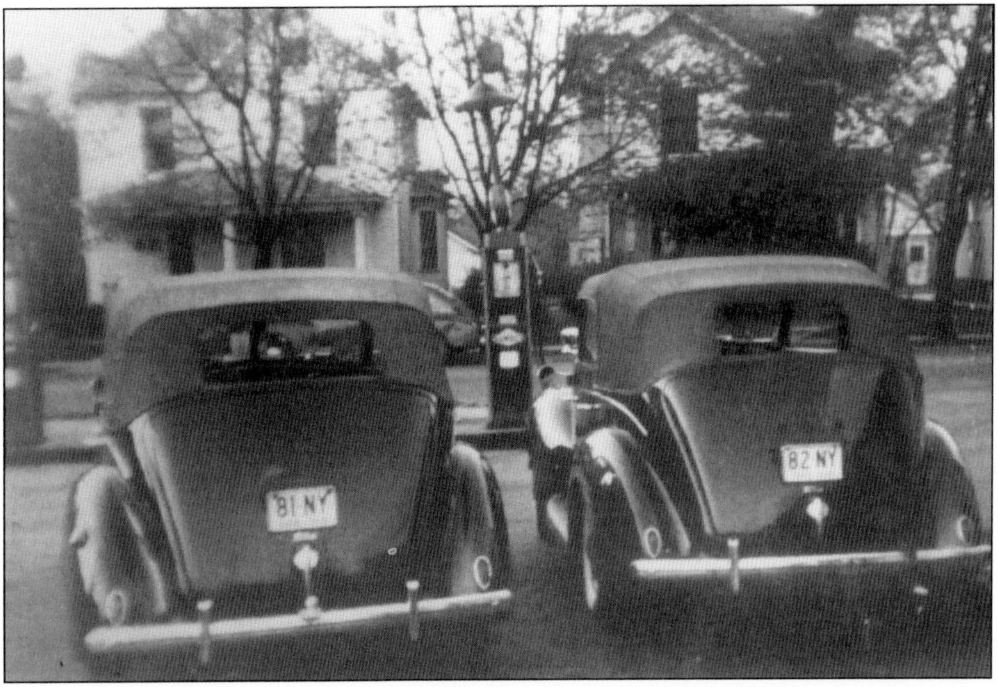

The matching '39 Ford convertibles of Bob Kuhn and Harold Michael. Note the consecutive license plates. Mike owned 81NY and Bob owned 82NY. (Michael collection, 1945.)

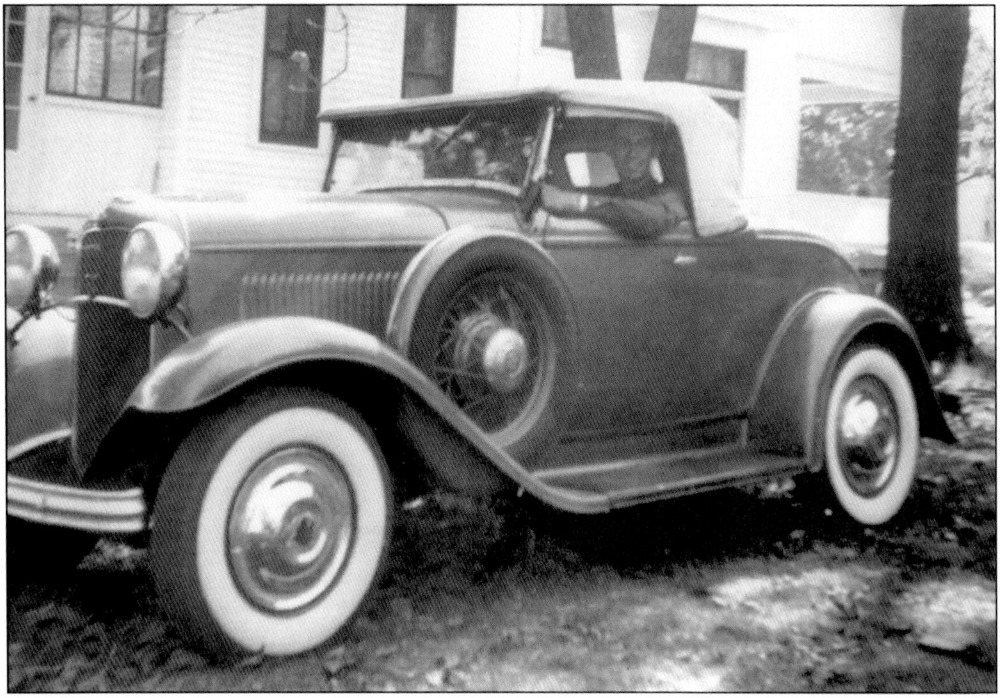

Harold Michael poses in his '32 Ford roadster with Mercury engine. Mike won his class at the opening drag race at Thorn Hill Drag Strip in Kenton, Kentucky, with this car. Note the Cadillac hub caps and DeSoto bumpers that were popular on '50s hot rods. (Michael collection, 1955.)

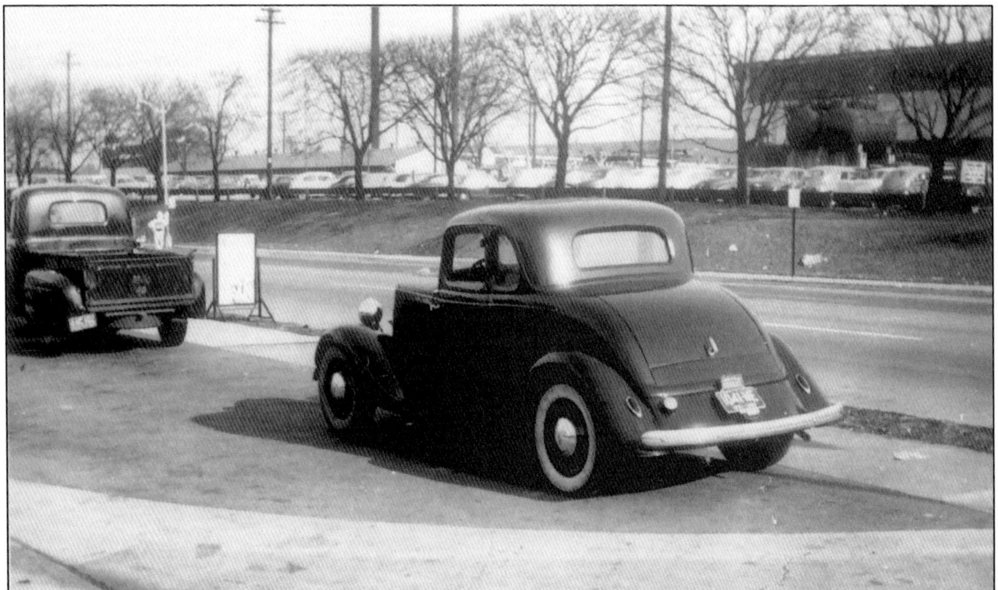

Herb Sebastian's first hot rod was this '33 Ford five-window coupe with Mercury V-8. It sat out front at his dad's Sohio service station serving as a beacon for Middletown hot rodders to stop in and chat. Note the '39 Ford tail lights. (Lakes collection, 1951.)

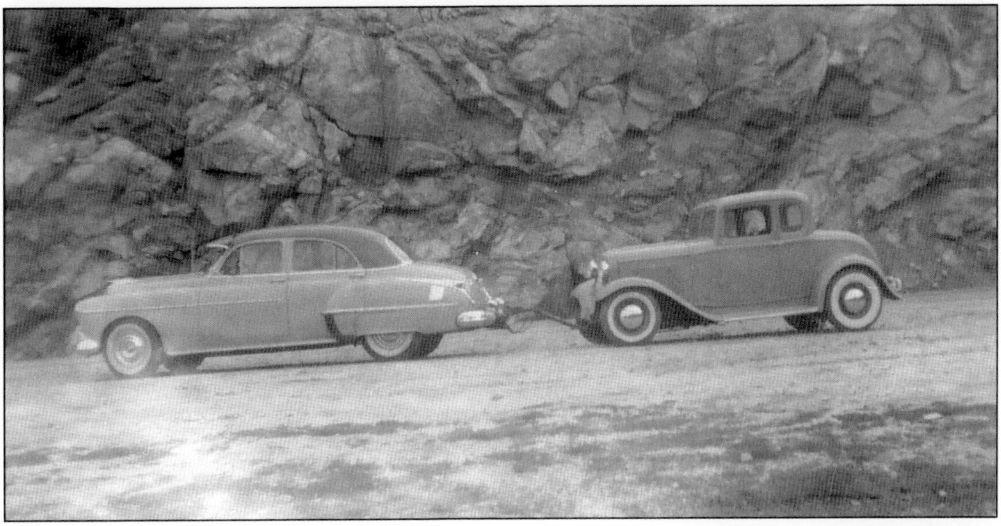

Herb Sebastian's 1932 Ford coupe with Olds engine is being towed behind our 1951 Olds Rocket 88 family car en route to Wendover, Utah, for the '55 Bonneville Speed Trials. (Roberson collection, 1955.)

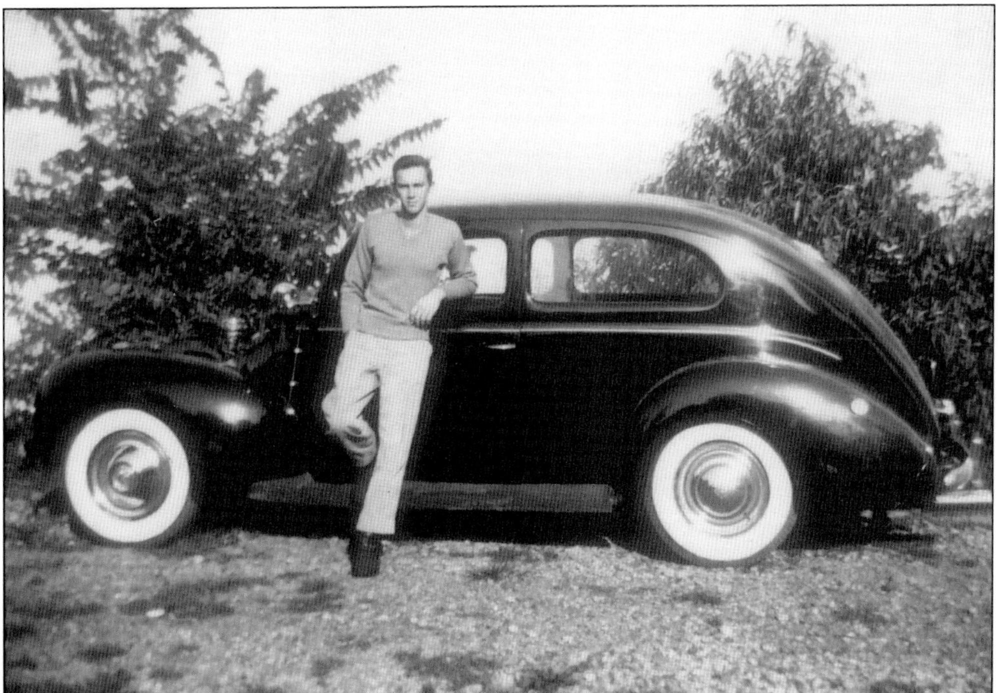

Carl Lakes strikes a Hollywood pose beside his 1940 Ford two-door sedan with Mercury power. (Lakes collection, 1952.)

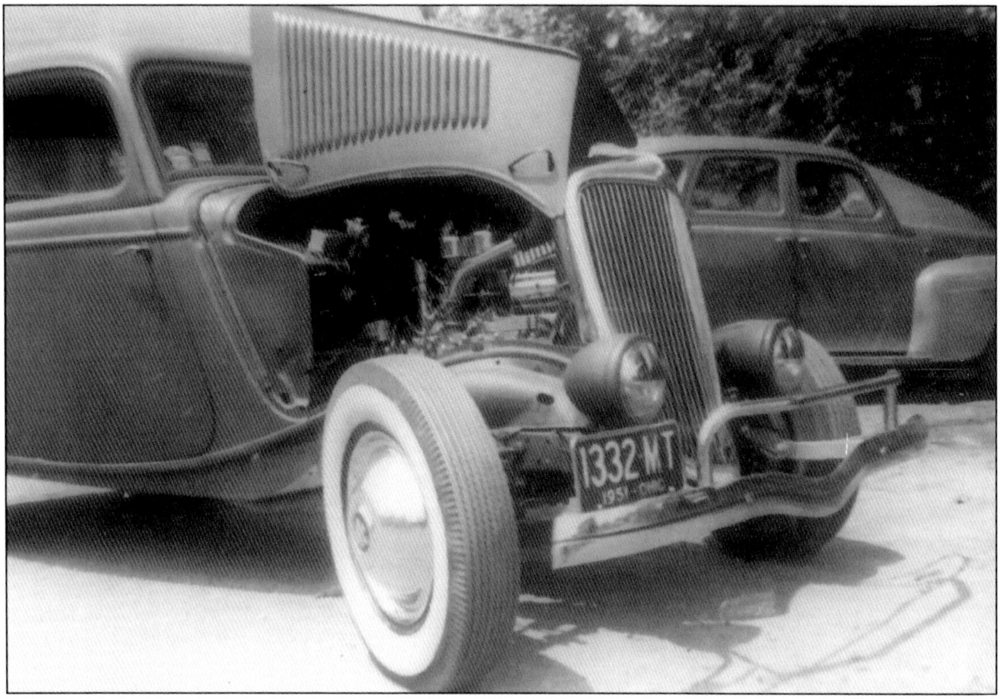

Carl Lakes drove this '34 Ford coupe with Mercury V-8 engine in 1951, one of the earlier hot rods in the area. It earned him the nickname,"Hot Rod" Lakes. (Lakes collection, 1951.)

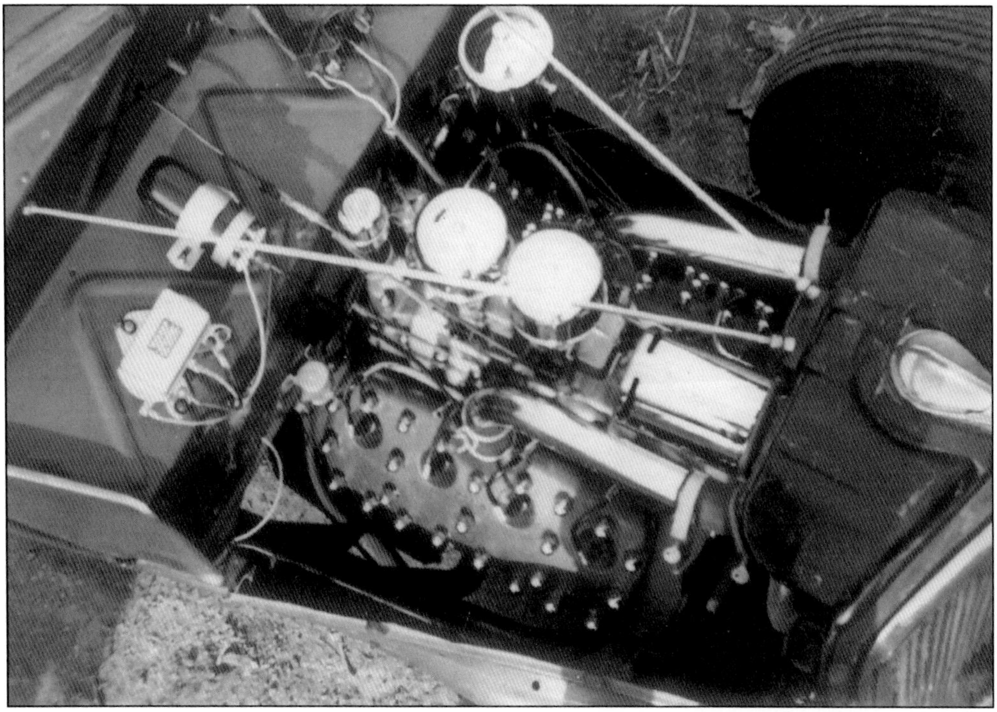

The Mercury V-8 in Carl Lakes '34 Ford coupe was bored out and featured twin Stromberg carburetors and lots of chrome. (Lakes collection, 1951.)

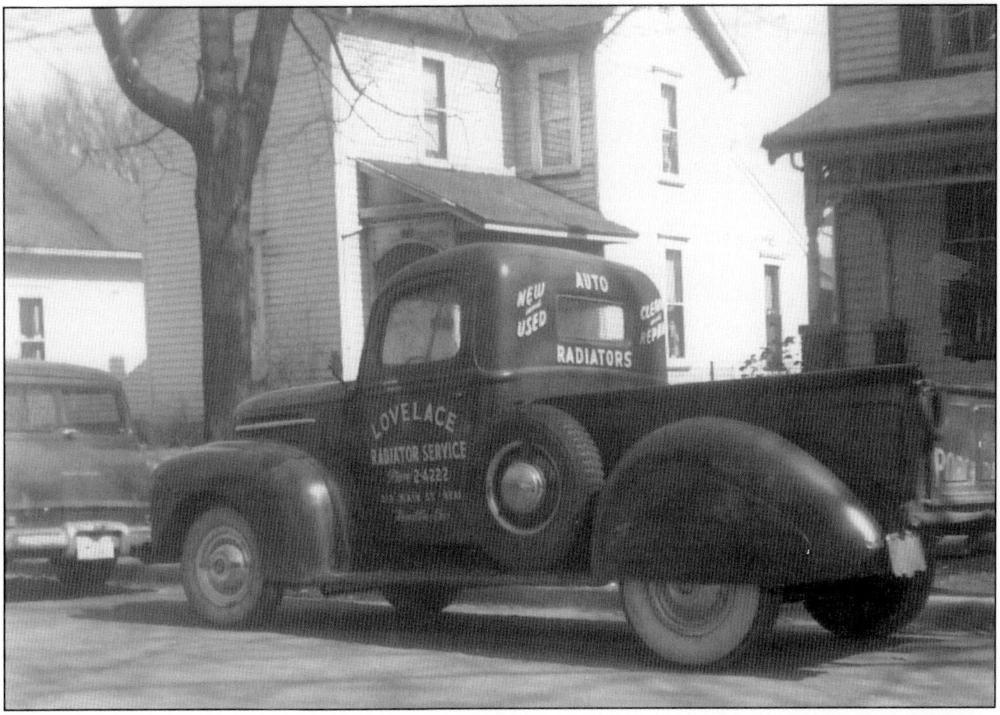

Dad opened the Hamilton branch of Lovelace Radiator Service in 1951 and built this Olds V-8 powered 1945 Ford pickup truck as his shop truck. The site is Grandpa Bill's house on Schafer Street in Middletown. (Roberson collection, 1951.)

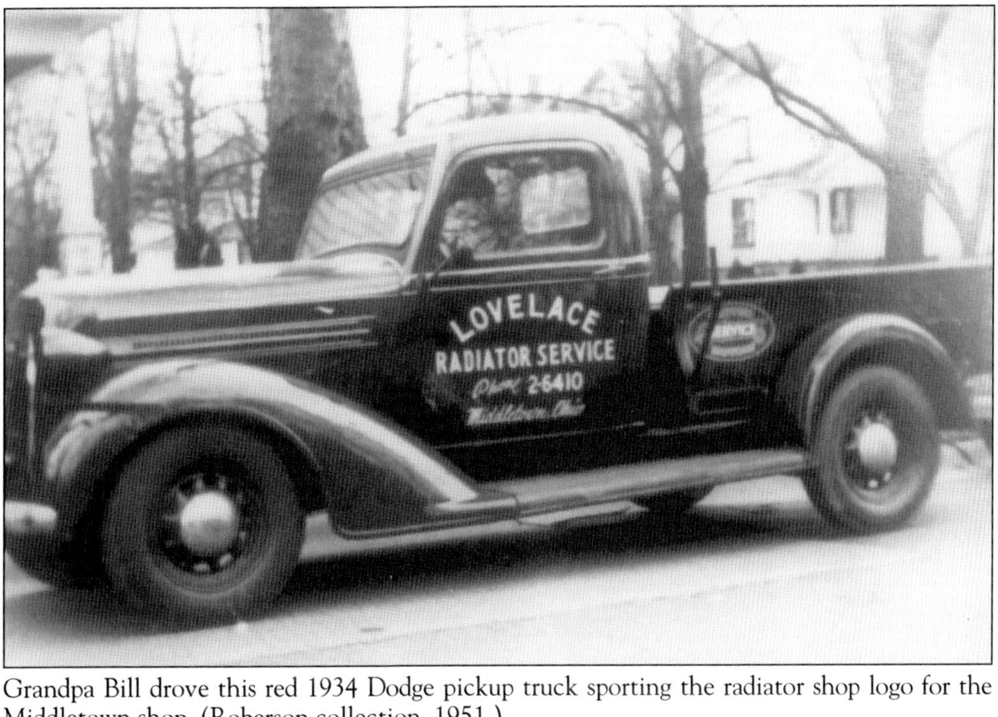

Grandpa Bill drove this red 1934 Dodge pickup truck sporting the radiator shop logo for the Middletown shop. (Roberson collection, 1951.)

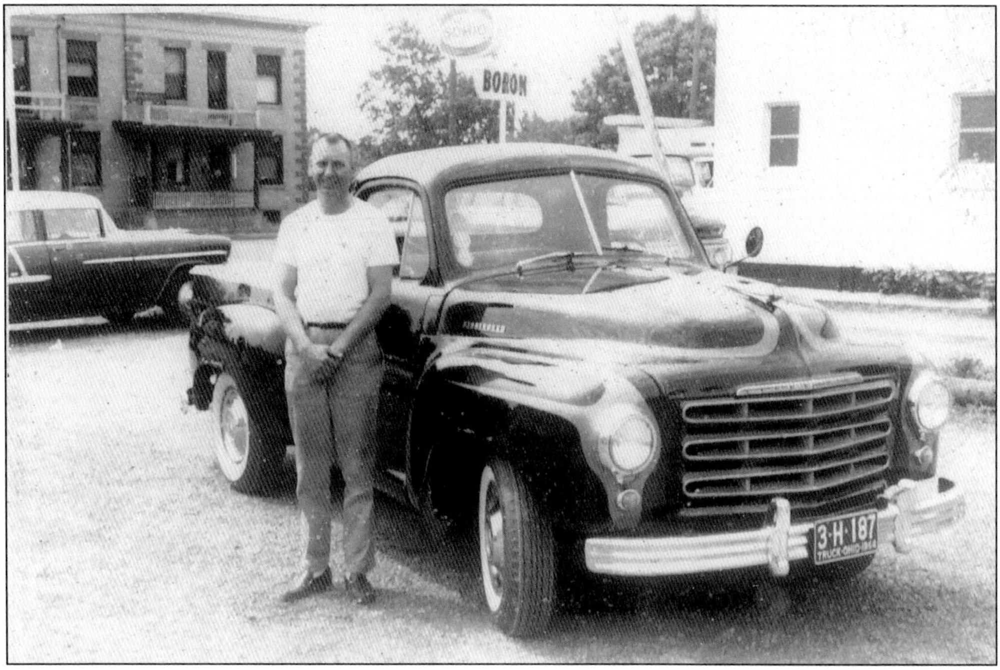

Dad poses beside the '50 Studebaker Shop truck built in 1959 just after its update to a 327 Chevy engine. Note the DeSoto bumpers, Caddy hubcaps, and gold scallops over black paint applied by fellow club member Gene Wells. This photo is set in the parking lot of Dad's radiator shop at 121 North B Street in Hamilton. (Roberson collection, 1964.)

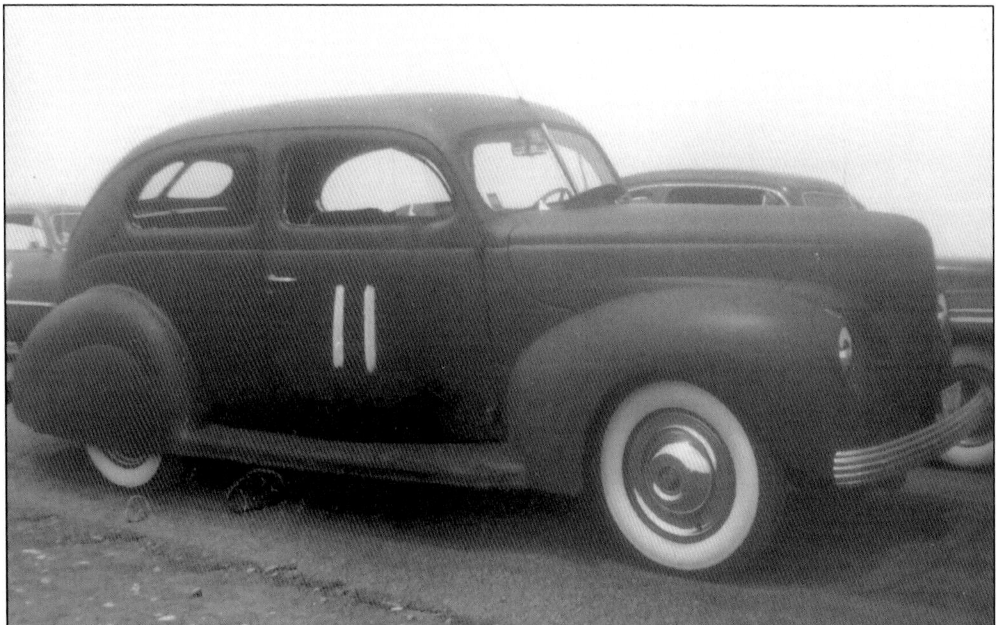

The 1940 Ford sedan of charter club member Tom Frebis appears bearing the number 11 at one of the club's early reliability runs. The car was Mercury powered. Note the fender skirts, Cadillac hubcaps and Plymouth bumpers, all typical '50's hot rod fare. (Lakes collection, 1952.)

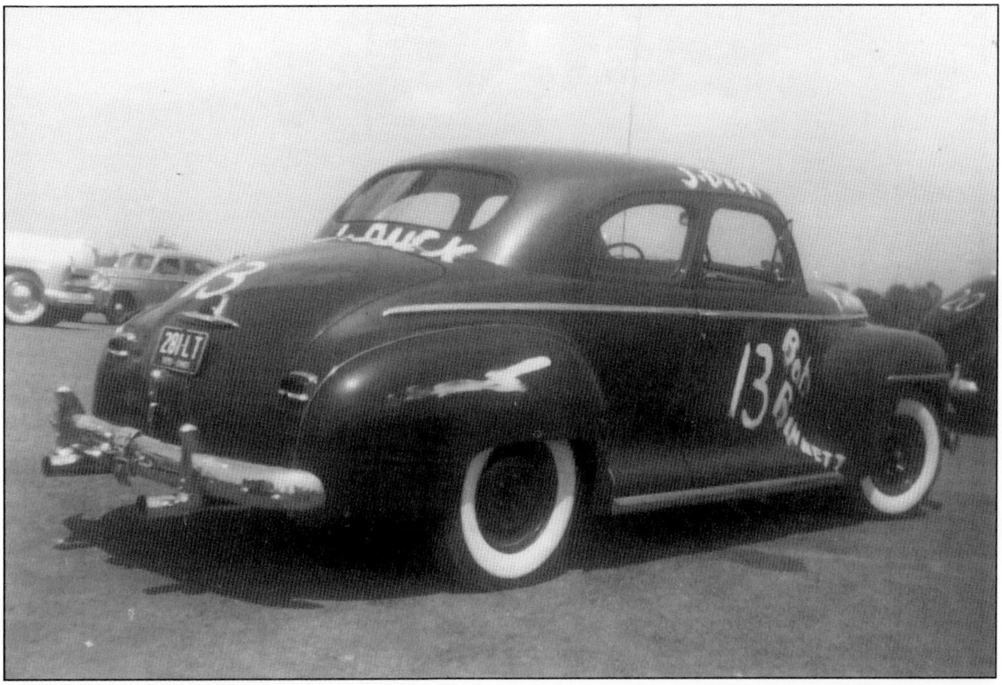

Early member Bobby Jay was obviously not superstitious about displaying the number 13 on his Plymouth coupe entered in an early reliability run. The car also sported some creative temporary graphics in white shoe polish. Note the lightning bolt over the rear wheel. (Lakes collection, 1952.)

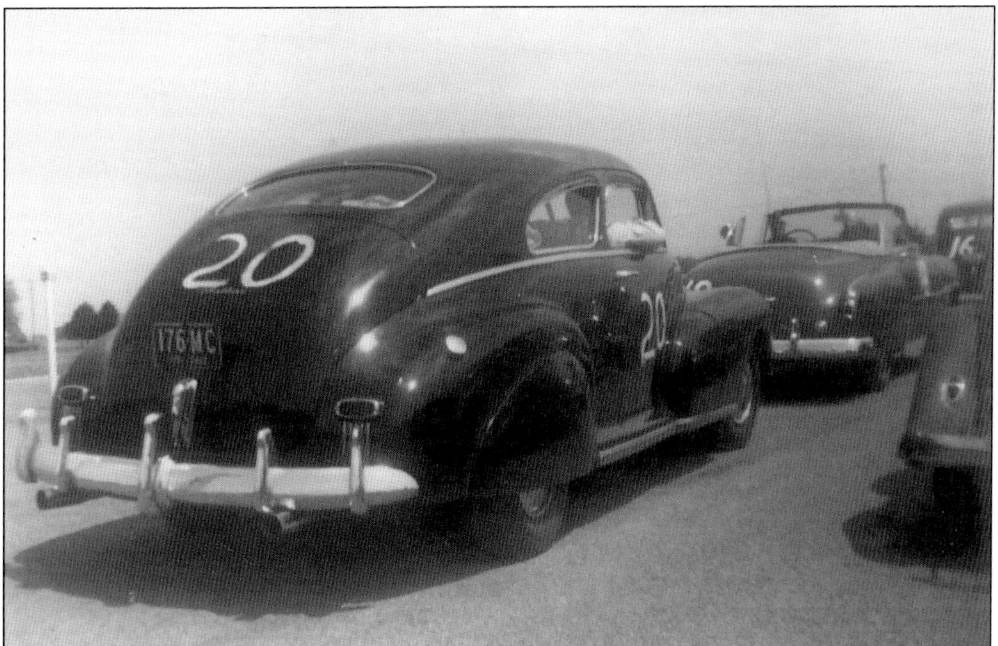

Charter club member Jim Tincher competes at the club's first reliability run at LeSourdsville Lake. The 1948 Chevy bore the number 20 for the competition. (Lakes collection, 1952.)

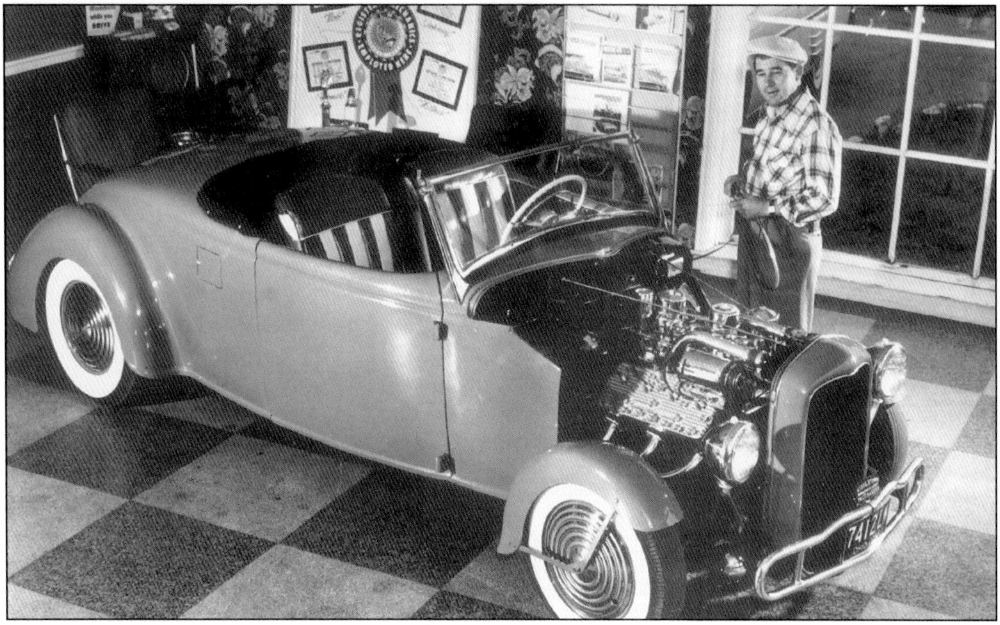

The always dapper Alex Slamka poses next to his customized '36 ford roadster at the local Mercury dealer show room. The car was channeled with filled fenders and smoothed doors. A hot Mercury engine with lots of chrome motivated the cinnamon beauty. Note the '50s style cycle fenders, nerf bars, and Deuce grille. Alex had a striking resemblance to actor Glen Ford. (Slamka collection, 1954.)

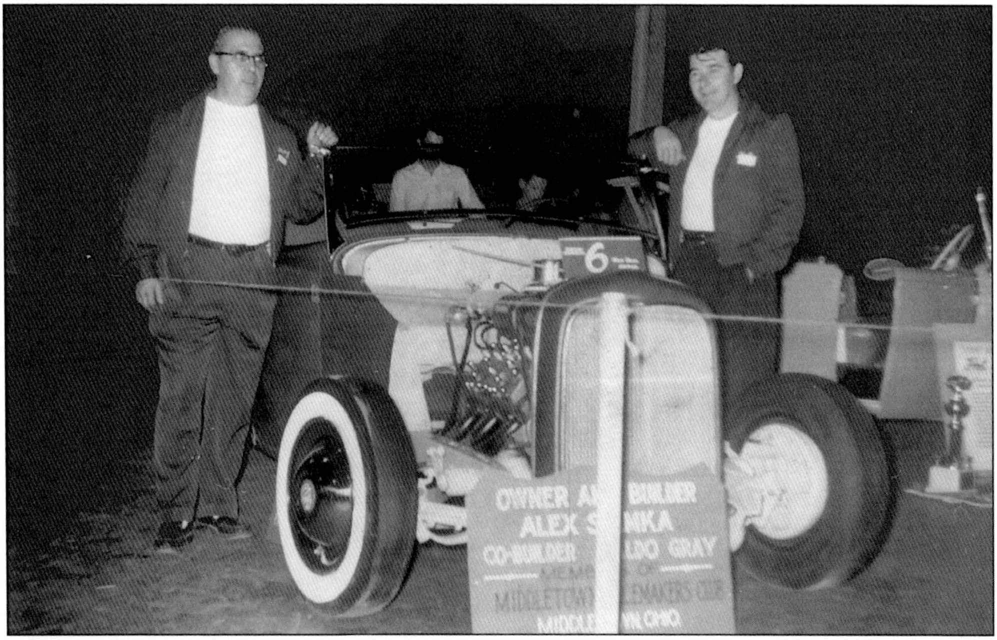

Waldo Gray (left) and Alex Slamka (right) pose by Alex's '36 roadster at a car show at the Dayton Field House. The sign in front of Alex's roadster says that it was built by Alex Slamka and Waldo Gray, and it identifies both as members of the Middletown Pacemakers. (Slamka collection, 1953 or early '54.)

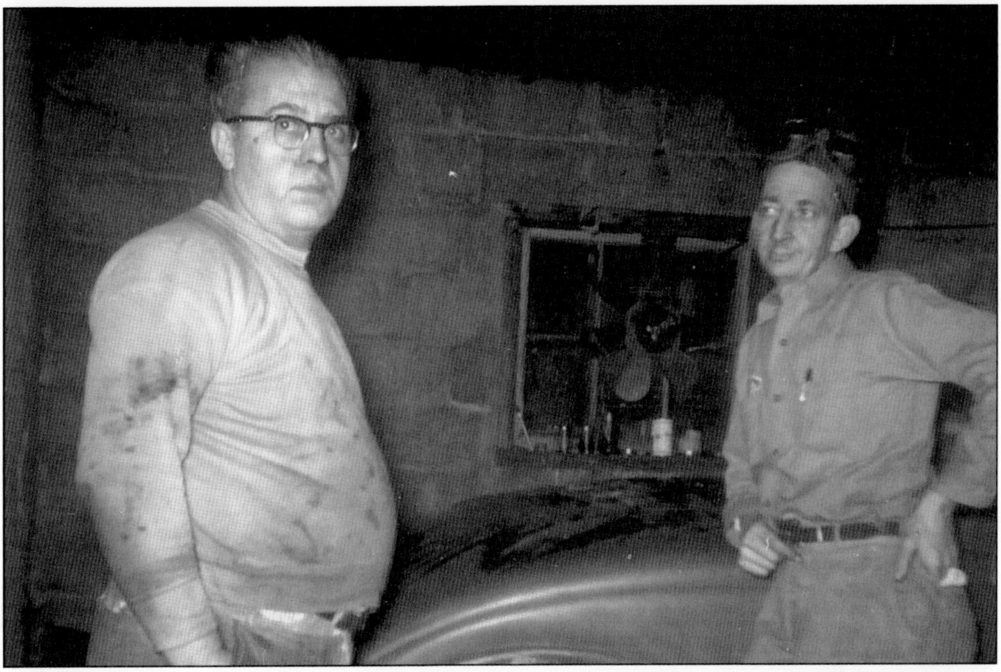

Waldo Gray and Sully Sullivan pose by Alex's roadster still under construction in Sully's body shop. Both men were early members of the Middletown Pacemakers. The car had filled fenders, where the joint between the fender and the body is lead-filled to make the body appear as one piece. (Slamka collection, probably 1953.)

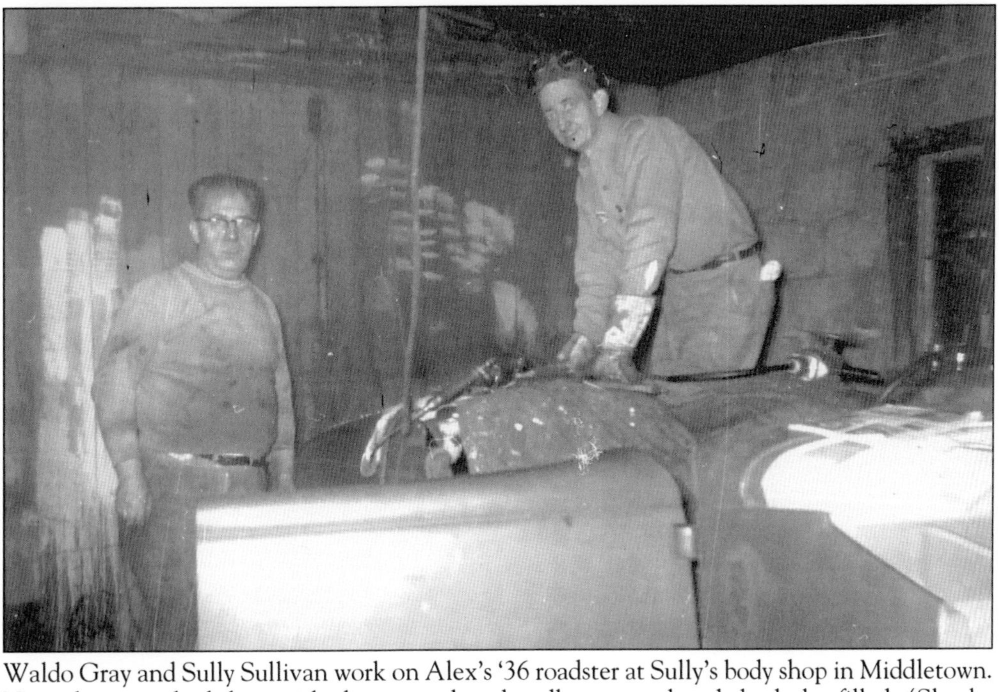

Waldo Gray and Sully Sullivan work on Alex's '36 roadster at Sully's body shop in Middletown. Note the smoothed door with the outer door handle removed and the holes filled. (Slamka collection, probably 1953.)

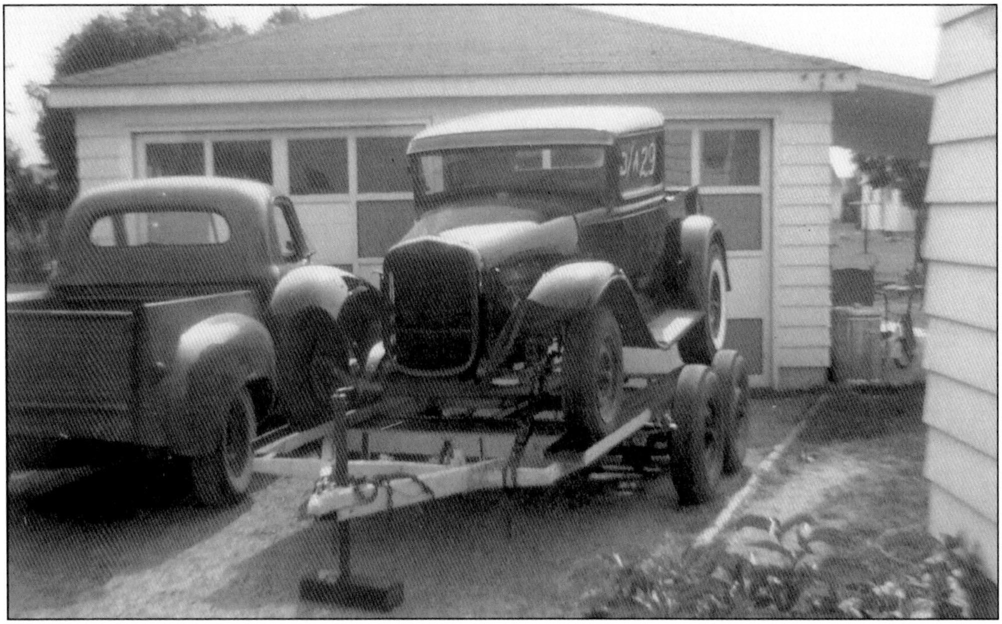

Dad's Model A truck in race-ready form rests in our driveway on South First Street in Trenton. The A ran in the B/Altered class at Beechmont Dragway using a 345 Olds for power. Next to the A is Dad's 1950 Studebaker shop truck on the road, but still under construction with a 283 Chevy engine. (Roberson collection, 1959.)

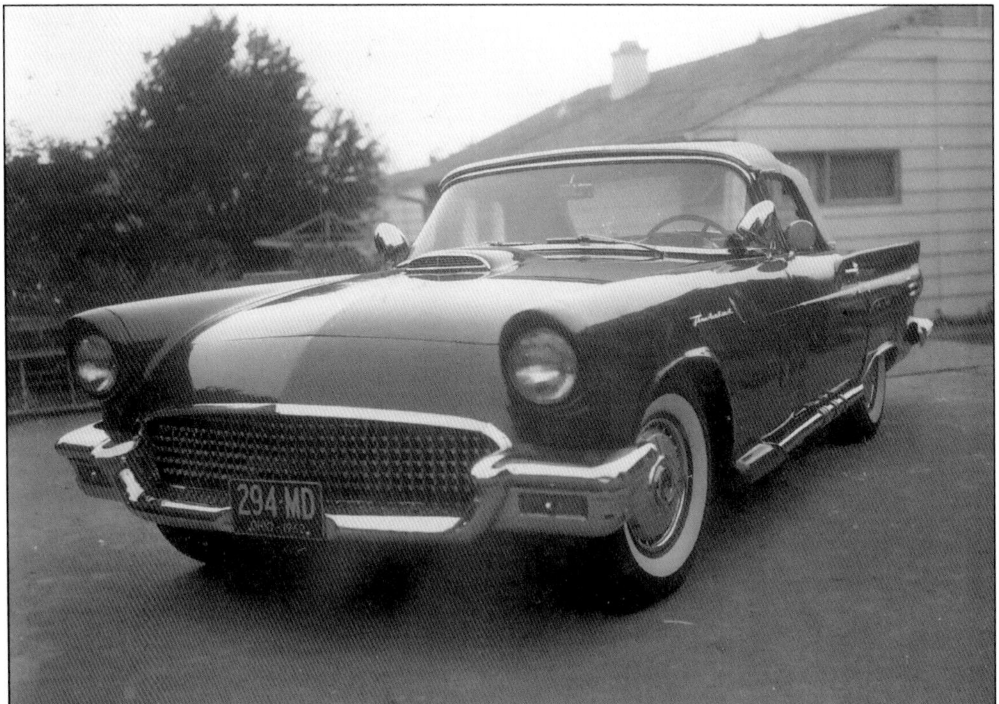

Alex Slamka's mildly customized 1956 T-Bird rests in his driveway in Middletown. The car was dechromed with side pipes and Edsel tail lights. (Slamka collection, 1962.)

Four

THE CAR SHOWS

You can't depend on your eyes if your imagination is out of focus.

- Mark Twain

In 1954, the Pacemakers made a huge stride by taking advantage of an opportunity that fell their way. They had been holding reliability runs that started and finished at the parking lot of LeSourdsville Lake Amusement Park on Route 4 between Middletown and Hamilton. They had obtained permission from the park to hold their runs there, and in doing so they made the acquaintance of the park president, Don Dazey. At one such reliability run, Don inquired about the possibility of a major custom auto show that would be held inside the amusement park. The park would provide a lump sum of money from which the show would be promoted and run including the cost of trophies for the entrants. The club would run the car show, including judging of the cars and presentation of the awards, and would pocket the unused portion of the money. This would be the Middletown/Hamilton area's first major custom auto show. If successful, it would be repeated annually. It would ultimately become the club's major fund raiser for the next 12 years.

This was a great opportunity for the club and for the area. The closest such shows to date had been the ones run at the Dayton Field House at the Montgomery County Fairgrounds, about 30 miles to the north. The Dayton shows were smaller than the anticipated show in the relatively roomy amusement park. LeSourdsville Lake offered lots of room for cars at a site that already had an audience.

The club got the word out by passing flyers to other clubs and posting specially printed posters throughout the region. The show would be held Saturday and Sunday, the second weekend in June. An article appeared in the *Middletown Journal* newspaper announcing the show and featuring photos of two entrants: the "Red Comet," a custom rocket-shaped car built by Stanley Eskin of Shelbyville, and a '32 Ford roadster hot rod built by Don Conrad of Covington, Kentucky. The article noted that this was the first custom auto show in the area, and it was drawing entrants from three states.

LeSourdsville Lake Amusement Park was built around a large man-made lake, as the name implies. Along one side of the lake was a beach area and swimming facility complete with diving boards built out on a narrow pier. Amusement park rides sprawled around two sides of the lake, and the lake itself served to accommodate a replica steamboat paddle wheeler and a contained course for small powerboat rides. The land side rides were the typical fare with bumper cars, Tilt-a-Whirl, Ferris wheel, turnpike cars, and a large wooden roller coaster. An arcade with games, a fun house, and a house of mirrors gave the park a carnival aura, and concession stands with corn dogs, cotton candy, and funnel cakes provided the proper aromas. The park also had a large cafeteria-style restaurant and a dance hall called the Stardust Gardens Ballroom that could accommodate banquets. Later renamed Americana Amusement Park, it was a well-planned and well-marketed facility that long survived the advent of the super theme parks. Later on the swimming facility was removed, and some of the rides were replaced with modern versions, but the park retained that old time amusement park feeling more than 40 years later.

The picturesque park was the perfect backdrop for a major custom car show. The lakefront design with lakeside walkway, and the rides all set back facing the lake, left ample room to display cars. It could easily accommodate a hundred or more. And since the show was inside the park, people had to pay to enter in order to see the cars. In those days the entry fee for the park was low, and the rides were sold through ticket purchases, so people would not be intimidated by a high gate fee if they just wanted to see the cars. But most folks made a day of it, looking at the cars and enjoying the park's attractions as well.

The results of the Pacemaker's inaugural 1954 Tri-State Custom Auto Show were as follows: Stanley Eskin's Red Comet, a rocket shaped, hand built three-wheeler with a Ford engine took "Most Outstanding Car of the Show." The show hot rod class was won by Charlie Mann of Indianapolis, with Alex Slamka's '36 Ford finishing second and Don Conrad's '32 ford taking the third place trophy. In the practical hot rod class Spud Parsley of Hamilton took first place, Elbert Freeman of Hamilton was second and Cass Michaels took third. The sports car class had Dick Dome of Middletown finishing first with a Nash Healey, Fred Gunther of Dayton was second and Voris Sebald of Middletown was third. The custom car class was won by Fred Kenter of Silverton, with William Johnston of Erlanger, Kentucky, finishing second and Wally Gordon of Rushville, Indiana, third. Finally, the antique car class was won by Ray Jones of Middletown with a '24 Dodge, Earl Zellner of Hamilton was second and Eddie Orman of Middletown was third.

The inaugural show was a huge success. The park set a weekend attendance record with 25,000 people going through the gates, including a single day attendance record of 15,000 on Sunday. This was quite an accomplishment since the park dated back to 1921 and had grown steadily in added attractions for 33 years. The Pacemakers became well known in the area, but the most important accomplishment of these early custom auto shows was the advancement of the sport of hot rodding in the eyes of the public.

Hot rodding had acquired a bad name in the 1950s through newspaper headlines reporting highway accidents resulting from street racing, and through the dramatization of such activity in Hollywood movies. The public for the most part considered hot rodders a nuisance, an undesirable element of society. One way to turn the public opinion around was to show the cars so people could appreciate the amount of time, talent, and effort that goes into a custom built car. The Pacemaker shows were open to all types of cars, including sports cars and antique cars, which further promoted the hot rodders by association with the more acceptable automotive groups. If a hot rodder drove his car on the street, maybe a hundred people would notice it in the course of a day. Some may be curious and give it a second glance, but most people really wouldn't appreciate what they had seen. By showing it in this car show, 25,000 people would see it in two days, and it would be displayed with a sign telling the story behind the car. People could then learn that one car took two years to build, or that another car has extensive body changes that required a lot of cutting and welding; they would see the chrome-laden engines and the immaculately clean undercarriages; they would see people who loved their unique machines and showed purpose in applying their craft: the public would see that these hot rodders could not possibly be delinquents, but talented, hard working craftsmen.

The Tri-State Custom Auto Show became an annual club event running through 1965, the club's last full year. (It continued well into the 1990s through other avenues, making it one of the longest running car shows in the country.) It was a prestigious car show for the area, sanctioned by the National Hot Rod Association. The cars were judged by club members, who were knowledgeable auto enthusiasts following established, standardized guidelines. Trophies were of high quality, and above all the show was fun. Who couldn't have fun at a custom car show in an amusement park?

The club usually added a second fund raiser in the form of a raffle car. They would purchase a car during the course of the year and apply some mild customizing or hop it up with aftermarket parts. Alex Slamka was usually responsible for the custom touches, and any number of guys would apply the hop up work. They would sell the raffle tickets over the course of the weekend show. The car would be displayed at the park entrance, which also served as the show's registration area and the temporary headquarters of the club for the weekend.

Several club members showed their own cars in the annual show, and sometimes the club's dragster would be displayed. A friend of Dad's, Bud Dickman of Hamilton, owned a Sunbeam roadster, which he liked to enter. Bud would have the car nicely detailed, and Dad would pick it up at his house, which was not far from the park, and he would drive it over and enter it. At the end of the show, he'd return the car to Bud along with any trophy he had won. Some years Bud would not attend at all in person, but the white, shiny Sunbeam would be prominently displayed.

The car shows were a lot of fun for me, because I got to spend the entire weekend in this neat amusement park. The last three years of the show, as an early teen, I took a more active roll in the car show. My friend Ron Leisner and I displayed our model car collection in conjunction with the club dragster display or with Bud Dickman's Sunbeam. This was fun, and we got a lot of attention from the club members who liked to check out the model cars. The display expanded each year, and Ron and I would plan for months ahead, selecting new model kits that would ultimately fit into the theme of the display.

The car shows were a lot of work, but there were always a lot of members to share the workload. Besides judging the cars, which includes tallying points to determine the first three places in each class plus special awards like best paint or best interior, the members had to run the car show registration and direct the cars throughout the park to the designated display spots. This was a long, drawn out process, because the cars didn't all arrive at the same time. They also sold raffle tickets for the car they were giving away. Many of the wives helped with these functions, since the registration desk service activities and ticket sales had to be continued all day.

The park management was very appreciative of the work that the club did on the car shows, and the subsequent record crowds that the show would bring into the park. The last night of the show, the park would treat the guys to a free chicken dinner in the park's cafeteria, after which they would hold some of the rides open after hours for the guys to have some fun. After two long days of busy detail work, the late night party was a great way for the guys to unwind. The most popular rides with the guys were the turnpike cars and the bumper cars, both of which offered driving opportunities of a competitive nature. What developed was something I will refer to as the Pacemaker 500.

It began with the turnpike cars ride, a miniature expressway winding through a miniature town on go-kart sized cars with fiberglass bodies reminiscent of mid-1950s Packards. The cars were powered by gasoline engines of about 10 horsepower and normally incorporated a throttle stop to keep speeds down to a reasonable level for an amusement park ride. However, in honor of the Pacemakers being a hot rod club, the operator would remove the throttle stops so the cars would take on a high performance mode.

On the scaled down course, the cars were quite interesting without the throttle stops. Similar rides today have a center guide rail along the road to prevent passing and to help kids steer the cars. But back then, no such rail was available, just a 360-degree bumper that would protect the car if it hit another or one of the guard rails that ran along either side of the paved road. The road itself was designed for touring and viewing the small buildings and scenery. It was not meant for racing. The entire course was not wide enough for passing, and the occasional narrowing of the road to single car passageways made the course that much more of a challenge at the relatively high speeds.

A typical late Sunday night after the annual Tri-State Custom Auto Show would find about a dozen or so of the car show regulars engaged in a no-holds-barred race, at half scale but with full scale drivers. All were car enthusiasts. All were highly competitive. And there were no rules. The race would have to be stopped periodically to untangle the pile-ups that would occur as the course narrowed down to one lane. More often than not, two cars would wedge in together only to be hammered tightly by the cars behind them, making the pile up that much harder to correct. The cars had no reverse, so the drivers would have to get out and push the cars back out of the entanglement. But the most memorable Pacemaker 500 of them all ended much more dramatically than a simple pile up at the chicane. One over zealous driver was racing full throttle to get to the narrow chicane ahead of the field when his car went into a broadside slide and wedged into the narrowing guardrails sideways! Of course the abrupt stop was followed by several other cars ramming his car deeper into the confinement. The car was seriously wedged in, and it took quite a while to get it out. There were no half scale tow trucks available, and manually freeing the car was difficult since the wheels were at 90 degrees from the necessary rotation. The operator was a bit unhappy and suggested that they try the bumper cars.

The bumper car version of the Pacemaker 500 seemed like a safe alternative since the cars moved more slowly and they were designed to withstand collisions. However, they were not designed for two or three drivers to team up on another one, nor were they designed for the no rules demolition derby that was about to erupt. The collisions became more and more intense until one driver took a full course running start to broadside another car, causing it to tip over onto its side! The operator had to cut off the power so the guys could upright the car carefully so as not to damage the mast that made the electrical connection with the ceiling, or get electrocuted in the process. This time the operator suggested that the guys go back to drag racing where they were safe.

The Pacemakers' car shows were among the club's greatest accomplishments. Certainly they were the first major custom auto shows in the immediate area, and such shows gave the sport of hot rodding a shot in the arm with some of the best public relations strides available. The car shows like the Tri-State Custom Auto Shows at LeSourdsville Lake offered thousands of people a peek at the sport and a chance to learn about hot rods and customized cars that otherwise would have remained distant oddities never to be appreciated or understood.

There were numerous custom auto shows throughout Ohio in the '50s and '60s that were put on by car clubs or civic organizations. The aforementioned shows at the Dayton Field House dated back to at least 1953, and the Pacemaker shows began in 1954. The following is a partial list of other Ohio area shows assembled from the car show schedules in the period car magazines: The Trotters in Columbus and the Northwest Ohio Timing Association in Toledo began putting on annual shows in 1957. In 1958, the Kiwanis club in Lima, the Flywheels in Marion, the Flying Angels in Mansfield, and the Road Knights in Evansville, Indiana, began annual shows as well as an unnamed group in Cleveland. In 1959, the Southern Ohio Timing Association began shows in Cincinnati. In 1960, the Kingpins of Steubenville held their first show, as did the Floor Shifters in Canton and the Indy Idlers in Indianapolis. In 1961, there were shows by the Squires Car Club in Cincinnati, the Rod Burners in Loudenville, the Nomads in Mansfield, and an unnamed group in Youngstown. Shows by the Cardinals in Dayton were first listed in 1963. Hundreds of similar shows dotted the country from coast to coast. Each of these shows and the dedicated clubs and groups that ran them helped to sell the sport of hot rodding to the public. Today's rodders, who enjoy a sport that is very much accepted, owe a debt of gratitude to these pioneer clubs and to the National Hot Rod Association that led them. Without them, the sport could have easily been legislated out of existence long before the first fiberglass T-bucket saw the light of day.

This poster advertises the fourth annual Pacemaker Tri-State Custom Auto Show held in June of 1957 at LeSourdsville Lake Amusement Park. It was given to me by Paul Scorti at the first Pacemaker reunion held in June of 1994, on the 40th anniversary of the first Pacemaker car show. (Roberson collection, 1957.)

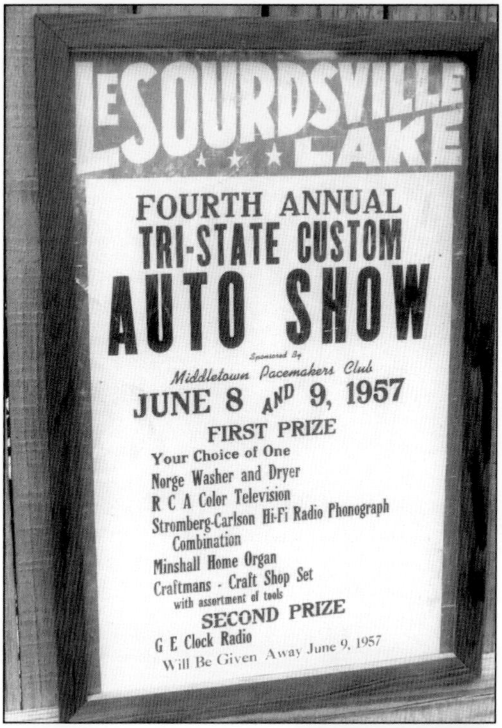

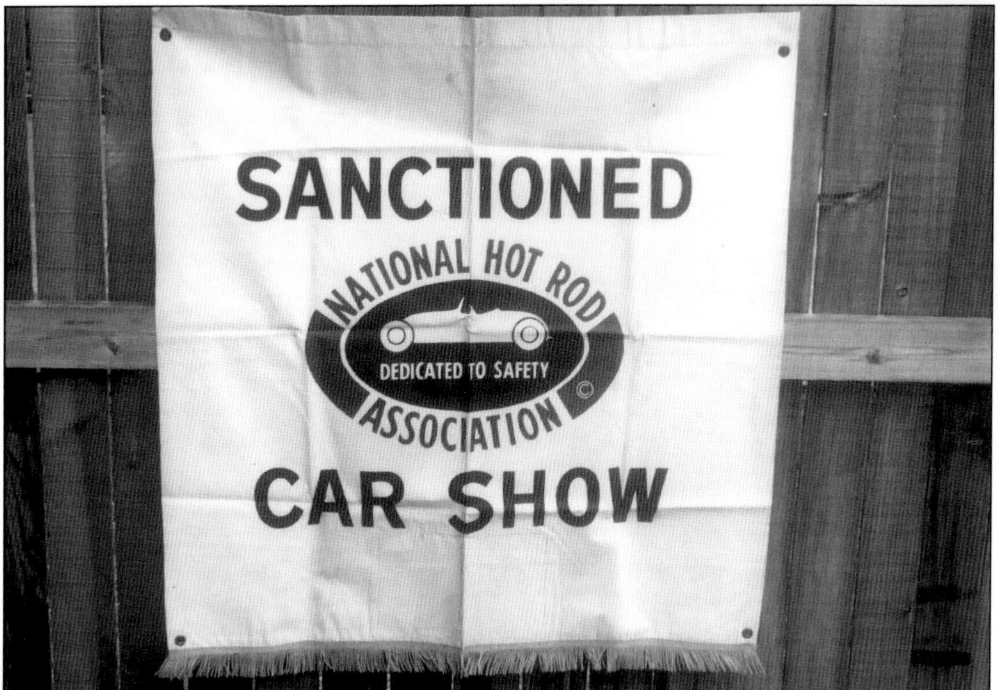

The car shows were sanctioned by the National Hot Rod Association as this banner indicates. The Pacemakers held the Tri-State Custom Auto Show at LeSourdsville Lake every year from 1954 though 1965. (Roberson collection, 1954.)

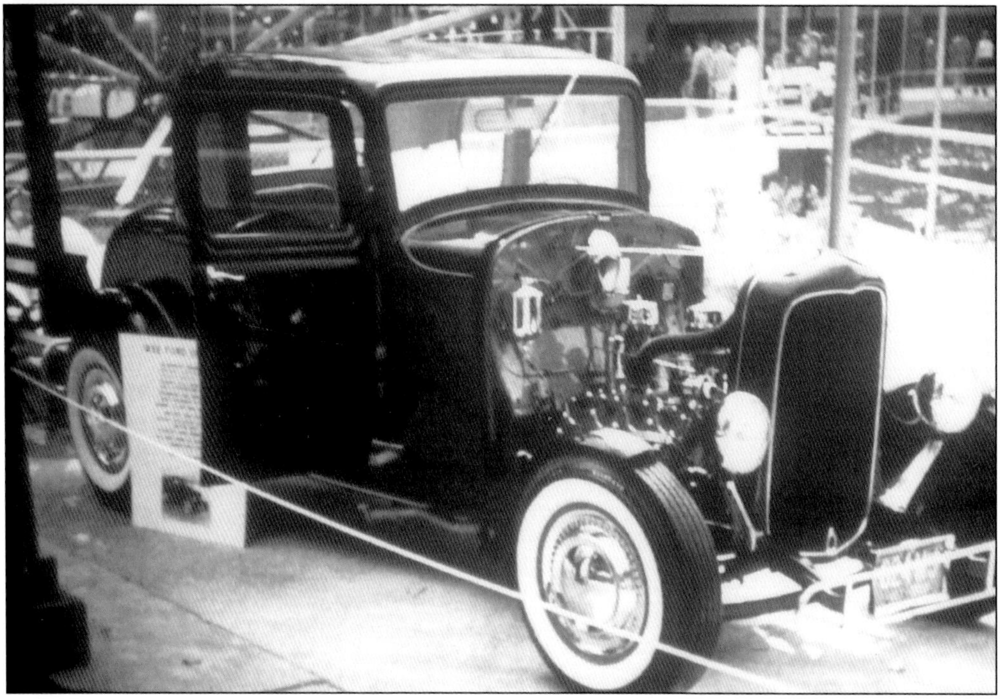

Club member Bill Burton's beautifully detailed 1932 Ford five-window coupe is displayed at the 1957 Pacemaker car show at LeSourdsville Lake. The midnight-blue coupe sports a '48 Mercury engine, but it was updated to a 345 Olds for drag racing the following year. (Burton collection, 1957.)

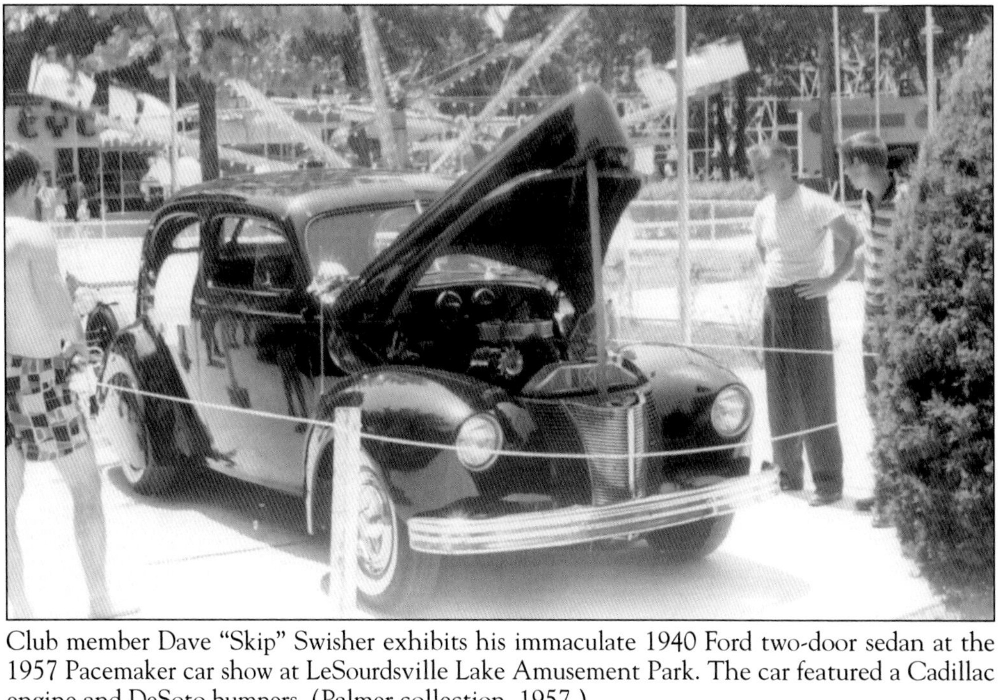

Club member Dave "Skip" Swisher exhibits his immaculate 1940 Ford two-door sedan at the 1957 Pacemaker car show at LeSourdsville Lake Amusement Park. The car featured a Cadillac engine and DeSoto bumpers. (Palmer collection, 1957.)

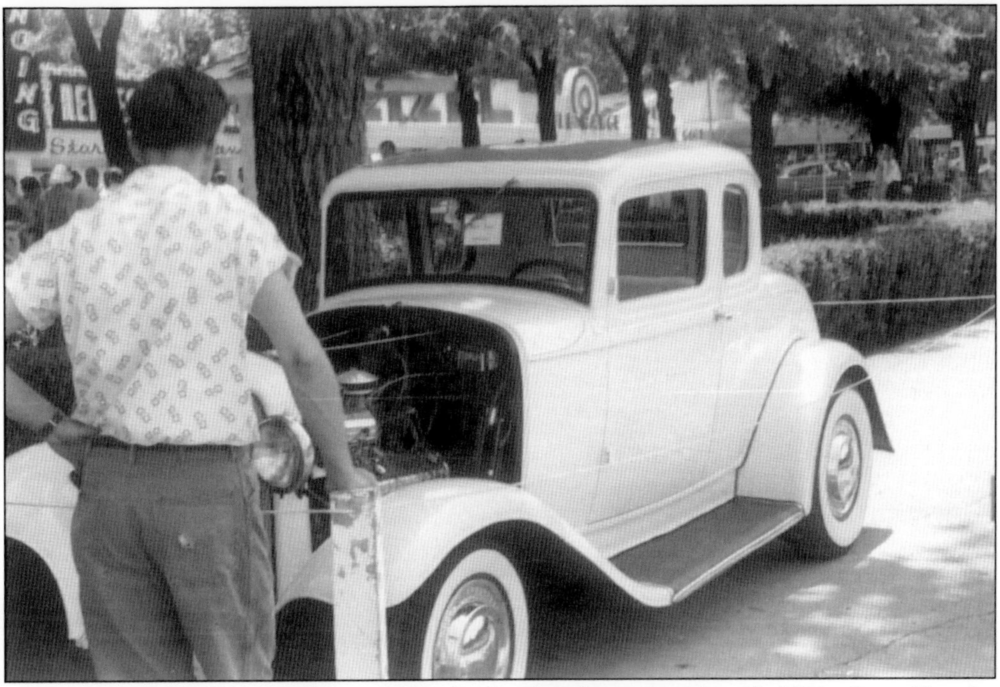

A beautiful '32 Ford five-window coupe is displayed in front of a ride called "The Pretzel" at the 1957 show. (Palmer collection, 1957.)

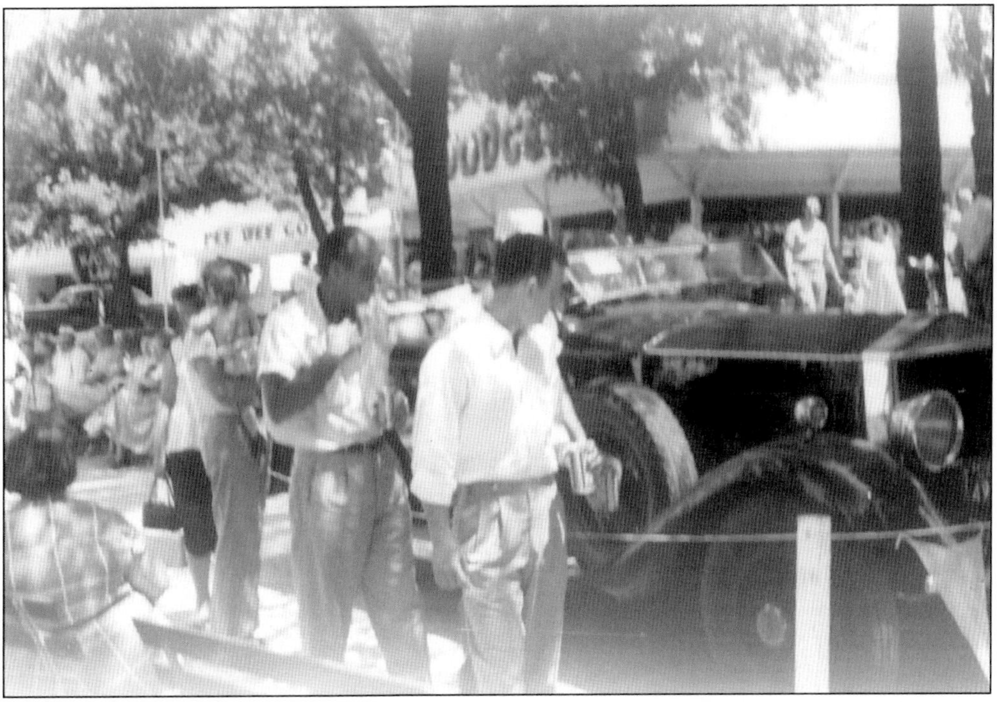

The Tri-State Custom Auto Show always drew big crowds to the lake as indicated by the group gathered around this vintage Rolls Royce. Note the "Dodge'em Cars" bumper car ride in the background. (Palmer collection, 1957.)

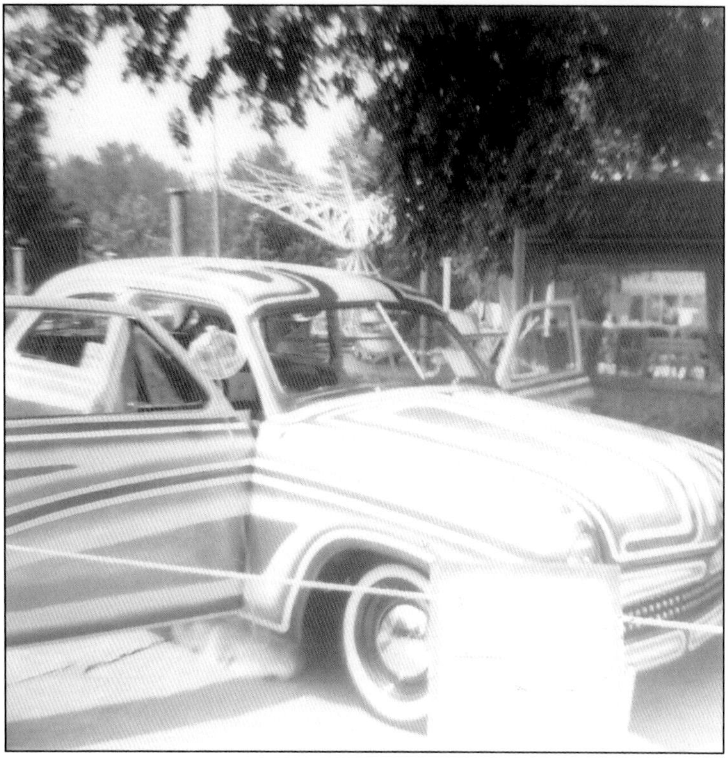

This customized 1950 Ford had a trick paint job that was state-of-the-art for the time. As I recall, it was pearl white with lavender and green accents. Note the custom grille. (Roberson collection, 1964.)

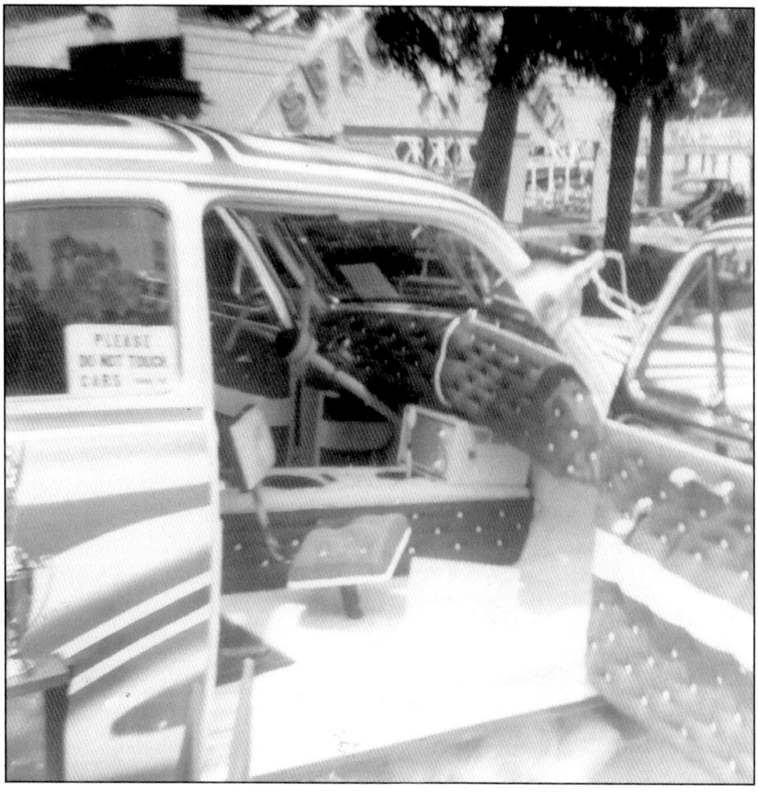

The '50 Ford's interior featured swivel seats, a padded dash and a television set. The identity of the owner is unknown. (Roberson collection, 1964.)

Local paint and body specialist Bill Neal's customized Ford Ranchero sported Edsel taillights, fender skirts, and a removable continental kit bearing the name "Maverick," after the hit TV show. Bill painted many of the show cars in the area. (Roberson collection, 1964.)

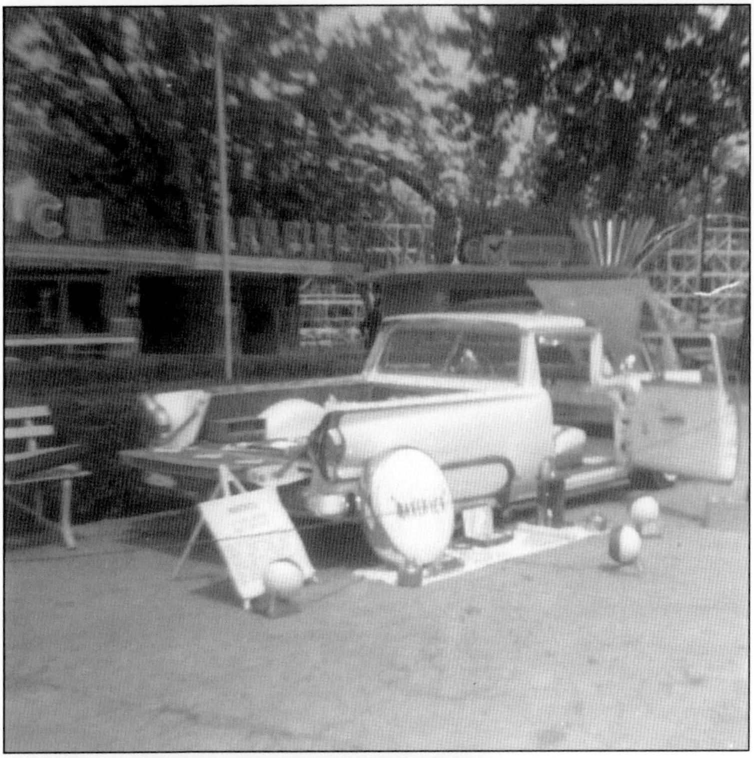

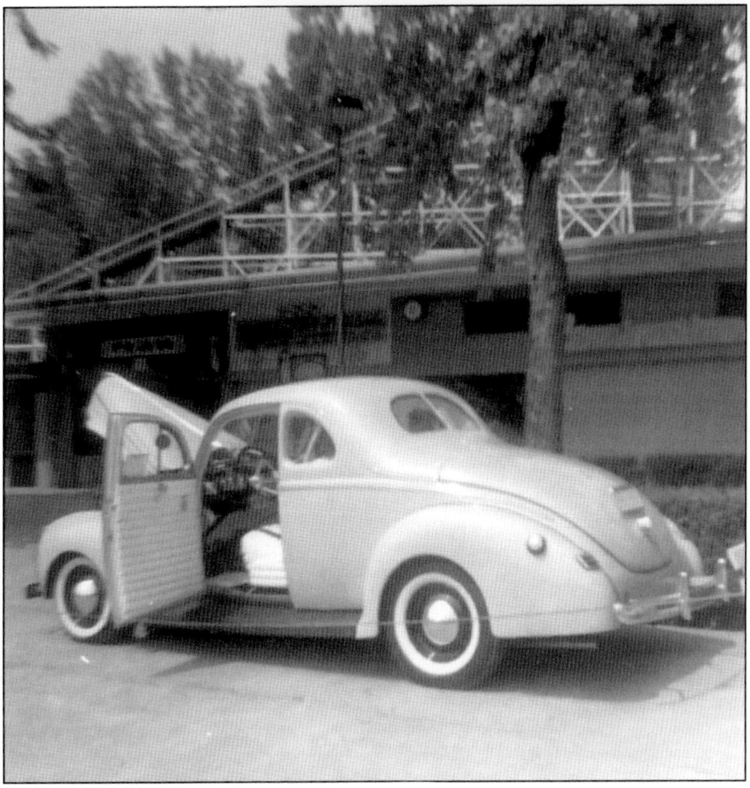

This 1940 Ford deluxe coupe had white tuck and roll upholstery. The framework of the park's wooden roller coaster is in the background. (Roberson collection, 1964.)

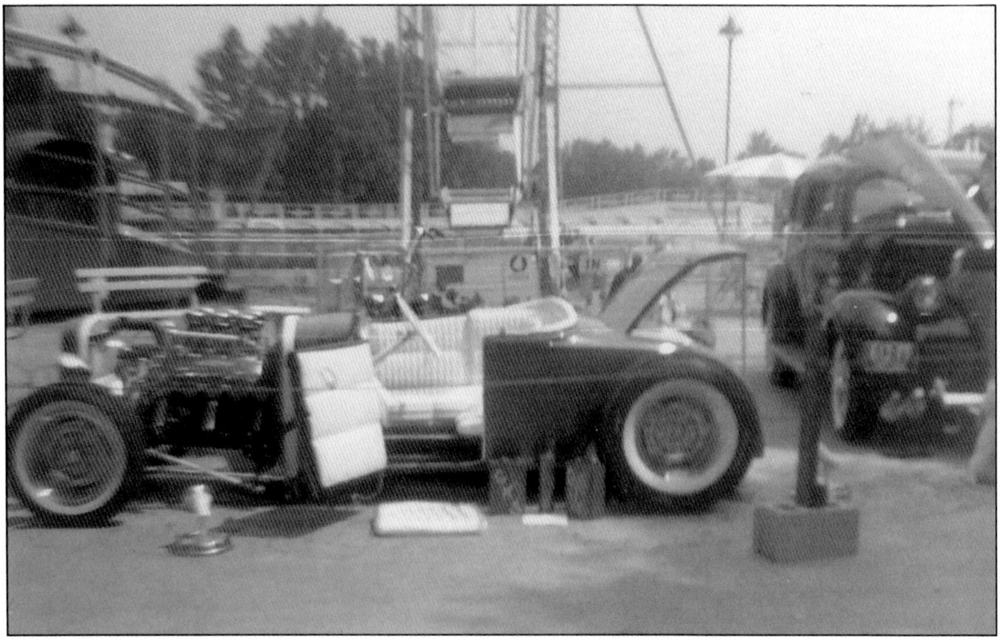

A channeled Model A roadster with an extra low silhouette sports a Chevy V-8 engine with six carburetors. People on the Ferris wheel that day got an aerial view of this beauty. (Roberson collection, 1964.)

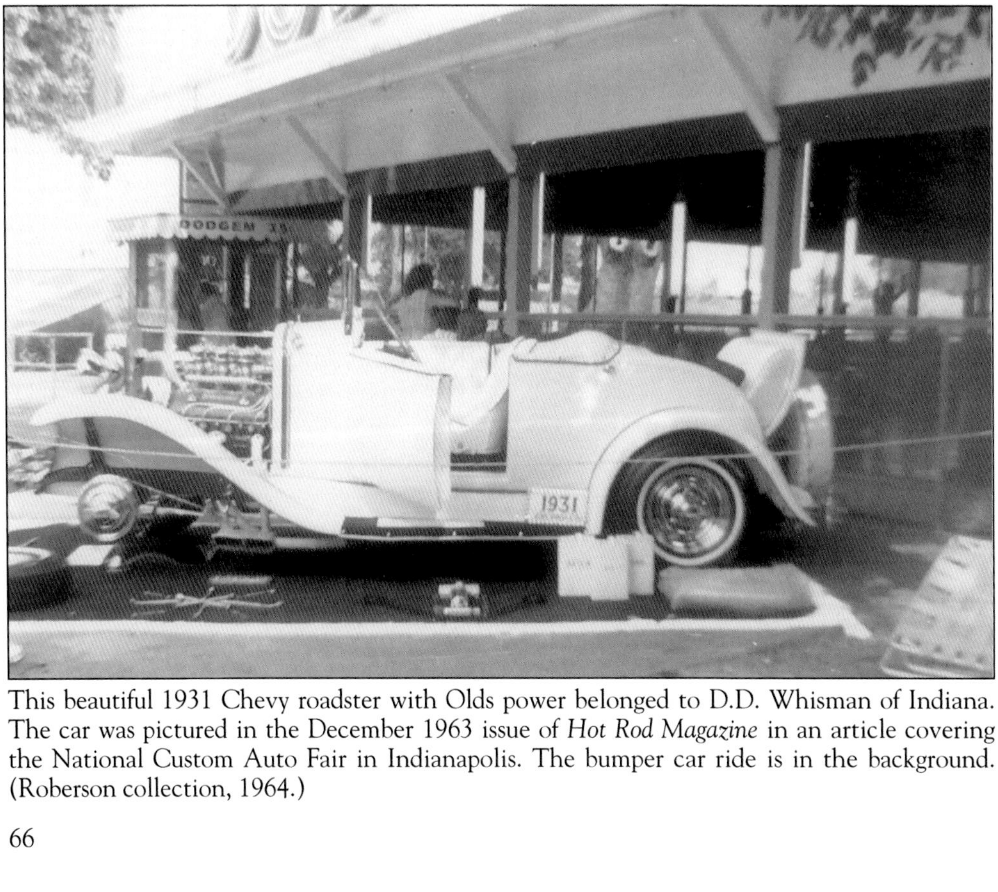

This beautiful 1931 Chevy roadster with Olds power belonged to D.D. Whisman of Indiana. The car was pictured in the December 1963 issue of *Hot Rod Magazine* in an article covering the National Custom Auto Fair in Indianapolis. The bumper car ride is in the background. (Roberson collection, 1964.)

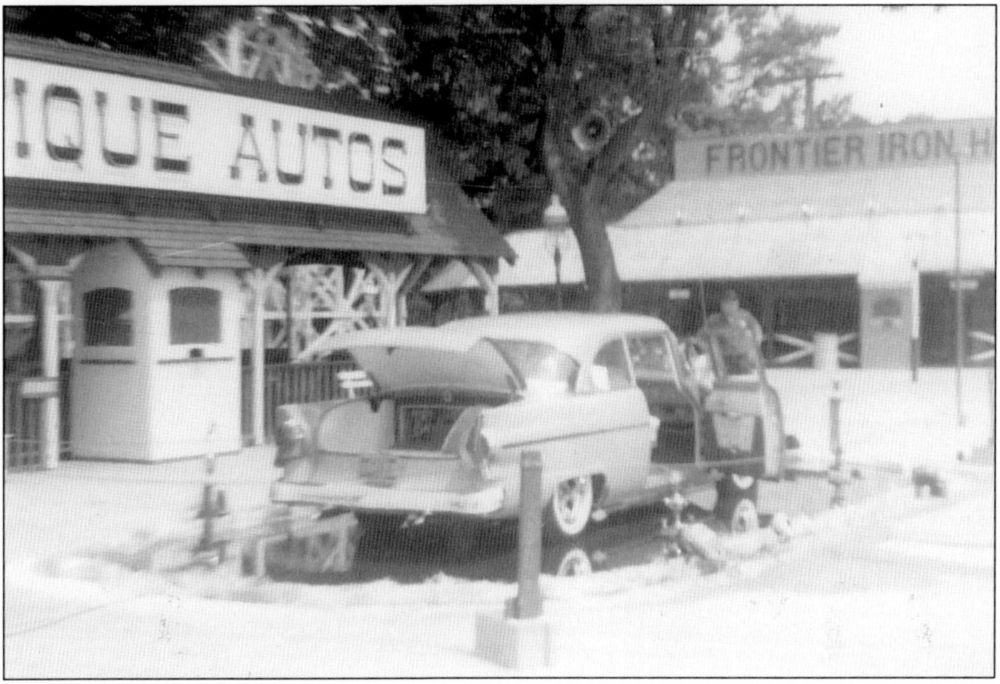

A customized 1955 Ford is displayed appropriately in front of the Antique Autos ride, although it was not an antique in 1964, when this photo was taken. The car sports Edsel taillights, a custom interior, and a detailed under carriage. (Roberson collection, 1964.)

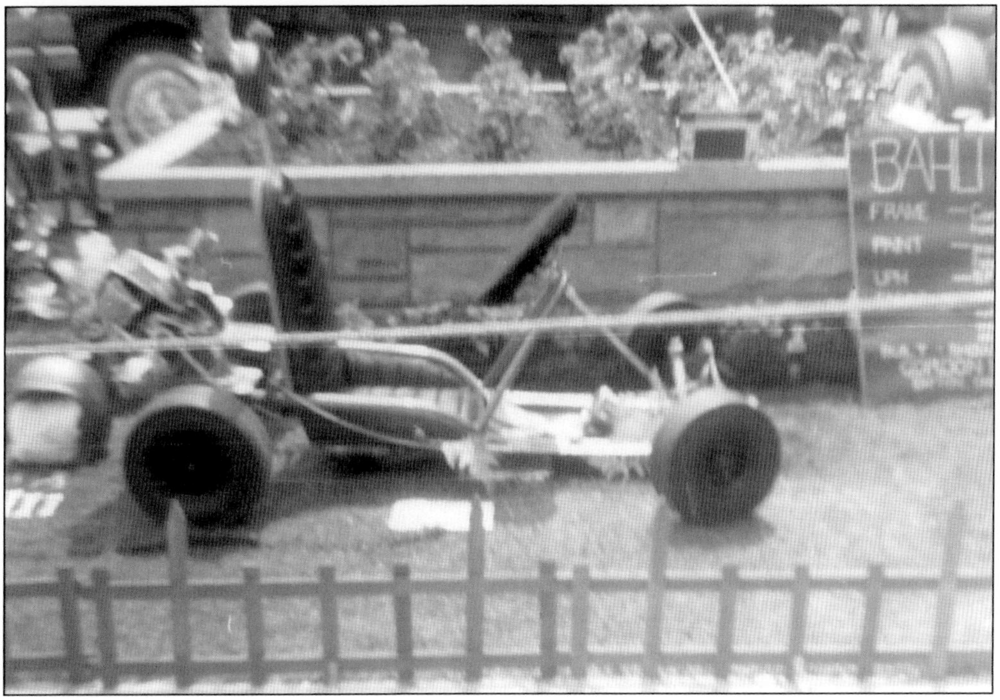

A customized go kart was enough to catch the eye of this photographer at age 13. (Roberson collection, 1964.)

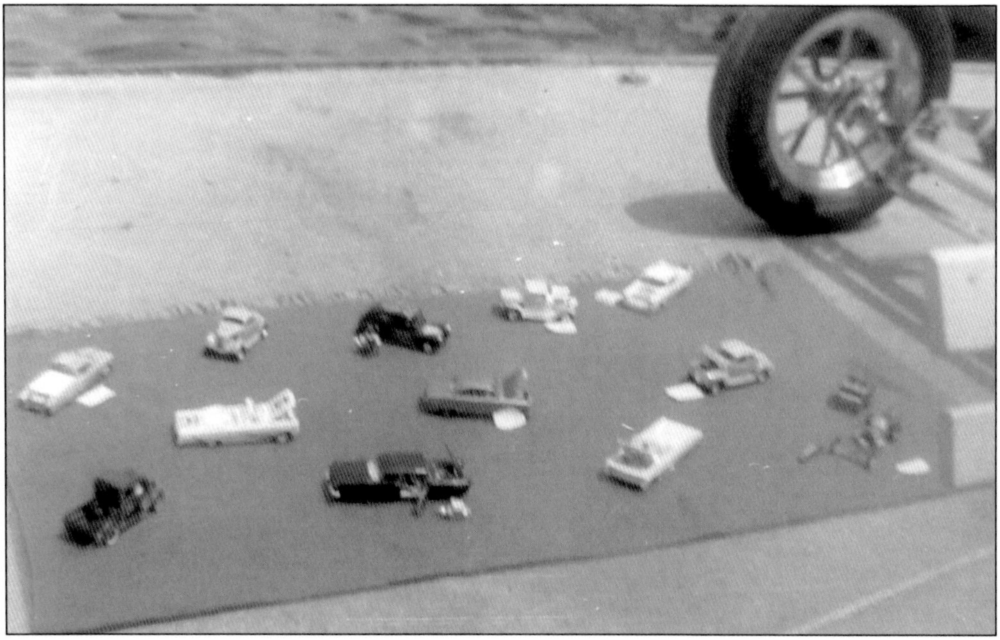

My friend Ron Leisner and I displayed our model cars at the 1963 show along side the "Pacemaker Special" dragster. Note the twelve-spoke mag wheel looming in the background. (Roberson collection, 1963.)

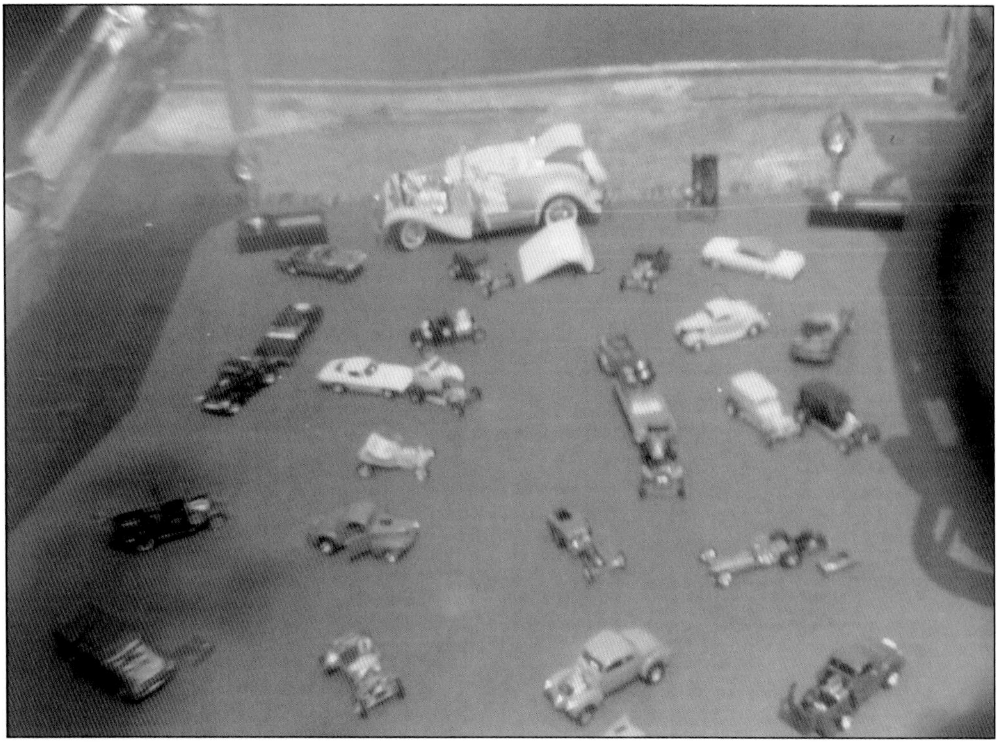

Our expanded model car display shares space with Bud Dickman's Sunbeam roadster. Note the trophies at the back of the display. (Roberson collection, 1964.)

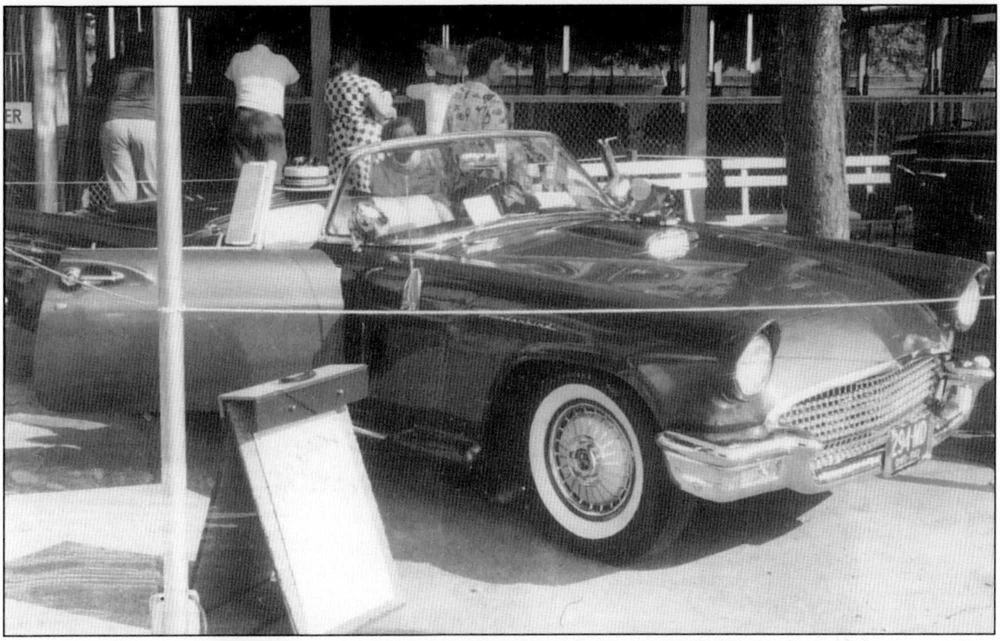

Club member Alex Slamka's mild custom 1956 T-Bird shines brightly at the 1964 show. That looks like the Arcade in the background. (Slamka collection, 1964.)

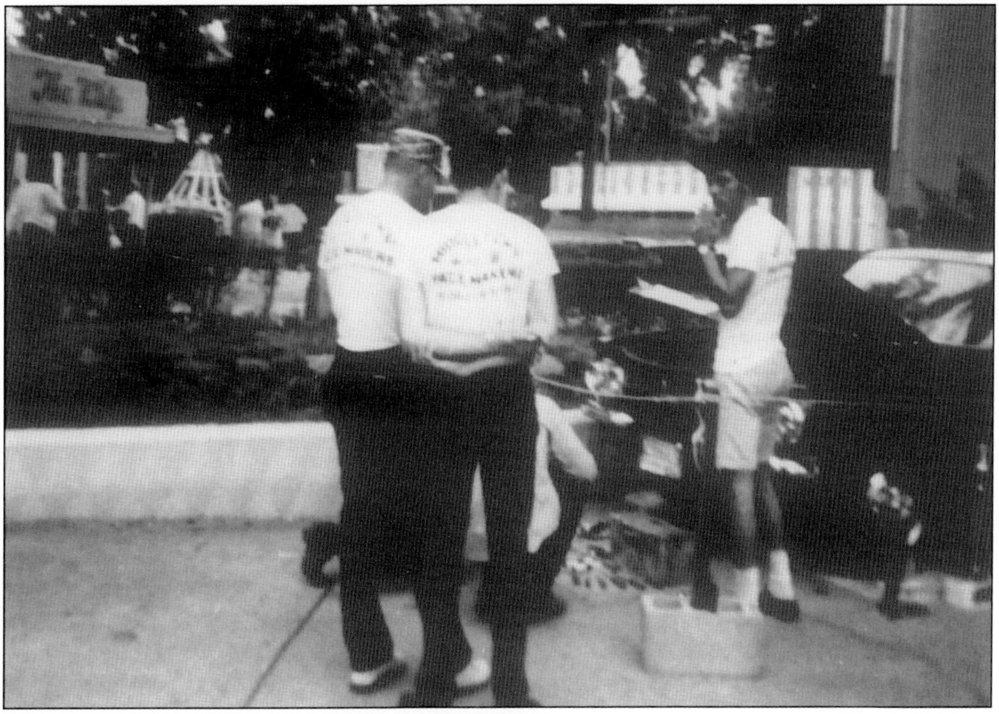

Judges inspect the cars at the 1965 show. From left to right are Dad, Tom Denniston, and Earnie Barnes (in the cowboy hat). Tom, a nonmember, worked in Dad's radiator repair shop, and volunteered to help judge the large field of cars that day. Note the Pacemaker tee shirts. (Barnes collection, 1965.)

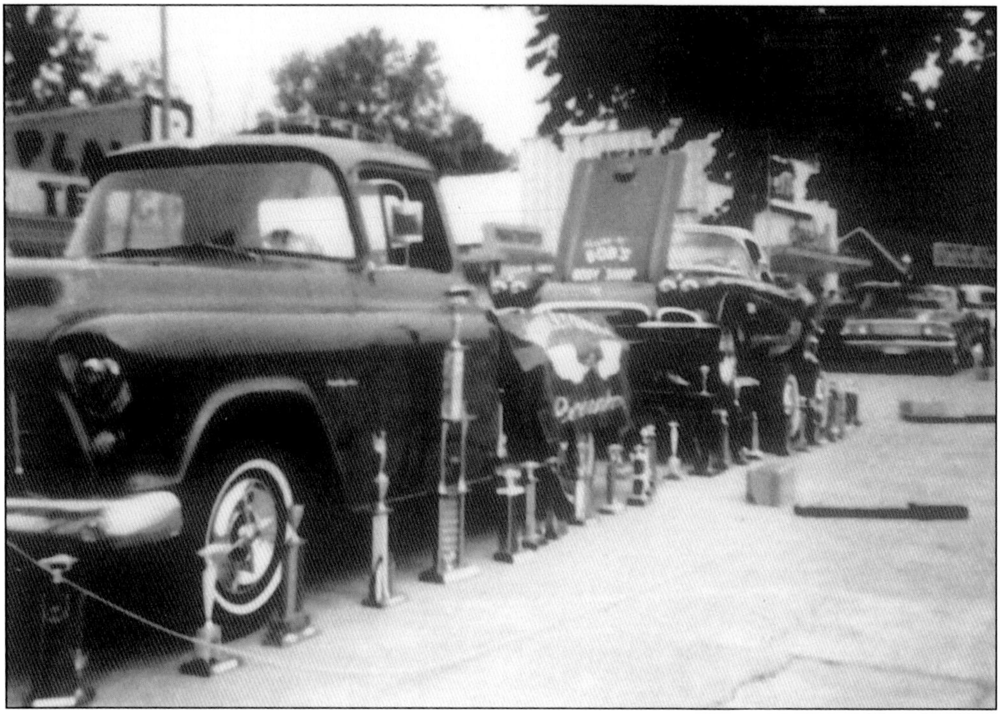

Harold and Earnie Barnes' '61 Corvette racecar and matching Chevy tow truck are flanked by a ton of drag racing trophies at the '65 show. Note the Pacemaker banner laying over the truck's rear fender. (Barnes collection, 1965.)

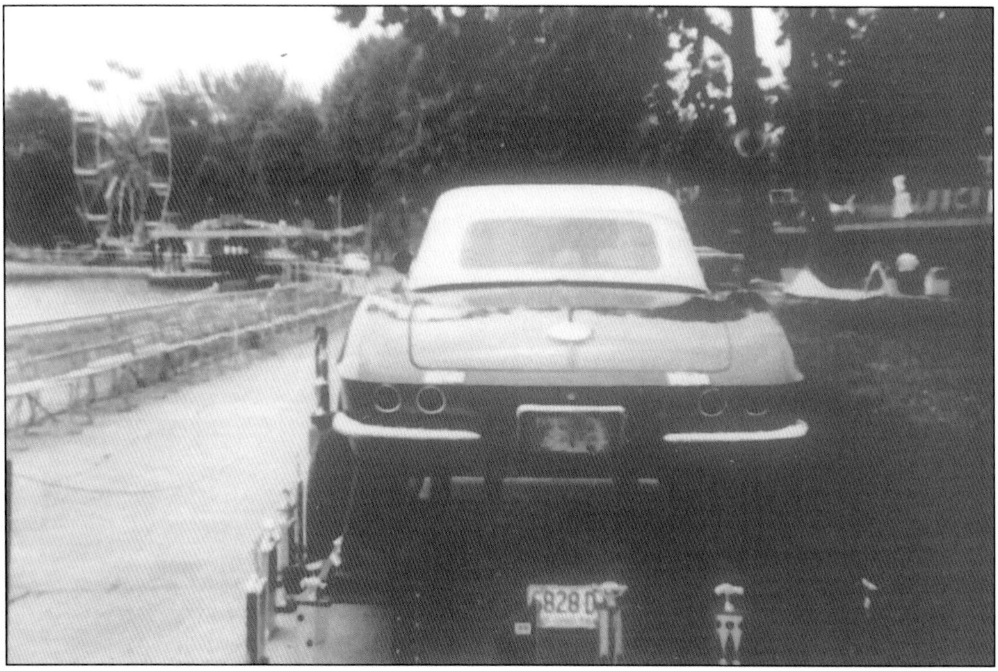

This rear view of the Barnes Brother's Corvette shows the lake and the Ferris wheel in the background. (Barnes collection, 1965.)

Five

Drag Racing
The Formative Years

To invent, you need a good imagination and a pile of junk.

- Thomas Edison

It has been said that drag racing's roots date back to the turn of the 20th century whenever the second person in a given town purchased a new horseless carriage. The natural tendency would be to see which one was faster, and a drag race is the simplest, quickest test. It is seemingly uncomplicated; a side by side acceleration contest in a straight line over a given distance, usually a quarter mile or an eighth mile. It is auto racing's version of the hundred-meter dash.

Today's highly refined dragsters run the quarter mile in about four and a half seconds, at top end speeds of over 325 mph. Sophisticated electronic systems provide the racer with electronic starting and elapsed times for 60 feet, 1,000 feet, and 1,320 feet as well as the top end speed and the driver's starting line reaction time. But when the Pacemakers' club formed in 1951, organized drag racing was in its infancy. If you could find a legal organized drag meet in the Midwest in the early '50s, there would be no timing devices at all, unless local police offered to monitor speeds with radar. Cars would be started by a flagman, and the winner indicated by two flagmen on either side of the track at the finish line. As the sport progressed, simple timing systems were developed to report the top end speed, since that figure was the early drag racer's gauge for performance. There were no elapsed times given until the mid '50s, when such timing systems emerged in an effort to explain why cars with slower top end speeds sometimes won races. There were no grandstands. Spectators sat on the hoods of cars lined along the track, and beyond the immediate crews and family members there were few spectators at all. There were sometimes guard rails, consisting of unsecured logs or hay bails, but never any lighting for racing after sunset. The vast majority of the racecars were driven to the event and breakage often left the contestant without a ride home. Drag racing today is a mega dollar sport with professional crews, major sponsorships and national television coverage, but the sport's early days were humble indeed.

The earliest organized drag races in the Midwest were probably those held on a naval base at Willow Grove, Pennsylvania, where a local car club reportedly held at least one meet in 1949. The earliest continuous organized drag races in Ohio were probably those held in Akron, which began on blocked off public roads in 1951. The local Sheriff's office and the Cam Jammers car club worked together to put on the races, which were later moved to the municipal airport.

The Pacemakers' first venture into drag racing was possibly the first organized drag meet in southwestern Ohio. The year was 1954. Akron was 200 miles from Middletown, so there was a need for something closer. The Pacemakers worked with Middletown Police and set up a quarter mile drag strip on a short access road outside of nearby Trenton. The cars ran singly using a flag starter, and top speed was measured with police radar. (Details appear in Chapter 2.) Complaints from local residents put a stop to the races after three or four events.

In 1954, NHRA began the traveling Safety Safari, which put on drag races across the country. That year they made stops in Akron and Detroit, which were close enough for the Pacemakers to attend. In 1955, an extended schedule brought more races into the Midwest. One site was Stout Field Air Force Base at Indianapolis, where Charlie Mann and his Cluster Busters car club promoted a Safety Safari event in July of 1955. This was closer to Middletown, only 110 miles away. Another Safety Safari event was held the same month in Columbus at Don Scott Field, hosted by the Pipers car club. This event was only 80 miles from Middletown, so drag racing was getting closer.

Top speeds at these events barely broke 100 mph, but many stars were in the making. George Montgomery of Dayton ran a 1934 Ford coupe with a Cadillac V-8 that topped 95 mph at the first Stout Field race, winning the B/Gas class, which he also won at Columbus. Don Conrad of Covington, Kentucky, ran a Model A roadster with an Olds engine that topped 97 mph to win the B/Roadster class at the Stout Field race. Other racers at these events included Ken Hirata, Dale Hartong, Ron Burkett, Otis Smith, and Charlie Mann.

These NHRA meets proved that the Middletown area had some fine racecars. They gave local racers the opportunity to be clocked with the same equipment that had timed other racers across the country, since the Safety Safari had its own timing equipment. It also introduced the concept of elapsed times to the area, since local tracks at best only had timers for top end speeds. The faster cars like George Montgomery's '34 Ford coupe ran the quarter mile in about 14 seconds.

The Safety Safari meets inspired the local clubs to follow with regular events, usually once or twice a month. Stout Field began regular races in 1955. Regular races also began about the same time at Mansfield, Ohio, hosted by the Gents car club, and a drag strip most handy for the Pacemakers opened at Thorn Hill Lake, Kentucky, near Covington. There was even one enterprising farmer in Farmersville, Ohio, who graded a dirt drag strip on some available farmland and began to promote drag races. The success of these mid '50s drag races was followed by more airfields opening their gates to car clubs (like nearby Wilmington AFB) and by the construction of single-purpose commercial drag strips with weekly races by the late '50s.

With the availability of regular drag race meets in the area by 1955, several of the Pacemakers had begun to race their hot rods. Among these were Ray Boyce in a '53 Ford; Dick Beckett, in a GMC powered Chevy; Danny Allen, in his Mercury powered '39 Ford; Carl Lakes, in his Mercury powered '40 Ford sedan; Ray Palmer, in a Mercury powered '41 Ford coupe; Harold Michael, in his Mercury powered 1932 Ford roadster; and Dad, who raced his Olds powered 1945 Ford shop truck. But the most successful of the racing club members by 1955 was Herb Sebastian, whose potent Olds powered '32 Ford coupe was a consistent winner. Herb could beat or hold his own with anyone in the area except for George Montgomery and his '34 Ford coupe. Herb's coupe topped 94 mph on the drag strip, which was a very respectable top speed for the day.

Dad and Herb would attend the meets together. They would tow the coupe behind Dad's truck and race both vehicles. This was a common practice of the day. The coupe's highly modified Olds engine was linked to a Lincoln Zephyr transmission and stock Ford rear end. The high output Olds engine attached to the stock drive line would often lead to broken parts, so it was wise to tow it to the track. Dad's truck had a milder Olds engine, which was not quite as prone to breaking the drive train parts, so it was the more reliable ride home.

When Thorn Hill Lake Drag Strip opened in 1955, Dad and Herb made plans to attend the opening event with both vehicles. Herb had a conflict at the last minute and couldn't go, but he insisted that Dad go and take the '32. Dad balked at first saying, "What if I take your car down there and scatter the transmission?" "So what?" Herb replied. "The junkyards are full of them." So Dad went to the meet without Herb but with his friend's coupe. Harold Michael went along with his '32 roadster and also entered.

As with the typical drag strips of the era, there were no electronics except for clocks to measure top speed. The rest was done by flagmen. The cars were separated into classes for stock cars, roadsters, gas coupes, and dragsters. They were flagged off in pairs, and two track officials at the finish line waved flags to indicate the winning lane. Two by two they roared down the course. When the dust cleared, Dad had won the C/Gas class, and Mike had won his roadster class. Then the two entered the elimination runs in which the class winners raced each other to determine the Top Eliminator.

Thorn Hill Lake Drag Strip was a primitive operation by today's standards. It was run by a local car club of which Don Conrad of Covington, Kentucky, was the star drag racer. When the facility first opened, the track surface wasn't paved. They had leveled off a dirt surface and oiled it down to control the dust. Later it would be paved in stages, beginning with the starting line and progressing down course until it was eventually paved the full length. But when it opened in the summer of 1955, it was dirt. This made for some exciting top end action as the cars would become unstable and squirrely on the dirt surface, especially the light weight flathead powered dragsters that had entered the meet. Herb's nimble coupe was well suited to the task and handled relatively well under the conditions. This was in part due to Herb suggesting that Dad put snow tires on the car, because he'd heard the track wasn't paved. Dad would get a jump on the dragsters and hold them off as their anticipated top end charges failed to materialize. He even put away Don Conrad's potent Olds powered Model A roadster. He won top eliminator at the event, and turned in the day's top speed at just over 90 mph.

I was about five years old during the '32 coupe's hey day, and I can personally remember only one story from the Thorn Hill racing days. It was a typical meet in 1956, with Dad racing the Ford shop truck and Herb racing the coupe. Dad was lined up to race and I was standing by the fence with Herb, watching the action. Dad took off and quickly began losing ground to a turquoise '56 Chevy. Due to my short stature I couldn't see the far end of the track. "Did Dad lose?" I asked. "Yeah," Herb replied. "He lost that time." Just then we heard some commotion in the pits behind us, and we turned to see a Corvette spurting long yellow flames out of the hoodless engine compartment about 50 feet away. Herb turned to me quickly and said, "Ronnie, you stay right here. Don't move." Then he ran off to get the fire extinguisher from his coupe. I remember looking around in fear at all the strangers that surrounded me, and seeing the flaming car and the commotion around it. People were shouting, and the helpless owner tried in vain to put out the flames with a beach towel. There was only one thing to do. I ran after Herb as fast as I could. Herb grabbed the extinguisher, ran up to the Corvette and put out the fire single handedly in an effort that can only be described as heroic. He didn't even know the car's owner. As the fire went out Herb stepped back and bumped into something. He turned and looked down to find that I had been standing right behind him all the time he was fighting the fire. With horror in his eyes he began to scold me for not staying put as I was told. It was the only time Herb ever raised his voice to me, but looking back it was rightfully so. Herb had no problem risking his own safety to save a fellow racer's car, but he was terrified to find out that I was at risk too. It is curious that at five, I was afraid of being left alone, but I had no fear of standing next to Herb while he fought the fire.

The duo ended the 1955 season with a trip to the Bonneville Salt Flats, where they entered the coupe in the 1955 Speed Trials. The wives went along, so they used our '51 Olds family sedan instead of the cramped truck to flat tow the '32. At the meet they encountered carburetor problems, and the coupe never ran up to expectations. Dad made a 101 mph run in the family Olds that was faster than any run either driver made in the '32 coupe all week long; they had anticipated running 125 mph on the salt, but the car never broke 90.

The year 1955 had been a banner year for drag racing. The California racers had perfected the use of nitromethane fuel to the point of producing some outstanding speeds. First Mickey Thompson broke a major barrier by exceeding 144 mph. Some had theorized that no dragster could ever exceed 144 mph in quarter mile acceleration, because that speed was the terminal velocity of a falling object. Then Lloyd Scott ran 151 mph on gasoline at Lawrenceville, Illinois, in a dual engine (Olds and Cadillac) backyard engineering marvel called the "Bustle Bomb." The year was ended with NHRA's first national championships at Great Bend, Kansas, with

California's Calvin Rice becoming the sport's first national champion.

Dad and Herb continued racing the '32 coupe in 1956. They painted the car and Dad's Shop truck in matching colors, white with red flames. The truck carried the shop logo on the doors in red and blue letters. They raced often at Thorn Hill and Stout Field at Indy. Herb still won some races, but the gap widened between his performance and that of George Montgomery. George had installed a larger 414 cubic inch Cadillac engine and had run 111 mph in less than 14 seconds in the A/Gas class. Top eliminator run offs at local tracks in those days had no handicapping system, so class winners ran each other heads up. Herb would win his C/Gas class, but he was never able to beat George in the eliminator run offs.

By the end of the year, Dad and Herb, with the help of several of the other club members, began construction of a dragster in the garage behind Herb's house on Brentwood Street in the Mayfield area of Middletown. The car was crude by today's standards, with a modified 345 Olds engine sandwiched between Model T Ford frame rails and a home-made body formed from thin sheets of mild steel. The driver sat behind the engine straddling the rear end slingshot style like the California cars of Calvin Rice and Mickey Thompson. They used a Ford truck transmission and rear end, because these units could link together without a driveshaft, allowing the engine to be set back as far as possible in the chassis. Dad built the Olds engine with a Pop Dreyer racing cam. The car utilized a hand brake and a hand operated pump to pressurize the fuel tank. For an induction system, Dad hand made a log-type manifold that would accept four Stromberg 97 carburetors. He also adapted the motor mounts and a made a simple two point roll bar. The car would wear white paint and carry the club logo in red letters. It was dubbed the "Pacemaker Special," and it represented the club's first single purpose racecar. All of the club's previous racecars were dual-purpose cars, which the owners also drove on the street. This car was not street legal, but was built rather for the sole purpose of racing.

The car was tested on a stretch of country road along Jackson Lane outside of Middletown. In those days, dragsters were push started with another car. With Gene Wells behind the wheel, the engine sputtered to life, popping and cracking and alarming the pigs and cattle in the nearby farms. Dad made a few adjustments and the engine smoothed. Gene rapped the throttle and popped the clutch to make a few quick launch tests on the slag roadway, and then he shut the engine off as the car rolled to the side of the road. That was as far as the car could be tested short of taking it to a drag strip.

Just as the car stopped, a Middletown Police patrol car pulled up, and the officer approached the group. The racecar at this point was still in primer, so the Pacemaker logo was not yet applied, but still the officer recognized the group as the club who ran the vehicle safety inspections for the city. The guys looked at each other nervously. They were breaking most of the vehicle safety laws by running this racecar on a public road. It was not licensed and had no amenities like headlights, turn signals, brake lights, or mufflers. For a club dedicated to road safety, they were in a very embarrassing position. The officer calmly asked what they were doing, and Herb explained. He looked the car over and was impressed by the fact that it was hand built. He wanted to hear it run, so the guys fired it up again, and Gene made a couple more short hops. He made a joke about hoping he never had to try to chase this one with his patrol car. Then he smiled and drove away.

The car made its racing debut at Thorn Hill Drag Strip in the late fall of 1956. It ran in the B/Dragster class and was an immediate success. With top end speeds of 111 mph, it began winning drag meets regularly at Thorn Hill and Stout Field. At first the driving chores were shared by Herb, Dad and Gene Wells, but eventually Gene became the regular driver. Gene's thin and wiry build gave him a 20-pound weight advantage, which showed up favorably on the elapsed time clock.

The 1956 NHRA Nationals were held Labor Day weekend at Kansas City, Missouri. The club dragster was not yet finished, so Dad and Herb entered Herb's '32 coupe, and several club members including Ray Palmer and Tom Bishop went along. The coupe had a dismal outing though, as the rear end gears failed on an early practice run. The only available spare was the street version rear end that had been removed in favor of one with a lower gear ratio. So they spent one day swapping them out, with the sounds of 500 racers roaring away in the background, knowing they would be disappointed by the performance. The car slowed noticeably, and Herb was eliminated early in the class run offs.

However, the '56 Nationals proved to be a learning experience for the guys. It was Dad's first close up look at the California cars that graced the pages of *Hot Rod Magazine*. He watched in awe as Bob Alsenz ran an unheard of 159-mph in a fuel dragster with a Chrysler engine. The officials were so dumfounded by the run that they stopped the meet and remeasured the speed traps to make certain the speed was correctly calculated. He saw the beautifully prepared "Glass Slipper" dragster, the "J.E. Riley Special" of defending champ Calvin Rice, and the famous "Bustle Bomb" dual engine car. But biggest surprise was in the Top Eliminator run offs, when an Oklahoma farmer named Mel Heath edged out both defending champion Calvin Rice and the speedy Bob Alsenz with a fuel Chrysler of his own to win the event. In addition to this, Akron's Art Arfons ran 150mph on gasoline with his "Green Monster" powered by a WWII aircraft engine. The California guys had invented drag racing, but the rest of the country was catching up.

The year 1957 was a banner year for drag racing. The speed records continued to climb. California cars had exceeded 165mph early in the year. By the end of the year, the fuel dragsters would exceed 170 mph and a Florida star named Don Garlits would emerge. NHRA would be so concerned over the rapid advances in speeds that they would put a ban on the use of nitromethane fuel that would last for over six years.

The Pacemakers continued winning with the little Olds dragster. They were even beating George Montgomery now, even though he had installed a supercharger, and was running 116 mph with his '34 Ford coupe. They restored a 1947 Buick sedan painted in a matching white scheme with red and blue lettering to tow the car to the races. They had no trailer, so the car was flat towed behind the Buick. This required an extra set of wheels and tires for the rear of the dragster so as not to wear out the newly acquired Inglewood racing slicks in transit. The first and last task at every meet was to change the rear tires. In 1958, the club purchased a trailer, and the tire changing ritual was eliminated.

Most of 1957 was spent racing at Thorn Hill and Stout Field, with occasional outings at special events elsewhere. Herb had sold his coupe, now spending all his effort in running the dragster. The dragster was disassembled at one point and the roll bar and body were modified. The modifications improved the looks of the car, but more importantly the car now afforded the driver better protection. Also during this time, the club members began to coordinate their clothing to give the crew a real team look. They were among the first drag racers to do this. At two-day meets, they would have two coordinated outfits, always with white pants and white shirts like the club tee shirts. These outfits coupled with the white race car and matching Buick tow car presented a real professional look, especially when you consider that they often fielded a crew of ten or more. They began to win awards for the best appearing car and crew at the various meets they ran.

By the end of the '57 season, the Pacemakers were already planning the next car. The little Olds dragster had served them well, running 111 mph in a class where the national record stood all year at 115. However, a B/Dragster at the '57 Nationals had set a new class record at 127 mph, and the car needed to be updated. The guys didn't enter the Nationals in '57. Rather, they spent the time planning the new car. It would have a custom built frame and use a much larger Olds engine, but it would have to follow a very tough act. The first "Pacemaker Special" had a win record that few racecars could ever claim. In its competitive life—a little over one race season—the car was never defeated except for breakage. Every race that it finished under power, it had won. But the best was yet to come, because the real accomplishment of the first "Pacemaker Special" was to act as the prototype for future cars. The Pacemakers were now ready to enter the national scene.

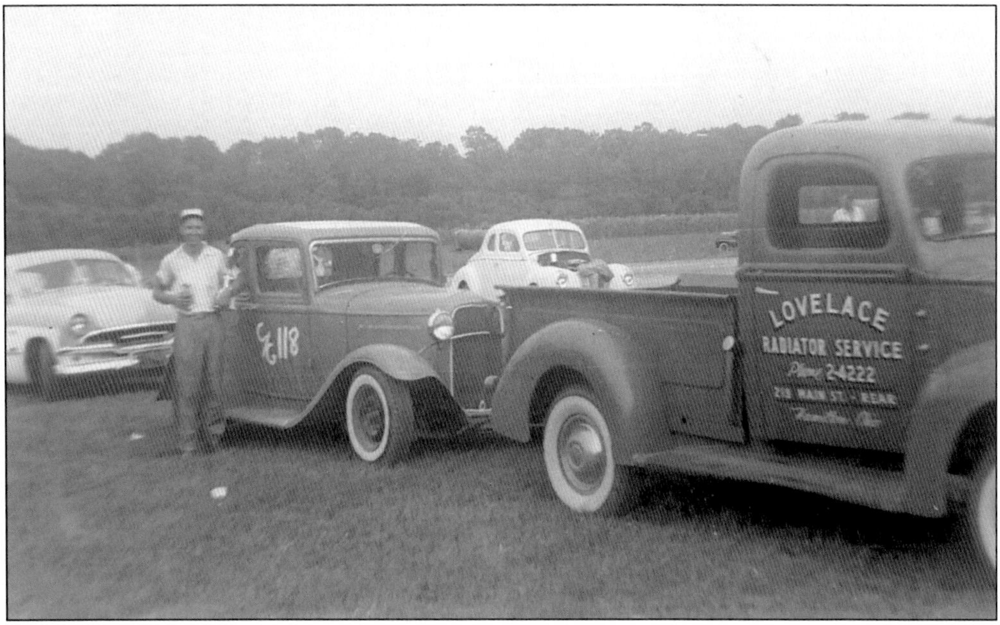

Dad poses with two trophies at the opening race at Thorn Hill Lake Drag Strip in Kentucky. Driving Herb Sebastian's Olds powered '32 Ford coupe, Dad won the C/Gas class, took Top Eliminator, and set top speed of the meet at just over 90 mph. The exact date is unknown, but it was in the summer of 1955. (Michael collection, 1955.)

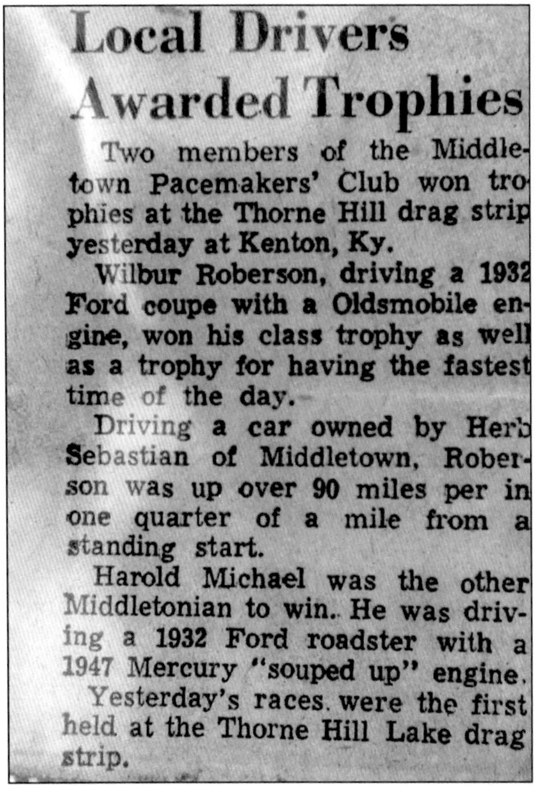

Local Drivers Awarded Trophies

Two members of the Middletown Pacemakers' Club won trophies at the Thorne Hill drag strip yesterday at Kenton, Ky.

Wilbur Roberson, driving a 1932 Ford coupe with a Oldsmobile engine, won his class trophy as well as a trophy for having the fastest time of the day.

Driving a car owned by Herb Sebastian of Middletown, Roberson was up over 90 miles per in one quarter of a mile from a standing start.

Harold Michael was the other Middletonian to win. He was driving a 1932 Ford roadster with a 1947 Mercury "souped up" engine.

Yesterday's races were the first held at the Thorne Hill Lake drag strip.

The *Middletown Journal* carried this article about Dad's win at Thorn Hill. Harold Michael also won his roadster class for a Pacemaker sweep. (Reprinted with permission of the *Middletown Journal*, 1955.)

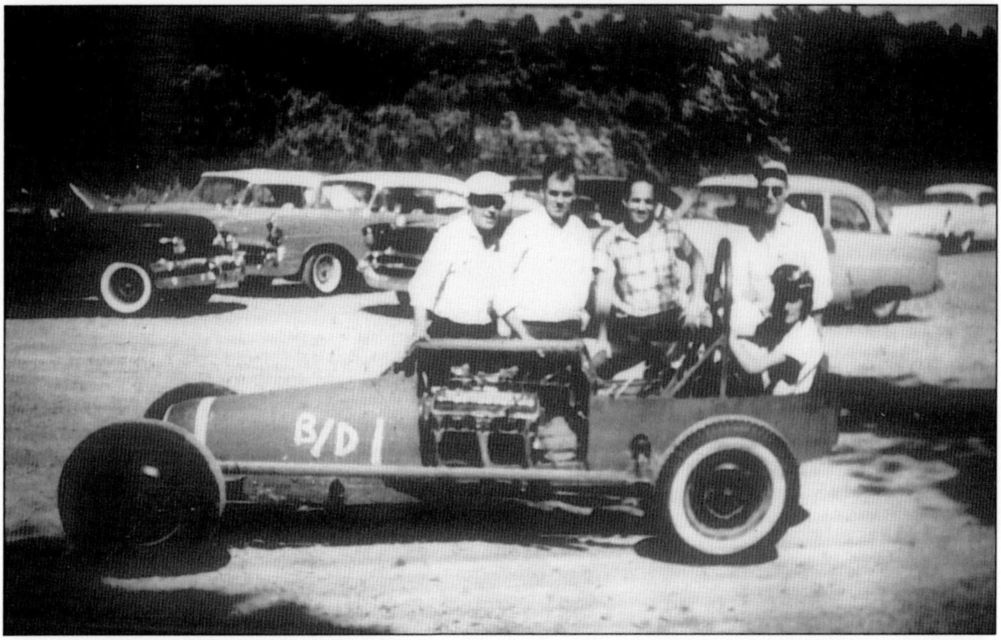

The first "Pacemaker Special" dragster is debuted at Thorn Hill Lake Drag Strip at the end of the 1956 race season. The Olds powered car is still in primer. From left to right are Herb Sebastian, Jerry Williams, Dallas Gardner, Dad, and Gene Wells (in the driver's seat). (Burton collection, 1956.)

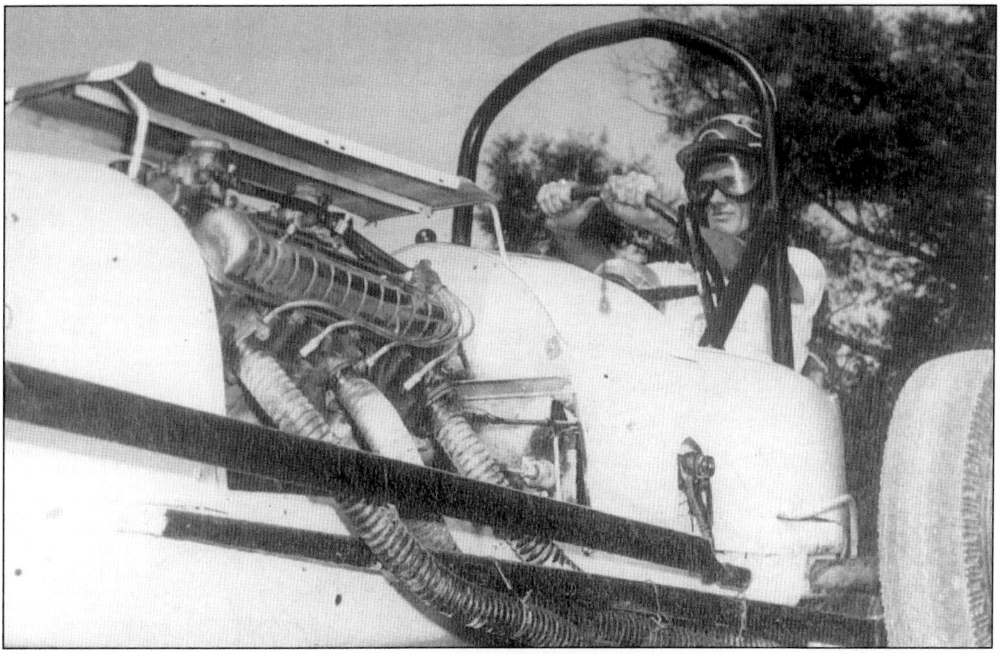

Gene Wells poses in the cockpit of the "Pacemaker Special" in this worm's-eye view of the car at Thorn Hill. Note the "dangle" style flexible exhaust pipes, the large steering wheel and the truck style rear tires. The photo either pre-dates the purchase of the racing slicks, or they have been removed for towing. (Michael collection, photo by Gilbert Gray, 1957.)

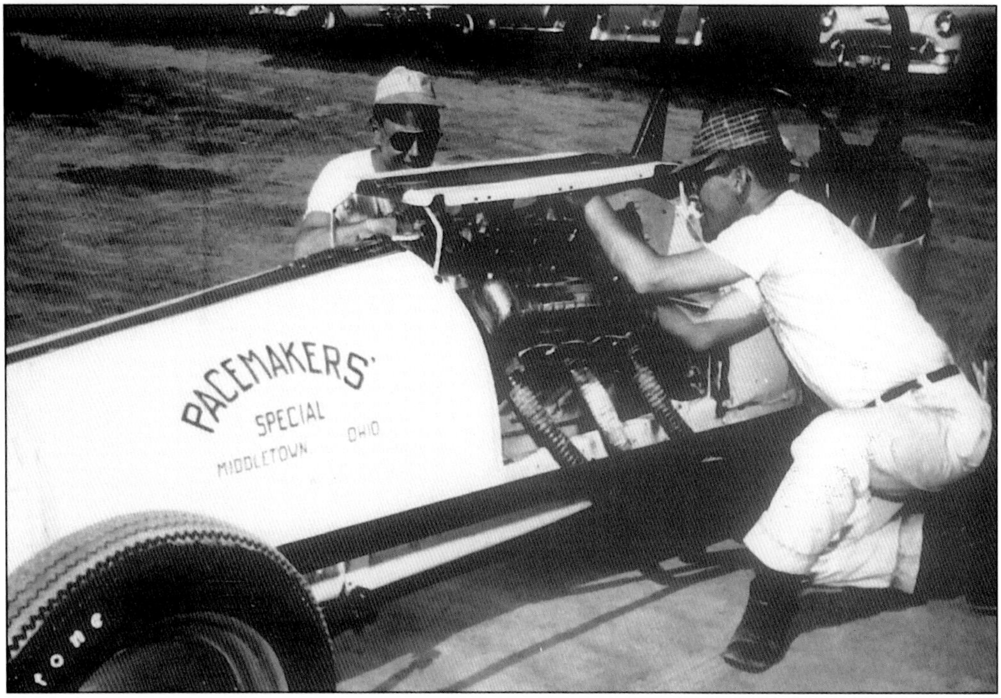

Dad (left) and Herb Sebastian (right) pose beside the "Pacemaker Special" at Thorn Hill. The Olds engine featured a Pop Dreyer racing cam and four Stromberg carburetors on Dad's homemade log manifold. Top speed was 111 mph running in the B/Dragster class. (Palmer collection, photo by Gilbert Gray, 1957.)

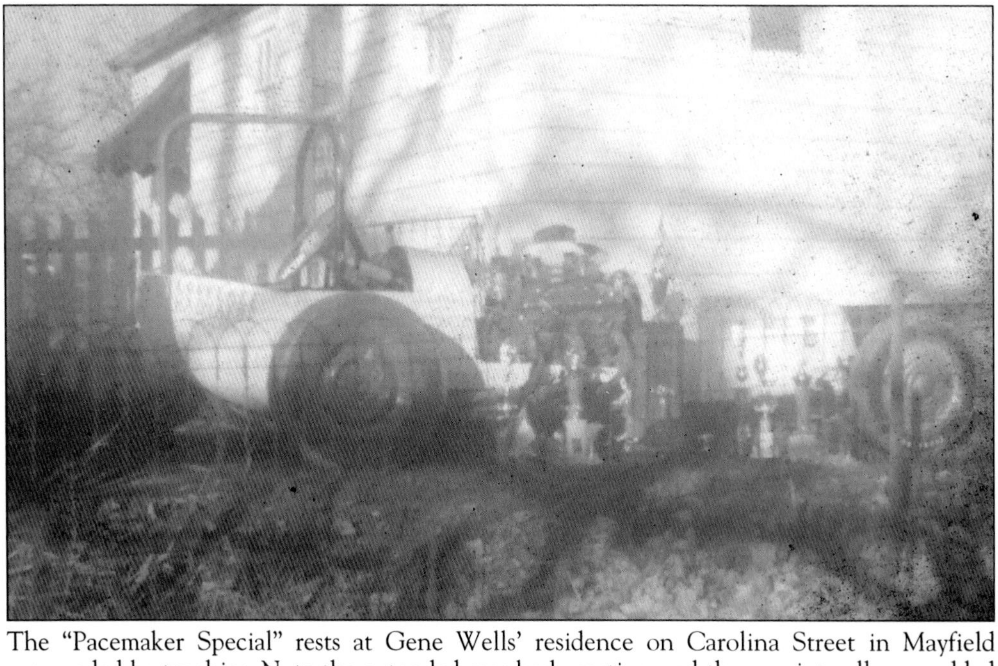

The "Pacemaker Special" rests at Gene Wells' residence on Carolina Street in Mayfield surrounded by trophies. Note the extended rear body section and three-point roll cage added mid season. (Roberson collection, 1957.)

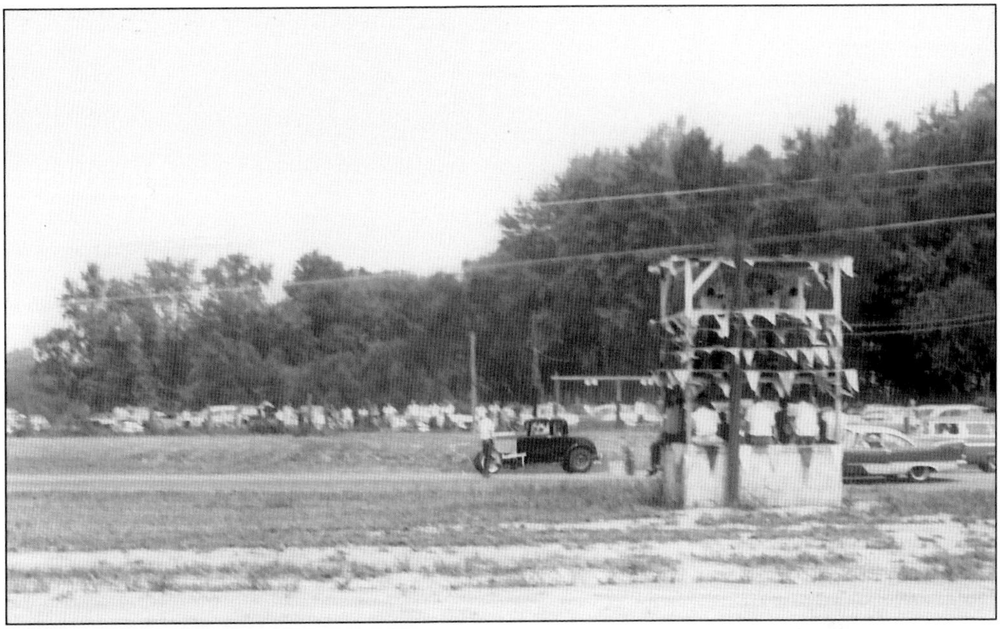

Bill Burton's '32 Ford coupe with Olds power smokes the treads at Beechmont Dragway in Cincinnati. Note the flag starter and the primitive "tower" at the starting line. This was state of the art in 1958. (Palmer collection, 1958.)

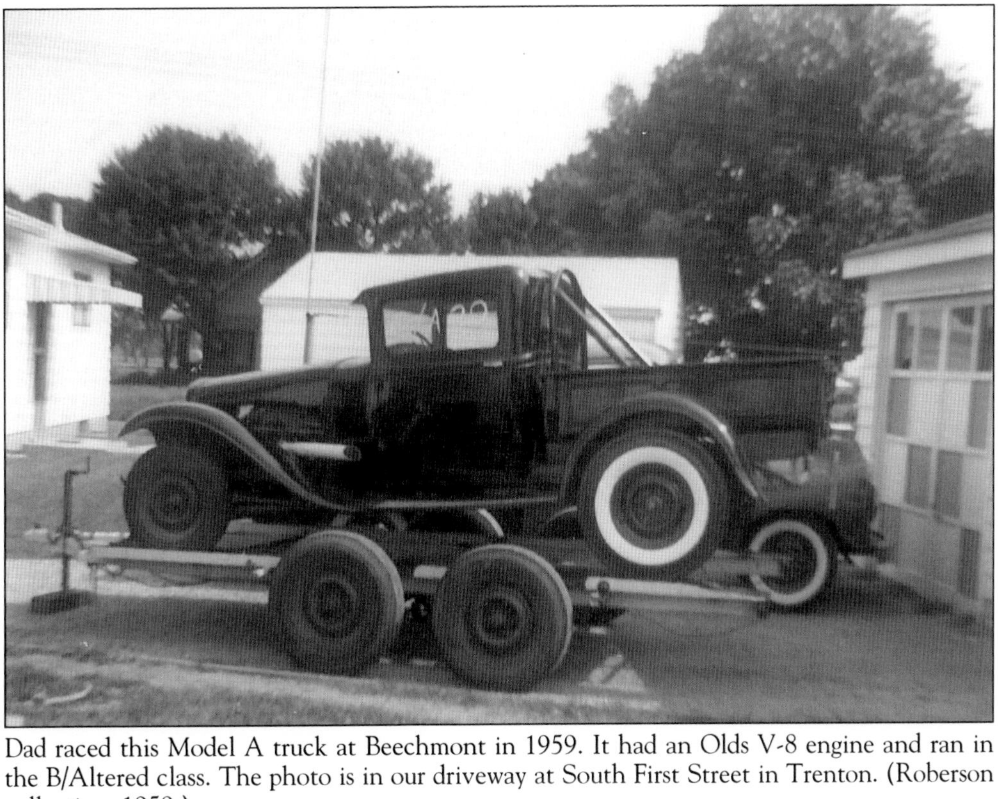

Dad raced this Model A truck at Beechmont in 1959. It had an Olds V-8 engine and ran in the B/Altered class. The photo is in our driveway at South First Street in Trenton. (Roberson collection, 1959.)

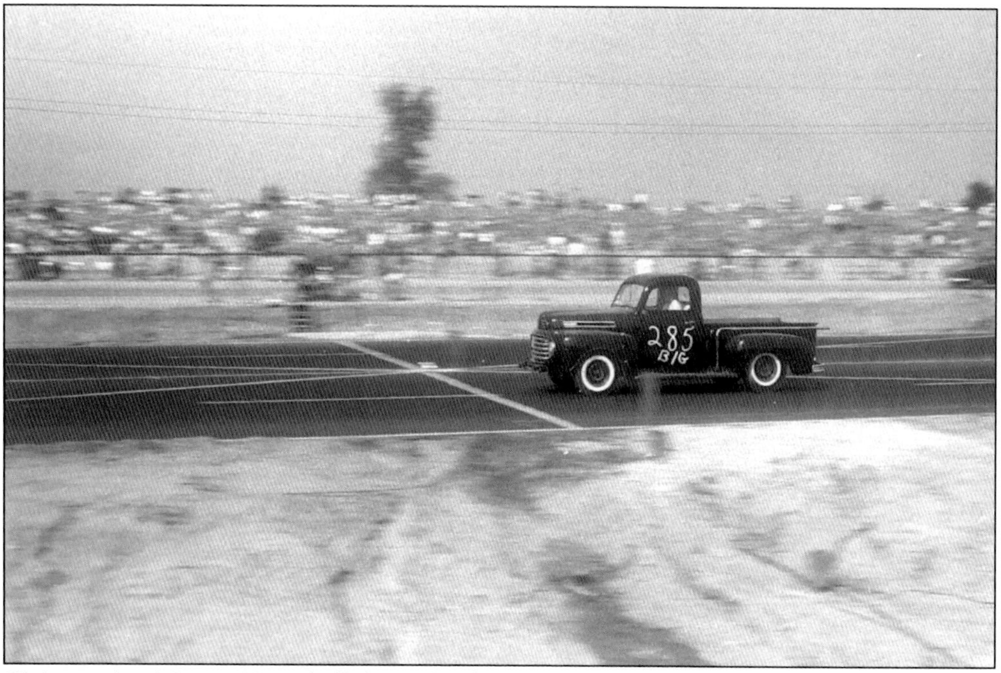

Club member Marion Hounshell drove this beautiful 1949 Ford pickup truck with a '57 Olds Rocket V-8 engine. It was his daily driver, but the truck also did drag strip duty as evidenced by this finish line shot taken at the '59 NHRA Nationals in Detroit. (Neely collection, 1959.)

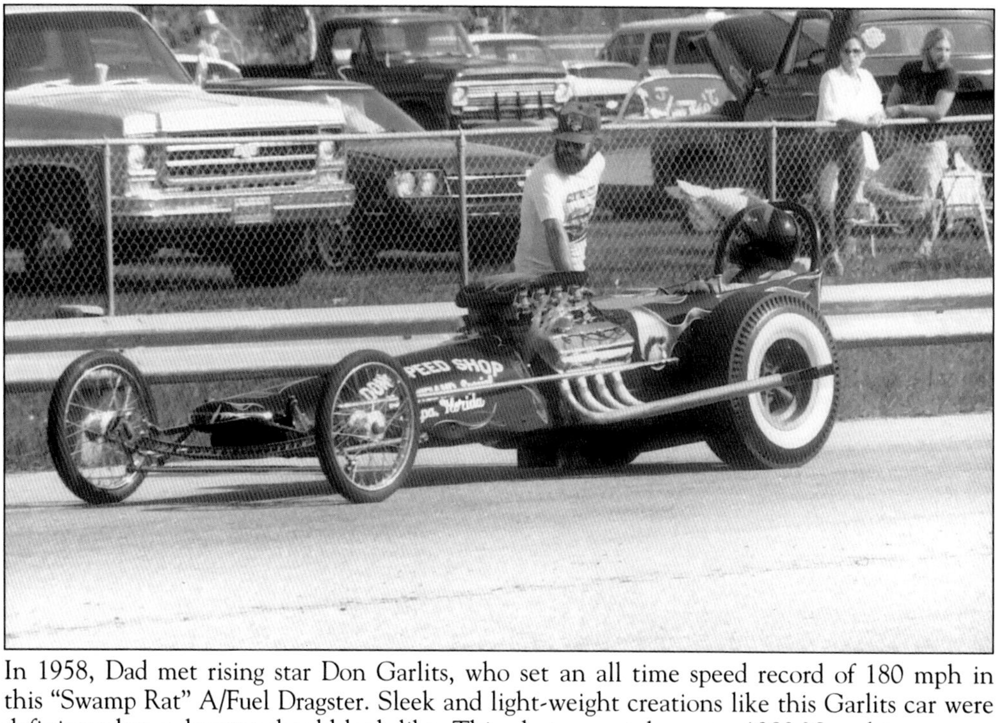

In 1958, Dad met rising star Don Garlits, who set an all time speed record of 180 mph in this "Swamp Rat" A/Fuel Dragster. Sleek and light-weight creations like this Garlits car were defining what a dragster should look like. This photo was taken at a 1982 Nostalgia meet at DeSoto Drag Strip in Bradenton, Florida. (Roberson collection, 1958.)

A busy Don Garlits takes time to pose with my son Jason at DeSoto Drag Strip in Bradenton, Florida. (Roberson collection, 1991.)

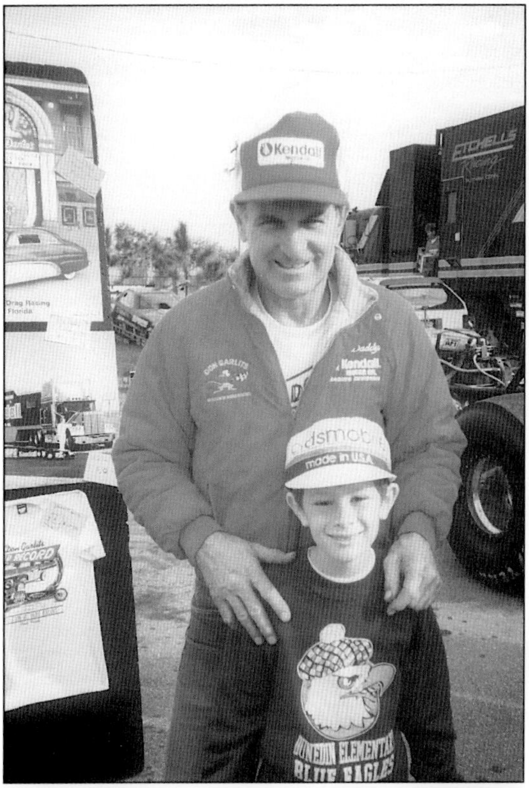

Don Garlits works on the engine of "Swamp Rat I" at a DeSoto Drag Strip nostalgia meet. (Roberson collection, 1982.)

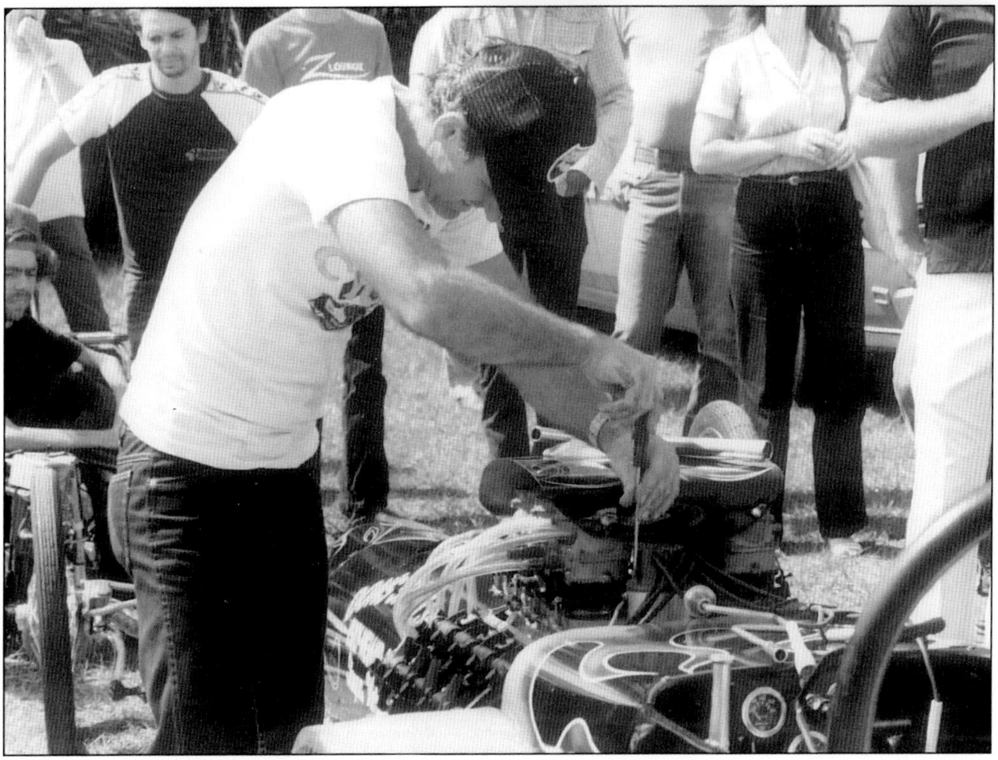

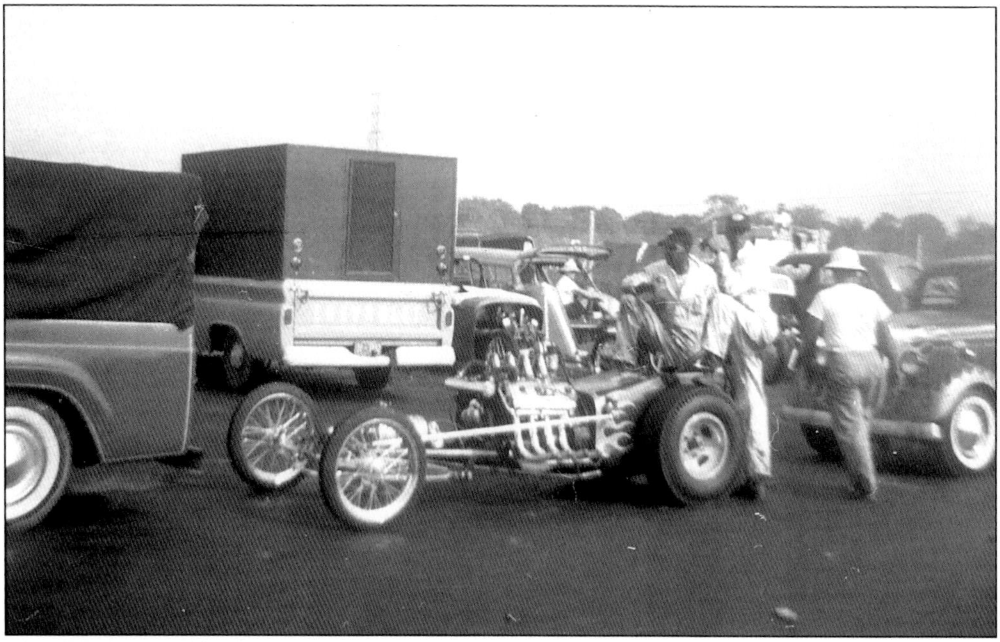

The Trotters, an all African-American club from Columbus, Ohio, won "Best Appearing Crew" at the 1960 Nationals. They ran this beautifully detailed B/Dragster and matching tow truck throughout the Midwest. (Roberson collection, 1960.)

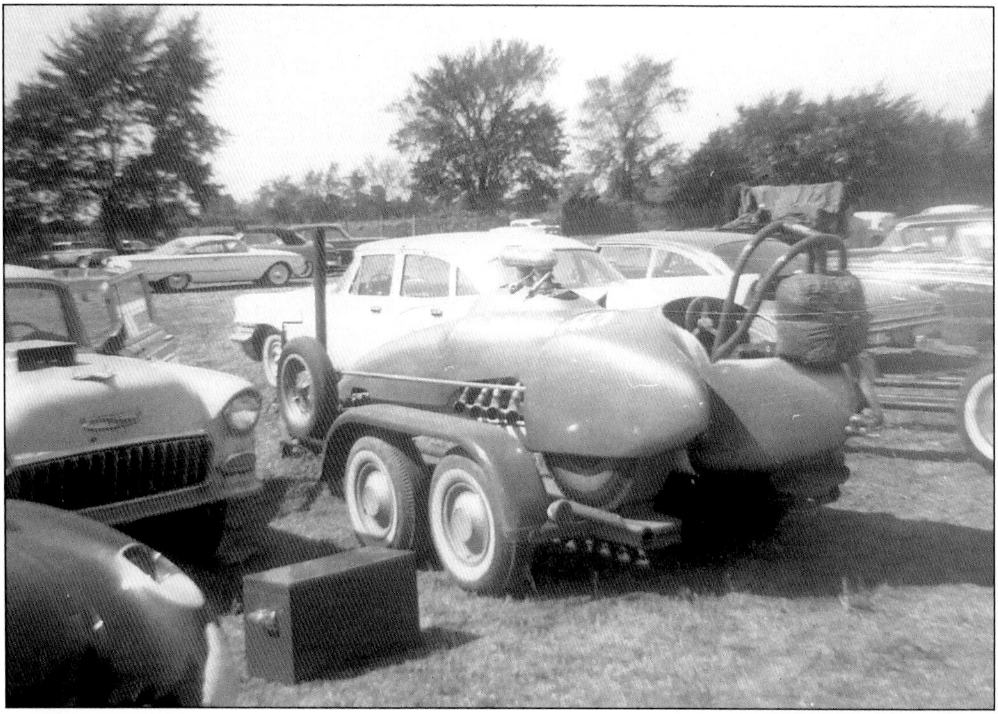

California's Mickey Thompson entered this dragster at the 1960 Nationals in Detroit. The photo was taken to highlight the still-rare parachute on the back of Mickey's car. (Roberson collection, 1960.)

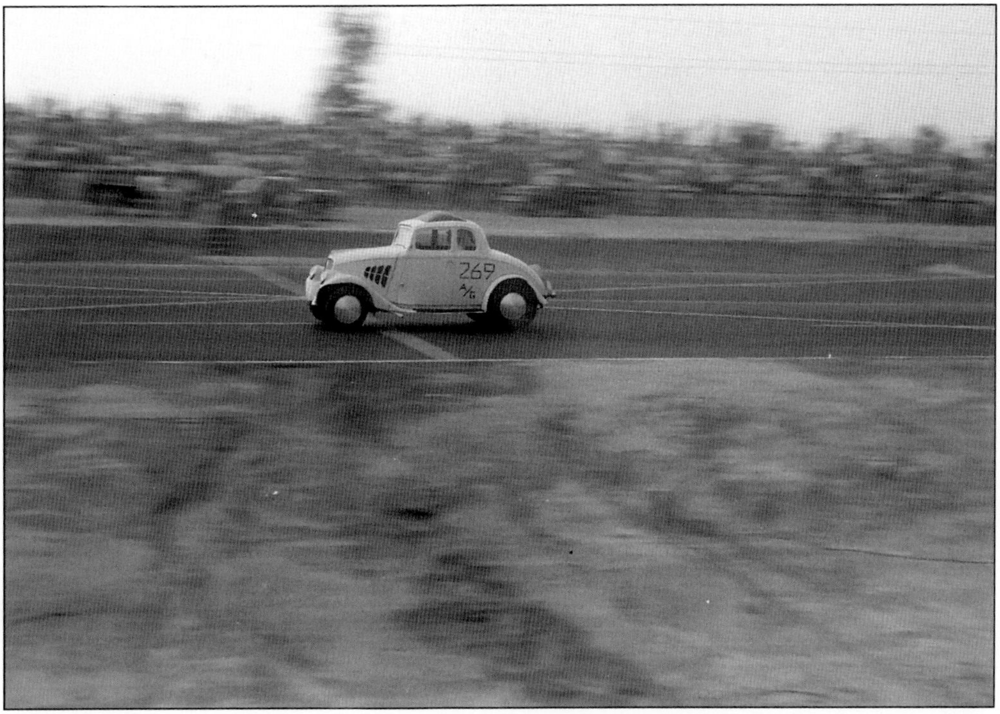

Dayton's George Montgomery roars past the finish line at the 1959 Nationals in his winning A/Gas Willys coupe with Cadillac engine. He would win Little Eliminator titles back-to-back at the '59 and '60 Nationals, becoming the first repeat winner in NHRA Nationals history. Note the vinyl top section bulging in the wind. (Neely collection, 1959.)

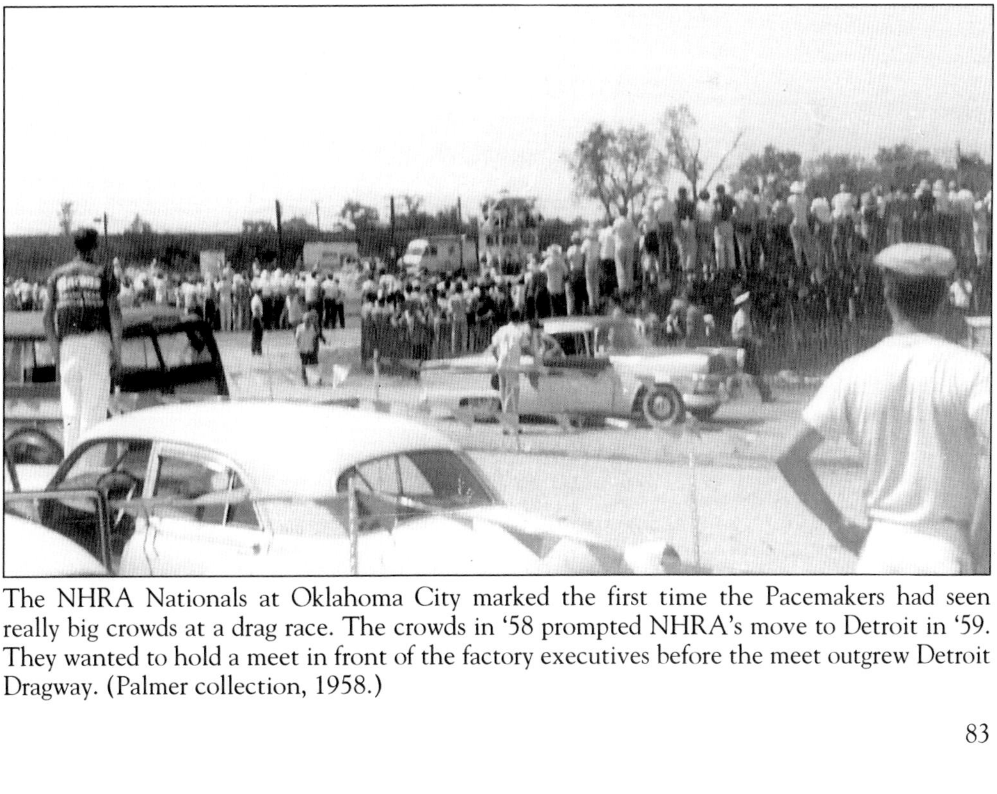

The NHRA Nationals at Oklahoma City marked the first time the Pacemakers had seen really big crowds at a drag race. The crowds in '58 prompted NHRA's move to Detroit in '59. They wanted to hold a meet in front of the factory executives before the meet outgrew Detroit Dragway. (Palmer collection, 1958.)

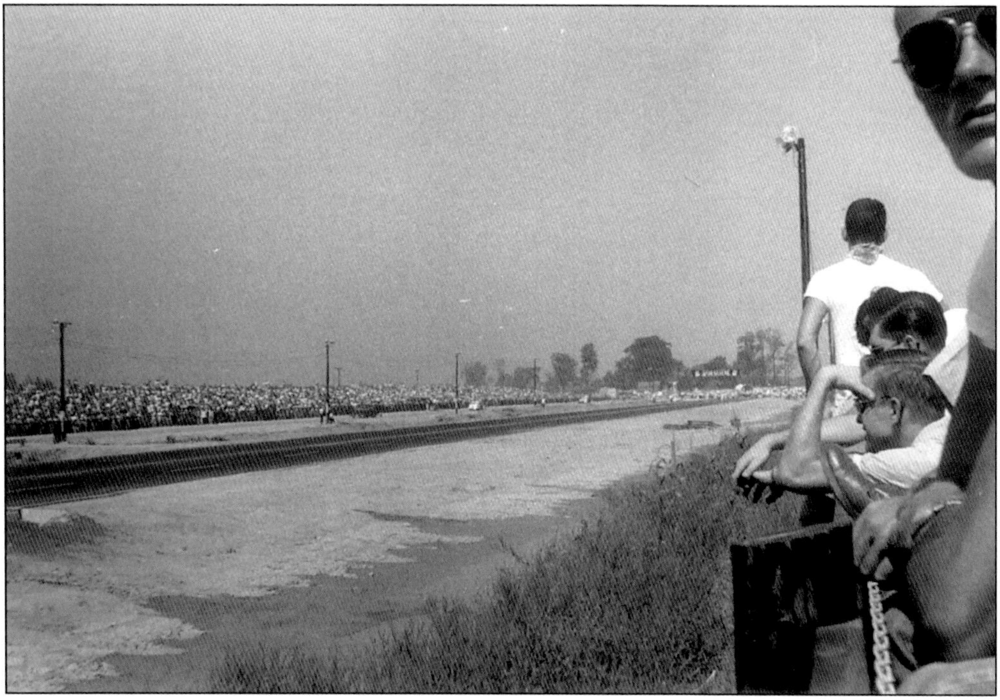

Gene Wells watches intently as the final runs of the '59 Nationals unfold. Note the complete absence of guard rails. (Neely collection, 1959.)

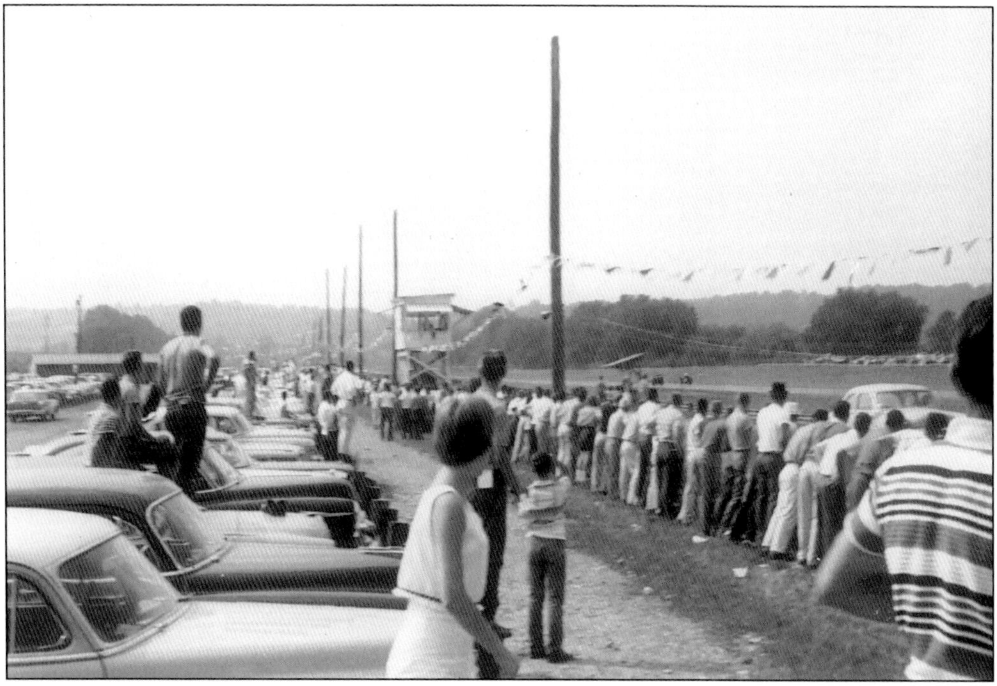

Early drag strips like Beechmont pictured here often had limited seating for spectators if any seating at all. Note the people lined along the fence and sitting on the tops of parked cars. (Palmer collection, 1958.)

Six

Drag Racing
At the National Level

Courage is the resistance to fear, mastery of fear—not absence of fear.

- Mark Twain

During the fall of 1957, the club members began assembling the materials, parts and pieces that would become the second "Pacemaker Special" dragster. It would be another slingshot design, with the engine set back and the transmission hooked directly to the rear end sans drive shaft, and the driver sitting behind the rear wheels. The design was proven, and all the top running dragsters of the day were being built that way. Dad decided to pattern the new "Pacemaker Special" after the famous Cook and Bedwell dragster from California.

Dad began the project in his radiator repair shop in Hamilton just after Christmas. Some of the guys had obtained some mild steel square tubing from the Armco Steel plant to make the chassis. Dad worked from chalk marks on the shop floor and built a custom chassis around an Olds engine block and mocked up drive train. When the chassis was complete, he moved the project to the garage at our house in Trenton. (We had moved from Mayfield to Trenton in 1956. With the birth of my younger brother Marty, we needed a larger house, so we took advantage of the move to shorten Dad's daily drive to Hamilton.) The shop at Main Street had limited space, and moving the project to Trenton also made it handier for the other Pacemakers to help with the assembly of the car.

Dad began building a monster 406 cubic inch Olds engine that had every trick he and Herb Sebastian had accumulated in three years of competitive drag racing with Oldses. The engine would feature a Pop Dryer racing cam and six Stromberg 97 carburetors on another of Dad's home-made log manifolds. The car also incorporated a hand brake and hand operated pump to pressurize the fuel tank, since good racing fuel pumps were at this point a thing of the future. Dad modified the heads himself, porting and relieving the intake and exhaust passages, and installing oversized intake valves, modified from another engine make.

The body on the "Pacemaker Special" No. 2 was a thing of beauty by 1958 standards. A sprint car-type rear section was fabricated using two Chevy truck hoods to form the "boat tail." The cowl section was enclosed, as well as the nose of the car, and a flat cover over the carburetors gave the body a look of continuity. A large two-point roll bar rose from the front of the cockpit, forming an archway over the large steering wheel. A small push bar protruded out the rear of the body, which was painted white to match the paint scheme of the Buick tow car. Moon hubcaps set it off nicely. The car would win many "best appearing" awards during the 1958 season.

The "Pacemaker Special" No. 2 was an instant winner on the drag strip, hitting speeds near 125 mph immediately. They ran often at Stout Field and at the new Beechmont Drag Strip that opened in Cincinnati off Beechmont Avenue. Early in the season, Gene ran 124.30 mph at Stout Field and established a new track record for B/Dragsters. But the real success came in May at the NHRA regional meet at Stout Field, with Gene winning Top Eliminator and setting top speed of the event at 126.93 mph—just 1/2 mph short of the B/Dragster national record. Within a month, Gene would top 128 mph, and later in the season they would travel to Crown Point, Indiana, and set the national speed record at 130.05 mph. The car seemed to win wherever it went, and they began to travel around the area looking for new cars to race. They would hear about a new hot dragster, and travel to the guy's home track to race against him. The car ran well, and they got the most out of it when pitted against the best competition they could find.

On one occasion the guys traveled to Akron just to run against Art Arfons and the "Green Monster." Arfons' car was powered by a 1,710-cubic-inch WWII Allison aircraft engine that would propel the mammoth beast to speeds approaching 160 mph. This was 30 mph faster than the new "Pacemaker Special," but the relatively nimble Olds dragster produced similar elapsed times to the heavier "Green Monster." In the match Gene took the early lead and held off Arfon's rapid top end charge. Art passed gene just beyond the finish line and blew by like a hurricane.

The opening of Beechmont Dragway during this period was a big step for drag racing in the Cincinnati area. It was a nice facility, and it was only about 30 miles from Middletown. Several club members raced cars there, including Bill Burton in his '32 Ford coupe and Don Klamo in his '32 Rockne coupe. The "Pacemaker Special" was often Top Eliminator at Beechmont. Two dragsters from Hamilton raced there regularly. One was the Chrysler powered car of Bob Kyle, who ran a local speed shop. The other was a Buick powered car, which was later updated to a Chrysler, run by Leonard Caldwell. Leo was a very likable guy, who sadly died an untimely death after a battle with cancer. Both Kyle and Caldwell belonged to the Shafters car club in Hamilton. Others who raced regularly at Beechmont included Dick Vest, Norm Reis, Bill King, and Ernie Weiser.

The worst accident the Pacemakers ever encountered while drag racing occurred at Thorn Hill the first time they tried to run the new car there. By 1958, Thorn Hill Drag Strip was paved over the entire quarter mile, but still had a dirt shut off area. Gene made his first pass at over 125 mph, and the car with the racing slicks seemed to speed up when Gene hit the brakes in the dirt. He went careening past the graded shut down area and headed through a cornfield, the car bouncing uncontrollably over the plowed rows. Gene managed to keep the car upright, but he was knocked unconscious, and the dragster's frame rails bent under the stress. He had pulled so hard on the hand brake that it was bent also. Dad took Gene to a Hospital in Covington, Ohio, to be checked out, and after a slow recovery to consciousness, Gene was declared okay. Dad straightened the car's frame the following week, but they never went back to Thorn Hill. Beechmont became the Pacemakers' home track.

The club closed out the 1958 race season with a trip to the NHRA Nationals at Oklahoma City. The car was running at the top of the large B/Dragster field, turning some of the best times in the class. It looked like they were on the way to a class championship, when the transmission let go against Gene O'Tanger of Texas in a late round. The class winners ran each other for Top Eliminator in those days, and the eventual B/Dragster winner, Al Ishenbaugh, was runner-up to the A/Dragster of Ted Cyr in the Top Eliminator final. Art Arfons turned top speed of the meet at 161 mph.

One of the highlights of the 1958 season for Dad was making the acquaintance of rising star Don Garlits. Dad and Mom took a vacation to Englewood, Florida, to visit Grandpa Bill who had retired there. The trip was an ideal opportunity to meet the new drag racing sensation that all the magazines were writing about. Don had built a new dragster (later to be called Swamp Rat I) that had set the drag racing world on its ear, when he clocked 176 mph at Kissimmee, Florida, in November of 1957. The California racers wrote it off to bogus clocks, not believing that an unknown could break the existing speed record by seven mph. After all, the technology for drag racing, especially using nitromethane, was centered in California, not the East Coast. How could such a thing be real? To find out, a Texas promoter had invited Garlits and three top West Coast dragsters to Houston for a showdown.

Dad went to Don's shop in Tampa and introduced himself to the amiable Garlits, eagerly telling him about the Pacemakers and their B/Dragster that had won the regional championship race at Stout Field. He asked Don about the big showdown in Texas that he had read about in the magazines. Don told him he was leaving for Texas the following morning, and asked if he would follow him to his house in Sefner to help load the car onto the trailer. Dad jumped at the chance, and followed Don to his house. Dad was impressed with the high quality of workmanship on the Garlits car, which indeed blew away the California cars when Don raced against them Texas. Dad did not realize it at the time, but he had witnessed the birth of the touring professional in drag racing: Garlits had made drag racing history by being among the first drag racers paid to travel to a drag meet.

Dad made a lot of friends racing over the years, but one that he admired most was Ray Godman of Memphis, owner and builder of the famous "Tennessee Bo-Weevil" modified roadsters. Ray was confined to a wheel chair, a paraplegic as the result of injuries from the Korean Conflict, but built and maintained a top running car using hired drivers. I was about six years old when I first met Ray, and I was fascinated with the guy and the way he would use his arms to muscle his way over the car to work on it. Dad has often told the story of how he was working on the "Pacemaker Special" at one meet, and noticed that I was missing. He searched frantically through the pits and found me at the "Tennessee Bo-Weevil" handing tools to Ray Godman.

The 1959 season turned disastrous before it began. In January, Dad took the car to the radiator shop in Hamilton and pulled the engine with the shop's chain hoist. Then he took the car back to our house in Trenton, since the shop had little spare room. In pulling the engine, he had not removed the valve covers and had bent the outer fins on the Offenhauser aluminum units as the chain tightened under the engine's weight. As he disassembled the engine later, he made a mental note to try and straighten the valve cover fins after the engine was back in the car. He completed the rebuild over the next few weeks and left the engine hanging on the hoist ready to drop into the racecar. He towed the car to the shop the next day and noticed broken glass at the shop's door. The previous night, a thief had broken into the shop and stole the record breaking Olds engine!

Nothing else was taken. The robbery was reported to the police and the guys began to scrounge parts to try to salvage the fast approaching race season. Meanwhile, the season opened at Thorn Hill, and word got back to the club about a '56 Olds stocker that ran over 100 mph at the opener. This was about 25 mph faster than a stock Olds would normally run, and the guy who owned it sometimes hung around the Pacemakers and the radiator shop. He lived in Cincinnati, so several of the guys drove down to pay him a visit, just to see how he would react. He was working on his car when they pulled into the driveway. As Dad walked up to the car and was recognized, the owner slammed the hood down quickly, but Dad thought he had seen enough to recognize the engine. The six carburetors had been replaced by a four-barrel, and it had the stock valve covers on it, so he couldn't be certain. Then Dad glanced around the area and saw the Offenhauser valve covers complete with the bent fins lying on the guy's garage floor. The owner nervously asked if the guys were going to the Reds' game at Crosley Field, and they said they were. He then excused himself, claiming he was late for a date and left. The guys went straight to the police and reported that they had found the engine.

The thief got nervous after the visit and pulled the engine out of the car. He began to dispose of parts, some going into the Miami River near the GE plant. The police arrested him and recovered the engine partly disassembled. They sent divers into the Miami River to retrieve parts, based on the guy's confession. Then they brought Dad and Bill Burton in to identify the engine. Dad described a gouge in the block he had made when he bored out the cylinders. Bill Burton had gotten the oversized intake valves shortened by a machine shop. He described the dimples in the valves that were placed there to test the hardening process. The police found the marks that the two described. The thief was convicted, and at the request of the Pacemakers, he served a parole term and reimbursed the club in installments instead of going to jail.

Dad reassembled the mighty Olds engine as best he could to try to salvage the racing season. The "Pacemaker Special" was modified considerably for the 1959 season. The nose section of the body had been removed to save weight, and the open sides of the cockpit were enclosed with aluminum panels. The large two-point roll bar was replaced with a smaller unit set farther back in the cockpit, directly over the driver's head. The body was still painted white, and Gene Wells was still the main driver. But the 1959 year would be disappointing. The big Olds engine had seen severe misuse by the temporary owner.

The club entered the '59 Nationals, held in Detroit. Gene Wells made a valiant showing in the large B/Dragster field, but the Olds engine blew during the class run offs. The blown engine ended the season for the Pacemakers, and it was Gene's final race as a driver, as he announced his retirement from racing.

The 1959 race season was another milestone year for drag racing. Don Garlits had traveled to the West Coast to run the California racers with admirable success. The Top Fuelers had gone to superchargers and were breaking 180 mph. The Top Gas dragsters were also supercharged and hitting 160. In a brilliant marketing move, Wally Parks moved the Nationals to Detroit and invited executives from the major auto manufacturers to attend. This move led directly to the factory super stock teams of the 1960s, once the execs saw the crowds and the cars' performances at the Nationals. The Ramchargers (a Detroit club made up of engineers at Dodge) emerged on the national drag racing scene with a wild looking '49 Dodge coupe called "The High and the Mighty." Rodney Singer won Top Eliminator in a supercharged Lincoln-powered dragster, and Art Arfons set top speed at 172 mph slowing the massive Green Monster with a newly developed parachute that fascinated the crowd. Arfons' speed at this meet prompted NHRA to outlaw aircraft engines in dragsters. Dayton's "Ohio George" Montgomery won the Little Eliminator title with a Cadillac powered '33 Willys coupe, and the rest of the country discovered one of the greatest drag racers of all time.

Arfons' car was not the first we had seen using a parachute. Dick Vest of Dayton began using one at the new Kilkare Drag Strip with his 160-mph supercharged Chevy Top Gas car. Although they may have already been used in California and in Akron, 200 miles to the northeast, Vest had never seen one on a racecar. He got the idea from World War II aircraft that sometimes used parachute brakes to stop on short landing strips. He bought a chute from an army surplus store and began to experiment. He tied it to the back of his pickup truck and had a buddy drive him around at various increasing speeds, while he would toss it out the back and observe what it would do. He finally tried it on his dragster and soon had it working.

Also in 1959, Dad made his return to the driver's seat in a racecar. Herb Sebastian got the itch to race again and began construction of a Model A truck for the drag strip. He chopped and channeled the truck and began to shoehorn in an Olds V-8, when he lost interest in the project. Dad bought the truck and completed it. He competed at Beechmont in the B/Altered class, and it ran pretty well with speeds around 103 mph.

Dad did not condone cheating on the drag strip, but one of his favorite drag race stories revolves around the one time that he did cheat while racing the Model A truck at Beechmont. Dad had won the B/Altered class and had worked his way into the final for Middle Eliminator against the winner of the A/Altered class. This was before electronic starting, and there were no handicap starts. He was going to have to race the higher class car heads up. Dick Vest was there that night running his Top Gas dragster. This was during the NHRA ban on nitromethane fuel, and the nearest track that ran fuelers was at Cordova, Illinois, where Don Garlits, Chris Karamsines, and Setto Postoian had run. Vest had been intrigued by the fast times that the fuel cars were running at Cordova, and he had considered switching to nitro. He had been secretly playing with a small percentage of the fuel mixed with gasoline and had told Dad about the performance gains he had seen. (He could get by with this at local tracks where they did not run fuel checks). Dick encouraged Dad to even things out by running this fuel mix in the final against the A/Altered. Reluctantly, Dad let the charismatic Vest talk him into the experiment, and Dick poured some of the concoction into the tank. Dad fired up the truck and drove to the staging lanes noticing no particular difference. He lined up against the A/Altered and got a mild jump at the start as the flagman waved them off. At mid track, the A/Altered began to pull back, and Dad fully expected the bigger engine to pass him, when suddenly the afterburner kicked in. Dad described it as a "rapid kick in the pants" as the little truck suddenly pulled away and stretched out the lead. Dad was clocked at106 mph and set a new class track record running the illicit mixture.

The reliability runs had gone by the wayside and the club had developed a new emphasis on drag racing—not by plan, but as a by-product of the success of the club dragster. Most of the new members were drag racers. In 1958, Jim Neely joined the club, with the goal of being the next driver of the "Pacemaker Special." At the end of the 1959 season Gene Wells retired from driving, and Jim took over as the main driver of the car for the next four seasons. Three others joined in 1959, and would have future success on the drag strip. The first two were the team of Don Klamo and Marion Hounshell, who campaigned their own dragster with partner Gary Rupp (who would later team with Pat Dakin in a successful Top Fuel dragster effort). The other was Darryl Hobbs, who would become the "Pacemaker Special's" main driver in 1964 and '65.

Another Pacemaker milestone in occurred 1959. The club purchased its own building, an oversized two-car garage at 406 Manatee Street off Oxford State Road in Middletown. This provided a place for club meetings and a place to build, maintain and store the dragster. Prior to the availability of the clubhouse, the car spent much of its time in our garage in Trenton. The new clubhouse was always abuzz with activity as many members worked on their cars on the large lot that came with the building. And it would be a center for wheeling and dealing in hot rods, parts and services. The building still stands today looking much the same as it did 40 years ago, and it still belongs to car enthusiasts.

The "Pacemaker Special" underwent a major change for 1960, including a switch to a new class, C/Dragster. The body was largely unchanged from 1959, but to make the lower class the engine was down-sized. They replaced the monster 406 Olds with a much smaller Chevy of 292 cubic inches. The six Stromberg carburetors were gone in favor of a Corvette Rochester fuel injection unit. The body was repainted in powder blue except for the cockpit's aluminum side panels. The Moon hubcaps were retained. The 1960 version of the car was not as pretty as the 1958 version, but it performed very well.

The little C/Dragster ran nearly as fast and quick as its B/Dragster predecessor—120 mph with 11-second elapsed times. The club immediately resumed the winning ways of 1958 as the 1960 season opened. And there were now plenty of places to run in the area. Besides Stout Field, Kilkare Drag Strip had opened near Xenia, Dayhio Drag Strip was running in Dayton, and Dragway 42 operated near West Salem. Muncie Dragway in Indiana was offering a great program, and Beechmont was still alive in Cincinnati, despite repeated editorials in a local newspaper about the evil hot rod element that was invading the city. The club began a very busy race schedule, which allowed freshman driver Jim Neely the opportunity to develop skills quickly.

The 1960 season was a successful one that culminated with a strong appearance at the Nationals in Detroit. Jim waded through a very large C/Dragster field to run in the class final against record holder Walt Markert of Massachusetts. Walt ran a Desoto-powered car that ran just well enough to win everywhere it went. He edged Jim out in the class final, and we settled for runner-up.

The 1960 Nationals saw the famous "Albertson Olds" with Leonard Harris at the wheel win Top Eliminator over the "Tennessee Bo-Weevil" Modified Roadster. George Montgomery became the first ever repeat Nationals winner by again taking Little Eliminator with his Cadillac-powered '33 Willys coupe. The award for best appearing car and crew went to our friends the Trotters, an all African-American club from Columbus.

A major highlight of the Pacemaker 1960 race season came after the Nationals. In September of 1960, NHRA opened its first major racing complex, Indianapolis Raceway Park. The huge facility was built to hold the Nationals, which had outgrown every available drag strip in the Midwest. IRP opened in September and held a major meet to inaugurate the new facility. Jim Neely in the "Pacemaker Special" won the event.

For 1961, the Pacemakers decided to stay with the C/Dragster class because of the 1960 successes. They gave the car a facelift over the winter. The main theme behind the facelift was to improve the car's looks and drop some weight in the process. The old patched up 1958 body was discarded, and the car was fitted with a smaller squared body that hugged the contour of the frame. It was painted in the familiar white Pacemaker paint scheme. The Chevy engine was freshened, but the same basic package was retained in 1961, complete with the Rochester fuel injection. A set of white wall racing slicks set the car off nicely although the classic Moon hubcaps were gone. The car would be basically unchanged for 1962, so this "Pacemaker Special" would be the final version of the old 1958 car.

During the 1960 season the car had used the Rochester fuel injection with the stock Corvette distributor. For 1961, they wanted to replace the distributor with a racing magneto. (A magneto combines the function of a distributor and generator or alternator by producing its own electricity and distributing that electric charge to the spark plugs. It eliminates the need for a generator or alternator and battery in a dragster). Converting to a magneto posed a problem. The original Corvette distributor drove the fuel pump for the injector by means of a cable similar to a speedometer cable. The racing magneto had no such drive, so they had to come up with a way to drive the mechanical fuel pump. The solution was simple and bordered on genius: the fuel injection unit was turned around on the engine, backwards from its stock placement. This placed the fuel pump at the front of the engine, where it could be driven by a pulley off the crankshaft. Dad fabricated a V-belt drive unit and they were in business. They raced the setup for most of the 1961 season, and only one person commented on the fact that the Rochester unit was on the car backwards. A ten-year-old kid pointed it out to his dad.

At the end of the 1961 season, they upgraded to a Hilborn fuel injector. The Hilborn unit was a great innovation of hot rodding. Stu Hilborn was one of the top California dry lakes racers when World War II broke out. While in the service he whiled away his spare time thinking of ways to make his lakester go faster once he returned to the U.S. The result of the day dreaming was the invention of fuel injection, which he began to develop upon his return. Soon he ran the first 150-mph run at the dry lakes with the innovation. He formed a company to build a commercial version, which became a leading performance parts company.

Also about this time, the local drag strips began to substitute cash awards for trophies. The club had been racing for trophies, as was the norm for the sportsman categories. NHRA's fuel ban beginning in 1957 had helped to make the Top Fuel dragsters into touring professionals as did the banning of aircraft engines in Top Gas in 1959. It was already becoming common to pay appearance money to guys like Don Garlits or Art Arfons to get their cars and the subsequent crowds to distant tracks. However, the local racers still raced for trophies, as drag racing was still largely an amateur sport. At the same time the costs of racing were beginning to mount. The cars had become more sophisticated, and more parts were coming from the speed shops and fewer from the junkyards. At the urging of the racers many tracks began to offer a cash value equivalent in lieu of a trophy for a class win. The racers jumped at the chance for the cash to offset racing costs, and soon the trophies all but disappeared.

The 1961 race season was another successful one for the Pacemakers, with the car winning regularly throughout the area. Don Klamo and partners Marion Hounshell and nonmember Gary Rupp had built their own dragster with a larger Chevy engine that put them in the B/Dragster class. Now the club was essentially running two cars, and often a local meet would come down to those two cars for the final run. The race schedule was becoming frantic with all the drag strips that were available within a hundred-mile radius, and the club could readily race three times a week. Darryl Hobbs began to get some seat time in the car in order for the club to keep up the pace, and soon Darryl began to develop driving skills of his own. And when neither Jim Neely nor Darryl Hobbs could make it, Herb Sebastian would drive. In May they won the C/Dragster class and the Middle Eliminator title at the NHRA regional meet at Dragway 42 in West Salem, Ohio. That same month at IRP they won Middle Eliminator with a 122.10 mph run in a quick 11.00-second elapsed time. In June, they won the C/Dragster class at the NHRA regional meet at Beechmont Dragway in Cincinnati.

It was about this time, probably 1961, that the club replaced the tired 1947 Buick tow car that had served them faithfully since 1957. The club purchased a 1954 Pontiac station wagon from a used car lot, and began a facelift that included a white paint job with red and blue lettering.

The 1961 NHRA Nationals was held at the new IRP track, and the club began the ritual of wading through the large C/Dragster class, which record holder Walt Markert still dominated. In July of 1960, Markert had shattered the C/Dragster national record with an elapsed time of 10.97 seconds and an incredible speed of 138.24mph—a record that would stand for over two years. Between Markert and the ample opportunity to break drive train parts while wading through a field of 30 to 40 cars, the class win remained elusive.

The 1961 Nationals saw the meteoric rise of a new star. Top Eliminator was won by an unknown engineer from Atlanta driving a spindly little light weight Chevy-powered car that out ran the bigger engines by such a wide margin that the officials refused to announce his times over the PA system. Pete Robinson came to the meet running 8.60s when all the top runners were just getting into the 8.90s. The officials thought his car was doing wheelstands and jumping over the starting lights, tripping the beam with the back wheels and getting bogus times. What they couldn't explain was the way he ran off and left the other cars when they ran side by side. Pete won the meet handily. Walter Knoch's "Walt's Puffer" A/Roadster from Dearborn, Michigan, took Middle Eliminator, shutting down the famous Ratican-Jackson Stearns Fiat from California in the process. Top speed of the meet was set by Dode Martin in the twin engine "Dragmaster Two Thing" at 177.87 mph.

The 1962 drag race season saw little change in the Pacemaker car. The crew had traveled to Miami, Florida, to run the Southeast Winter Championships in February, and Don Klamo wound up winning Top Eliminator at the event, earning a photo in the June '62 issue of *Hot Rod Magazine*. The photo has him running against Darryl Hobbs in the Pacemaker C/Dragster, which had also won its class. It was a clean sweep for the club. After the Miami meet, the car was prepped for the regular season with little more than an engine freshening and a new blue paint job. The car still won locally and regionally. They traveled to Memphis and won Junior Eliminator at the NHRA southwest divisional drag meet, running 124.82mph in 11.10 seconds. But the Nationals in 1962 produced the same story. The class was won by Walt Weney of Pennsylvania as the class domination by Walt Markert was beginning to wane. Markert still held the class speed record at 138.24 mph, but another C/Dragster from Oregon held the elapsed time mark at 10.48 seconds. The highly competitive field of C/Dragsters was catching up to the king, and it was clearly time for the Pacemakers to update their car.

The 1962 Nationals saw Jack Chrisman take Top Eliminator in a Pontiac-powered gas dragster owned by Mickey Thompson, beating Don Garlits in the final. The "Tennessee Bo-Weevil" won Middle Eliminator, and Junior Eliminator was won by Michigan's Walter Knoch.

Sadly, during this period our favorite drag strip, Beechmont Dragway at Cincinnati, had come and gone. Pressures stemming from a series of condemning editorials in a local newspaper had closed the great little drag strip nestled along the Ohio River. Indeed, everyone in Ohio was not sold on drag racing. Nonetheless, Beechmont Dragway was a great track, and many good racers got their start in its four-year span. If not for tracks like Beechmont to carry the sport through the development years, there would be no mega facilities today like Indianapolis, Houston, Topeka, or Gainesville. The little commercial facilities of the '50s and '60s paved the way for bigger and better things.

In a final note for 1962, Dad purchased a large building in Hamilton on B Street near the Champion Paper mill and moved the radiator shop to the new location. The building dated back to the early 1900s and had once housed the old Hamilton city traction lines. It looked like 1963 would be a very good year.

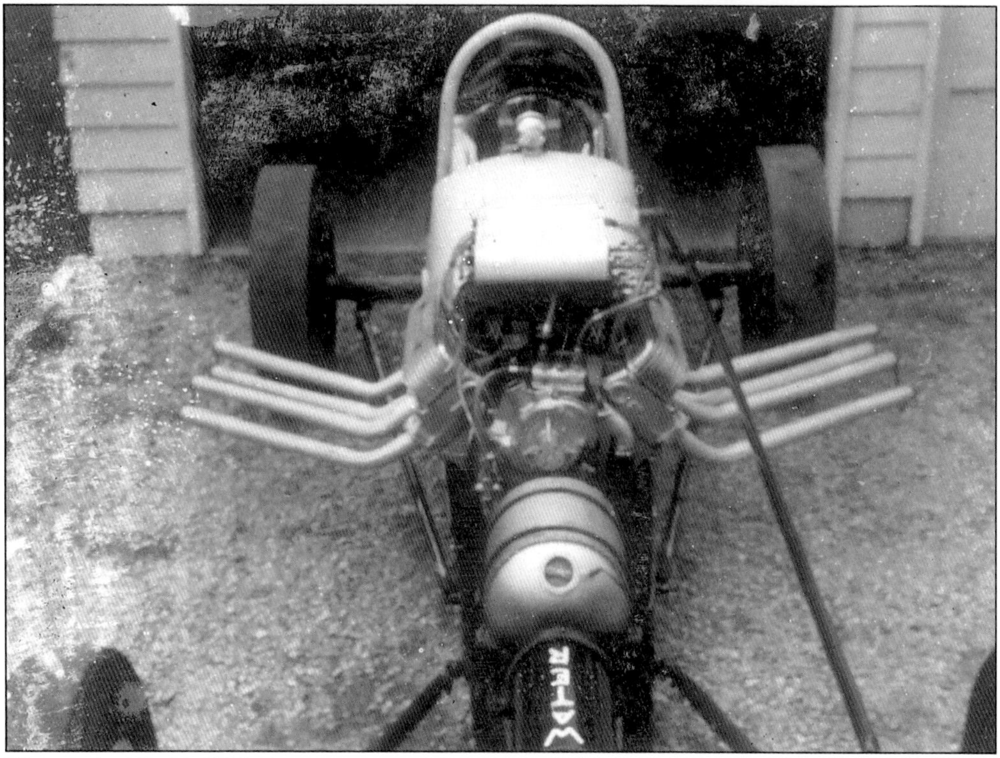

"Pacemaker Special" No.2 sits near completion at our house on South First Street in Trenton. The monster 406 Olds engine ran six Stromberg carburetors on Dad's homemade log-type manifold. The body's nose section is not yet installed. (Roberson collection, 1958.)

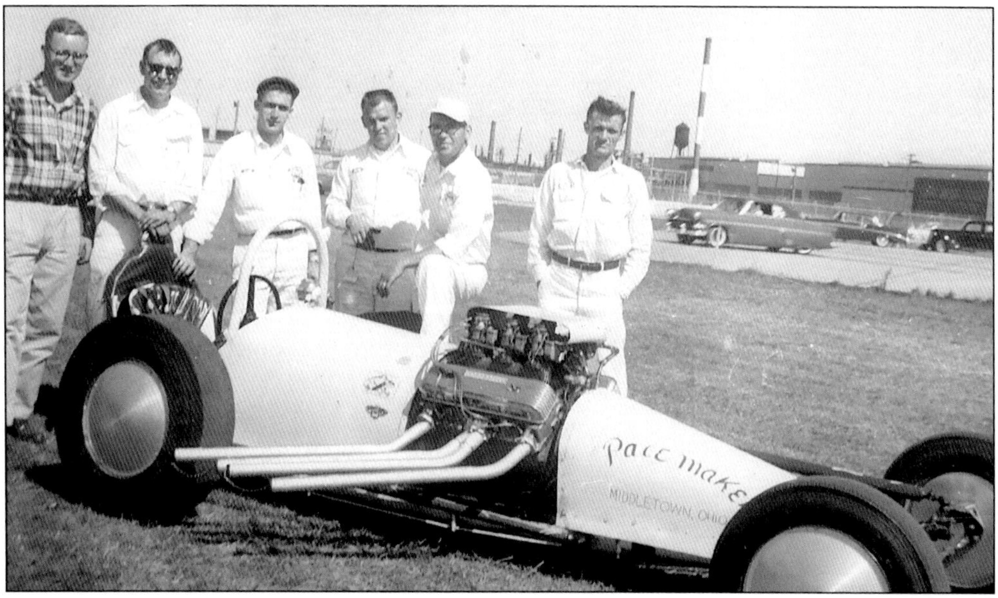

The Pacemakers' crew poses around the car at Stout Field, Indianapolis, where they just won Top Eliminator at the NHRA Divisional race in May of 1958. From left to right are Jim Neely, Dad, Bill Burton, Jerry Williams, Herb Sebastian, and driver Gene Wells. (Michael collection, 1958.)

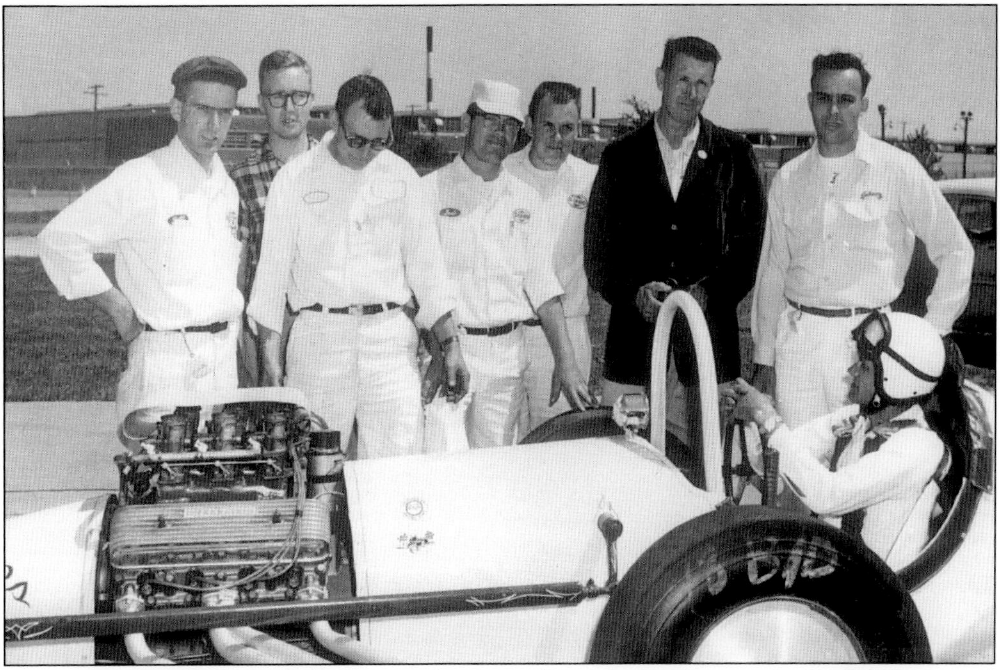

The crewmembers pose with the "Pacemaker Special" No.2 after winning the NHRA Divisional race at Stout Field at Indianapolis in May of 1958. From left to right are Bill Burton, Jim Neely, Dad, Herb Sebastian, Jerry Williams, NHRA President Wally Parks, an unidentified race official, and Gene Wells (seated in the car). Gene is evidently telling Dad about a problem with the car, and Dad is looking down at the car in response. (Roberson collection, 1958.)

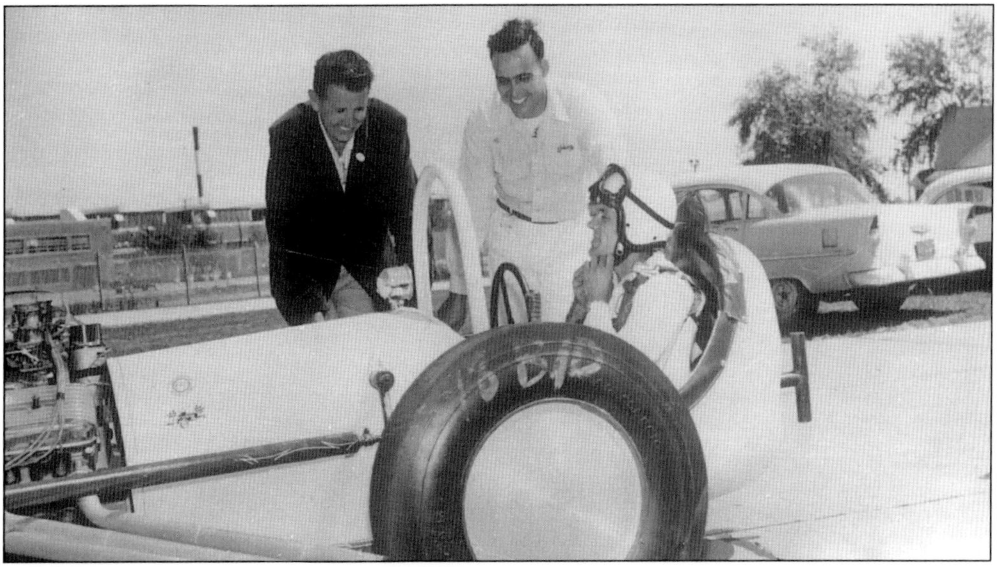

Gene Wells unhooks the chinstrap of his helmet at Stout Field as NHRA founder and President Wally Parks and an unidentified race official from the host club Cluster Busters look on. Gene set top speed of the meet at 126.92 mph, earning an NHRA jacket with "126 mph" emblazoned on the breast pocket. Later at Crown Point, Indiana, Gene would set a new B/Dragster national record of 130.05 mph. (Roberson collection, 1958.)

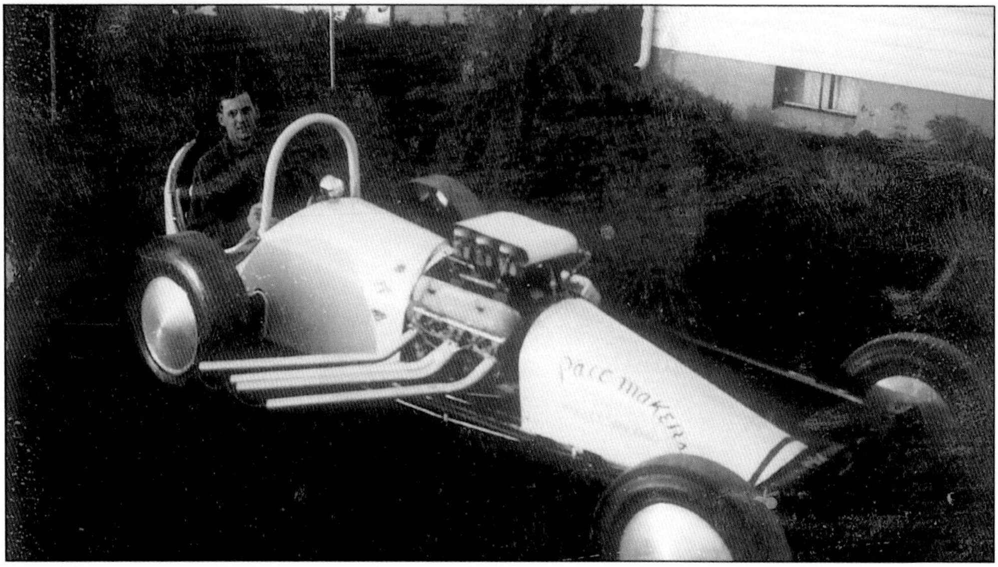

Harold "Mike" Michael poses in the "Pacemaker Special" No. 2 at our house in Trenton. Mike, then the motor sports reporter for the *Lebanon Star*, once drove the Pacemaker dragster through the quarter mile while describing the action into a portable tape recorder. (Michael collection, 1958.)

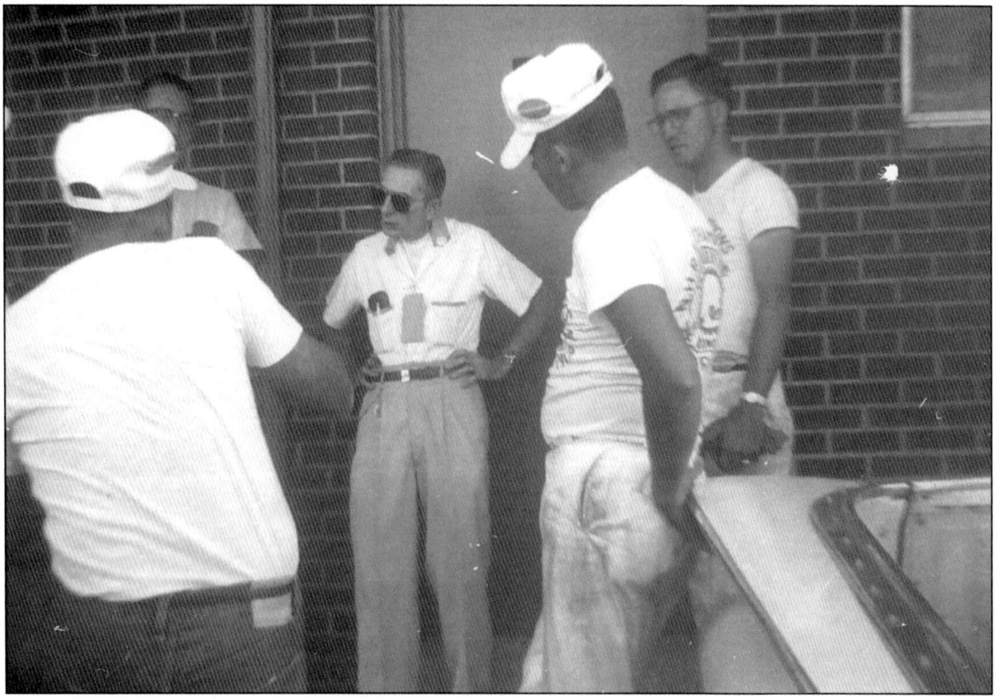

The Cluster Busters car club ran the drag races at Stout Field in Indianapolis. The man at the center of the photo in sunglasses is Charlie Mann, a pioneer drag racer and racing journalist, who acted as the coordinator for NHRA for the first Safety Safari meets in Indiana. From left to right are two unidentified men, Charlie Mann, and Pacemaker members Jerry Williams and Jim Neely. (Roberson collection, 1959 or 1960.)

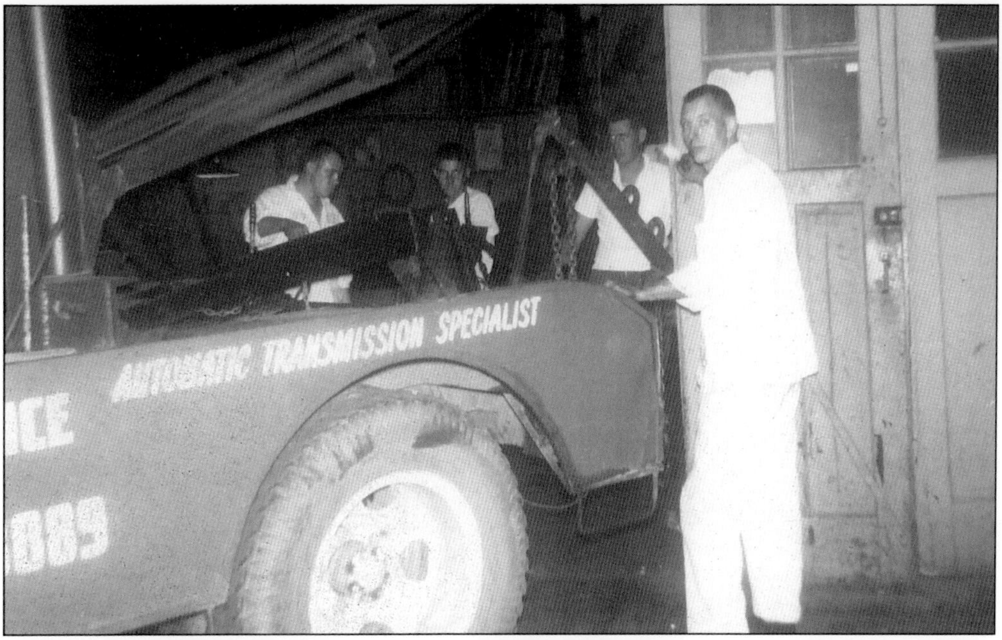

The recovery of the stolen dragster engine at Dad's radiator repair shop in Hamilton. Barely visible through the tow truck hoist, from left to right, are Jerry Williams, Don Klamo, Marion Hounshell, and Dad, who looks a bit surprised by the camera. (Roberson collection, 1959.)

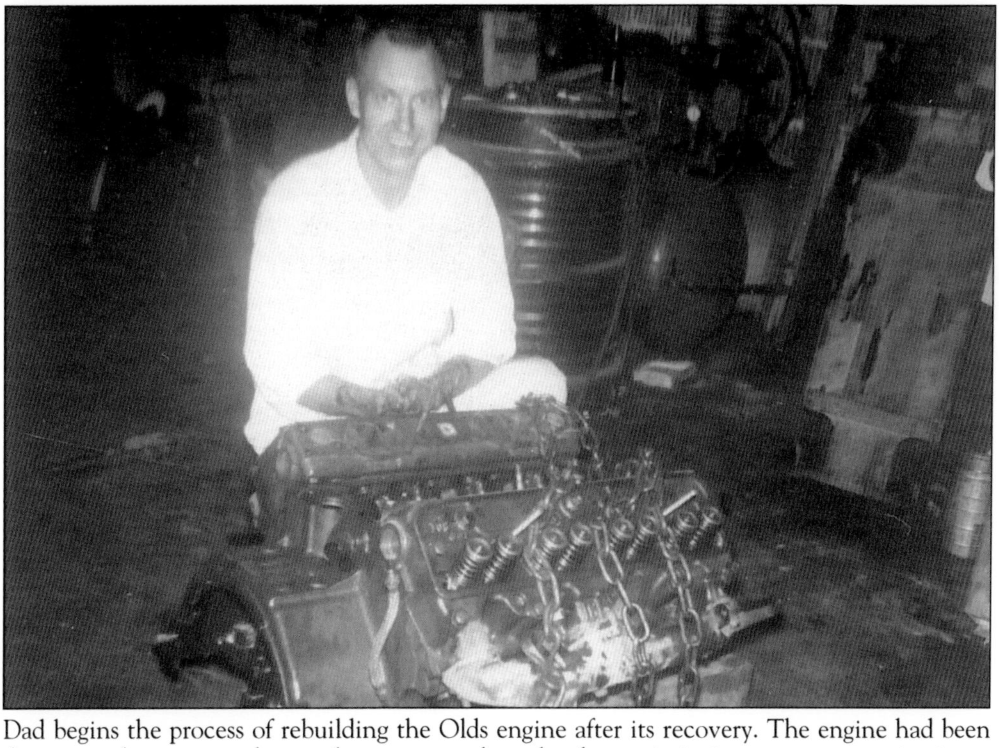

Dad begins the process of rebuilding the Olds engine after its recovery. The engine had been driven on the street and severely over revved on the drag strip in its temporary service in an Olds "stocker". (Roberson collection, 1959.)

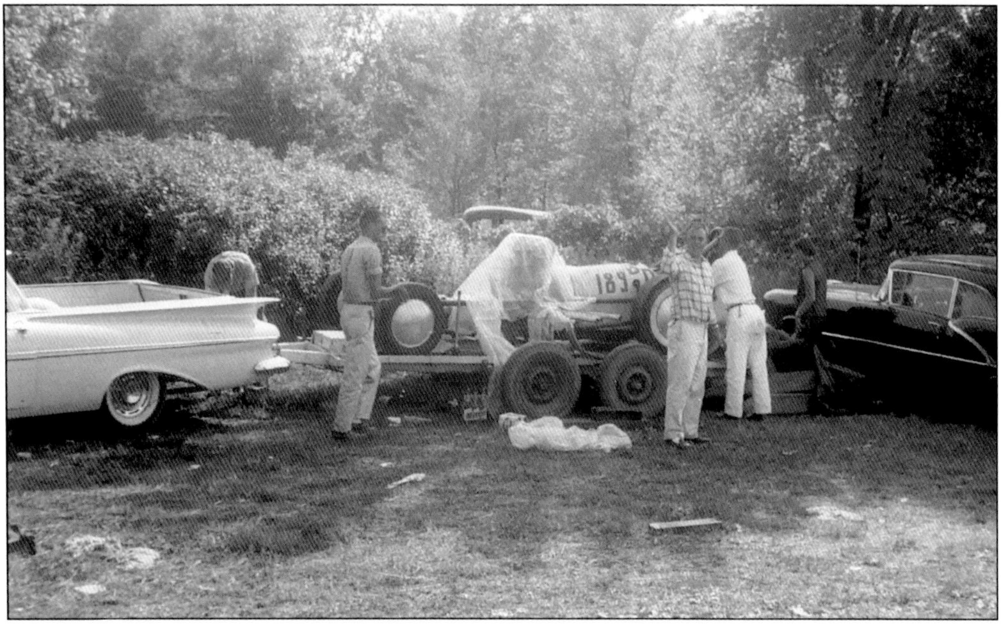

The season ended at the '59 Nationals when the tired Olds engine blew. Note that the body nose section was removed and the roll cage rebuilt from the 1958 version of the car. From left to right are Darryl Hobbs (behind the tow car), Gene Wells, Jerry Williams (waving), Herb Sebastian, and an unknown onlooker. (Neely collection, 1959.)

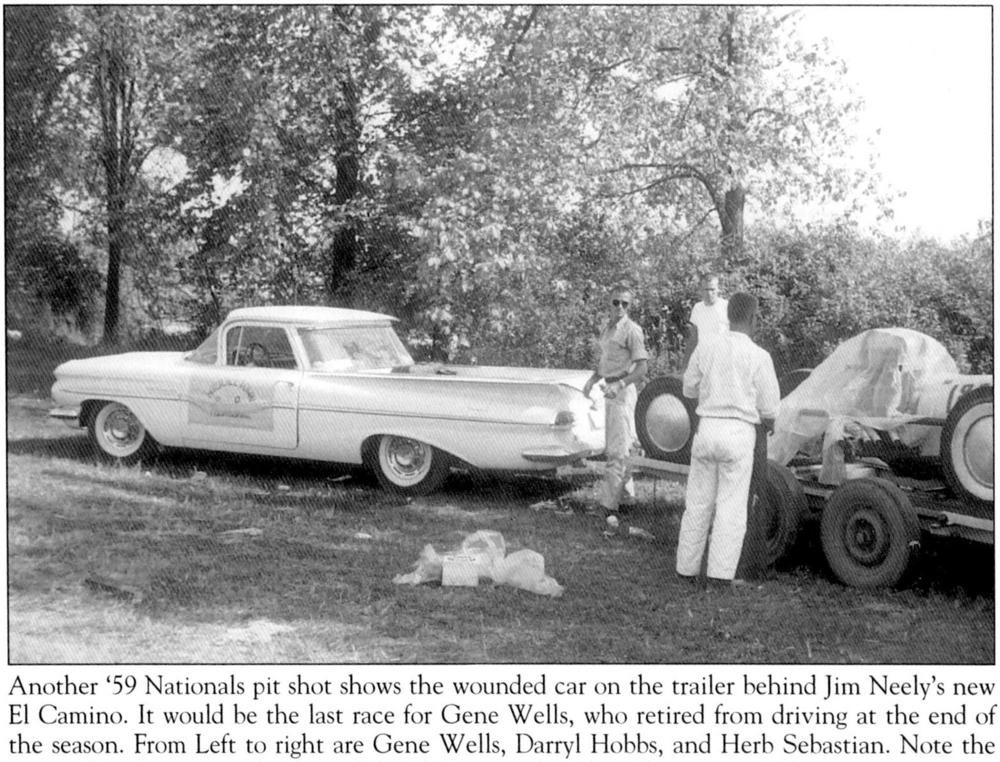

Another '59 Nationals pit shot shows the wounded car on the trailer behind Jim Neely's new El Camino. It would be the last race for Gene Wells, who retired from driving at the end of the season. From Left to right are Gene Wells, Darryl Hobbs, and Herb Sebastian. Note the Pacemakers banner on the door of the El Camino. (Neely collection, 1959.)

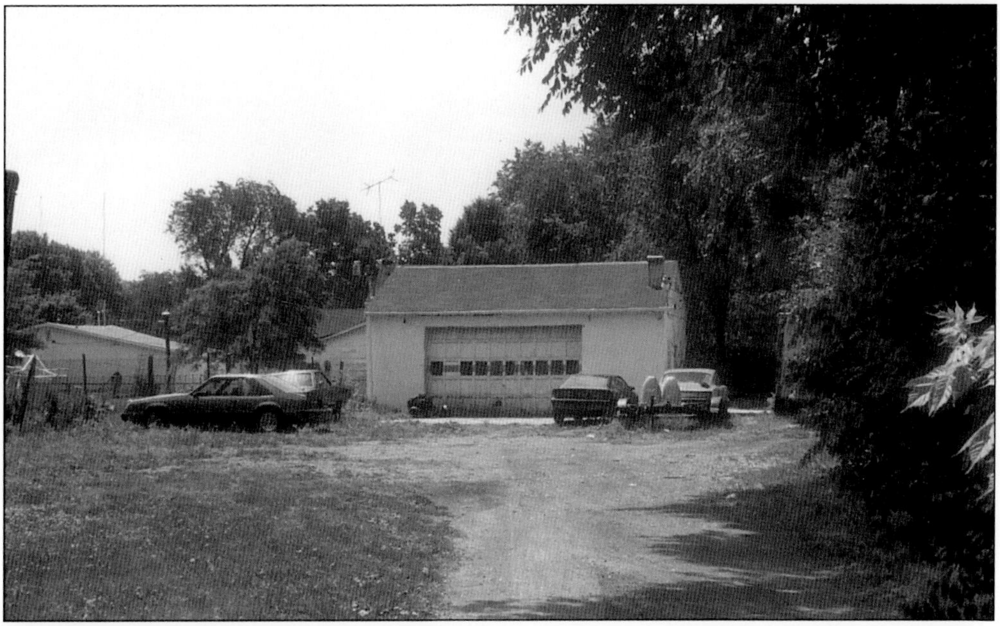

The club purchased this property at 406 Manatee Street to serve as the club's meeting place and project garage. This 1994 photo suggests that the building still belongs to a car enthusiast. (Roberson collection, 1959.)

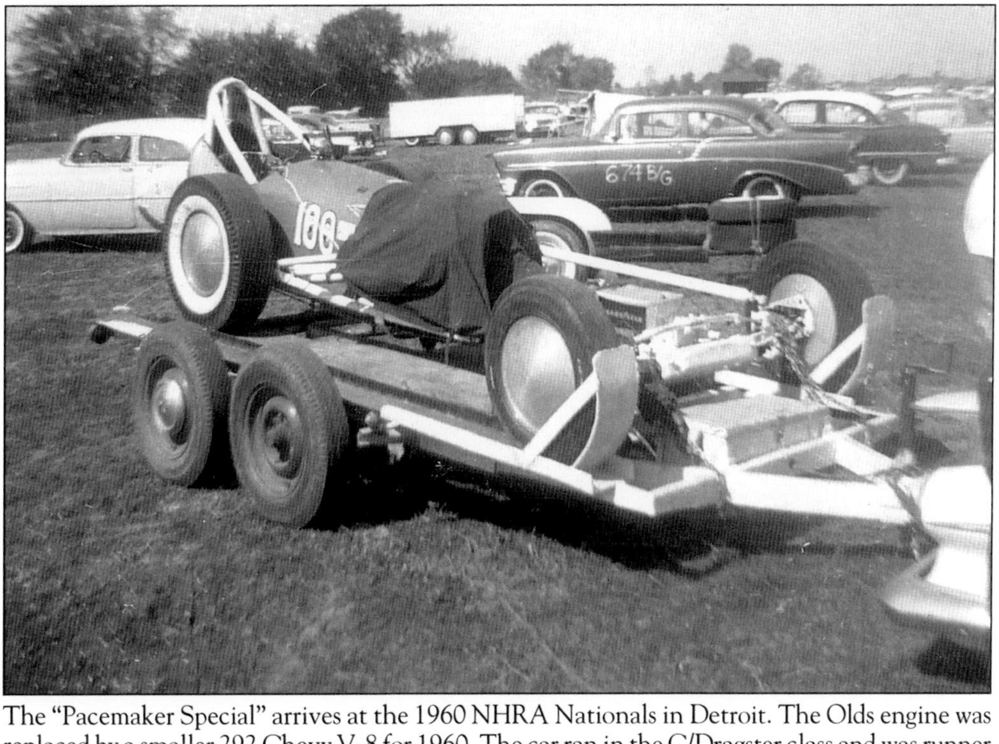

The "Pacemaker Special" arrives at the 1960 NHRA Nationals in Detroit. The Olds engine was replaced by a smaller 292 Chevy V-8 for 1960. The car ran in the C/Dragster class and was runner up to Walt Markert for the class trophy at the '60 Nationals. (Roberson collection, 1960.)

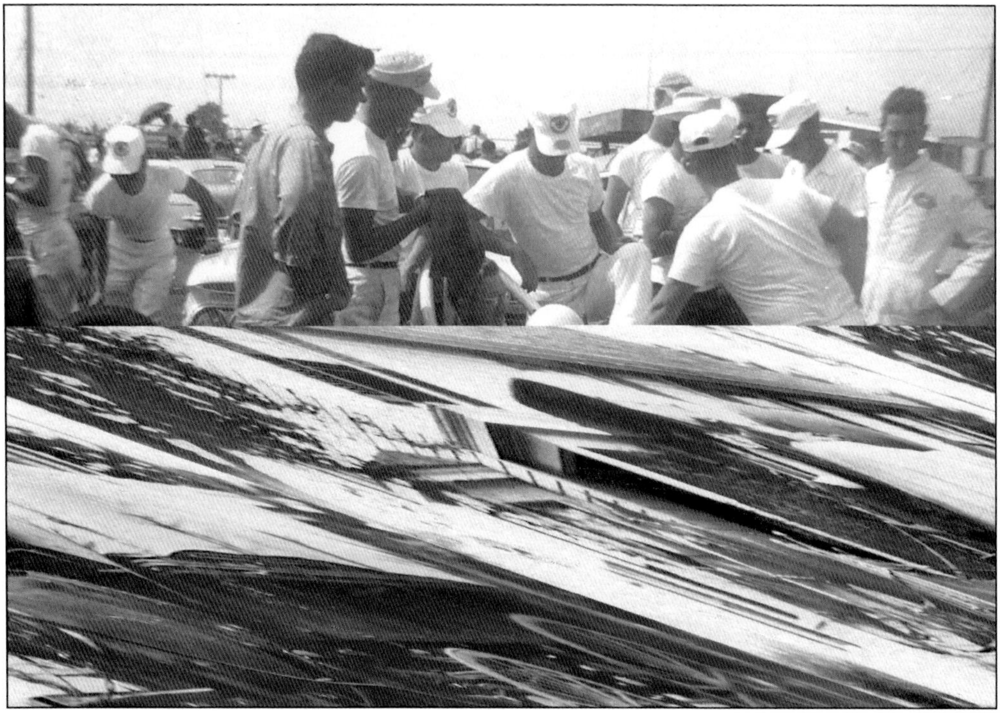

The crew tends to the car in the staging lanes at the '60 NHRA Nationals as driver Jim Neely sits anxiously in the cockpit. Dad is standing over Jim wiping his hands on a shop rag. Others are unidentified. Note the dragster's Rochester fuel injection mounted in the conventional position. (Roberson collection, 1960.)

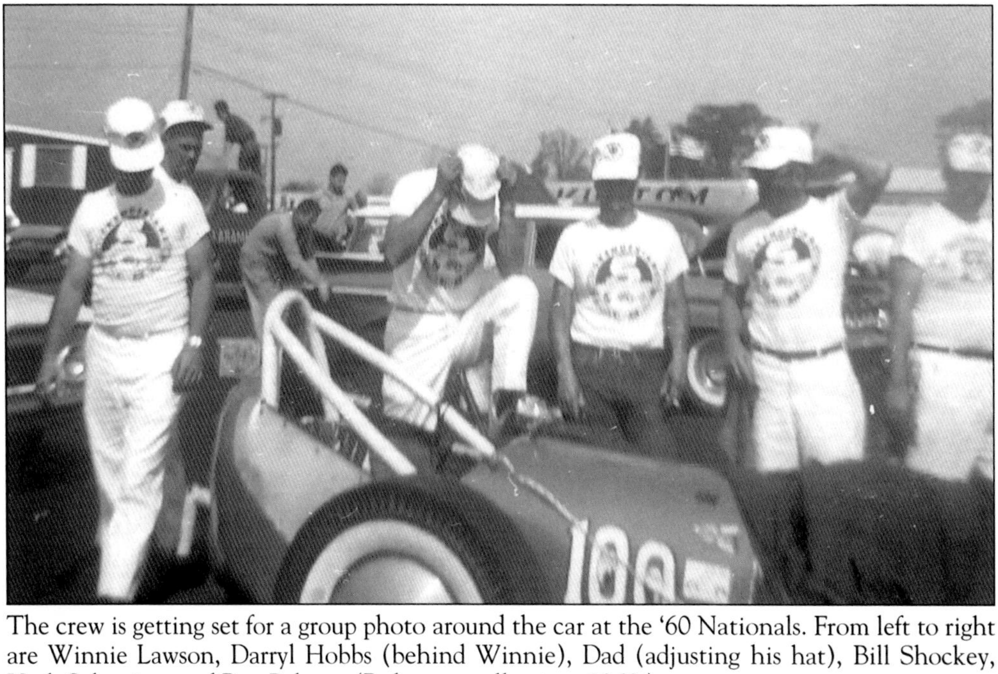

The crew is getting set for a group photo around the car at the '60 Nationals. From left to right are Winnie Lawson, Darryl Hobbs (behind Winnie), Dad (adjusting his hat), Bill Shockey, Herb Sebastian, and Ray Palmer. (Roberson collection, 1960.)

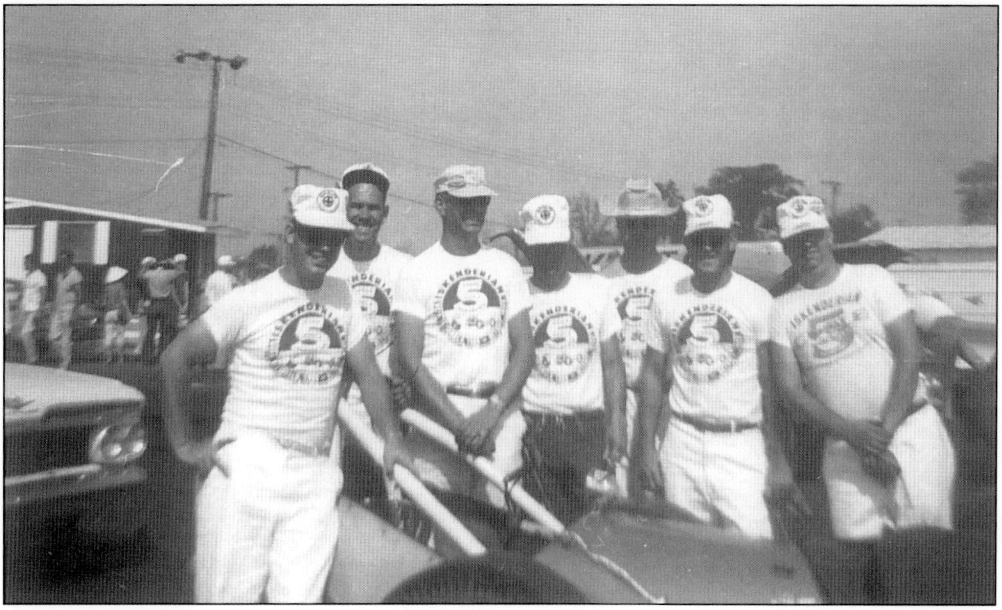

The crew poses in matching Iskenderian Racing Cam tee shirts at the '60 Nationals in Detroit. From left to right are Winnie Lawson, Darryl Hobbs, Dad, Bill Shockey, Jim Neely (in cowboy hat), Herb Sebastian, and Ray Palmer (leaning toward Middletown). (Roberson collection, 1960.)

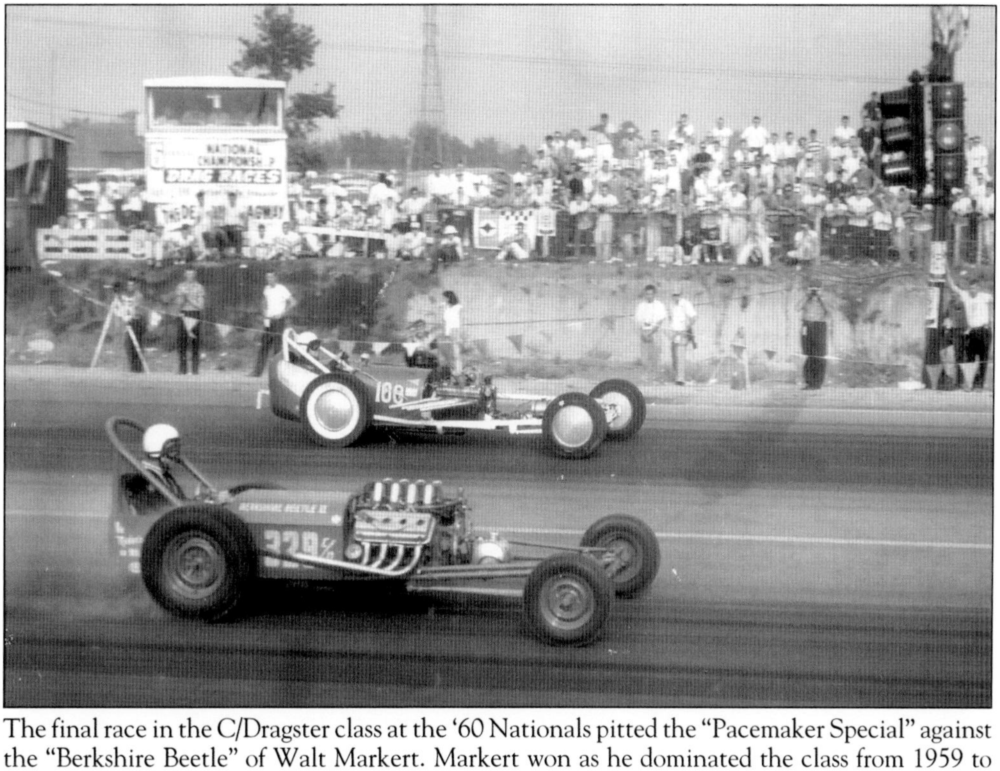

The final race in the C/Dragster class at the '60 Nationals pitted the "Pacemaker Special" against the "Berkshire Beetle" of Walt Markert. Markert won as he dominated the class from 1959 to 1962. (Neely collection, 1960.)

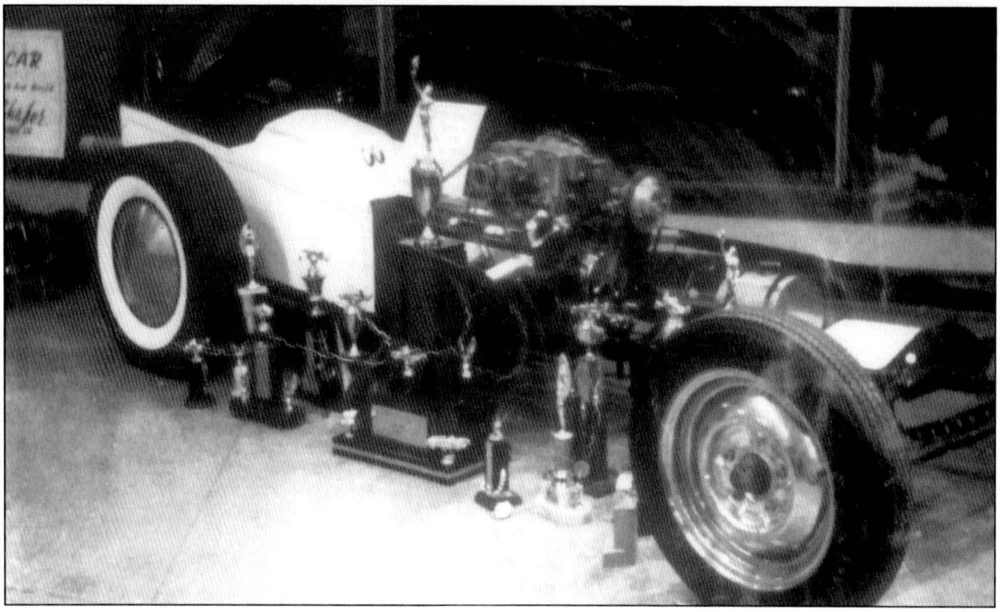

The last rebuild of the 1958 car resulted in this "Pacemaker Special." It sported a new body complete with a cowl made from a refrigerator panel and a 292 Chevy engine. Dad's homemade drive unit for the fuel pump of the backward-mounted Rochester fuel injection unit is visible in this photo. By the end of the year, they would switch to a Hilborn fuel injection unit. For the 1962 season the car would be painted blue, but largely unchanged from this 1961 format. (Palmer collection, 1961.)

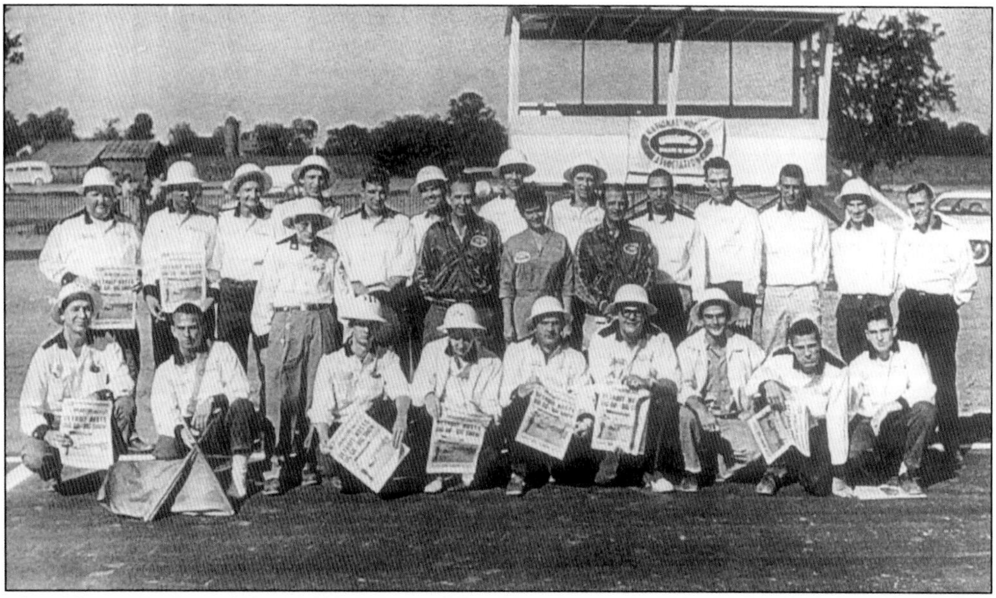

The Cluster Busters club members pose with the Indianapolis Timing Association group that hosted the inaugural race at Indianapolis Raceway Park in September, 1960. Standing in the center row, from left to right, are Charlie Mann, NHRA Technical Advisor Manual Venis, and NHRA Divisional Directors Eileen and Bob Daniels. Others are unidentified. (From the collection of Bob and Eileen Daniels, 1960.)

Seven

Drag Racing
Records and Championships

You can't build a reputation on what you are going to do.

-Henry Ford

In September of 1962, Top Gas racer Jim Minnick of Nitro, West Virginia, put his old Chassis Research chassis up for sale as he started to build his new car. The club purchased the chassis for $175 and had the basis for the next and last "Pacemaker Special." The new car would stay with the tried and true Chevy V-8 engine. They had planned to build another C/Dragster, when a rule change fell their way.

NHRA made some sweeping rule changes for 1963 that included the separation of supercharged cars from normally aspirated cars and the consolidation of similar cars into single classes. They combined the modified roadsters (open body) with competition coupes (closed body) into one class called Competition, or Comp for short. These cars were essentially slingshot dragsters with lightweight fiberglass bodies that were replicas of Model T roadsters, or Fiat and Bantam coupes. The supercharged cars were separated into a double A (AA) class, and normally aspirated cars were designated as single letters A and B, with the B class having smaller engines in heavier cars.

NHRA had set the minimum elapsed time record for the new A/Competition class at 10.25 seconds. This was an educated guess as to where it should be, based on the performance of the supercharged cars that previously ran in the class, but would now be designated as AA/Comps. The records for those classes at the end of '62 were 9.51 seconds for A/Modified Roadsters and 9.77 seconds for A/Competition Coupes, both class records being held by supercharged cars. NHRA reasoned that the absence of the supercharger for 1963 would slow the cars by about a half-second and chose the 10.25-second minimum. The new A/Comp class would probably not be as crowded as the popular C/Dragster class. Since the '63 "Pacemaker Special" would be basically what they were already running, but with a bigger engine and a lightweight roadster body, making the 10.25 second ET look soft for the more powerful car, they decided to build it as an A/Comp.

The car was built in the Pacemaker clubhouse on Manatee Street. They purchased a fiberglass replica 1923 Model T body molded in the thin-walled competition style format and mounted it on the Minnick chassis. Openings had to be cut out of the roadster body to clear the new M&H Race Master slicks, mounted on American mag wheels. The front end was a traditional transverse leaf spring with radius rods and twelve-spoke mag wheels, which were so common for the period altereds and dragsters. Jim Neely prepared the 327 Chevy engine, and it would be the only club dragster engine for which Dad was not the main builder. It featured an Iskenderian cam and Hilborn fuel injection. The transmission was a manual shift unit with two speeds, using third and fourth gears from a Chevrolet four speed in a heavier Pontiac case.

I was 12 years old when this car was built, and I had graduated from little kid to crew gofer. I actually got my hands on the car and helped as much as a pre teen could. I was proud of this new position, and I reveled in the fact that I was the only kid on our block that knew how to set up a Hilborn fuel injector.

The finished car was a thing of beauty. It was painted metallic blue, like the 1962 C/Dragster. It had little chrome, but it was tastefully detailed. Darryl Hobbs' wife Kathy was a commercial artist, and she lettered the body in white letters with red highlighting. The car, with the small 327 engine, turned out to be a bit heavy for the class. They briefly considered adding weight to make the B/Comp class, but the initial outings on the car netted nine-second elapsed times at 140 mph, and it appeared that the "Pacemaker Special" No. 3 would be a very competitive racecar in the A/Comp class.

Jim Neely was still the main driver, but Darryl Hobbs was driving more and more often in order to meet the hectic race schedule that the tri-state area offered. In April, Seattle's Harold Gunderson set the A/Comp records at 10.20 seconds and 139.96 mph. Our first record meet for the season was on July 7th at Muncie Dragway in Indiana, and by that time, the record had been whittled down to 10.17 seconds and the speed upped to 140.76 mph by Campbell and Gibson of Oklahoma. When we arrived at Muncie, another A/Comp run by Wayne Morgan of Dayton had already made an attempt at the record, falling short with a 10.19-second ET. By the time we prepared the car and warmed it up, Morgan had made two more runs, both also at 10.19 seconds. We fired up the car, and Neely staged coolly. He ran straight as an arrow, posting an elapsed time and new national record of 9.96 seconds. Later Jim beat Wayne in the class final with a 9.87-second ET, which unofficially broke our own record. We didn't win Competition Eliminator though. That honor went to fellow Pacemakers Don Klamo and Marion Hounshell in their "D&M Special" B/Dragster. It was a Pacemaker sweep.

Our record stood one week and was lowered to 9.93 seconds by Ron Salisbury from Oregon, who also upped the speed record to 144.58 mph. Salisbury's record stood through the Nationals. Just after the Nationals, in September with Darryl at the wheel, the "Pacemaker Special" bumped the record down to 9.87 seconds. It was a short-lived celebration, because that same weekend the elapsed time record got lowered to a blistering 9.67 by Seattle's Harold Gunderson. That record held until spring. Curiously, Gunderson's record was very close to the two ET records from 1962—the 9.77 and 9.51 held by the supercharged versions of the same cars. Drag racing was progressing quickly.

As the cars progressed, so did the drag strip equipment. NHRA announced a new starting system for the 1963 Nationals. Flag starters would be replaced by an electronic lighting system that would become known as the Christmas tree. California's Mickey Thompson, one of the most innovative racers of all time, first suggested the concept of an electronic starting system. Racers would be started by a system of lights resembling a modified traffic light. The early trees worked as follows: The starter motioned the cars forward into the starting beam. (The stage and pre stage lights would come later.) He would start the tree sequence by pushing a button on a hand held controller. A series of five yellow anticipation lights blinked down the tree at half-second intervals resembling a dropping ball. The green light would light up at a half second behind the last yellow signaling the start, and a red foul light would indicate that a driver left too soon and was disqualified. Trees with three anticipation lights, 0.4 second gap pro lights, and the single yellow 0.4 second pro start, would come much later.

The Christmas tree starting system opened a new facet to drag racing, as the lanes could work independently of one another, and a handicap start could be designed into the run. Since the beginning of the sport, no one had ever come up with a fair means of giving a head start to a car of a lower classification, when it had to run against a higher-class car. Some tracks had a system of spotting a car so many car lengths per class level, but these rarely produced close races. Most tracks just ran the class winners against one another heads up, which always gave the higher classes the advantage. But with electronic handicapping, a slower class car could receive a head start by getting a green light ahead of the faster class car, and the amount could be determined by the difference between the two class ET records. For example, a car with a national class record of 10.00 seconds could run against a car with a class record of 9.00 seconds, and the starter could dial in a one-second head start for the slower car. The car that ran the closest to the national record would theoretically win the race, if both drivers reacted to the start lights at an equal rate.

This in turn lead to another new rule: the break-out rule. Since handicap starts were based on the difference between the class national elapsed time records, it was now to a racer's advantage to not set new records. A new record would put your class at a disadvantage, because you would now spot slower cars by a larger margin and receive a lesser head start from faster classes, making it harder to win handicap races. NHRA's answer was to limit the margin by which a competitor could exceed the national record in a competitive handicap race. If a car won a handicap race by running more than 0.10 seconds faster than the class record, it would disqualify the car. This was losing by breaking out. Today's NHRA class racing is handicapped by an index system based loosely on the national records, but in 1963 they used the class records.

By the time of the Nationals, the class record still stood at 9.93 seconds, which meant that we could run as quick as 9.83 seconds in a handicap race without breaking out. We had enjoyed a very successful year at that point, winning often in the new car. Besides the record at Muncie, we had won the A/Comp class at the 500 Gas & Fuel Challenge at Indianapolis Raceway Park in May, and the divisional championship at west Salem in July. A good showing at the Nationals would be icing on the cake.

The "Pacemaker Special" was entry No. 37 at the '63 Nationals, and Jim Neely was entered as the driver. The new Christmas tree starting system was in effect, and many drivers were obviously clumsy with the new system. Another innovation for drag racing occurred at this meet: ABC's Wide World of Sports was taping the meet for the first-ever national television coverage of a drag race. Drag racing had certainly progressed from the civic programs of the previous decade to now be included in the "thrill of victory and the agony of defeat" drama of national sports television. The Nationals was also drawing in excess of 50,000 spectators.

The Nationals goes slowly for a competitor. With so many cars, it is a long time between runs. Thursday was tech day. Friday and Saturday afforded some practice runs. Then Sunday we had the class run offs. Round by round Neely shut down the competition, and worked his way into the class final. We watched with great anticipation as Jim lined up beside the Buick-powered "Big Iron" machine with Bill Bagwell of Collier, Tennessee, driving. The lights blinked down, and the two took off together. Bagwell's car had a '27 T body that looked physically bigger from the back, so it was difficult to tell who was ahead from our vantage point in the tow car. It looked liked Jim was out front, but we couldn't be sure. Then the win light came on at the finish line like a lightning bolt from the heavens—in Jim's lane! We had won the class at the Nationals! That elusive national class championship was ours. We were ecstatic! Jim had gone 143.26 mph in 9.82 seconds. Luckily, the break out rule didn't apply in heads-up racing.

At the far end of the track, the guys were hugging each other like long lost brothers. We took the car through the technical inspection required for the winners. They reweighed the car and checked the fuel tank for illegal additives. They checked the engine displacement with a device that fit into a spark plug hole. The car passed, making the victory official. We still had the run offs for Competition Eliminator the next day, so we headed back to the hotel. The guys checked out the car while Kathy Hobbs added lettering to the turtle deck. "1963 National Class Champions" was proudly displayed across the back of the car when we entered the track the next day.

Neely worked his way to the semifinals, where we had to run the "Plain Vanilla" A/Altered of Charlie Smith of Oklahoma City, one of the top Competition Eliminator cars in the country. Smith had a handicap head start, but Neely edged him out on the far end. In the other semifinal run, the local B/Dragster of the Yount Brothers edged out the "Tennessee Bo-Weevil" AA/Comp for the win. We were to run the Younts in the final, a team from Indiana that we often raced at IRP and Muncie, and we'd had pretty good luck against them. Things were looking good for the Pacemakers in the final.

The Yount's car was a B/Dragster with a smaller Chevy engine and a 4-71 GMC supercharger.

Neely lined up beside John Yount for the Competition Eliminator final; the engine of our "Pacemaker Special" popping and cracking in crisp response to Jim's right foot coolly jacking the throttle in rhythmic anticipation of the starting lights. The B/Dragster was a slightly faster class, and had to give us a mild handicap start. The yellow anticipation lights came down, and Neely nailed the throttle, picking up the front wheels slightly on a picture perfect launch. The B/Dragster wasted no time in chasing him down. Neely still had a slight lead at the shift point, but the car refused to shift into high gear! Neely quickly jammed it back into the low gear and hit the throttle again in vain as the B/Dragster flew by. The Yount brothers were running awfully well, and certainly deserved their championship title. They had won the heavily populated B/Dragster class, set a new speed record of 154.90 mph, and had beaten no less than the "Tennessee Bo-Weevil" to get to the final. But I've often wondered what would have happened if our transmission had held up for just one more run.

The 1963 Nationals stands among the best national championship events of all time. It was the first with the Christmas tree starting system and the first drag race ever covered by ABC Sports. Top Gas dragster was hotly contested with Don Garlits' Dodge wedge engine car falling to the local Hirata-Hobbs-Vodnik team in the final. The super stock classes were wildly popular with the Ramchargers edging out Al Extrand in an all Dodge final. Dave Strickler won Little Eliminator in an A/FX (Factory Experimental) Chevy. But the most popular class and peak drama surrounded the A/Gas Supercharged cars as local favorite George Montgomery edged out the heavily favored Stone Woods and Cook California car and went on to win the class.

The Pacemakers did not want this dream season to end. They decided to travel to Alton, Illinois, to race at the NHRA Division 3 Finals. They decided to run the regular meet at Kilkare then drive all night to Alton. The meet at Kilkare had a lot of cars entered and ran late. The "Pacemaker Special" went all the way to the eliminator final, and scattered the transmission on the final run. There they were, at midnight in Xenia, Ohio, due to race in Alton, Illinois, the next day—and now they had a transmission to rebuild. They piled into the '54 Pontiac station wagon and headed for Alton, some 300 miles away. The crew that night consisted of Dad, Jim Neely, Darryl Hobbs, Harold Barnes, Bill Shockey, and Kenny Miller.

They arrived at the track at Alton at about 7:00 a.m. The gate was closed, so they pulled over to the side of the road and went to work. With the car still on the trailer (these were still the days of open trailers), they pulled the transmission and laid it on the tailgate of the Pontiac wagon. Dad and Neely began to rebuild the transmission with the spare gears they always carried. Other early arrivals began to line up behind them. Soon the gates opened. They pulled inside the facility and resumed the work while the rest of the guys unloaded the car and took it to the tech inspection. Dad and Neely were buttoning up the transmission, when Harold Barnes came running up. "Robbie, we need the transmission. The car weighed in too light." They quickly hand carried the transmission to the race car—still sitting on the track scales—and dropped it into the seat, while 250 other contestants waited in line. The car passed tech, and the guys installed the transmission back in the pits.

It was Darryl's turn to drive the car. He systematically won the class, and then proceeded to wade through a large field to win the Competition Eliminator title. The win made the Pacemakers the Divisional champs for 1963. It was a storybook ending for the best racing season the club would ever enjoy. They had held the national record twice, won their class at the Nationals, were runner up for Competition Eliminator at the Nationals, won the Division 3 Finals, and were Divisional champions for Competition Eliminator. It had been quite a season.

The guys wasted no time in getting ready for 1964. The 9.67-second ET record set by Harold Gunderson in September was proof enough that 1964 would be a tough year. They wanted a larger engine and a lighter, less restrictive front end. They purchased a new engine block, and Dad built a 368 cubic inch engine, which was calculated to cut the weight-to-cubic-inch limit of the class more closely. The updating of the chassis was a major project. Dad made a completely new front section for the frame, which extended the wheelbase from 96 inches to 116 inches. The old style transverse leaf spring suspension was replaced by a torsion bar unit, which Dad made from a Volkswagen front end. The twelve-spoke mag wheels were replaced by motorcycle-type wire wheels, which were being run by the Top Gas and Top Fuel cars of the day. The longer chassis with a much lighter front end placed more of the car's static weight to the rear wheels.

The result of these changes was immediately apparent as the season opened. The car picked up two tenths of a second and five to six mph from the previous fall. We began the season running speeds at 148 mph and winning virtually everywhere we went. Darryl Hobbs had become the main driver of the car, because Jim Neely had entered into a project of his own.

Jim Neely and fellow club member John Buehl entered into a partnership on a new Plymouth super stocker for the 1964 season. The factory super stock wars were in full swing in 1964 with Dodge, Plymouth and Ford fielding heavily backed factory teams. General Motors was officially out of racing, but still worked with selected teams on a less formal basis. Dodge and Plymouth had introduced a new version of the hemi head engine that had been discontinued in 1957, in order to scale up the Chrysler Corporation racing effort. They placed the awesome 426 Hemi engines into lightweight sedans and sold them to an eager racing market. Neely and Buehl had caught the super stock fever and bought one of these awesome machines. The car would run the quarter mile in about 12 seconds at 125 mph, roughly the same performance as the 1958 "Pacemaker Special" B/Dragster. They raced the car under the name "Twilight Zone", named after the popular TV series.

Another race team had emerged from the Pacemakers in 1963. Harold and Earnie Barnes began racing a 1961 Corvette under the name "Cracklin' Rose" in the B/Sports class. The car was powered by a Rochester fuel injected Chevy engine. Earnie drove the car and Harold tuned it. The little maroon screamer ran low 13-second to high 12-second elapsed times at 106 mph, and won often.

Yet another super stock team emerged in the club in 1964. The father and son team of John and Dick Kauffman purchased a Ford super stocker and had success at the local level. The car ran under the name "Little Red I," and Dick did the driving. The team of Klamo, Hounshell & Rupp still campaigned their rapid little B/Dragster, bringing the total to five Pacemaker entries at many of the local meets.

One of the most memorable races for the Pacemakers for 1964 came early in the season at a meet at Muncie, Indiana. Darryl Hobbs was making an otherwise normal run when the fiberglass Model T body flew off of the car and broke into a bazillion pieces. Without the T body our car was classified as an A/Dragster, and although the car was quite heavy for the class, that was where we ran while we waited for a new T body. Surprisingly, the car ran about a half second quicker with the T body off and no other changes. We ran over a month that way and ran a best elapsed time of 9.05 seconds recorded at Tri-State Drag Strip. With the new body installed in early August, we were back to 9.60s and 9.70s.

The new T body was a new style that had been developed just for drag racing. It had a molded cover over the top around the cockpit. The design prevented the body from catching too much wind by routing the air over the body instead of creating turbulence by trying to collect inside the body. The car picked up a little top end speed over the old T body, and we were dancing around the150 mph mark on the better tracks.

On August 16th, the *Middletown Journal* newspaper ran a feature article on the club, the racecar and Darryl. The article carried three photos and relayed the club's history with quotes from both Darryl and Dad, who was the club's president at the time. The local newspaper was always supportive of the club, reporting its events and racing accomplishments over the years, but this article was by far the best coverage the club had ever gotten.

Darryl had adapted well to the Christmas tree starting system, which all the tracks had by 1964. He usually got the jump on the other driver and rarely fouled. The early days of the Christmas tree starting system did not include the reporting of the driver's reaction times as is done on today's drag strips. A driver had to adjust his or her reaction time by cutting the lights closer and closer until a foul start occurred, then backing off on the next run. Needless to say, this was a slow process, since the foul start put you out of competition until the following meet.

Darryl had a natural sense of timing that won many races when the car did not necessarily hold a performance advantage. His talent became evident at the Nationals in '64.

Frank Smith, of Oklahoma City, had moved from the gas coupe classes to A/Comp for 1964. His car was not significantly different from ours except that it was professionally prepared and had the best and latest of everything. Frank was the identical twin brother to Charlie Smith of "Plain Vanilla" A/Altered fame, and both ran very well. Frank had set the A/Comp ET record at 9.60 seconds and 149.00 mph in May. By the time the Nationals rolled around, Frank Smith had dropped the A/Comp elapsed time record to a blistering 9.34 seconds, and all the class competitors feared this awesome red-orange, T-bodied car. Frank was winning so many races in Texas and Oklahoma that people hardly noticed when Harold Gunderson set a new speed record at 151.00 mph in July.

At the Nationals we put the car through tech, which at that time was still held at a shopping center in town. The next day we began practice runs that were disappointing. After tweaking the car all day, the best we could do was 9.60s. Frank Smith had already run some 9.40s, so things were not looking so good. We were breaking 150 mph on nearly every run now, and Frank's speeds were not significantly different from ours; but his elapsed times were still two-tenths of a second better.

The A/Comp class was called over the P.A. system to line up in the staging lanes for the class run offs. We pushed to the staging lanes to find an almost comical scene: Frank Smith had gotten there first, and several other A/Comps were holding back at the entrance, balking at lining up behind him. They had planned to avoid the record holder for a few rounds in hopes that he might go out with breakage. We rolled past them and pulled in line behind Frank.

The cars fired up for the run, and Darryl lined up beside Frank on the starting line. The lights came down and Darryl got a huge jump at the start. Frank began to pull back, but he didn't have enough top end speed to catch Darryl. The win light came on in our lane, and the guys went wild cheering. Then we heard the unbelievable times announced over the P.A. system. Darryl had run a 9.66 second elapsed time, beating Frank's 9.46! It was the grand-daddy of all hole shots. As we progressed through the class runs, the car kept getting faster as Dad was getting it dialed into the track conditions. Darryl went on to win the class, running a best of 9.57 seconds at 151.00 mph, which unofficially tied the class speed record. We had won the class a second consecutive year. Topping off the Pacemaker class win was a fine showing by the Barnes Brothers' Corvette, which finished as runner-up in the B/Sports class, barely losing in the class final.

The Competition Eliminator run off on Monday included some really tight racing. The eliminator was expanded to fourteen classes, and any one of the fourteen class winners was capable of winning. Darryl raced the B/Comp winner, Dave Weber, in a car called the "Pussycat," and won with a 9.51 at 150.25 mph. This was our quickest elapsed time of the meet so far. The next round put us in a rematch from last year with Charlie Smith in the "Plain Vanilla" A/Altered. In the closest race of the eliminator, Charlie edged Darryl at the finish line. Neither driver knew who won until we got to the other end with the tow car carrying the news from the track announcer. Darryl had run a best ever 9.48-second elapsed time at 151.51 mph in the losing effort. Charlie went on to win the eliminator title, beating Joe Davis in the Davis and Ingram Fiat in the final.

After the eliminations NHRA had blocked some time for official record runs, and we wanted to take a shot at the speed record. It stood at 151.00 mph, and we had been running right on the record all weekend. Darryl needed to go and collect the contingency money for the class win, a time consuming task that required going to the manufacturer's tents for all the various products we ran (e.g., spark plugs, tires, oil, camshaft, etc.) Time was running short to collect those prizes, and waiting our turn to run might cause him to miss some of the manufacturers. The solution was a simple one: Don Klamo would drive the car on the record attempt.

Don drove a similar car in the B/Dragster class, but he had never driven the "Pacemaker Special" A/Comp car. The cockpit had been built around the six-foot stature of the original driver Jim Neely, and while Darryl Hobbs' similar height posed no problem, Klamo's small stature was a concern. Don was a full six inches shorter, and the seat and pedal placement made things hard for Don to reach. But Don was a driver who knew no fear, and he jumped at the chance to set a national record.

Dad went over the strategy: "Remember to drive an arc." This was an old drag racing trick to set speed records. The quickest way through the quarter mile was to drive as straight a course as possible. But on a run where you want top end speed, and don't care about the elapsed time, it is to your advantage to make the track a little longer by drifting side to side prior to entering the speed traps at the end of the track. The extra distance, even though it is only a few feet, gives the car more time to build up speed. Don nodded in agreement.

We watched the run from the vantage point offered by the tow car near the starting line. Indeed, Don went from side to side as the car sped down the track, just as Dad had instructed. Don skillfully ran the car within inches of the white sidelines, which marked the point of disqualification. The announcer reported that Don had gone 152.28 mph, setting a new record and running the fastest speed of the meet in our class.

When we got to the end of the track, Don stood by the car reaching over into the cockpit. Dad told him he had done a great job of "driving an arc," and it obviously worked since he had posted our fastest speed ever. Don replied excitedly, "Arc, nothin'! Look at this!" He pointed to the small bracket that anchored the car's steering column to the rear end third member. The bracket had broken loose, which allowed the steering wheel to roam free throughout the confines of the cockpit. Don demonstrated the elusive steering wheel, which he could move from one side frame rail to the other, and from the floor to a position that put the steering column nearly vertical with the wheel pointing to the sky. "I didn't drive an arc on purpose, it was all I could do to hang on!" It was his first time in the car, the steering column came loose, and he had set a national speed record all in about nine and a half seconds.

The 1964 NHRA Nationals was another classic full of hints of what was to come. Drag racing in the 1960s was in its golden age. Cars were still hand built with lots of individuality. Dragsters used Chrysler, Olds, Chevrolet, Pontiac, and Ford engines. Many Top Gas dragsters had two engines. The Nationals that year saw the return of Top Fuel cars for the first time since they were banned in 1957. Connie Kalitta turned the sport's first 200-mph run at an NHRA national event. Jack Chrisman had put a supercharged Ford engine into a Mercury Comet stocker and produced an exhibition car that many people point to today as the first fuel funny car. George Montgomery repeated his win in the A/GS class complete with another Midwest crowd-pleasing win over California's Stone, Woods and Cook. The factory experimental cars included some Dodge and Plymouth cars with the rear wheels moved forward about two inches, which was hardly noticeable, but moved about 100 pounds of the car's static weight to the rear wheels, greatly improving the car's traction. These famous 2% cars were the forerunners of wilder things to come from those factories.

Don Garlits won the Top Fuel trophy over Jack Williams. Gordon Collett of Portsmouth, Ohio, won Top Gas Eliminator over Pete Robinson. Roger Lindamood's "Color Me Gone" Dodge won the Top Stock trophy over the Ramchargers similar car with Jim Thornton at the wheel.

The Jim Neely-John Buehl Plymouth super stocker venture went through some major changes during the course of the season. The factory super stock wars were torrid in that year, and the independent racers were at a tremendous disadvantage. The factory teams had access to highly developed parts and pieces that were not available to the independents. The Neely-Buehl team became frustrated with the scene and converted the car to the C/Altered class by the 1965 season, returning Jim to Competition Eliminator.

The winter of '64-'65 saw few changes in the "Pacemaker Special." Dad built a new Chevy engine of 376 cubic inches. We added a parachute to accommodate a new rule that any car with a class record above 150 mph had to carry a parachute. The club decided not to run a project car in '65, so Dad, Herb Sebastian, Darryl Hobbs, and Ray Palmer bought the car from the club and raced it under the club name. Herb Sebastian also made a return to the driver's seat in 1965, filling in on occasion when Darryl was not available. It had been at least four years since Herb had driven competitively, and the car was about 30 mph faster than anything he had driven before, but he did an admirable job running over 150 mph and winning on a regular basis.

The other club cars remained pretty much in tact for the 1965 race season. Neely and Buehl campaigned the Hemi Plymouth in the C/Altered class. The Barneses ran the B/Sports Corvette, and the Kauffmans ran the Ford super stocker. The Klamo-Hounshell-Rupp B/Dragster began the season on a fast note, winning the class at the inaugural NHRA Spring Nationals held at Bristol, Tennessee. They immediately sold the car to the Barnes brothers, and debuted a supercharged Olds powered AA/Gas Dragster. The Barneses campaigned both the Corvette and the B/Dragster simultaneously, with Earnie driving both cars, a feat made possible by the fact that the two classes competed in different eliminator categories.

Sometime in 1965 or '66, the Neely-Buehl Plymouth was badly damaged in a towing accident, but was rebuilt with the wheelbase altered like the new "funny" cars coming from the Dodge and Plymouth factories. The rear axle was moved forward by fifteen inches to distribute the car's weight to the rear wheels. The new version of the car was painted white and ran under the name "White Tornado" in the C/Altered class. It ran quite well in the new format, and became one of the first funny cars in our area.

In 1965, the match race craze was accelerating like a fuel dragster. It had actually begun when NHRA had first banned nitromethane fuel in 1957. The guys who wanted to run nitro had to race in exhibition matches around the country. Banning the aircraft engine dragsters in 1959 created even more exhibition racers, and soon special exhibition cars were being built like Tommy Ivo's four-engine dragster. The highly popular A/GS cars often ran in exhibition match races as did the factory experimental stockers, and the new equally popular altered wheelbase funny cars were following suit. It was only logical that the "Pacemaker Special" would wind up in a few match races.

The first one came to us on a lark. We were invited by a drag strip in Huntington, West Virginia, to come and race the local favorite, the Fisher brothers' A/Comp, in a best-of-three match race. The Fisher brothers' car was a good running and very good looking Ford-powered car that had posted some good times at the track, and the promoter wanted to match them with the national class champion. We had not run at this track before, but it was a nice facility built along the riverbed like most tracks in the Midwest, since the riverbeds were often the only naturally flat land. The track was well run also, and it had the first track newsletter we had ever seen. We beat the Fisher car in the first two runs and won the match. We returned to the track the following week to run at a big money meet they were promoting, and wound up winning Top Eliminator.

Darryl was intrigued with the concept of the match race. We had been paid just to show up at the track and received additional money for winning. We had also been celebrities at that meet and were treated like royalty. The fans gathered around the car like we were Don Garlits. Darryl immediately began working on the next one.

Norman Ries of Cincinnati had campaigned a B/Comp car in 1961 and won notoriety by finishing in the top ten NHRA national points chase. He had dropped out of racing for a few years, but was back with a beautifully detailed A/Comp car that was featured in the July '65 issue of *Hot Rod*. His partners were Glenn Hall and Joy Fernandez, the latter being a very attractive young blonde lady, who drew as much attention in the pits as the green, yellow, and chrome show-quality racecar. Darryl saw the magazine article as an opportunity and sold the idea of a match race to the promoter at Kilkare. The "Pacemaker Special" would run a best-of-three match race with the Fernandez, Ries and Hall A/Comp.

That night we had problems with the car, and it barely ran at all in the practice runs. Dad found the problem. He had set the timing back home in our driveway with a myriad of neighborhood kids running around. He left the car to get a wrench to tighten down the magneto, and one of the smaller kids turned the magneto while he was gone. This had changed the timing drastically, and caused us some frantic moments at the track. With the timing set correctly the car ran best ever elapsed times of 9.27 and 9.15 to take Norm two straight.

For the 1965 Nationals, we retained entry number 171, which we had in '64, and fittingly the event was almost an exact repeat of '64 for the A/Comp class. We had held the speed record at 152.28 over the winter, but by April Harold Gunderson had broken it at 153.97 mph. Frank Smith had whittled the elapsed time record down to 9.28 seconds in May, then knocked it down to a miniscule 9.15 seconds at 157.43 mph in June. In August, Frank bumped the speed record up to 158.94 mph, and he seemed unbeatable. His first run off the trailer at Indy was 9.28 seconds, and he had the rest of the field shaking their heads wondering where his car got all that power. We were running consistent 9.40s, but Frank definitely had the performance edge.

Norm Ries raced Frank Smith in the first round, and Ries lost when his transmission failed. Round by round we eliminated cars, as did Smith, until we were the last two. Darryl had been running consistent mid 9.40s, and Frank was running low 9.30s. Darryl earned his way to the final by shutting down Andy Sheehan in the popular "School Bus" A/Comp. The final run came, with Darryl knowing he needed another hole shot to win. Frank's bright red-orange car and our metallic blue twin fired up side by side and the two drivers carefully staged the cars. The yellow anticipation lights came down and the two leaped from the start with Darryl taking the early lead. We watched from the starting line as the two disappeared down the course together. We couldn't tell who was ahead from our vantage point. Then like a sign from the heavens, the win light came on in Darryl's lane. The times were announced, and Darryl had run a 9.40 second elapsed time against Frank's 9.32. Darryl's top speed was 153.58 mph, and Frank ran a blazing 156.62 mph in the futile chase. For the second year in a row, Darryl had taken out the record holder with a huge hole shot. At end of the track the two warriors stood beside their cars, shaking hands. Frank was shaking his head saying in his Oklahoma drawl, "Ah cain't believe it! Ya done it to me again!" That night at the hotel, Kathy Hobbs painted new lettering on the side of the T body turtle deck, "'64 & '65 National Class Champs," and we returned to the track for the eliminator run offs the next day advertising the previous day's victory.

Competition Eliminator at the Nationals was won handily that year by Pete Shadinger in a D/Dragster powered by a straight eight Buick. Pete dominated that class in the '60s, and enjoyed a huge performance advantage in '65. He beat Francis O'Connor's AA/Altered roadster in the final. Darryl lasted a couple of rounds, but it was Shadinger's year.

The '65 Nationals saw our eliminator deluged by the new altered wheelbase funny cars out of the Dodge and Plymouth factories. They had been intended to run in the factory experimental classes, but NHRA ruled that they had gone too far with the modifications of a "stock" car, and threw them into the Competition Eliminator ranks. Most fell into the C/Altered class or B/Altered class, depending on whether or not weight had been added. Jack Ditmars of Harvey, Illinois, waded through a whole bunch of these cars and won the B/Altered class in a '34 Ford-bodied car. The crowd was really behind the little Ford, because it had the appearance of a home built hot rod against the factories. Stone, Woods and Cook won the A/GS class when Montgomery went out early with a giant wheelstand. Cook beat the John Mazmanian Willys in an all California class final. Top Gas Eliminator was won by the local Indiana team of Hirata and Hobbs over Ohioan Gordon Collett. The Top Fuel final saw a young Don Prudhomme overtake TV Tommy Ivo. The Nationals in '65 would be the last great Pacemaker drag racing triumph. Within a year, the club would disband.

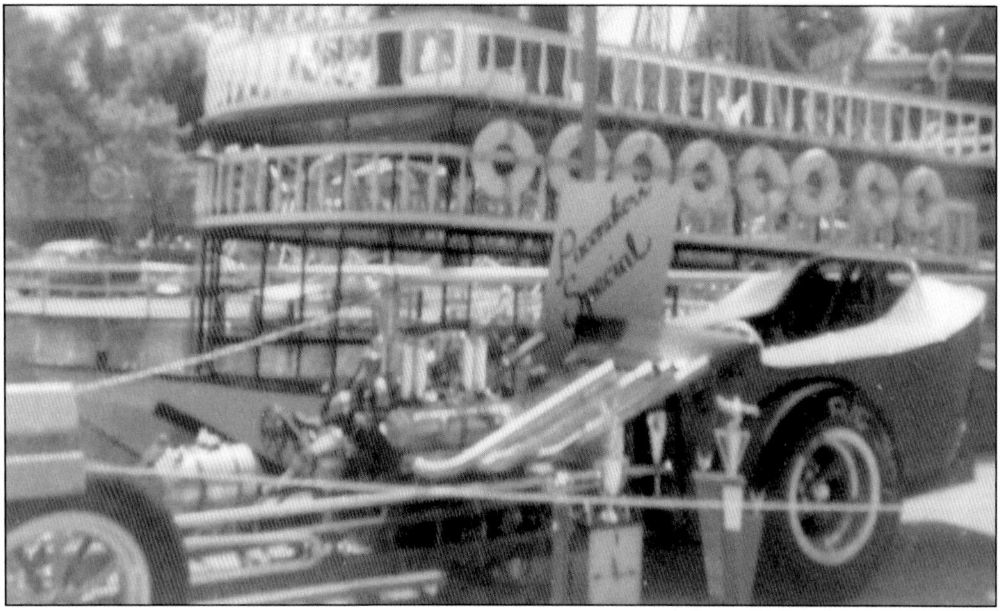

"Pacemaker Special" No. 3 A/Comp is displayed at the Tri-State Custom Auto Show at LeSourdsville Lake Amusement Park in June of 1963. The car is located in front of the Showboat ride, which circled the lake numerous times during the day. The car is new and the body is still unlettered. The model cars that Ron Leisner and I displayed that year were at the front of the car out of frame. (Hobbs collection, 1963.)

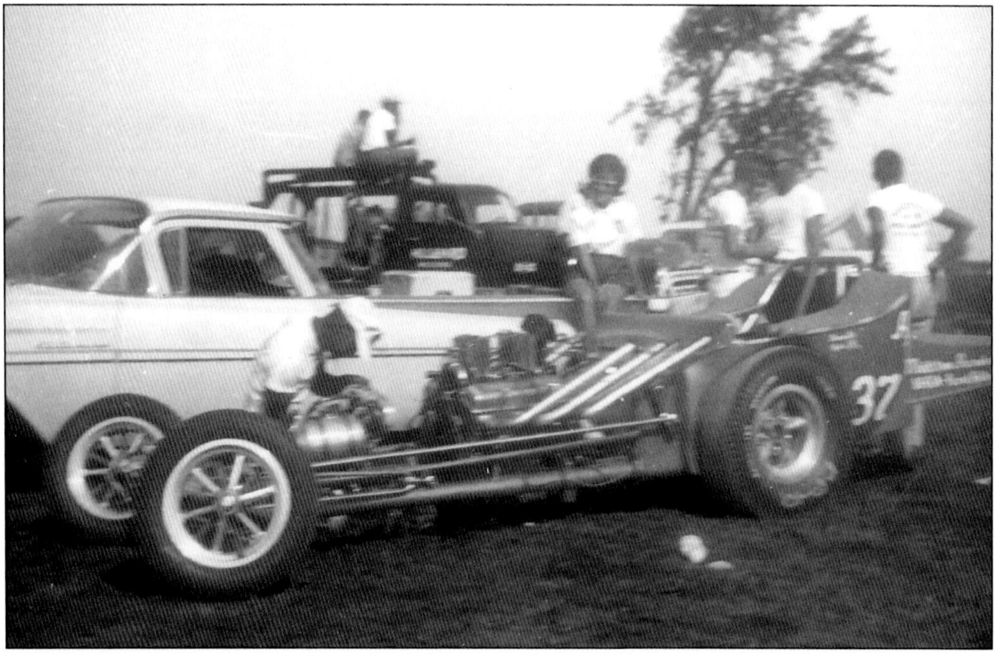

In this 1963 Nationals pit scene, Dad (stooping behind the Moon fuel tank) appears to be changing a jet in the Hilborn fuel injection return line as Kathy Hobbs looks on. Jim Neely (with glasses) is standing by the roll bar talking with Bill Shockey. Another club member at far right is unidentified. (Hobbs collection, 1963.)

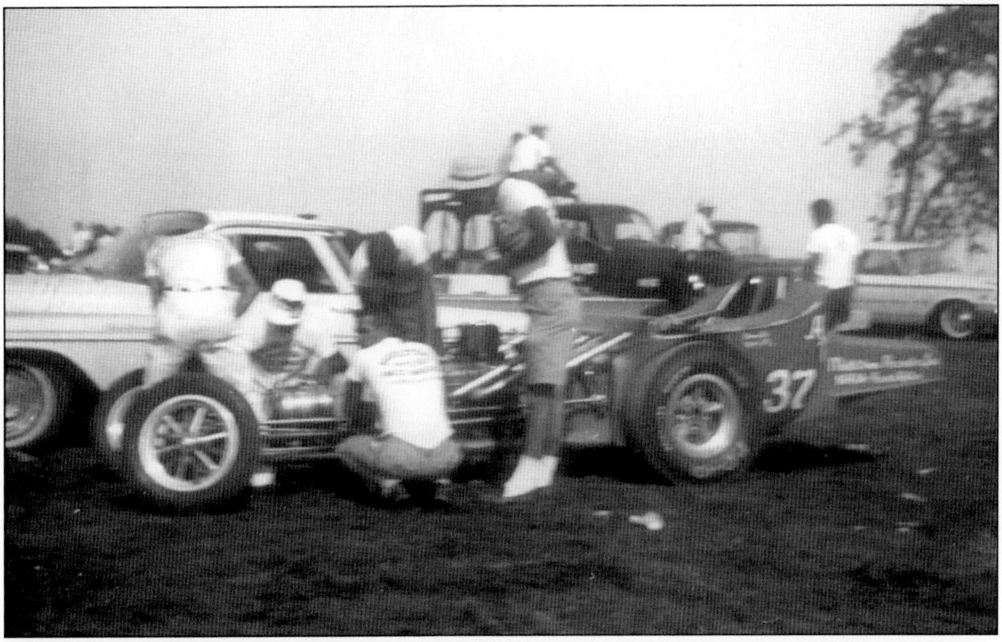

The crew is working on the A/Comp at the '63 Nationals. Dad (white baseball cap) appears to be looking into the fuel tank. Harold Barnes (stooping at center, back to camera and looking left) appears to be in conversation. Darryl Hobbs (standing at right in shorts and hat) looks on. Others are unidentified. (Hobbs collection, 1963.)

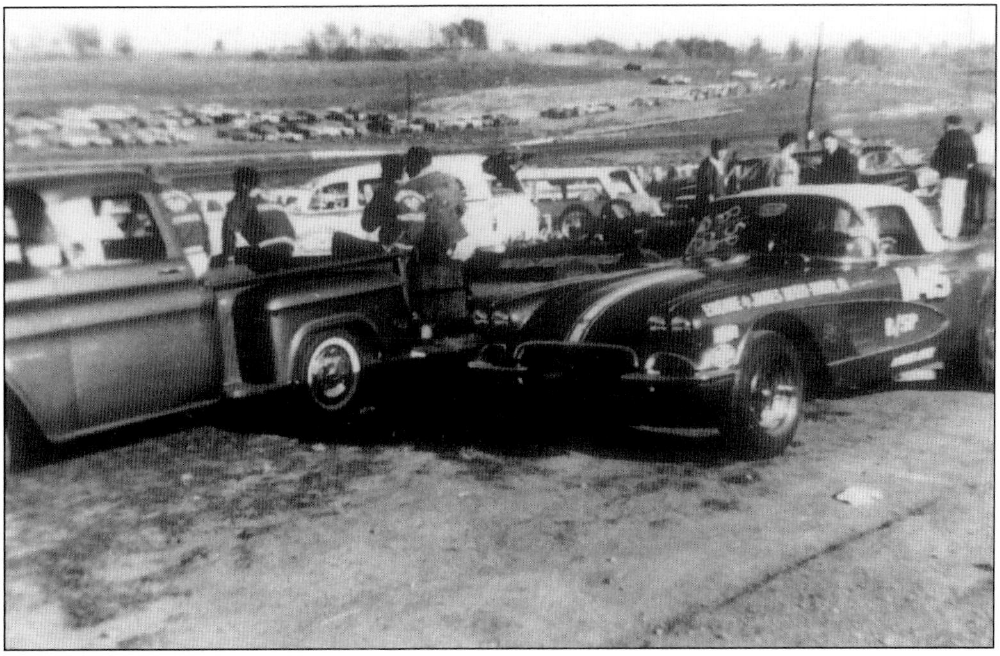

This pit shot highlights the Barnes brothers' B/Sports '61 Corvette with matching Chevy tow truck at Bluegrass Raceway in Lexington in September, 1964. Several unidentified club members in Pacemaker jackets are watching the action seated in the back of the pickup truck. The Pacemakers' '54 Pontiac station wagon is in the background. (Barnes collection, 1964.)

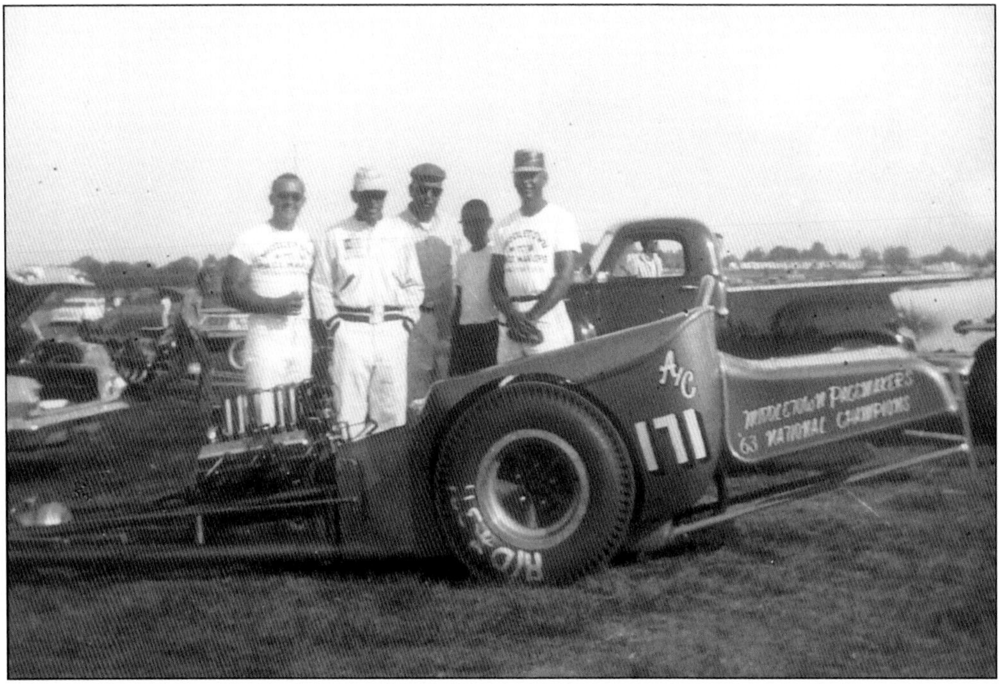

The crew poses for a group shot at the '64 Nationals. From left to right are Phil Norris, Darryl Hobbs, Tom Bishop, the author (at 14), and Dad. Note that the roll bar has been raised to accommodate a new minimum height rule. Dad's '50 Studebaker truck is in the background. (Hobbs collection, 1964.)

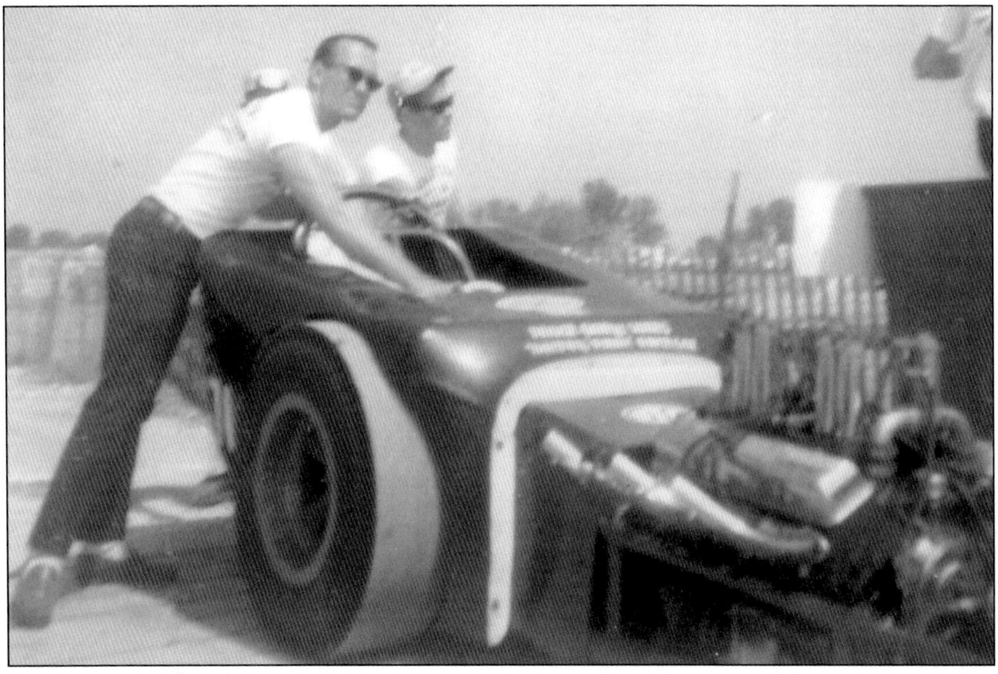

Phil Norris (left) and Darryl Hobbs (right) push the car in the staging lanes at Indy. (Hobbs collection, 1964.)

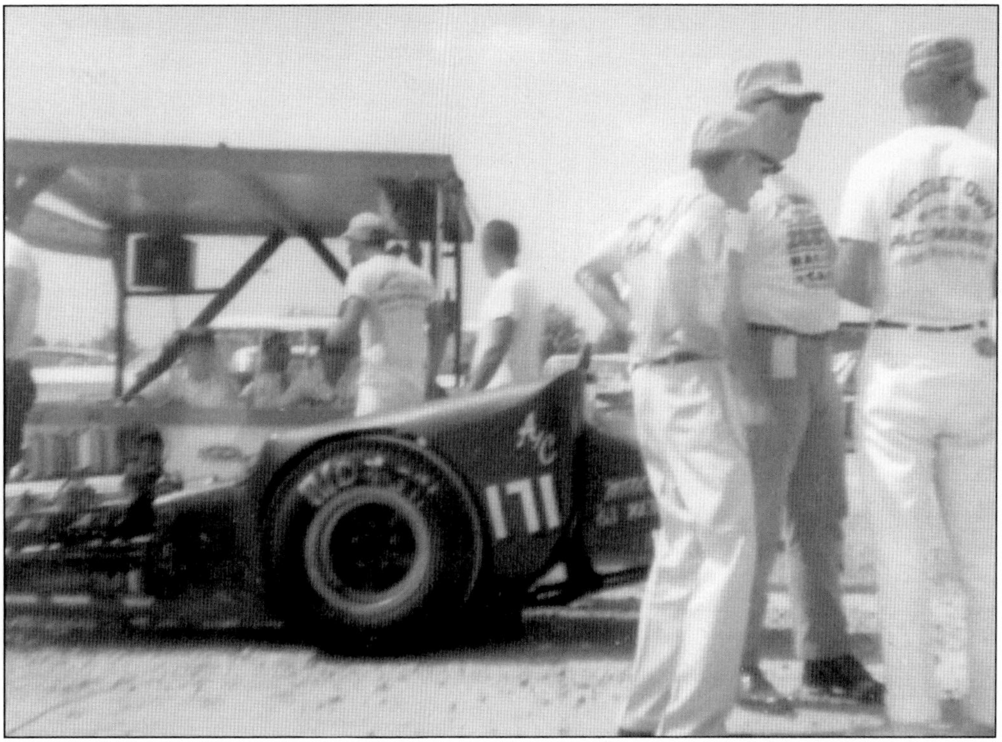

Cluster Buster stalwart Charlie Mann is helping to tech the "Pacemaker Special" at the '64 Nationals. Standing, from left to right, are Darryl Hobbs (behind the car in the baseball cap), Don Klamo, Charlie Mann, an unidentified track official, and Dad. (Hobbs collection, 1964.)

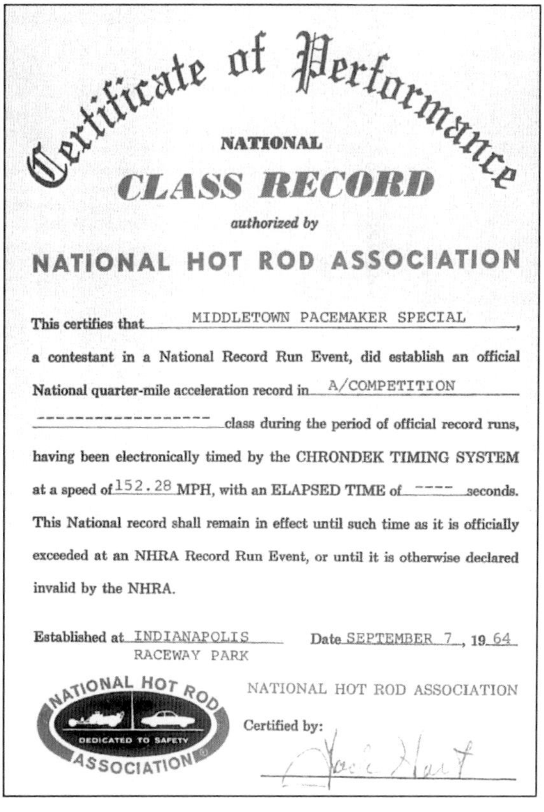

Certificate of Performance

NATIONAL

CLASS RECORD

authorized by

NATIONAL HOT ROD ASSOCIATION

This certifies that MIDDLETOWN PACEMAKER SPECIAL,

a contestant in a National Record Run Event, did establish an official National quarter-mile acceleration record in A/COMPETITION

------------------ class during the period of official record runs, having been electronically timed by the CHRONDEK TIMING SYSTEM at a speed of 152.28 MPH, with an ELAPSED TIME of ---- seconds.

This National record shall remain in effect until such time as it is officially exceeded at an NHRA Record Run Event, or until it is otherwise declared invalid by the NHRA.

Established at INDIANAPOLIS RACEWAY PARK Date SEPTEMBER 7, 19 64

NATIONAL HOT ROD ASSOCIATION DEDICATED TO SAFETY

NATIONAL HOT ROD ASSOCIATION

Certified by: Jack Hart

This NHRA certificate of performance signed by Jack Hart was presented to the Pacemakers for Don Klamo's record run of 152.28 mph in the "Pacemaker Special" A/Comp at the '64 Nationals. (Roberson photo, Palmer collection item, 1964.)

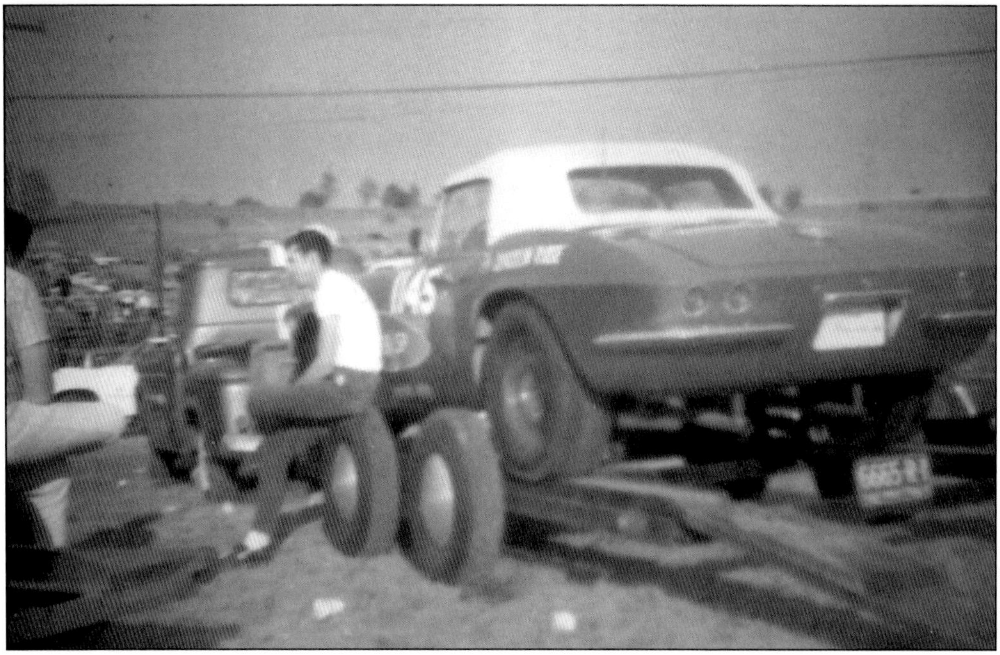

Club members Earnie and Harold Barnes raced this 1961 Corvette in the B/Sports class under the name "Cracklin' Rose." The car had a fuel injected engine and sported maroon paint, as did the matching Chevy tow truck. Harold Barnes strikes a pensive pose sitting on the trailer tire. He's wearing the club tee shirt. (Barnes collection, 1964.)

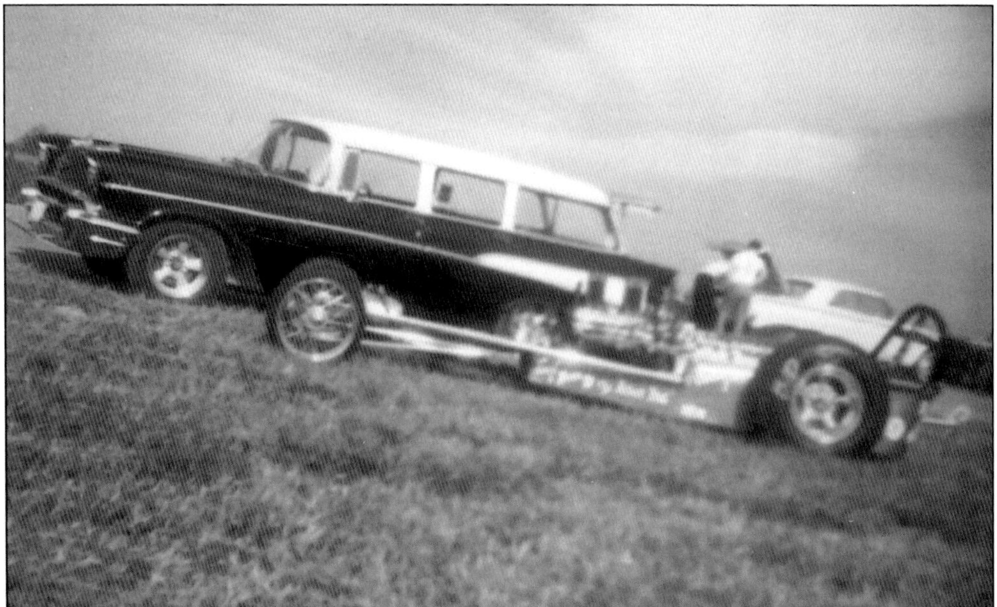

The Barnes brothers purchased the B/Dragster of Klamo-Hounshell-Rupp just after Don Klamo won the class at the inaugural NHRA Spring Nationals. They ran the car under the name "Cracklin' Rose II" and K-H-R debuted a new supercharged Olds powered AA/Dragster. (Barnes collection, 1965.)

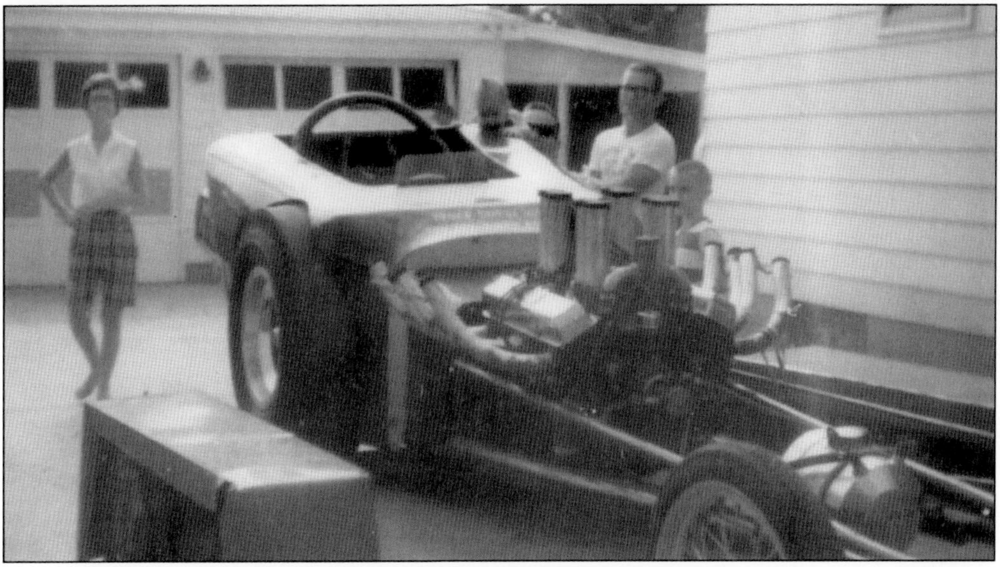

The "Pacemaker Special" rests on the trailer at our house in Trenton, ready to head out to a local track. From left to right are Betty Palmer, Darryl Hobbs (holding baby daughter Cheryl up to the car), Herb Sebastian, and Mike Palmer. (Hobbs collection, 1965.)

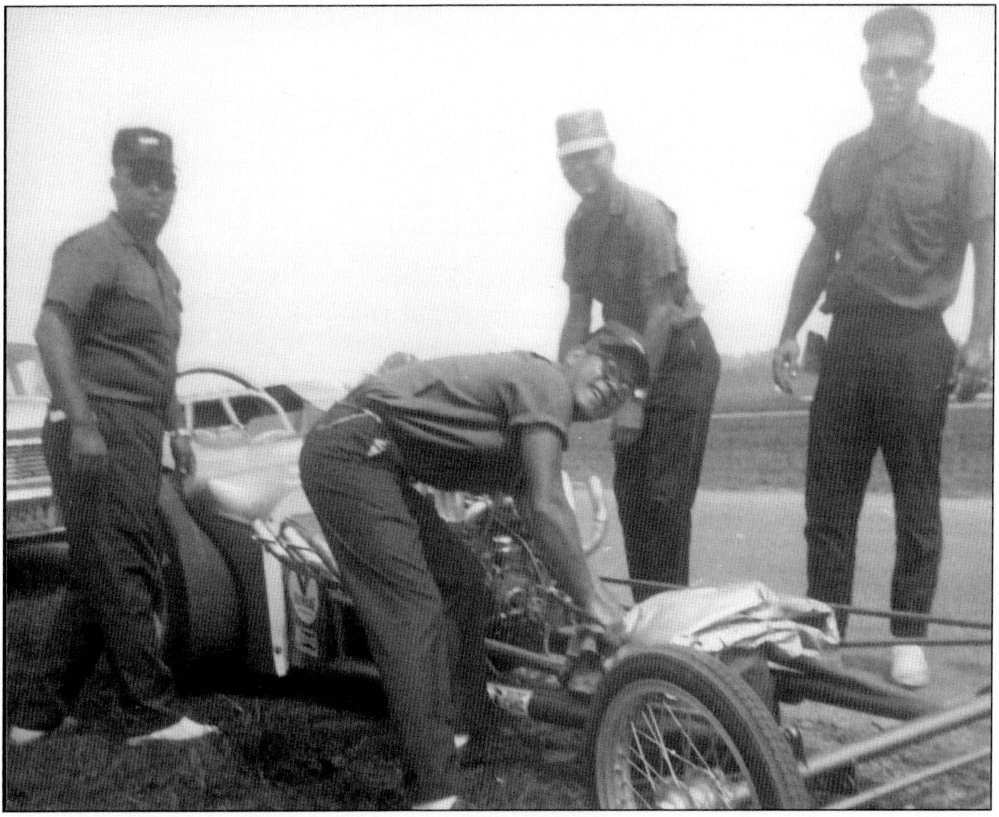

The crew readies the car for the class run offs at the '65 Nationals. From left to right are Ray Palmer, Herb Sebastian (bending toward camera), Dad, and Darryl Hobbs. (Hobbs collection, 1965.)

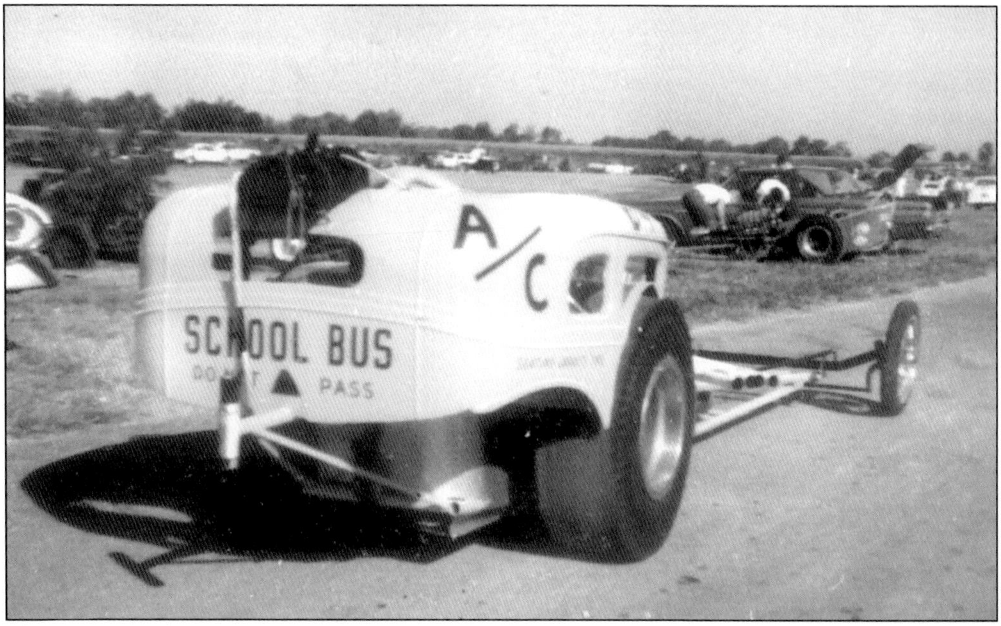

The most popular car in our A/Comp class at the '65 Nationals was Andy Sheehan's "School Bus" from Connecticut. The yellow Bantam coupe body said "Do not pass" on the back, and "Seating capacity one" on the side. Darryl raced Andy in the semifinal in the class run offs. (Hobbs collection, 1965.)

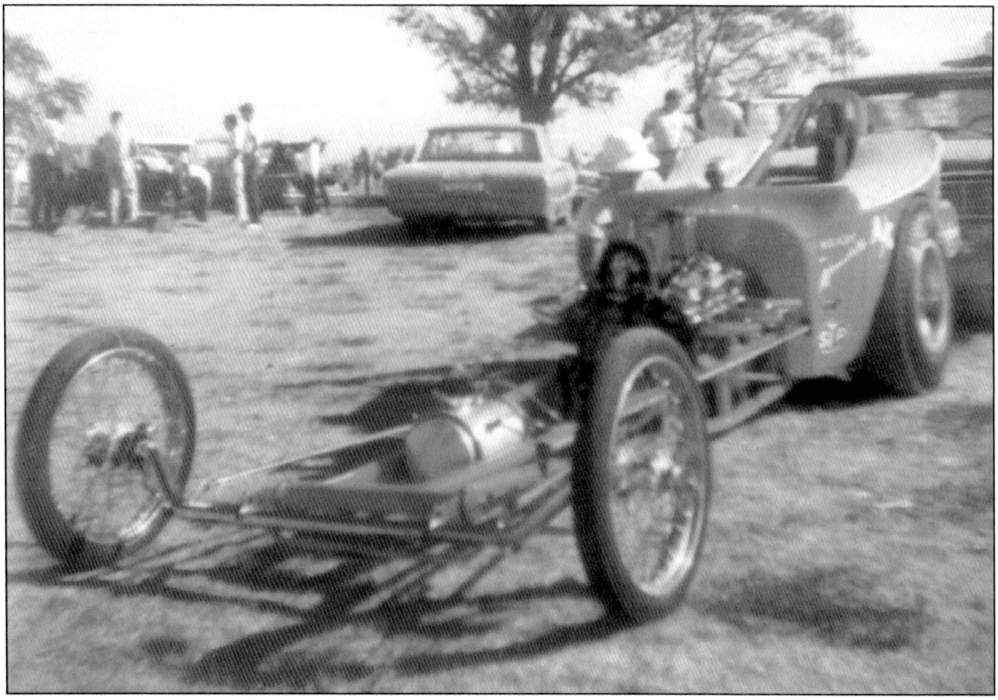

Frank Smith's awesome A/Comp from Oklahoma was easily the fastest and quickest in the country. Darryl beat Frank in the class final at Indy with a "hole shot" 9.40 ET against Frank's quicker 9.32. (Hobbs collection, 1965.)

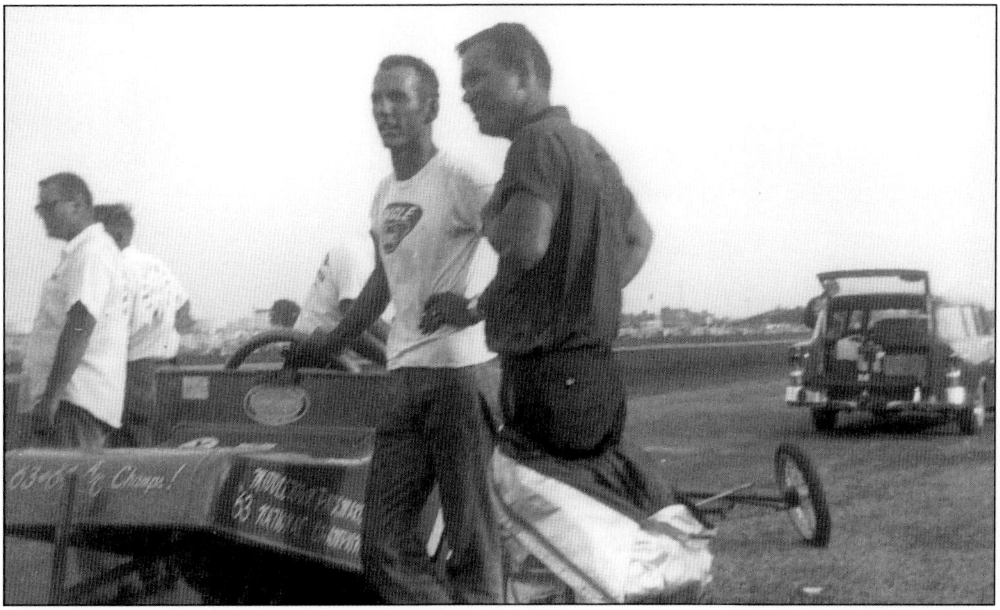

Frank Smith (left) and Darryl Hobbs (right) talk at the far end of the track after the '65 Nationals class final. Frank and twin brother Charlie were dominant forces in Competition Eliminator in the mid '60s; Frank in A/Comp and Charlie in A/Altered. Track officials at the far left are unidentified. (Hobbs collection, 1965.)

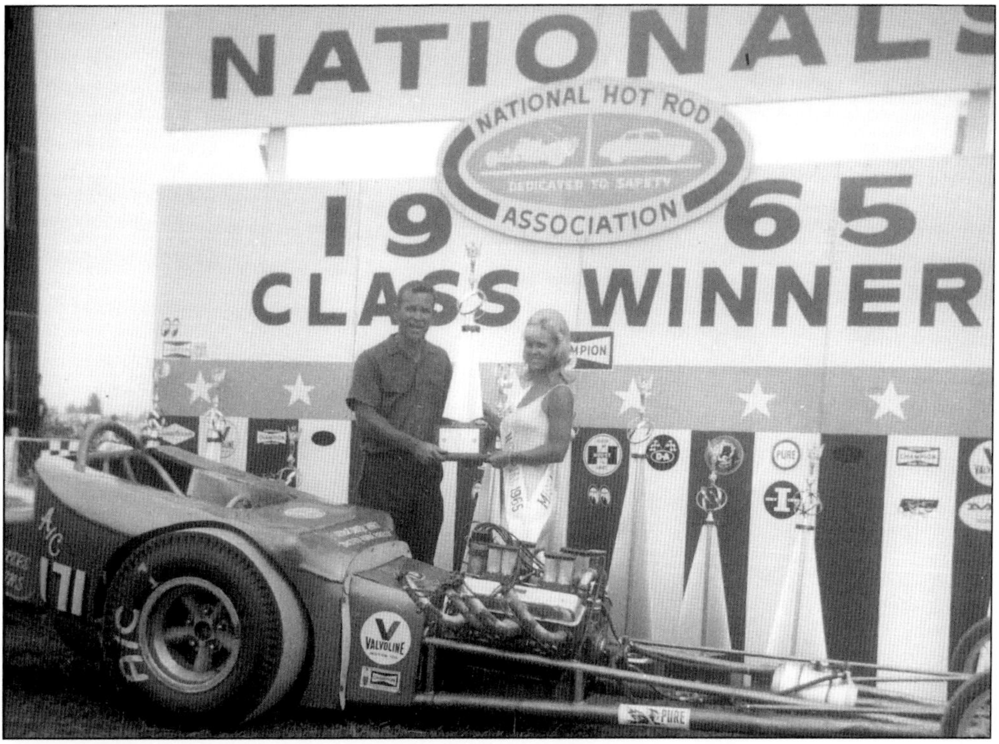

Darryl Hobbs accepts the class trophy from the trophy queen at the '65 Nationals. (Hobbs collection, 1965.)

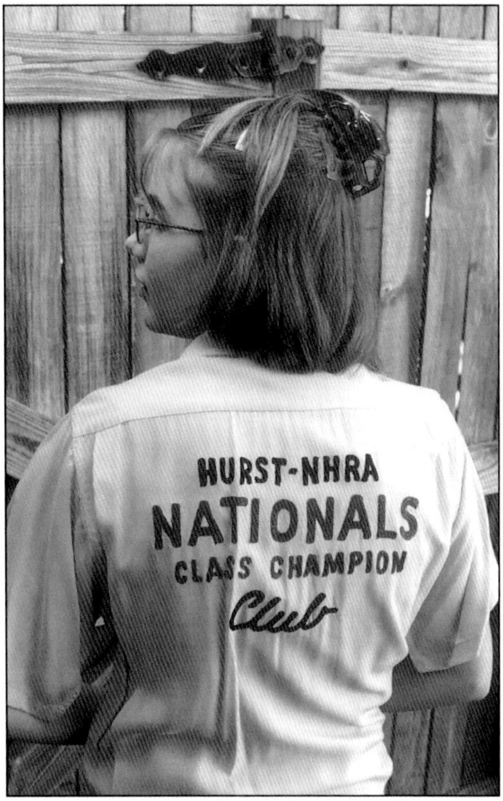

My daughter Jessica models a 35-year-old Nationals class champion shirt from the Hurst Shifter Company. (Roberson collection.)

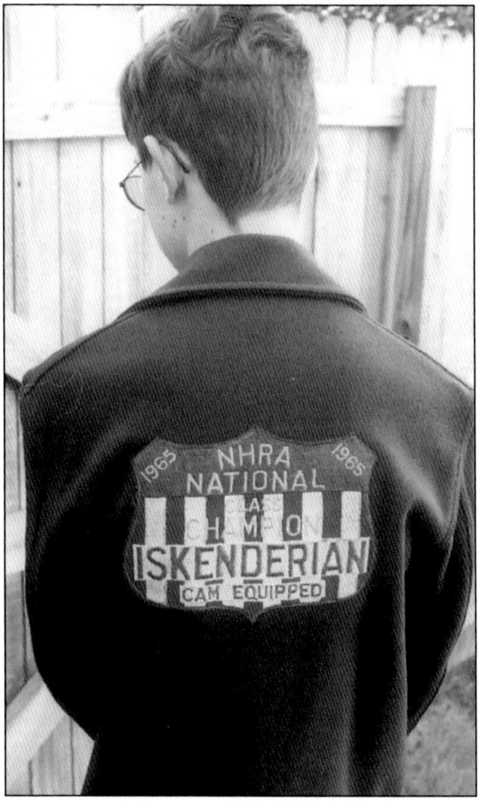

My son Jason poses in his Grandpa's 35-year-old Nationals class champion jacket from the Iskenderian Racing Cam Company. (Roberson collection.)

Eight

The Final Days and Life After the Club

Why are our days numbered and not, say, lettered?

- Woody Allen

In the 1964 model year, Pontiac introduced a special high performance version of the Tempest and gave it a name that hinted at a racing heritage—the GTO. It was a diversion from the high performance cars of the era, which were largely big, heavy cars with powerful engines, like the 409 Chevies and 390 Fords. The GTO was a smaller mid-size sporty car with a big, powerful engine—389 cubic inches with 325 horsepower. It would do 0 to 60 in 7.7 seconds and run 93 mph on the drag strip in 15.8 seconds off the showroom floor. It was not a limited production car built just for racing; it was a mass-produced hot rod built for daily use. It was perfectly timed for the baby boomer market, and its sales were fantastic. It was the first muscle car of the 1960's and '70's muscle car era. It was fast, and it was more affordable than the Corvette. The other companies followed suit, and soon the showrooms were full of Chevelle Super Sports, Olds 442's, Dodge Chargers, Ford Mustang Cobras, Camaro R/S's and S/S's, Plymouth Barracudas, Pontiac Trans Ams, and AMC AMX's all with large powerful engines in light-weight cars that performed and fulfilled a desired image. The muscle car era was on, and the traditional hot rod with its club support system was dying.

There was no need to build a hot rod when you could buy one off the show room floor and make monthly payments. It even had a warranty. If you could buy a hot rod, you didn't need the collective talent of a club to build one. There was no bartering for parts or services required. The club function, as a support mechanism for home built cars, was gone. By 1966, the country was full of commercial drag strips with hired staffs. There was no need for a car club to run a drag strip. The large-scale car shows were also commercialized with a nationwide show circuit and points system. Car clubs were no longer necessary to run the major car shows. The car clubs had changed the nation's view of hot rodding and built a support mechanism that was now self-supporting. Drag racing was big business by 1966. The speed equipment industry supporting drag racing and oval track racing was huge. The industry and the racing supported each other. The club function in running the car related activities was gone.

The car clubs of the 1950s and '60s by design were self-defeating. The car clubs developed drag racing and drag strips. Drag racing developed a market for the car manufacturers to produce muscle cars. Muscle cars replaced hot rods. The sport grew, but the seed was no longer necessary. It would take more than a decade, the legislated death of the muscle cars, and a nostalgia wave across the country to revive the car clubs. And the new wave hot rod would have a new name—the street rod.

By 1966, the Pacemakers had been around for 15 years. They had essentially seen a generation change. The guys who were older in the club's early days, like Bill Lovelace, Herb Dome, Sully Sullivan, Ray Palmer Sr., and Al Frebis had dropped out of the scene. The guys who were in their twenties in the beginning, like Dad, Herb Sebastian, Ray Palmer Jr., Alex Slamka, and

Mike Michael were now in their forties. They had businesses to tend to, or kids nearing college age, and life in general had many distractions that left little time for club activities. The younger guys who were into drag racing, like Darryl Hobbs, Jim Neely, Don Klamo, Dick Kauffman, and the Barnes brothers really didn't need the club to continue racing. The club had served as their racing school, and they had graduated with honors.

The Pacemaker club had served a purpose. It gave Middletown area hot rodders a place to meet and trade knowledge and ideas. It gave them legal and safe activities to attend with other car enthusiasts. It presented hot rods and rodders to the public in a proper gentleman-like image. It seriously curbed street racing in the area.

The twelfth annual Tri-State Custom Auto Show in June of 1965 would be the last for the club, although the car show survived through other promoters and continued well into the 1990s. The 1965 Nationals class win would be the club's last drag race triumph. Darryl Hobbs and partner Dave Armbruster, owner of Dason's Hardware in Middletown, purchased the A/Comp for the '66 season. The club sold the property at 406 Manatee Street and the Pontiac tow car, and by the summer of 1966 the Pacemakers were gone. I turned 16 that August, the birthday that would have qualified me to become a full member.

It was a sad time, but it seemed like a fitting thing, because the whole world seemed to be changing. A war was escalating in Southeast Asia that would prove to be unpopular and promote anti war demonstrations. The Civil Rights movement would lead to riots and the untimely death of Martin Luther King. Rich/poor class distinction would lead to the assassination of Robert Kennedy. The times were becoming complex, and the pure and simple sport of hot rodding, a throw back of the 1950s, didn't seem to fit in.

In 1966, Darryl Hobbs and Dave Armbruster campaigned the A/Comp with few changes from the '65 season. Armbruster shared the driving chores, and the team ran quite well, earning a class runner up spot at the Nationals. In 1967, Darryl bought out Dave's share, and Armbruster approached Dad and Herb Sebastian to build him a car. The team built an A/Comp late in the season, and debuted it at the Nationals. The brand new Chevy small block engine had a crack in the block that allowed one cylinder to fill up with water, and put the car on the trailer before it made its first pass. For 1968, the car was converted to a B/Dragster, which ran quite well and bore the name "Pacemaker Special." It ran a Chevy engine, which Dad had built, and utilized one of the new M&M Clutch Flite transmissions, made by modifying a Plymouth Torque Flite.

They towed the car to the Winternationals in 1969, a long haul from Middletown to Pomona, California. At the '69 Winternationals, they posted such good numbers that it drew the attention of Funny Car engine builder Ed Pink, who wanted to know the builder of the hot Chevy. Pink was interested in building a sportsman Hemi, and began to pitch the idea to Armbruster, knowing that this team would get the most out of his engine. After several conversations with Pink, Armbruster decided to purchase a Chrysler Hemi from Pink's shop in California. According to Pink, it was the first unblown, gasoline Hemi that he had built, and it registered 640 horsepower on his dynamometer. The team started the Midwest '69 season with the Pink Hemi powered B/Dragster, and the car was awesome. It ran mid 8-second times at nearly 170 mph and won often. It nearly won the B/Dragster class at the Nationals, losing on a hole shot in the final. But after the '69 Nationals, Dad began to lose interest in the team. With the professionally built engine, the game had lost its challenge. Besides, Dave was now an experienced racer and was learning to do his own tuning.

The swan song with Armbruster was the inaugural Gatornationals, which was run at Gainesville, Florida, in February of 1970. (Later the meet would move to mid March.) Dad and Dave towed the car to Florida along with Don Klamo, who agreed to a one-meet driver deal. With cool weather and dense low-altitude air, Dad soon had the car dialed in, and the veteran driver Klamo was running below the class elapsed time record nearly every pass. They qualified easily, but faced a dilemma when the elimination racing started. Don had trouble seeing out of the car, which had been built around a taller driver, and he couldn't judge where to shut off to keep from breaking out (i.e., running faster than the record would disqualify you in competition). So Dad would quickly drive the push car down the return road while Don slowly staged, and he'd park at the spot where he wanted Don to back off the throttle. This method got them to the semi-final round in Competition Eliminator, when Don broke out against Tommy Shinholster, who won the meet one round later in the final. After the Gatornationals, Dad left the Armbruster team.

A free agent, Dad was immediately contacted by old buddies Darryl Hobbs and Don Klamo. After the '66 partnership with Dave Armbruster, Darryl sat out of racing for a short time. Don had continued to run his AA/Dragster with partners Marion Hounshell and Gary Rupp, then split from the team and went back to a Chevy-powered B/Dragster, which ran under the name "Quarter Horse." Marion turned the AA into a show car, and Rupp built his own Top Gas dragster, then went on to field a series of Top Fuel cars with driver Pat Dakin. In the process, Gary Rupp became one of the most respected independent Top Fuel crew chiefs in the sport, running competitively against the big dollar teams that had major sponsors. Together Rupp and Dakin won the inaugural NHRA LeGrand Nationals Top Fuel title in 1971, repeated in 1973, and went on to be a top runner in NHRA and IHRA Top Fuel competition.

Darryl was itching to get back into racing for the 1970 season, and he had bought a Chrysler Hemi engine from Dayton's Paul Frost that Paul had run in a super stocker. He proposed that Dad rebuild the Hemi and they shoe horn it in to Don's nimble little dragster chassis. Dad had never built a Hemi, but had learned a lot about them running Armbruster's car. He jumped at the chance to build one, and teaming with the two old friends and die-hard racers was enough to put the spark back into the sport for Dad.

Dad went to work on the engine, and on the modification of Don's car, which had to be widened to accept the mammoth engine. He replaced the Hemi's stock pistons with domed versions to raise the compression, and added a Vertex magneto, a gear drive Crane cam, and Hilborn fuel injection. The team of Klamo-Hobbs-Roberson debuted the car with a few break-in runs at Edgewater and ran an 8.40 elapsed time on the car's fifth run. The class record stood at 8.41, so they were quite happy with the shakedown runs. Then they traveled to Milan, Michigan, to run an NHRA record meet. At Milan, Klamo made an off-the-trailer run of 8.26 seconds! The competition stood in awe. Division 3 Director Bob Daniels came over to them and placed a seal on the engine and asked if they wanted to make the required back up run to establish a new national record. The team decided not to pursue the record, since they had no idea if they could remain competitive in the handicap system with it. After all, it was the car's first competitive meet. Dad with his engine building skills, and Darryl and Don with their respective driving skills had mastered the powerful Hemi just as they had the scrappy small block Chevy. These veteran drag racers with a limited budget, a used engine, and an old chassis made quite a team.

The team of Klamo-Hobbs-Roberson had an outstanding season in 1970. They won at the local tracks nearly everywhere they went. In July, they went to another semi-final round at the inaugural Summernationals in York, Pennsylvania. They had gotten by the local B/Dragster team of Schmitz and Wallace (of later top alcohol dragster fame) in the first round, driver Bill Wallace being a Middletown resident. Tom Smith won the meet, but the guys were pleased with the showing. Dad's good friend Roy Roberts worked on the crew that year. Roy was an excellent photographer and left us with numerous high quality photos of the Klamo-Hobbs-Roberson dragster. But 1970 would prove to be Dad's last race season. He had recurring problems with phlebitis, blood clots forming in his legs as a result of the WWII wound, and in 1971 he began to consider the sale of the radiator shop and an early retirement.

The '60s were drag racing's Golden Age. The decade came in with innovative racecars, still largely home built with parts from junkyards and local machine shops. It went out with professionally built cars and professional racers. The '60s saw the development of the funny car, the pro stockers, electronic starting systems, nationally televised drag races, and the building of the first super tracks. The Ohio drag strips hosted some of the best racers in the country by the end of the decade. The Rod Shop team, the Ramchargers, Jeg Coughlin, Sam Giannino, Joe Schubeck, Gordon Collett, George Montgomery, Fred Hurst, Sam Parks, Paul Longnecker, Bill

King, and many others were likely to be at the meets we ran. And the professional match race circuits brought us all the best top fuelers, funny cars, and fuel altereds from all over the country. Drag racing was maturing quickly, and it was getting very expensive to race competitively. Soon the numbers of competitors would begin to drop, and it would take the innovation of bracket racing to revive the grass roots segment of the sport.

I graduated from Trenton High School in 1968, and started college at Miami University's Middletown Campus that fall. I moved to the Oxford campus my junior year and graduated with a B.S. in chemistry in June of 1972. Dad sold the shop that same month, and the family moved to Clearwater, Florida. I had not yet found a job in the depressed chemical industry, so I followed them. I got a job with Stauffer Chemical Company in Tarpon Springs, Florida in September, working in the newly expanding environmental field that had been prompted by the 1970 federal acts that formed the EPA and OSHA.

Dad was restless at first in retirement, and nearly drove Mom crazy. A chance encounter got him back into racing. My brother Marty was still in high school when we moved, and he and I immediately found the local drag strip—Sunshine Drag Strip in St. Petersburg. We began to frequent the Friday night meets there. The complex also had a quarter mile paved oval track, which ran on Saturday nights, but we only attended the drag races at first. We got to know some of the drag racers, and I always checked the local newspaper, which printed the box score results each week for both tracks. One Sunday, I happened to look at the oval track results and saw the name Earnie Barnes listed as third in one of the heats.

By the time we left Ohio, Jim Neely and John Buehl had sold their funny car, and Jim had concentrated his efforts on a tune up business that he had opened in Middletown. The Kaufmans were no longer racing their super stock Ford. Hobbs was running a B/Dragster, and Klamo was still running his B/Dragster. The Barnes brothers had moved to Florida in the late '60s, but we didn't know exactly where. Earnie came by the shop one day in 1970 or '71 while vacationing and visiting relatives. He told us they were racing round track cars in Florida, but we failed to get his address. After all it was a big state, and what were the chances of winding up in the same area? My Grandpa Bill had retired to Englewood, Florida, in 1958, and we visited him several times before he moved again, this time to Arizona. After that, we had vacationed in Florida regularly, spending a week in Daytona and a week in St. Petersburg, and Mom and Dad had not yet picked the area to which they would retire. When we did get to Florida, we did not know that the Barneses lived in the same county.

I showed the newspaper to Dad and encouraged him to come with Marty and me to Sunshine Speedway. Marty and I were determined to find out if it was indeed the same Earnie Barnes that had been in the Pacemakers. Dad was a much better racer than he was a spectator, and he was reluctant to go, but we talked him into it.

At the track, we found out that the pits were closed to spectators until after the racing was over. Being drag racers, this seemed odd, but we took our seats in the stands and watched the action. The racing was great with several classes, including Late Models and the Thunder Car class in which Earnie competed. We watched him run the first heat in his '55 Chevy. He had a problem and coasted to the infield. He got out of the car and sat on the fender watching the remainder of the heat. When we saw the slightly built figure emerge from the car we knew we had the right Earnie Barnes. After the last race, we went into the pits and had a surprise reunion with Earnie, Harold and their brother Jim, or "J.D.," whom we had barely known before. We were introduced to their buddy Frank Barfus, who ran a similar car. Harold immediately asked Dad if he could build them an engine, and within a few weeks, both Earnie and Frank's cars were running Dad's engines. We were back into racing, and Dad spent the mid '70s building round track engines. In addition to Earnie and Frank, he built engines for J.D. Barnes, Bob Pennington, Woody Miller, Fred Lane, Dave Riddlebarger, and some others who ran at Sunshine. It wasn't drag racing, but it was fun, and since Dad began his race career with a midget racer, he had come full circle back to oval tracks.

In addition to the round track engines, Dad would occasionally build a street engine for some of the local street machine crowd. In a few years, the Barneses got out of racing, and Dad soon lost interest. He still had the phlebitis problems and long hours standing on the garage floor didn't help. He again got out of racing, but the tinkering didn't stop. Marty and I had both acquired VW powered dune buggies, and Dad wound up building high performance VW engines for both cars.

Marty had graduated from Clearwater High School in 1974 and attended St. Petersburg Junior College for two years. On August 19, 1977, he eloped with his high school sweetheart, Linda Conkel, and went to work shortly thereafter at the Square D plant in Clearwater. I had met my future bride, Sherrill Erickson, in 1976, and we were married in a small ceremony at her parent's home in St. Petersburg on August 18, 1979.

We kept in touch with a lot of former club members. Darryl Hobbs and family visited Florida each spring, and Darryl ran the Gatornationals several times in the mid '70s with a rear engine Hemi-powered A/Dragster driven by later NHRA Divisional Director Keith Ferrell, former campaigner of the famous "Dog Catcher" Willys gasser. Former club member Bob Kuhn and his wife, Shirley, had also retired to Clearwater, as had Alex Slamka's widow, Marge, with her new husband, Middletonian Bob McFeeters. Mike and Polly Michael often visited Clearwater to see their long time friends. Other members popped in from time to time, including Don Klamo, Herb Sebastian and Gene Wells. Marty and I would rush to Mom and Dad's house to see any of the old Pacemakers that were visiting, especially Mike, who was such a good story teller and whose racing roots went back to the '40s.

In 1977, I began to assemble a Pacemaker scrap book using a few photos and some articles from some old car magazines I had found. It was a start, but the club history still had a lot of holes in it. The following spring, Darryl and Kathy Hobbs came to Florida and saw the scrapbook. They had lots of photos from 1963 to '65 and sent them to me when they got back to Ohio. This increased the scrapbook considerably and gave me lots of clues to identify photos from those three years. I began to find more and older magazines at swap meets, and each new find provided lots of information. The magazines provided dates and places and events that were often guessed at from loose, undated photos. Soon the club history began to gel.

In 1981, Marty, Bill Haggerty and I got into racing radio controlled scale model cars. We belonged to the Pinellas (County) Electric Auto Racers, or PEAR club, but raced as a three-man team under the name "Pacemaker Racing Team." We had team shirts, and through 1986 we carried on the name of the Pacemaker club in one-twelfth scale. We competed at two Winternationals in Orlando and raced in the state points series for several years, traveling throughout most of Florida in the process.

In 1992, Mike and Polly Michael were visiting Florida, and as always I went rushing over to see them with the latest expansion of the scrapbook in tow. I suggested that we hold a club reunion and offered to put the scrapbook on slides for the occasion. Mike told me he would pass the word along and see if anyone was interested. It took two years to make it happen, but the first reunion of the club took place in June of 1994 (on the 40th anniversary of the club's first car show) at the historic Manchester Inn in Middletown. The reunion consisted of a banquet at which I presented a slide show that depicted the club's history. Over 40 people attended with many bringing memorabilia that was displayed for all to see. There were jackets, tee shirts, arm bands, trophies, and two large banners. Paul Scorti brought a poster from the 1957 Tri-State Custom Auto show and gave it to me. I was also given some photographs and two copies of the club's code of ethics. Bill Burton brought some slides from the 1958 Nationals and showed them. There were lots of hugs and laughs, tears and stories, and we left the room planning the next year's reunion.

The following year we held a second reunion, this time a picnic at Armco Park near Lebanon, Ohio. Mike and Polly had brought photos of Mike's 1940s round track roadster. Darryl Hobbs showed up a bit late. He had attended his high school reunion in Ashland, Kentucky, the night before and had driven all night to get to the Pacemaker reunion. Ray Palmer brought some home movies that he loaned to me. I hand carried them on the airplane back to Florida, and anxiously threaded the film through my ancient Super 8 projector. As I watched the flickering images of the first two "Pacemaker Specials" racing on the screen, I felt like Indiana Jones discovering the Holy Grail.

In 1996, a third reunion was held at the Country Buffet Restaurant in Middletown. At that reunion I was showing Gene Wells a photo of the 1958 "Pacemaker Special" dragster. "Look how primitive it looks today," he said. "You know, I went 130 mph in that car. What in the world was I thinking?" We took turns telling stories to the group that night, and I told the story of Fred May nominating me for honorary membership when I was five. The 88-year old gentleman laughed and admitted that he did not remember the story. He told me later that night that he wanted to design a club tee shirt for the next reunion, as he had designed the club jacket logo some 45 years earlier. He passed away a couple of months later. But the real guts of the matter came in a conversation that night between Dad and Dick Miltenberger. Dick had been ill and missed the '95 reunion. He was nearly blind and was emaciated from his illness, weighing about half what he weighed in football form. He and Dad sat and talked about old times for a while, and then Dick summed up the story of the Pacemakers in a simple proclamation: "We had some great times back then, didn't we Robbie?" Dad agreed as Dick continued. "And we didn't do one thing that anyone should be ashamed of." Six weeks later Dick passed away.

I remember one day at the drags when I was about seven or eight, Gene Wells had made a run with the dragster, and in those days they pushed the car back to the pits with the tow car. This required a driver, and the guys would take turns in the cockpit often letting me ride along on their laps. This time Dad took the wheel, and naturally I was riding on his lap, wide eyed and in seventh heaven, straining to see over the cowl and past the massive Olds engine with its six carburetors. As the '47 Buick pushed us down the return road toward the pits, we passed three teenagers standing by the fence near the pit entrance. As we made the turn into the pit area we heard one of them say, "Man, look at that lucky little kid!" I didn't have to look around to see where he was pointing. I knew exactly who that lucky little kid was. And I was having the time of my life.

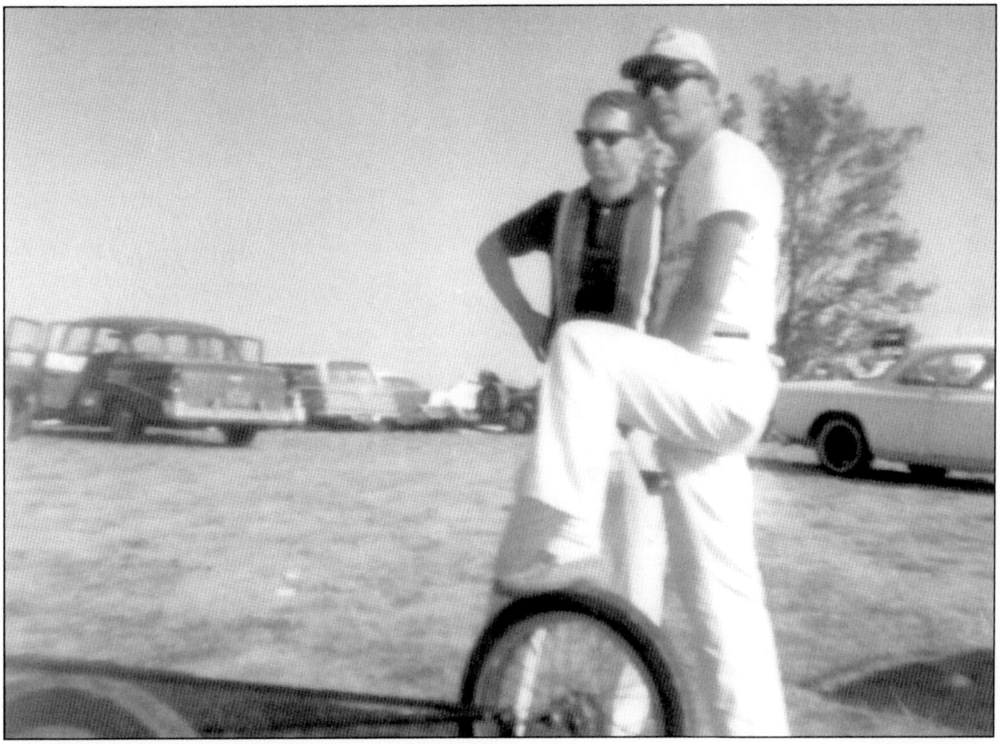

When the Pacemakers dissolved in 1966, Darryl Hobbs (right) bought the "Pacemaker Special" with partner Dave Armbruster (left), owner/operator of Dason's Hardware in Middletown. The team raced the 1966 season, ending with a runner-up in the A/Comp class at Indy (Hobbs collection, 1966.)

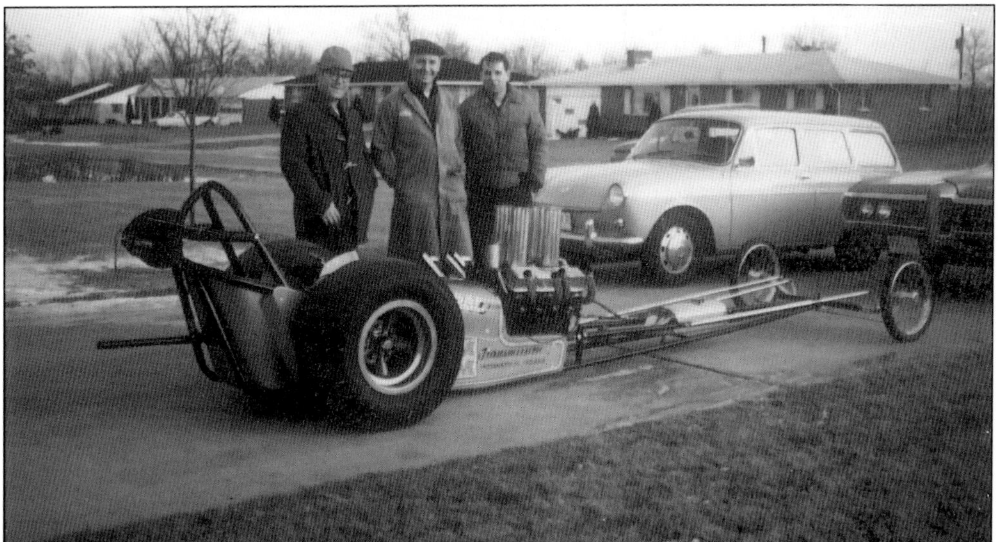

Dave Armbruster ran his own car beginning in 1967 with an A/Comp built by Dad and Herb Sebastian. For 1968, the team revamped the car into this B/Dragster with Chevy power. From left to right are Herb Sebastian, Dad, and Dave Armbruster. (Roberson collection, 1968.)

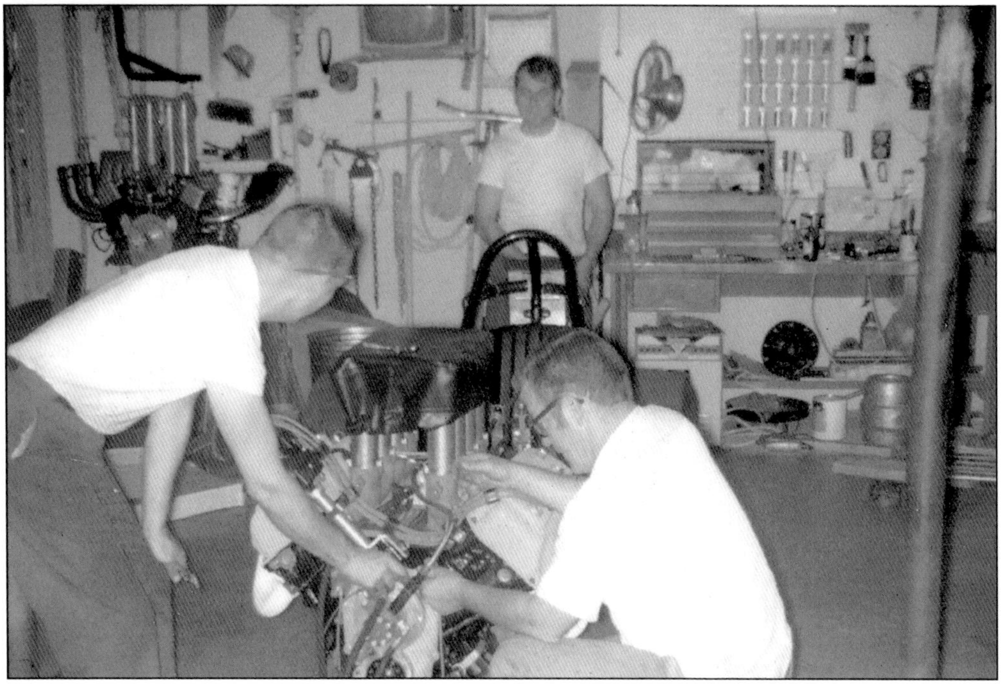

After meeting California engine builder Ed Pink at the '69 Winternationals, Armbruster bought a Hemi engine from him. Dad and Herb work on the installation at Dave's residence outside of Franklin. Note the Chevy engine on a motor stand in the background. From left to right are Dad, Dave Armbruster, and Herb Sebastian. (Roberson collection, 1969.)

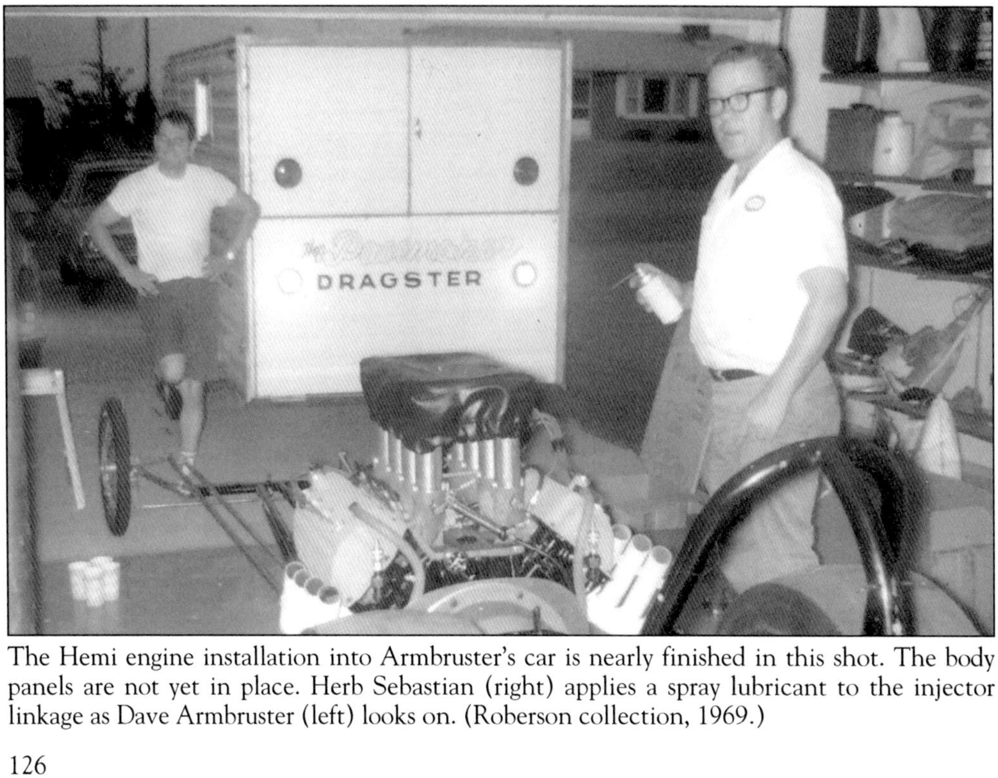

The Hemi engine installation into Armbruster's car is nearly finished in this shot. The body panels are not yet in place. Herb Sebastian (right) applies a spray lubricant to the injector linkage as Dave Armbruster (left) looks on. (Roberson collection, 1969.)

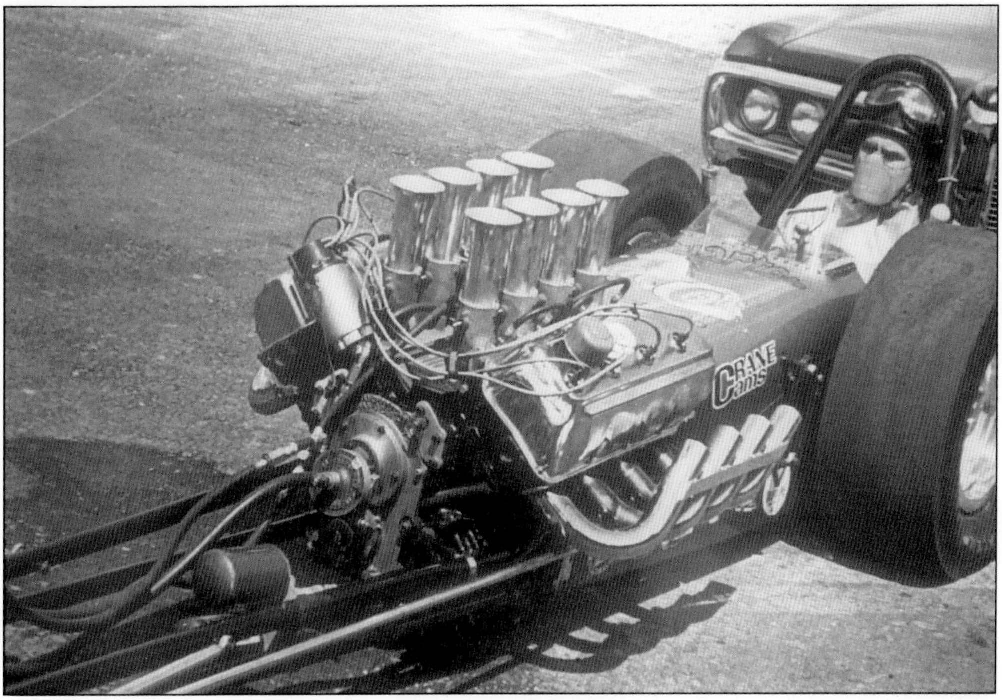

For 1970, Dad teamed with Darryl Hobbs and Don Klamo in a Dad-built Hemi-powered B/ Dragster. In this Roy Roberts photo Darryl Hobbs looks intensely over the injector stacks as the Hemi fires up on its maiden voyage. The car is shown still painted in Klamo's previous "Quarter Horse" theme. (Roberson collection, 1970.)

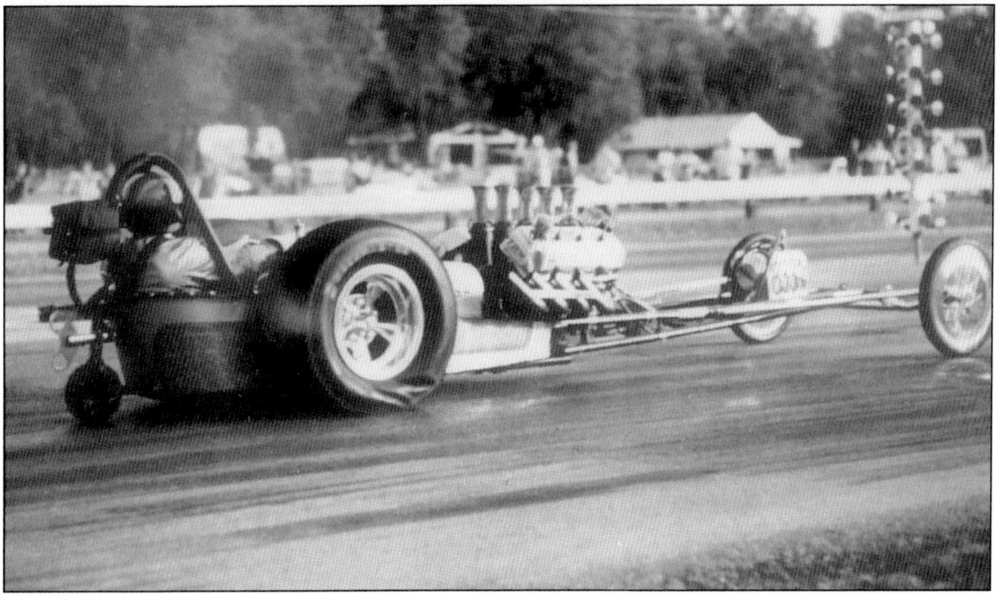

Sporting a new paint job, the Klamo-Hobbs-Roberson dragster wrinkles the slicks as Don Klamo launches the car. After some shake down runs at Edgewater, the car ran 8.26 seconds against an 8.41 national record in its first competitive meet at Milan, Michigan. (Hobbs collection, 1970.)

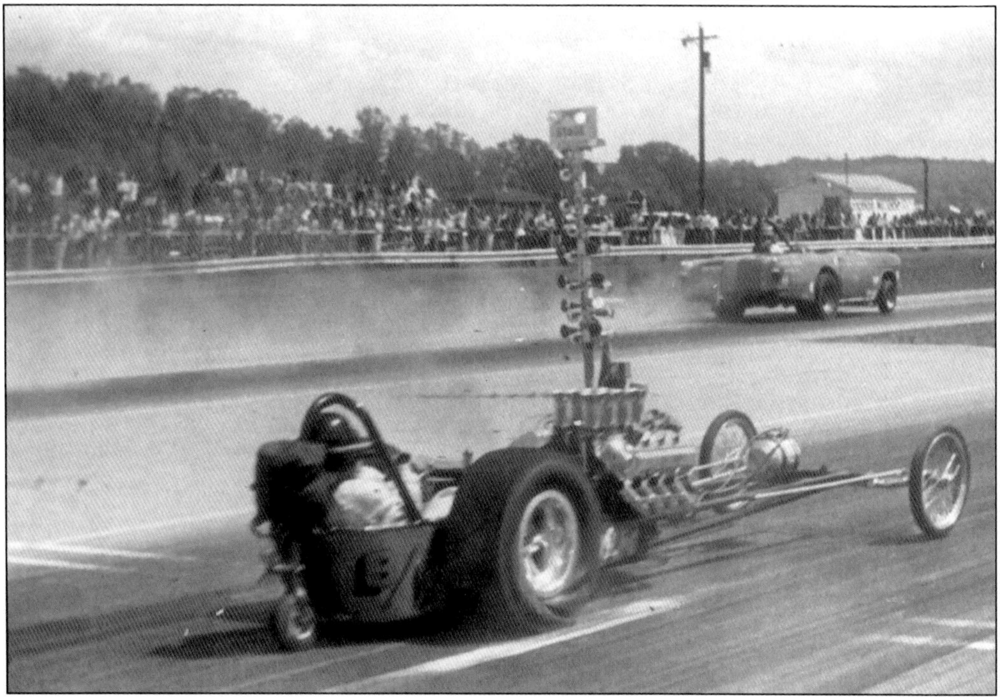

Don Klamo in the Klamo-Hobbs-Roberson B/Dragster takes off in hot pursuit of a funny-car-style '55 Chevy altered at Edgewater Dragway in this Roy Roberts photo. Note the low pressure racing slicks wrinkling under the stress. (Roberson collection, 1970.)

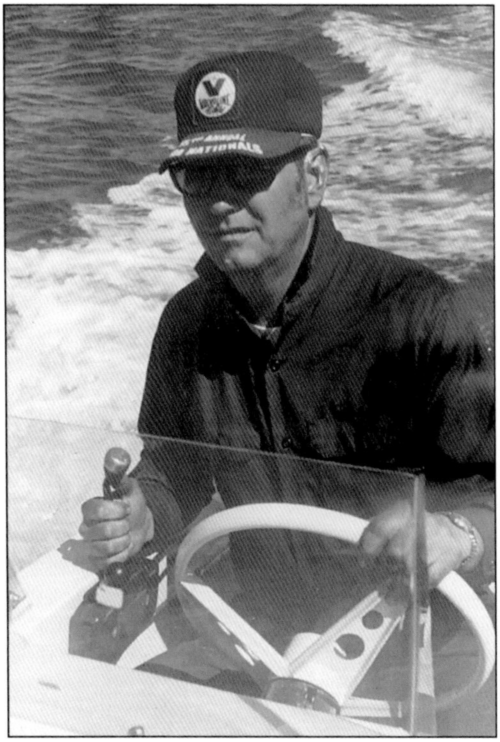

After recurring problems with phlebitis, Dad sold the radiator repair shop and retired to Florida. Here he is at the helm of his pleasure boat in a Roy Roberts photo. He looks at home on the water, but the drag racing cap indicates a link to land. (Roberson collection, 1972.)

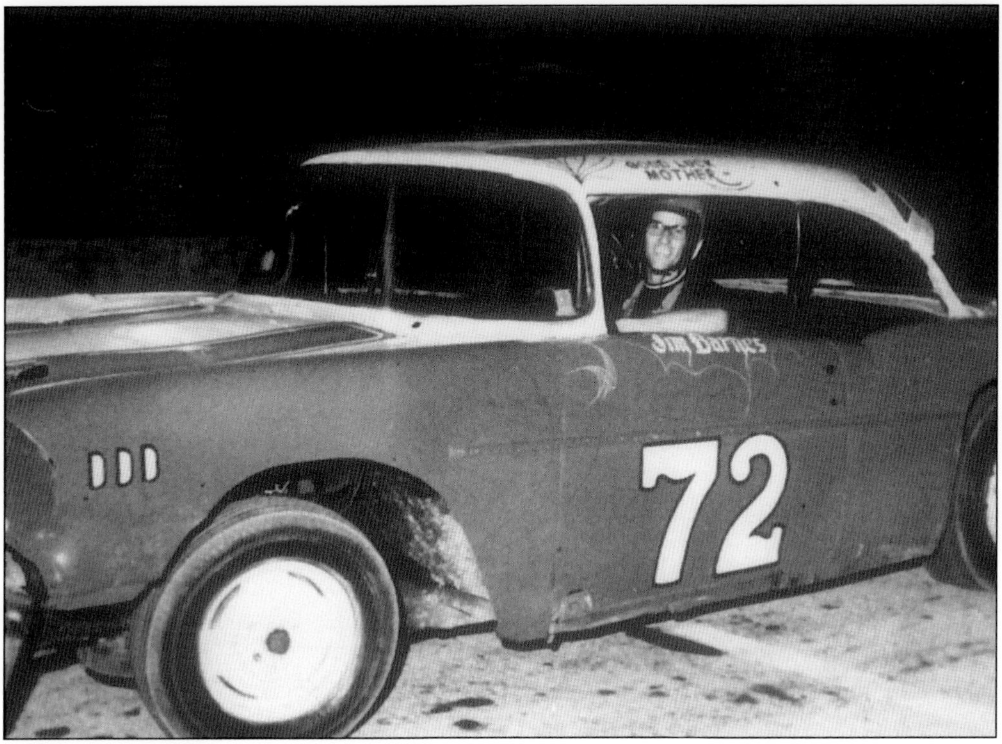

Once in Florida, Dad began a second racing career building Chevy engines for round track racers. Shown here is Jim "J.D." Barnes, brother of Pacemakers Earnie and Harold, at the wheel of his '55 Chevy Tornado car at Sunshine Speedway in St. Petersburg. J.D. played on Middletown High's championship basketball team with Jerry Lucas. (Barnes collection, 1973.)

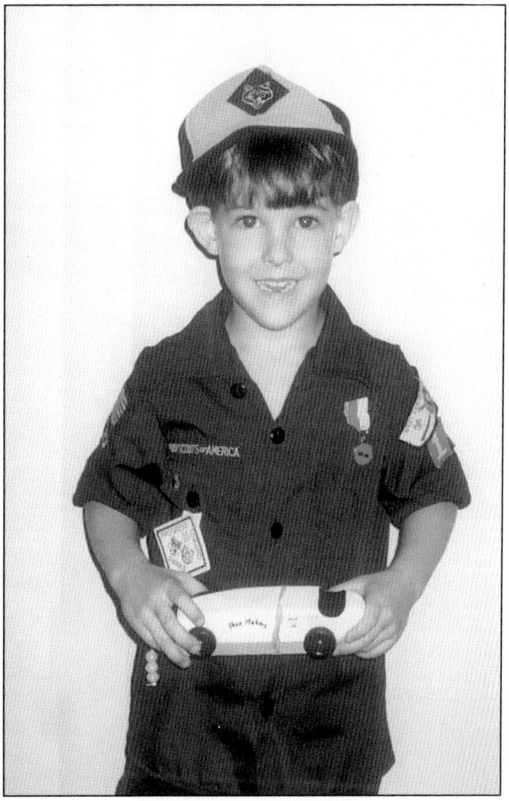

My son Jeremy poses with his Pinewood Derby racer, a near scale model of "Pacemaker Special" No. 2. The car is attached to a small board to protect the wheel alignment prior to the race. (Roberson collection, 1997.)

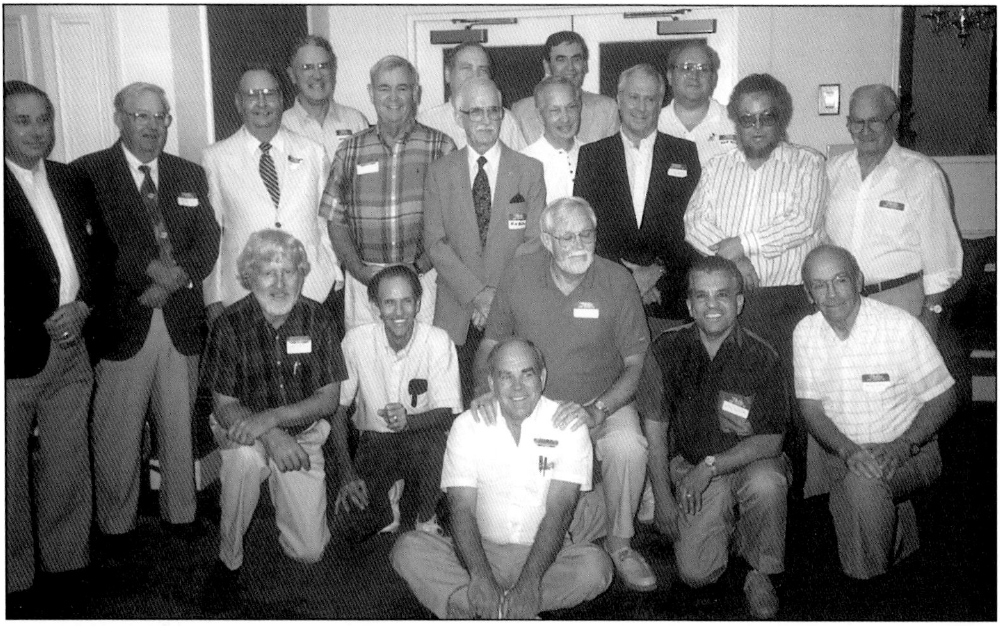

The first Pacemaker reunion was held on the 40th anniversary of the club's first car show. The club members, from left to right, are as follows: (front row) Jim Neely, Earnie Barnes, Darryl Hobbs, Carl Lakes, Paul Scorti, and Danny Allen; (back row) Winnie Lawson, Ray Palmer, Dad, L.G. Meade, Dick Miltenberger, Bill Burton, Bob Yauch (behind Burton), Don Skaggs, Harold Michael, Tom Frebis, Kenny Miller, Jim Tincher, and Fred May (Lakes collection, 1994.)

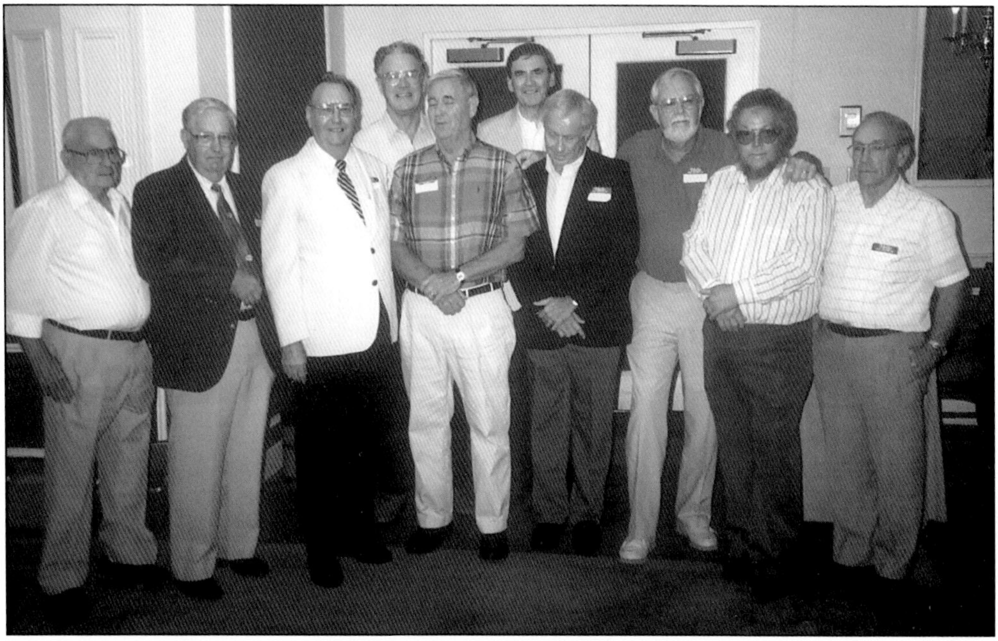

These charter members (from March 1951) posed at the first reunion in June of 1994. From left to right are Fred May, Ray Palmer, Dad, L.G. Meade, Dick Miltenberger, Harold Michael, Tom Frebis, Carl Lakes, Jim Tincher, and Danny Allen. Jim Tincher, who turned 16 on May 2, 1951, lied about his age to join in March. (Lakes collection, 1994.)

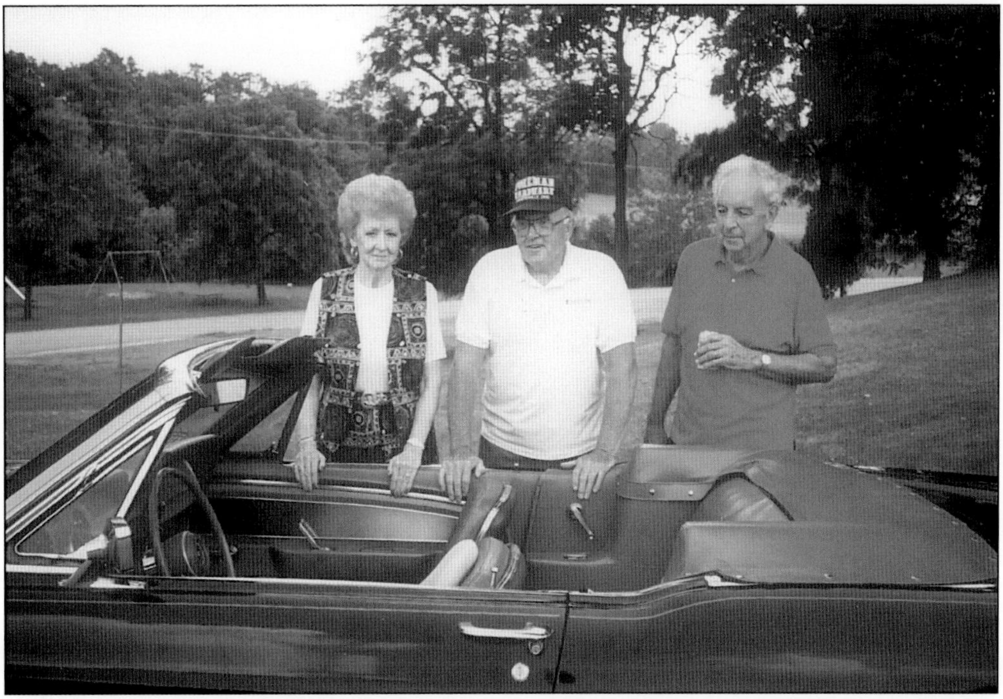

From left to right Polly Michael, Dale Foreman, and Tom Bishop admire Dale's early Mustang convertible at the second Pacemaker reunion at Armco Park in 1995. (Roberson collection, 1995.)

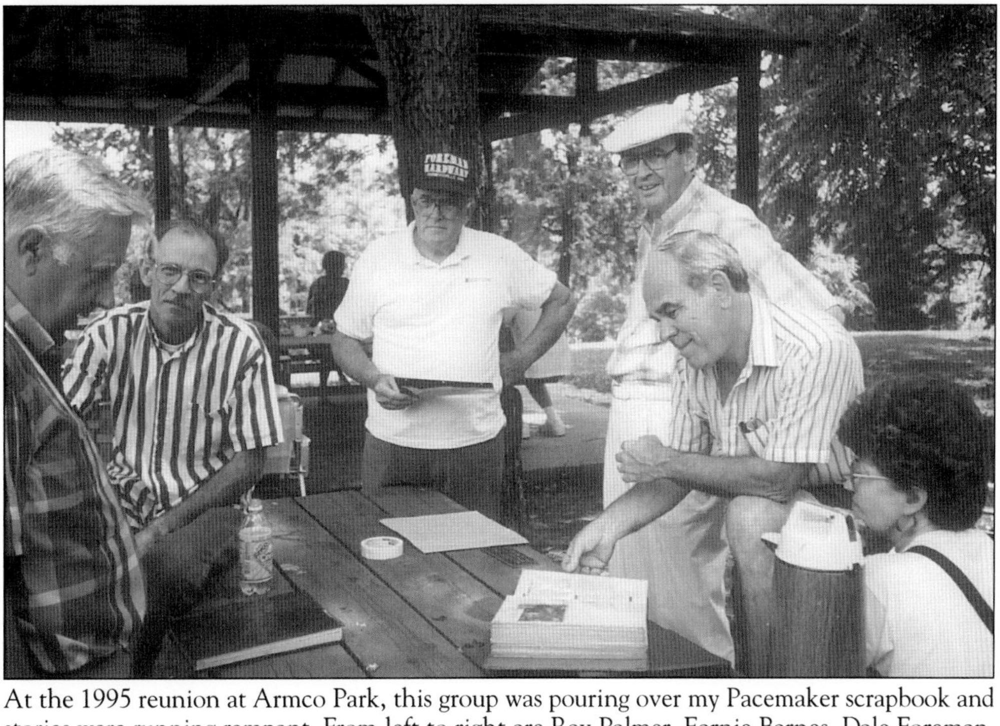

At the 1995 reunion at Armco Park, this group was pouring over my Pacemaker scrapbook and stories were running rampant. From left to right are Ray Palmer, Earnie Barnes, Dale Foreman, Harold "Mike" Michael, Darryl Hobbs, and Barbara Finfrock. (Roberson collection, 1995.)

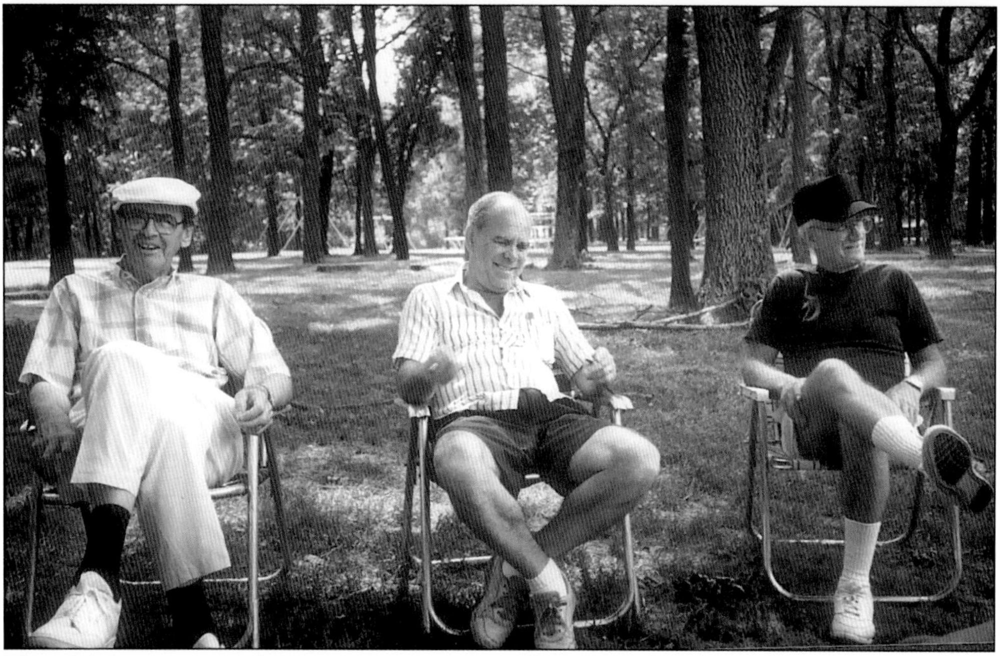

Three Midwest pioneer drag racers swap stories at the Pacemaker reunion at Armco Park. From left to right are Harold Michael, Darryl Hobbs, and Bill Burton. (Roberson collection, 1995.)

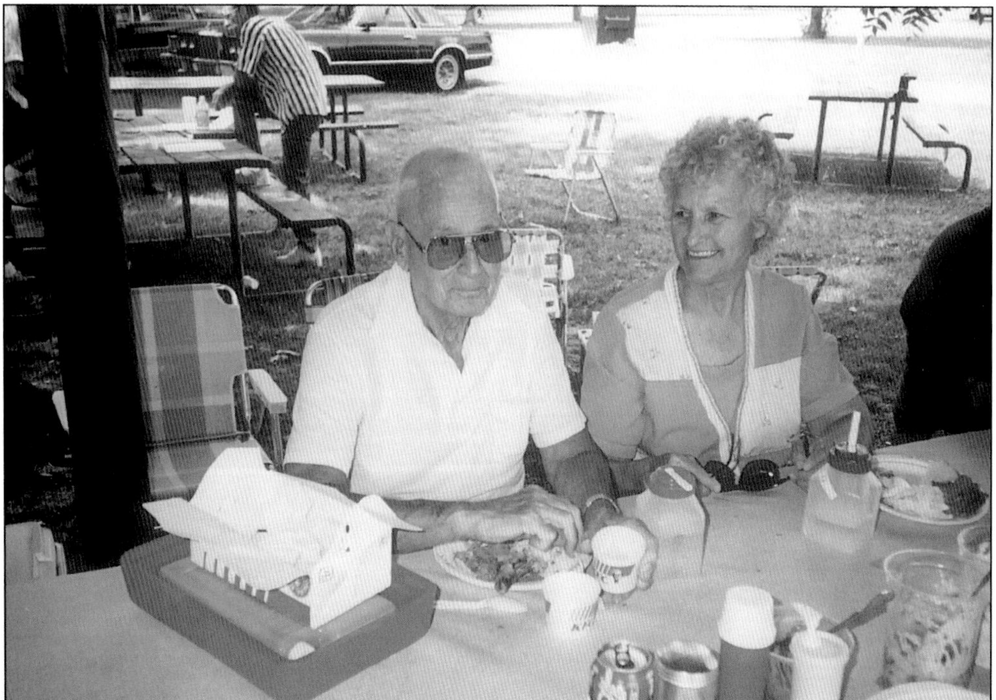

The first to arrive at the 1995 Pacemaker reunion was 87-year-old Fred May and wife Dolly. Fred designed the logos on Pacemaker jackets and tee shirts in the '50s. (Roberson collection, 1995.)

Nine

Humor on Wheels
Part I

The human race has one really effective weapon, and that is laughter.
- Mark Twain

The humor chapters are dedicated to the memory of Herb Sebastian, the Pacemakers' resident comedian and a pioneer drag racer, who passed away on November 13, 1997.

Everybody Knows Hobbs

In 1965 we traveled to Huntington, West Virginia, by invitation to run a match race with the Fisher Brothers' car. Darryl Hobbs was originally from nearby Ashland, Kentucky, and had made arrangements for all of us to stay with various members of his family. He had given us directions and told us that if we got lost, we could ask anyone for help. "Everybody in Ashland knows Darryl Hobbs," he assured us.

Herb Sebastian rode with us, and as we entered downtown Ashland, he asked Dad to pull over to the curb. A well-dressed elderly lady stood waiting to cross the street. "Excuse me Ma'am," Herb said politely. "Do you know Darryl Hobbs?" The lady thought for a moment, then answered, "No, I don't believe I do." Herb thanked her, and then he turned to Dad and said, "See there, everybody in Ashland doesn't know Hobbs!"

Assault on the Salt

In 1955 Dad and Mom and Herb and Betty Sebastian made the long trip from Middletown to Wendover, Utah, to compete at the annual Bonneville Speed Trials. They flat-towed Herb's 1932 Ford coupe racecar behind our family car, a 1951 Olds Rocket 88. The entire trip was a comedy of errors spiced with memorable quips from Herb.

The first day, Dad noticed that the '51 Olds seemed to be down on power, so they stopped early for the night in Indiana in order to work on the Olds. They soon found the problem. The '32, which was supposed to be towed in neutral, had been left in high gear causing the extra drag on the tow car. The two ace mechanics had run an entire tank of gas through the Olds racing engine!

The next episode occurred while towing the car through mountains. Dad got behind an elderly lady in a Cadillac who drove very slowly through the switchback turns, and sped up only mildly on straight sections. That is until Dad tried to pass, at which time she would gun the Caddy enough to keep the Olds with race car in tow from getting around her. After a few failed attempts at passing, Herb told Dad to pull over, and he ran back to the '32 and got in. When Dad pulled up behind the Caddy again, Herb fired up the racecar, and the loud dual Olds powered mountain train went flying by the wide-eyed old lady, who nearly lost her dentures in the process.

At Bonneville, the guys struggled with the coupe, which refused to perform on the salt. It would run 94 mph on the drag strip back home, and they expected to run 125 on the Salt Flats. But the '32 mustered a best speed of 87 mph all week at Bonneville. No matter what they did to it run after run with both guys taking turns at the wheel, she ran a best of 87 mph in the thin Utah air. To add insult to injury, Dad ran the family Olds through the course at 101 mph.

They rented a storage garage for the coupe in Wendover and made a side trip to Billings, Montana, so Mom could visit relatives. Mom was about seven months pregnant with my brother Marty at the time, and her condition was obvious. They stopped at a roadside cafe for lunch, and the waitress noticed Mom's condition and asked if she wanted anything special. "Hey, " said Herb. "Nothing but the best for them. They're on their honeymoon!"

Next, the four visited Yellowstone Park. As they drove through the park in the '51 Olds, they came upon a large grizzly bear lumbering slowly across the road toward some of the park's garbage cans, which he apparently intended to raid. Dad stopped the car to avoid hitting the bear, and the bear slowly turned toward them. He stood momentarily like a large dog at the front of the car starring at the two Pacemakers in the front seat, as the wives shivered at the mere size of the beast from their vantage point in the back. Herb had the window rolled down about two inches on his side of the car, and the scent of food carried inside the car led the bear that way. As they watched in awe, the bear was soon standing on his hind legs with one front paw on the front fender and the other on the car's roof, and his wet runny nose was crammed inside the opening next to Herb. Without batting an eye, Herb immediately spoke to him, "Just look at you! Will you please wipe that runny nose?" Then he proceeded to produce a Kleenex and wiped the bear's nose! The bear grabbed the Kleenex in his mouth, and backed away from the car, scratching the car's paint with both sets of claws in the process. Dad quickly took advantage of the opportunity, and drove away before the bear realized that the prize was not food. Herb would go to any lengths for a laugh.

The next stop was the Park's famous geyser, Old Faithful. It was due to erupt in a few minutes, and they were standing around waiting to watch it. Both Dad and Herb were sporting leather cowboy boots, western belts and white cowboy hats that they had bought on the trip. They were also wearing their navy blue Pacemaker club jackets to fend off the cool September air. Several people came by and asked them questions. They gave directions to the rest rooms and gift shop several times before they realized that their outfits were causing them to be mistaken for park rangers. Shortly after this revelation, an elderly lady came up to them and asked what time Old Faithful was due to go off. Herb looked at his watch and replied, "We're getting ready to go down and light the fuse right now."

A VW at Daytona

A most unusual Pacemaker drag racing story took place in the mid '60s. NASCAR's founder Bill France had built Daytona Speedway in 1959 taking on a huge debt in the process. He moved the local NASCAR beach races to the new facility, and it was a huge success with the stock cars hitting all-time high speeds on the 2.5-mile high-banked oval. He began to look for added events that would take advantage of his stock car crowds and produce more income for NASCAR. This led to NASCAR getting into drag racing, and often these drag races would coincide with NASCAR's major races. A huge Winternationals drag meet was held at Daytona at the nearby municipal airport at night during Speed Week in February of 1960. This first meet was held in conjunction with NHRA, but NASCAR soon began to hold separate races. At least one of these was held on the backstretch of the Daytona Speedway. Dad and Herb Sebastian made the trip to Florida in Herb's 1960 Volkswagen Karmen Ghia just for the event. This was the middle of winter, and the "Pacemaker Special" was still under re-construction, so they had no entry. Herb decided to enter his Karmen Ghia in the stock classes. Herb raced the diminutive sports car occasionally after the advent of the electronic handicap starting system, and he had good success with the car. It fell into such a low class that he would receive huge handicap starts that made the competition cringe over the long wait for their green light.

The guys were fascinated with the speedway with its high-banked turns and came up with a plan to test the facility. The races were run on the backstretch, and the infield road-race course was used as the return road. Herb had noticed on his initial runs that there was no one posted to stop the cars from going around the stock car track instead of the intended infield return road. He suggested to Dad that they take the long way around in order to experience the high-bank turns. When Herb got in line for his next practice run, Dad was in the car with him. They made the run turning the expected 65 mph in about 20 seconds. Then instead of going back on the road course, the two headed for the 3-4 turn as fast as the car would go and took the turn up on the bank. Dad recalls this stunt as one of the scariest they had ever done. He looked over at Herb and it appeared that he was looking almost straight down. It was like an amusement park ride. He could see the flat ground of the track's apron zipping past Herb's head out the side window. Going flat out at about 80 mph, it was all that the little German sports car could do to stay up on the bank. It gave Dad a whole new respect for the stock car boys who go fender-to-fender at more than twice that speed. When they got back to the pit area, they were met by a race official who politely asked them not to repeat the stunt. He didn't have to worry. They had already decided to stick to drag racing on nice flat, straight drag strips.

Miltenberger the Tire Man

One of the great personalities in the club was Dick Miltenberger, a former Middletown High football star, who sported a Dick Butkis build and a heart of gold. Dick had the wide-shouldered, no-neck look of an NFL football player and the enormous strength that went with the look. He willingly took on any job in the Pacemaker pit crew that required brute strength.

The first Pacemaker Special dragster was built in late 1956 and run throughout the 1957 race season. The car was flat towed to the track, because the club had no trailer until 1958. They had invested in a set of Inglewood racing slicks, and preserved them by towing the car with street tires and changing to the racing slicks at the track. Miltenberger often worked the afternoon shift at Armco, but he could make most of the Thorn Hill Lake, Kentucky meets, which ran on Sundays. He'd have to leave the track about 2:30 or 3:00 p.m. in order to make his 4:00 p.m. start time at work. He would remove the street tires and put the racing slicks on the car upon the morning arrival at the track, but would then have to leave before the meet was over. This presented a problem, because once Dick tightened down the lug nuts on the wheels, no two guys in the club could get them loose. More often than not, they would have to tow home on the racing tires.

Alex's Gift of Gab

One of the finest gentlemen I ever knew was charter member Alex Slamka, the club's resident customizer. Alex's cars were beautifully detailed showpieces, and Alex himself was always dapper, wearing button down shirts, dress pants and dress shoes while the rest of us wore tee shirts and work pants. This mode of dress and a striking resemblance to actor Glenn Ford earned him the nickname "Slick."

When I was about four or five, Alex would drop a nickel on the ground behind me, then point it out. "Look Ronnie, pick that up and put it in your pocket." While I was picking it up, he'd drop another one behind me. He'd repeat this with me spinning around to pick up coins until I'd completely cleaned him out of nickels and dimes. At first I didn't catch on to this and just thought he was great at finding change.

Alex was a very bright guy, who had amassed a tremendous amount of knowledge of 1930s and '40s Ford automobiles, but he had an interesting quirk. Like Jimmy Durante, Leo Gorcey and Norm Crosby, Alex loved to sprinkle conversations with malapropisms, a fancy word for using the wrong word in the wrong place.

For example, Alex and his wife Marge took vacation trips to Naples, Florida, which Alex always referred to as "Maples, Florida." Marge would correct him, and he would do it again a few minutes later. He once told us that he had to go home for dinner, because Marge had a "carrousel" (casserole) in the oven. He was so fluent with these grammatical gems that nobody could tell if he was joking or had poor hearing or just didn't care for the language as it was traditionally spoken. The Pacemaker meetings followed *Robert's Rules of Order*, but instead of making a motion, Alex would always make a "notion." The club motto, "Dedicated to Safety," became "Dictated to Safety." He built go-karts with Tecumseh engines, named for the famous Native American tribal chief, whom Alex turned Polish by calling them "Tecunski" engines. The Florida grocery chain Wynn-Dixie became "Wynn-Dickie," and his car was painted a "castel" color instead of the pastels that were popular in the '50s.

Alex passed away in 1971 after a long bout with cancer. He was a great guy, and the malapropisms helped make him an unforgettable character.

Alex the Spark Plug Guru

Dad was the crew chief for Dave Armbruster and his B/Dragster from 1967 through '69. At the Nationals in '69, we were pitted adjacent to the Autolite Spark Plug trailer. Today at major drag racing events there is a manufacturers' midway with large displays that traverse the country in gigantic tractor trailer rigs. In those days it was a bit more casual. Many manufacturers had tents or trailers, but they were usually just makeshift offices with card tables and folding chairs where you could pick up stickers or contingency money. Some had parts for distribution like the Autolite trailer, which came stocked with boxes of spark plugs that were handed out to racers like candy. This was handy for us, because Dave had acquired an Ed Pink built Chrysler Hemi that year, and with the engine switch from Chevy, we also switched spark plug brands from Champion to Autolite.

Alex Slamka came with us to the Indy Nationals that year, and as usual Alex was much better dressed than the typical crewmember. He had on gray dress pants and shiny black dress shoes with a golf style white shirt and a navy blue jacket that had a Ford emblem on the breast. He had visited the Autolite trailer and returned sporting an Autolite baseball cap. The dapper Mr. Slamka looked for all the world like a Ford executive. Pretty soon a guy came up to him and asked him to read the coloration on a spark plug. The ever-polite Alex obliged and told the young man his car looked a bit too lean. Soon there was another fellow asking for advice, and it wasn't long before a small crowd was gathered around Alex asking for advice on fuel mixtures. Alex was well aware that he had been mistaken for someone else, but on the other hand he was also perfectly capable of answering the questions. After a while he got tired of the game and asked the group if he could be excused from further consultation. "I'm really not here to answer questions," he told one guy. "I'm just doin' a little figuring for Ford."

Mike and the Granatellis

Harold "Mike" Michael and Heber "Snip" Dreher were two charter club members who raced an oval track roadster prior to the formation of the Pacemaker club. They raced a Mercury V-8 powered Model A roadster (later replaced by a more aerodynamic Model T roadster) throughout Ohio and Indiana, but occasionally they ventured up into northern Illinois and Wisconsin to run the famous Hurricane Circuit of the Granatelli brothers, Vince, Joe, and Andy. The circuit raced at several tracks, but the biggest races of the circuit were held inside Soldier Field, which had been constructed in the 1930's, and today serves as the home field for the Chicago Bears football team. Auto racing began at Soldier Field in 1947, and Mike and Snip's No. 25 roadster was in the first race held there.

Soldier Field had lots of seating for spectators, and the Granatellis were superb marketing promoters. As the racing progressed there in '47 and '48, they drew larger and larger crowds and the purses became some of the highest in the nation. This produced an influx of out of state racers, eventually pulling big names all the way from California. During the early meets with the first influx of out of town cars, which included the No. 25 of Mike and Snip, the local racers had mixed emotions. The Granatellis not only promoted the races, they also campaigned a car and were among the top racers. So some of the local racers resented the visitors, but others welcomed them openly, because they were tired of Vince and Joe Granatelli racing in the circuit they promoted and winning their own prize money. Mike and Snip's car ran very well in '47 and '48 with hired driver Don Beard, and a few of the local racers saw them as possibly dethroning the Granatellis, and therefore they befriended them immediately. But the fans in the grandstands overwhelmingly favored the local racers over the out-of-towners.

They were racing the Hurricane Circuit one night at Milwaukee, which was part of a weekly circuit that included five race tracks. The racing was very competitive, but Don Beard was the fastest qualifier that night, and as such he started the feature race at the back of the field. "Beardy" was fast making his way to the front, but he got a little too anxious and soon found himself and the No. 25 run into the wall. The car had severe front-end damage and caught fire in the process. Crewmembers from several teams and some spectators ran out onto the track from the infield and began to throw dirt on the car to put out the fire. One local fan seemed more intent on aiming the dirt into the carburetor than onto the fire, but soon the fire was out and the car was moved to the infield.

Mike, Snip and Don surveyed the damage and decided that they would have to drop out of the race and head back to Middletown. Then a local racer who had taken a liking to the team approached them and asked about the damage.

"Well I could take the engine apart and clean the dirt out of it," Mike said. "But, we don't have another front axle."

"The man looked at the damaged axle. "What's it out of?" he asked.

"A '40 Ford," Mike answered.

The man turned and called a couple of young, tough looking guys over. "My friend here needs a '40 Ford front axle," he told them. "Can you deliver one to his motel tonight?" One of the guys nodded and they disappeared.

Later at the motel Mike and Snip had removed the intake manifold and were cleaning the engine, when the two young toughs drove up in a pickup truck. They unloaded a '40 Ford front axle, complete with brakes, spindles and wheels, set it gently next to the race car and proceeded to leave.

"Hey, what do we owe you guys?" Mike asked.

"Nuttin'," came the reply. Then they left as quickly as they had appeared.

Mike and Snip installed the axle and silently readied the car for the next day's racing. Finally Mike spoke. "Where do you think they got that axle at this hour? All the junk yards have got to be closed." It was nearly 4:00 a.m.

"Don't know," said Snip. "Don't want to know."

They raced in Illinois the next day, but Mike felt uneasy all day. All he could think about was that somewhere on the streets of Milwaukee, some guy walked out the front door to go to work and found his '40 Ford setting flush on the pavement with no front axle.

Bill Burton and the Nose Cone

Bill Burton joined the club in 1955 and started work on a 1932 Ford five-window coupe hot rod. He built a beautiful car that first ran a '48 Mercury engine, but he began to drag race and eventually fitted it with an Olds Rocket engine. He was also a regular on the dragster crew until about 1960, when he opted to spend more time on his other hobby, operation of a ham radio. Bill worked at Armco Steel's research lab and became an expert in high temperature measurement.

Armco's plant was a huge operation, which sprawled along the south side of Middletown.

In the course of producing many tons of steel, the plant produced some recoverable waste, which wound up in one of several designated scrap piles. All good club members, who worked at Armco would periodically scour the scrap piles looking for usable hot rod building materials. The company would often let employees take designated scrap as long as they had filled out the proper permission form and obtained a gate pass to do so.

The late '50s harbored the birth of the space age, which had been foretold by science fiction movies like *The Day the Earth Stood Still* and *Forbidden Planet*, and was accompanied by modern sounding car models such as Olds Rocket 88's, Ford Galaxies and Plymouth Satellites. The space age was officially announced with the Russian launching of Sputnik I on October 4th, 1957. It was just about that same time that the Pacemakers began building the 1958 "Pacemaker Special" dragster, which was a thing of beauty and a study in backyard ingenuity. It sported a tubular frame of Dad's design and a full body patterned after the famous Cook and Bedwell car of California. The body was hand formed of sheet metal. It featured a semi boat tail section, which Dad made from two Chevy truck hoods, and a rounded cowl section and tapered nosepiece reflecting the combined body shop talents of several members including driver Gene Wells. The nose section matched the lines of the cowl section nicely and tapered almost to a point, leaving a small round opening at the front about the size of a cantaloupe.

About the time the body was being finished, Bill Burton was scouring the Armco scrap piles and found a light-weight steel cone about the diameter of a cantaloupe. With some modification this could be the perfect nosepiece for the body. He got the proper paper work and gate pass to legally remove the item from the steel mill. He delivered it to Dad at our house in Trenton, where the car was receiving its final touches prior to painting. Dad looked it over and mentally planned the cuts and welds required to fit it to the body. It was indeed a great match. He took it to the radiator shop and set it aside until a proper lull in the day's business would allow full attention to the job.

Later that day, the phone rang, and it was Bill Burton. With a shaky voice he began a conversation that went something like this. "Hey Robbie, do you still have the cone I gave you?"

"Yes."

"Have you cut on it or welded on it?"

"Not yet."

"Good! Don't! I've got to get that thing back to the mill as soon as possible."

"Why?"

"That thing was custom made by Armco for some kind of experimental rocket. It's one of a kind and worth a fortune. It got onto the scrap pile by mistake."

So Dad handed back the rocket nose cone, which Bill returned to Armco, and in doing so the Pacemakers did their small part to help usher in the space age. The car never received a pointed nose, but some twelve years later, fellow Ohioan Neil Armstrong walked on the surface of the moon. That's one small step for a hot rodder ...one giant leap for drag kind.

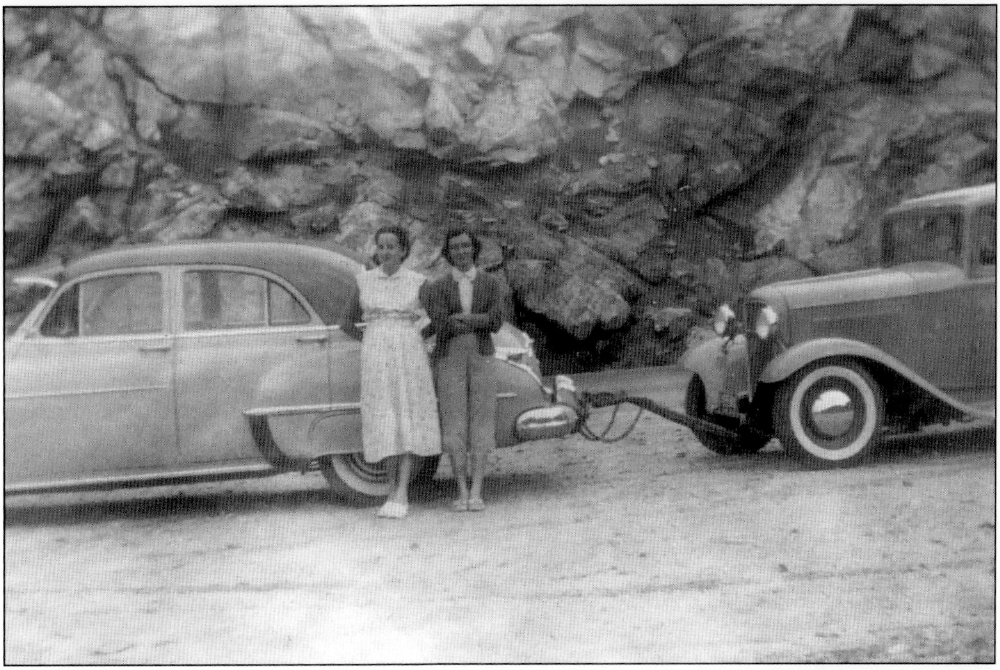

Mom (left) and Betty Sebastian (right) pose next to our '51 Olds and Herb Sebastian's '32 Ford coupe en route to the 1955 Bonneville Speed Trials. Mom is pregnant with my brother Marty, who was born the following January. (Roberson collection, 1955.)

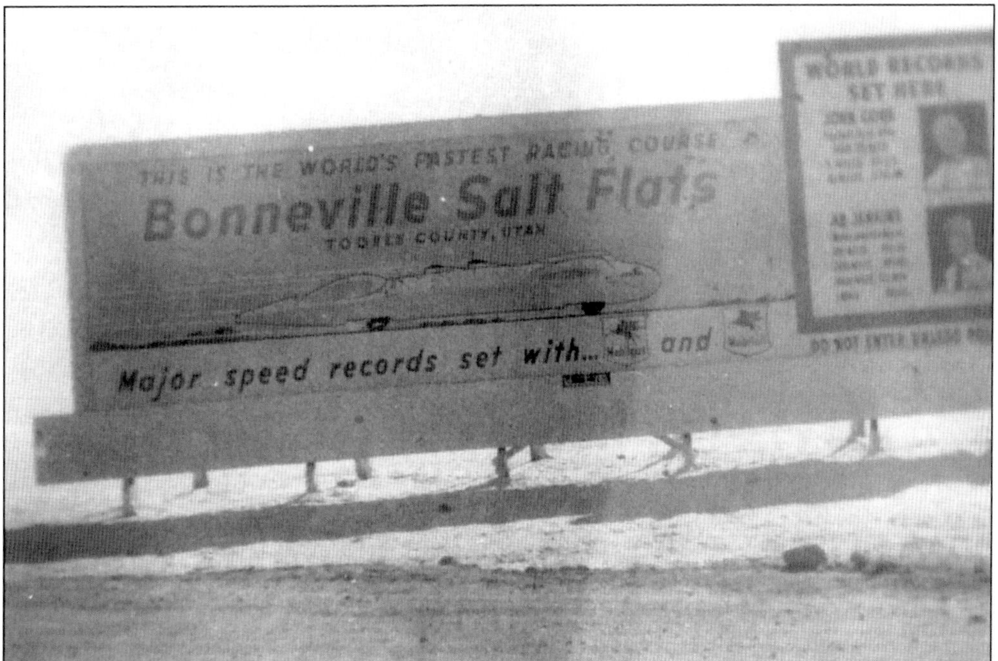

This sign welcomed all to the Bonneville Salt Flats in 1955. It read, "This is the world's fastest racing course." The land speed record at that time was 394 mph, set by John Cobb in 1947. (Roberson collection, 1955.)

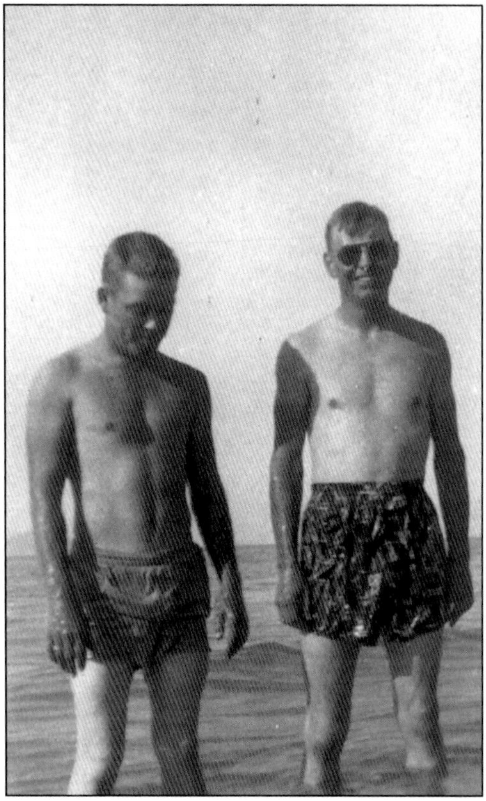

Herb Sebastian (left) and Dad (right) pose for the camera during a swim in the Great Salt Lake. (Roberson collection, 1955.)

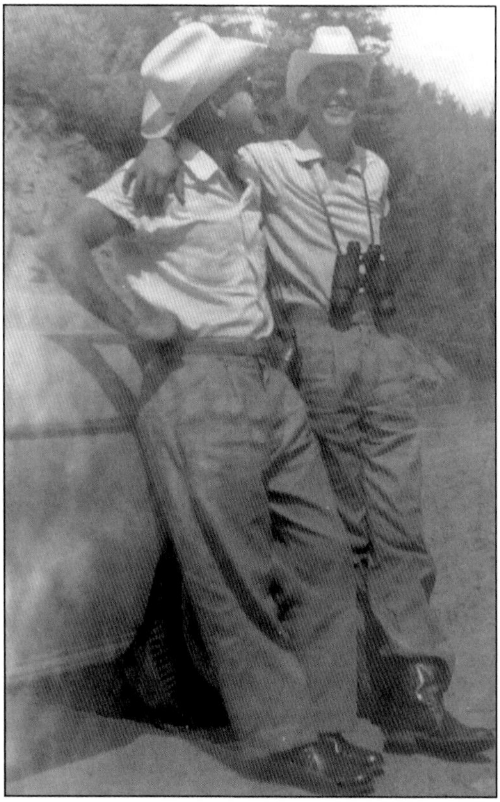

Herb (left) and Dad (right) mug for the camera in their matching cowboy hats and boots. When they added the navy blue Pacemaker jackets, they were mistaken for park rangers at Yellowstone. (Roberson collection, 1955.)

The clown prince of the Pacemakers, Herb Sebastian models a makeshift sun bonnet in an attempt to beat the Detroit heat at the 1959 Nationals. (Neely collection, 1959.)

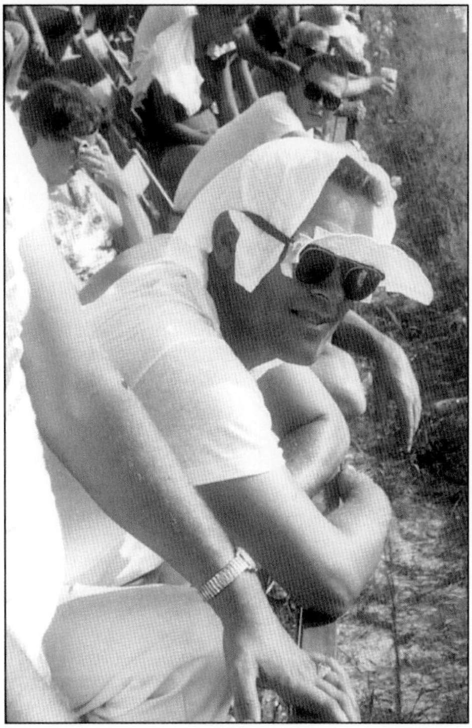

Dad and Herb Sebastian tend to the "Pacemaker Special" after the third consecutive Nationals class win at Indy. From left to right are an unidentified track official, Don Klamo (behind Dad), Dad, and Herb Sebastian. (Hobbs collection, 1965.)

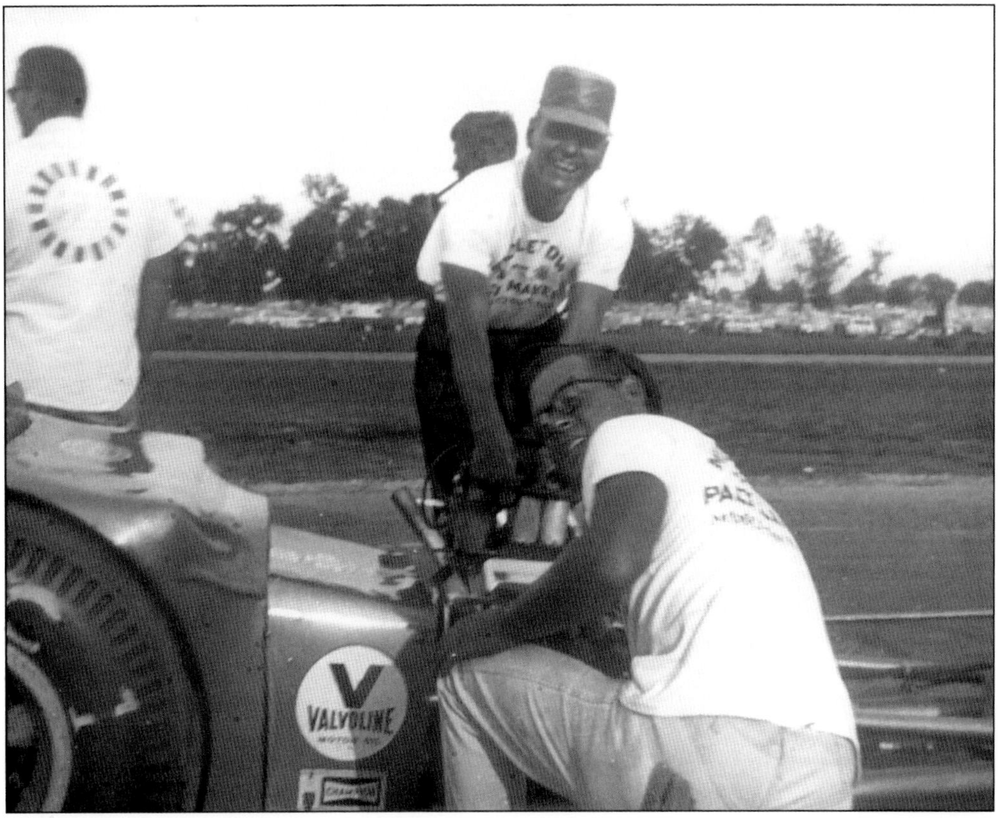

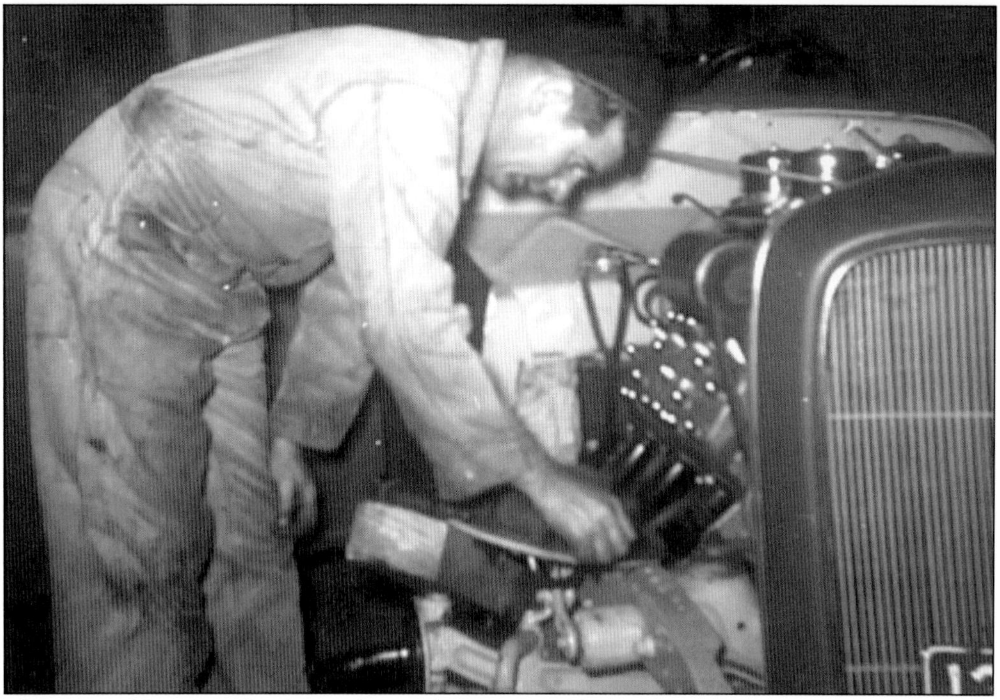

The inimitable Alex Slamka works on the engine of his 1936 Ford roadster. The car is just about ready for its initial outing. Alex appears to be either tuning or detailing. (Slamka collection, 1953.)

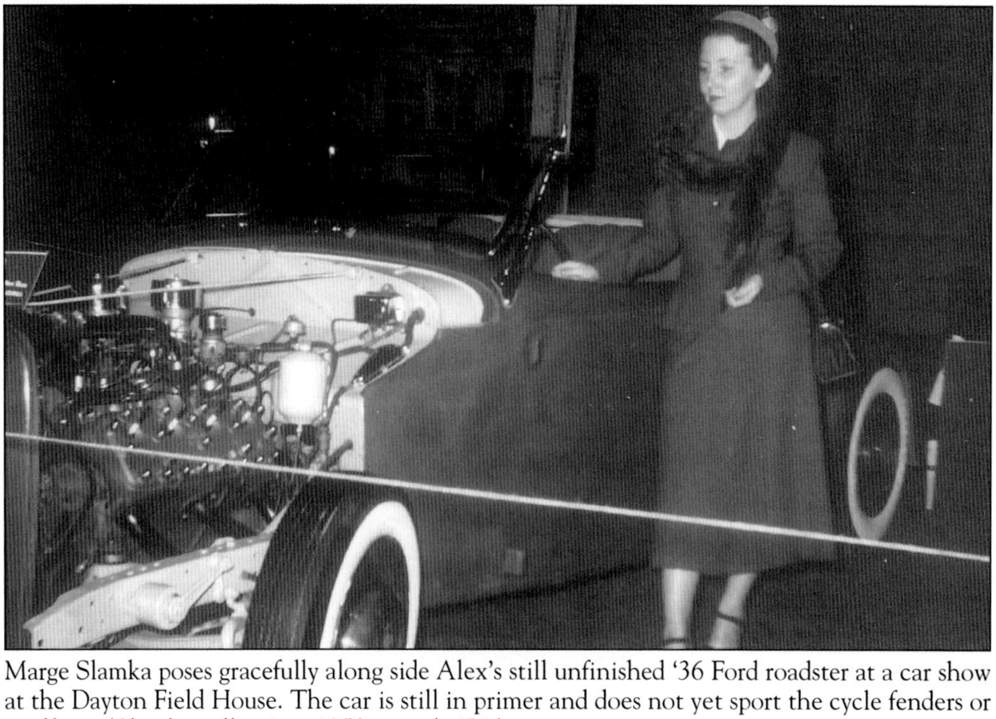

Marge Slamka poses gracefully along side Alex's still unfinished '36 Ford roadster at a car show at the Dayton Field House. The car is still in primer and does not yet sport the cycle fenders or nerf bars. (Slamka collection, 1953 or early '54.)

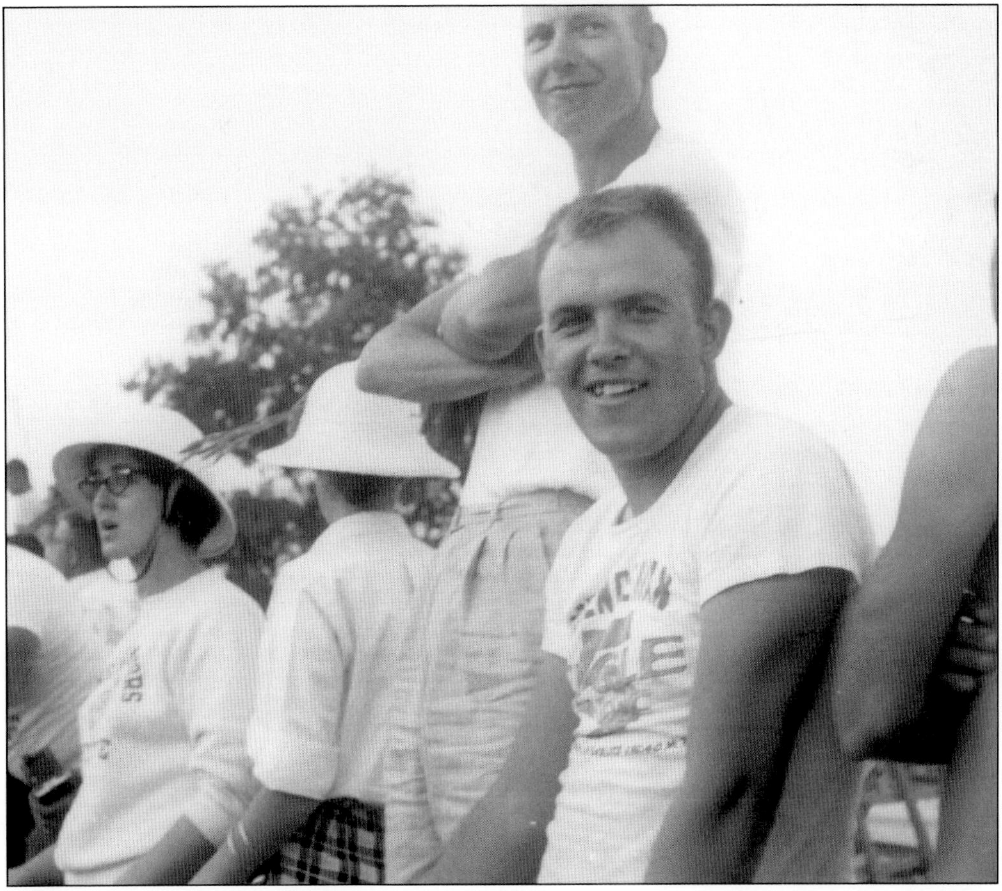

Popular and likeable Jerry Williams poses at the 1959 Nationals in an Iskenderian Racing Cams tee shirt as Dad mugs for the camera behind him. Jerry's wry and unpredictable sense of humor always kept the club members on their toes. (Neely collection, 1959.)

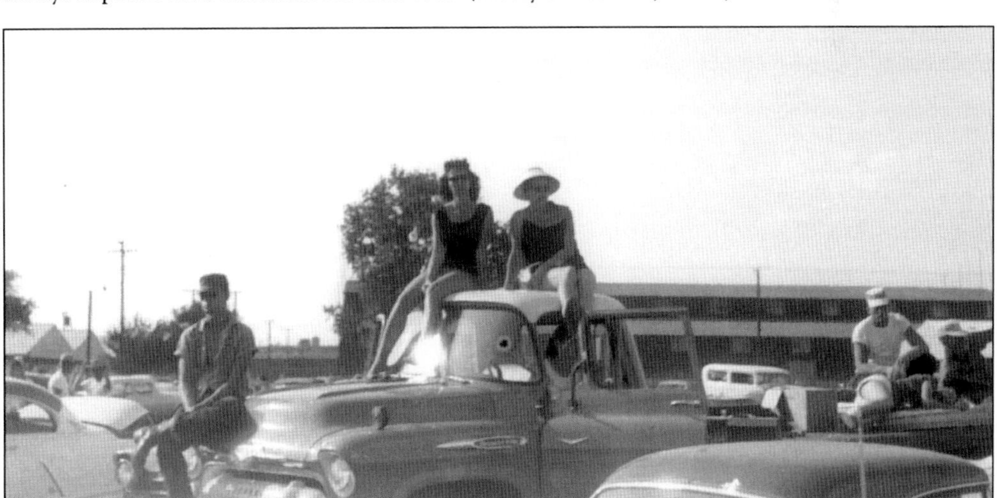

Drag racing was growing in popularity, but drag strips still had limited fan seating in 1958. These young ladies have "top row" seats atop a Chevy pickup truck. (Palmer collection, 1958.)

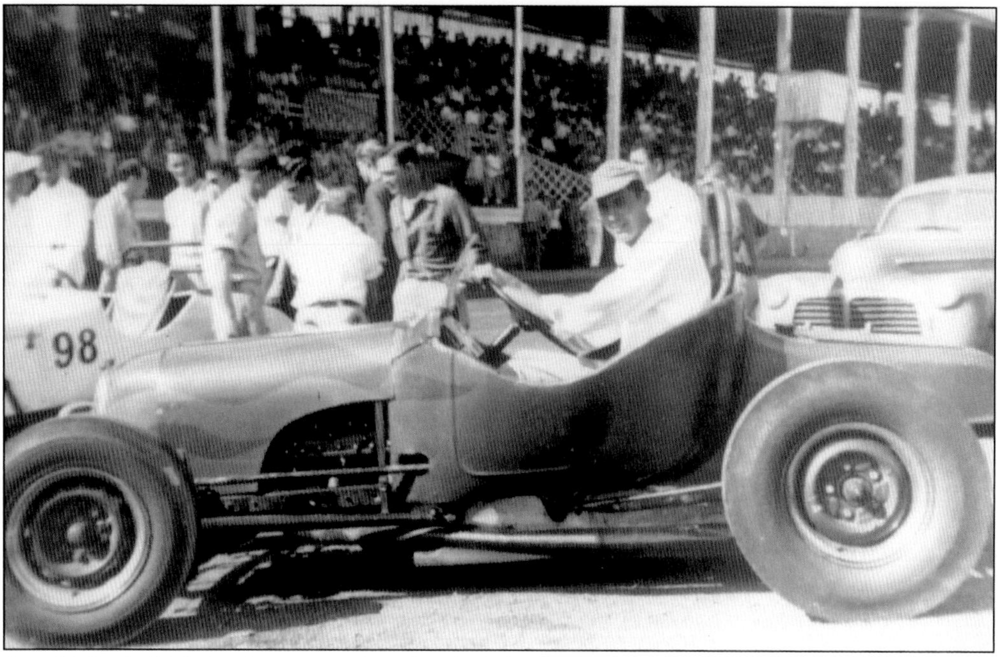

Harold "Mike" Michael poses at the wheel of the Dreher-Michael oval track roadster as fans look on. The No. 98 Jr. seen in the background is the Erickson Mercury V-8 driven by Larry Crocket. (Michael collection,1949.)

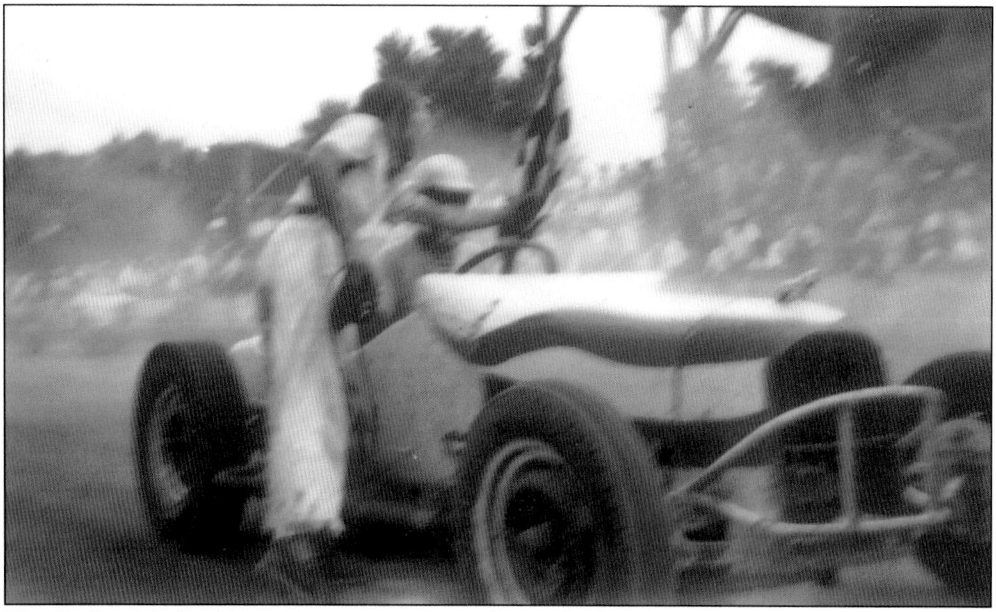

The Dreher-Michael No. 25 racing roadster takes a checker flag. It was these racing roadsters that were first called hot rods in the 1930s. (Michael collection, 1949.)

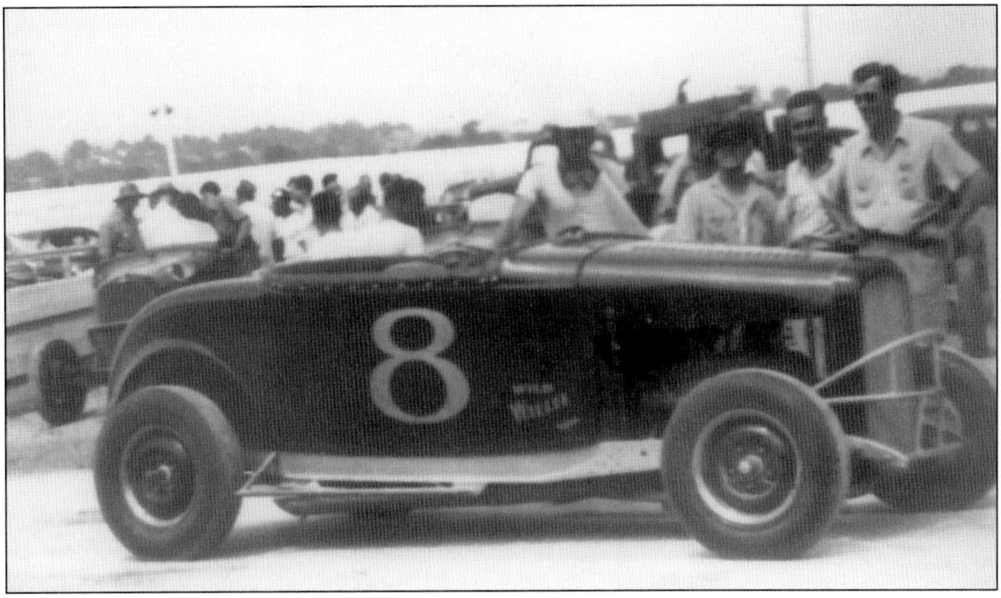

George McHenry of Chicago raced the "8-Ball" '32 Ford in the Hurricane racing circuit, which was run by the Granatelli brothers. By 1948, George was their longtime rival dating back to the Granatellis' street racing days. (Michael collection, 1948.)

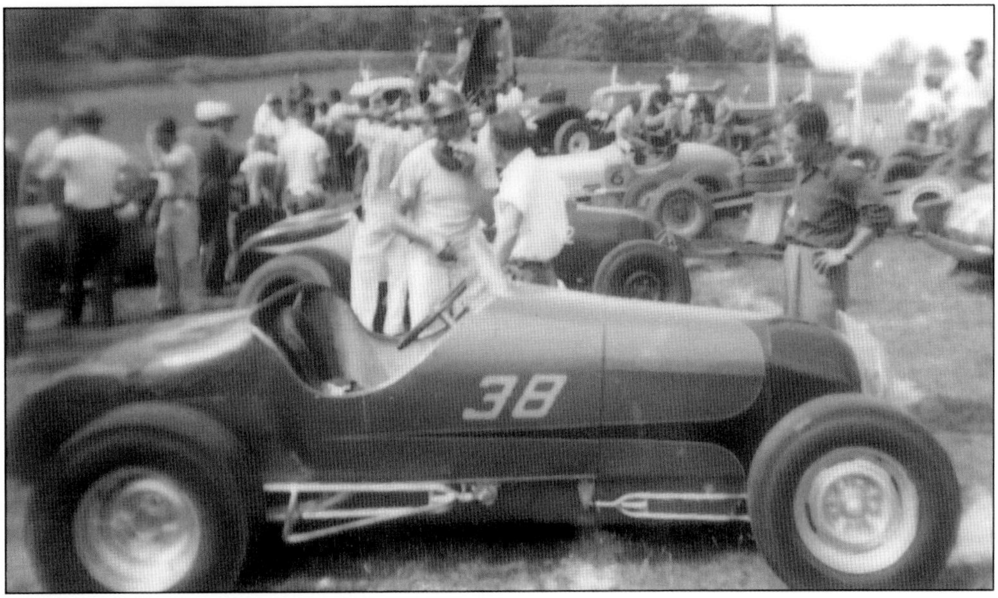

Tom Cherry's No. 38 roadster at Muncie, Indiana. Tom was one of the best among the Midwest roadster drivers. He was The Mutual Racing Association champion in 1941, and he won the famous "Little 500" in '50, '52 and '54. The car was later rebodied into a sprint car. (Michael collection, 1947.)

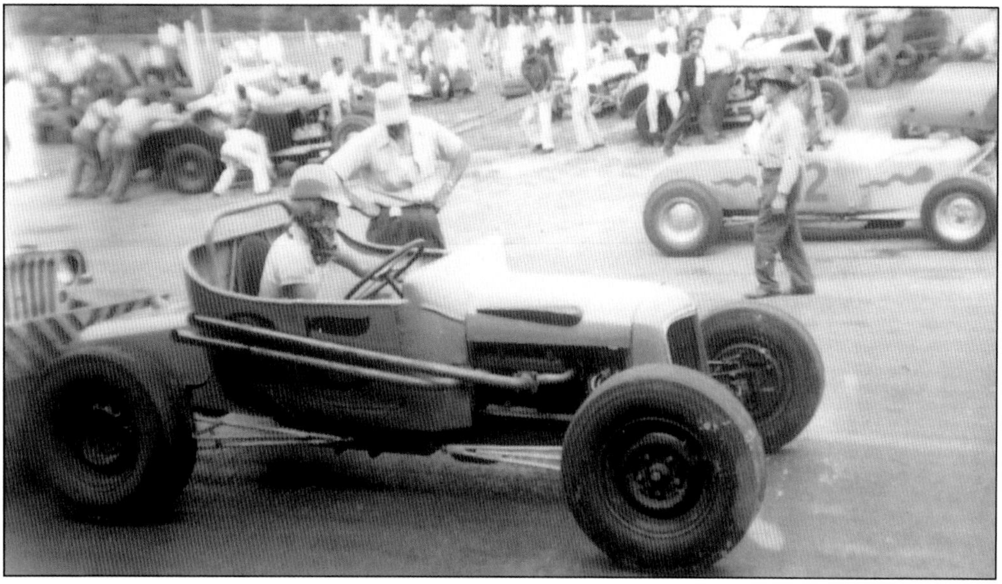

Californian Red Amick, who later raced at Indy (1959 and 1960) is push started in his car, another No. 25. Red was among the influx of top California racers who drove the Midwest's Mutual and Hurricane circuits in the late '40s. Car No. 12 in the background was owned by local racer Lee Izor. (Michael collection, c. 1948.)

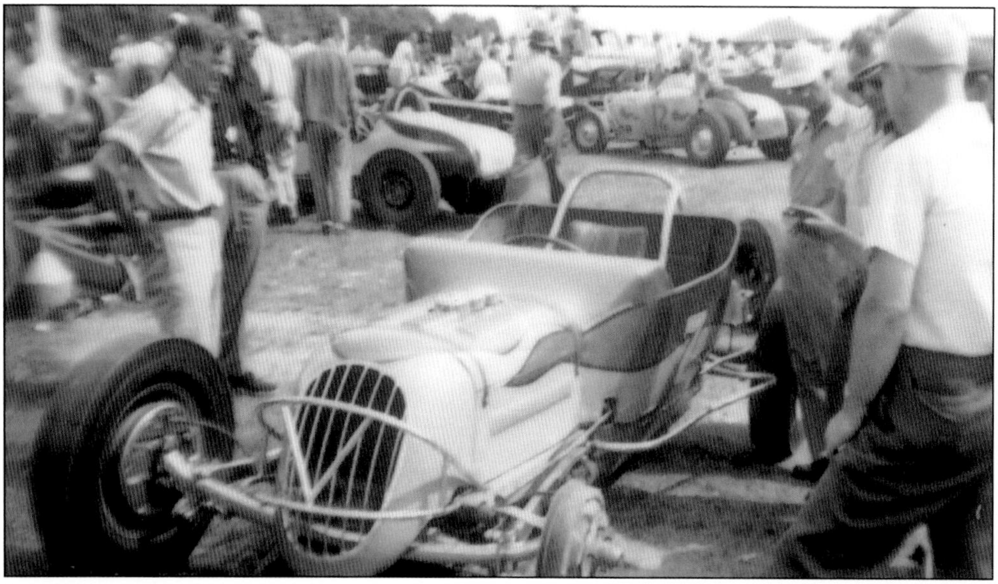

Roy Prosser's No. 7, a California car, sets a new track lap record at Winchester, Indiana. The record was formerly held by a AAA sprint car, proving the performance capability of the lowly roadster. Roy was a former jockey who gave up racehorses for horsepower. (Michael collection, c. 1948.)

Ten

Humor on Wheels
Part II

From the moment I picked up your book until I laid it down, I was convulsed with laughter. Some day I intend reading it.

- Groucho Marx

Don Klamo's First Ride

Don Klamo joined the club in 1959 as a skinny kid with an ambition to build and race hot rods. He produced a progression of hot rods, including a hopped up '48 Ford sedan followed by a Buick-powered '47 Ford coupe. His best hot rod was a beautiful 1932 Studebaker Rockne coupe with a 301 Chevy V-8 engine, which he drag raced in the B/Gas Coupe class at Beechmont. But Don had a strong desire to drive the club's dragster, and in 1960 he approached Dad and asked if he could make a run in the car. At that time the club ran a C/Dragster that used a fuel injected 292 cubic inch Chevy engine and was capable of running the quarter mile at 125 mph in about 11 seconds. Jim Neely was the regular driver, and the cockpit was designed around his six foot, 180-pound frame. Dad took a look at Don, who stood about five-foot-six and weighed about 120. Don was only 22 and still hadn't filled out yet.

"Are you crazy?" Dad asked. "This is a powerful car, and it could get away from you. It's a lot faster than your coupe." But Don was persistent, and week after week he kept asking Dad for a turn at the wheel.

One night at Kilkare Drag Strip in Xenia, Ohio, Neely was detained, and the guys were discussing the issue of who might drive the car on the warm up pass. Neely would be there later, but someone else had to drive the car if a shakedown run were to be made at all. That night the track was offering a tee shirt to anyone who ran faster than 100 mph and thereby joined the track's 100-mph club. Don saw his chance to get his first ride in the dragster and earn the much-coveted tee shirt. He approached Dad anxiously, and after some hesitation, Dad agreed. After receiving some intense coaching on safety, Don strapped on Neely's helmet and eagerly climbed into the cockpit. The helmet was a bit large, and the clutch and gas pedals were a little hard to reach, but Don didn't care. He had his first ride. His excitement mounted as the '47 Buick tow car pushed the dragster, and the crisp Chevy engine came to life.

Don followed the flagman's directions and carefully staged the car with Dad's words echoing in his mind. "Now don't let it get away from you! This car's a lot faster than anything you've ever driven." But any fear melted away, when Don thought about that tee shirt.

The starter waved the flag, and Don popped the clutch with a heavy foot on the accelerator. He was thrown back in the seat, and the oversized helmet immediately swiveled around on his head and covered one eye. Undaunted, he stayed on the accelerator. Then the car veered quickly to the right, and he had to let off. He straightened it out and hit the accelerator again. Again, the car veered right, and again he let off. He straightened it out once more and hit the accelerator again. Again it went right, but he steered it back and crossed the finish line peering through the errant helmet with one eye.

Dejected, he thought that Dad must be right. He just wasn't big enough to handle the horsepower. As the car silently rolled to a stop, he heard the speed announced: "One hundred and two miles per hour." At least he had the tee shirt! They towed the car back to the pits, and he told Dad, "You were right. I couldn't handle the car. I just couldn't keep it straight." His dream of driving a dragster had crumbled in about thirteen seconds, but at least he had the shirt.

Meanwhile, Jim Neely arrived and they prepared the car for the first round of competition. Neely strapped on the helmet and climbed into the cockpit, both of which fit him nicely. They pushed the car, it fired up, and Neely proceeded to the line. The flag dropped, the car veered to the right, and Neely shut it off and coasted to a stop. They pushed him back to the pits, and Neely climbed out of the car and immediately sought out Don Klamo.

"You went 100 mph in this car?"

"Yes," Don answered, already wearing the prize tee shirt.

"You idiot! The car's got a broken axle!"

The dragsters of the '50s and '60s ran junkyard rear axles that tended to break under the additional horsepower of the highly modified engines. A few years later special hardened axles would become available that solved the problem, but it was a problem indeed in that era. A broken rear axle put all the power to one side and would steer the car sharply toward the wounded side. It was also possible with some makes for the wheel to come completely off the car, so Don's situation was a dangerous one indeed when he unwittingly kept applying power to the wounded car.

Don built his own dragster the following year, a Chevy powered B/Dragster that he campaigned with partners Marion Hounshell and Gary Rupp. He won Top Eliminator at an NHRA winter series meet in Miami, Florida, in February of 1962, earning a photo in *Hot Rod Magazine*. At the '64 Nationals, he set a speed record in the Pacemaker Special A/Comp. In 1965, he won the B/Dragster class at the inaugural NHRA Spring Nationals in Bristol, Tennessee. In 1969, he traveled to Florida and won Competition Eliminator at the inaugural Turkey Trot National Open. He would build and drive numerous dragsters over four decades including a 180 plus mph AA/Dragster in the '60s, another B/Dragster in the '70s, a hiatus from the sport in the '80s, and since the '90s he and his driver/son Tom have campaigned a 190-mph nitrous oxide Super Comp dragster. This long and successful drag racing career began one night in 1960 at Kilkare Drag Strip, when a skinny kid with an oversized helmet earned a 100-mph tee shirt driving a dragster with a broken rear axle.

The Bad Headlights

In a group the size of the Pacemakers it is no surprise that practical jokes would be popular, but sometimes they transcended the fine line of good sense. One Saturday evening, probably 1960, they were towing the car home from Muncie, Indiana, and Dad was driving the '47 Buick tow car. Dad was getting tired and asked for someone else to take over the wheel. Jerry Williams, always eager to help, offered to drive. As the sun was beginning to set behind them, they pulled to the side of the road. The two switched positions and Jerry took the wheel.

As soon as he took over, Jerry turned on the car's headlights, since the sun was going down rapidly. A few minutes went by, and he began to complain about the headlights. "Boy these headlights are getting bad. We need to replace those beams."

The guys looked at one another, and then Herb Sebastian spoke. "They look okay to me," he countered.

"Me too, " Ray Palmer chimed in. Then in turn they all told Jerry that the headlights looked okay to them, including Darryl Hobbs, Jim Neely and Dad.

Jerry drove on, squinting to see in the diminishing light. A few minutes later, he repeated the complaint. "Dang guys, these headlights are really bad." The complaints were now accented by the occasional slip of a trailer wheel off the side of the pavement, bouncing the car and trailer around as Jerry corrected the course of the Buick. Again the passengers countered by saying that the car's lights looked fine.

Moments later Jerry exclaimed, "Guys I can't see well enough to drive. If you think these headlights are okay, then one of you drive!" Again the car and trailer bounced and swerved down the highway as the trailer wheels slipped off the pavement as if to accent Jerry's plea.

"No need to do that," Dad told him. "Just take off your sunglasses."

Jerry Williams' Disappearing Act

The Pacemakers at one point had 130 members, and any group that size is bound to have a few real characters. The club indeed had its share of characters, and in fact it seemed to have more than the normal statistical scatter would predict. One of the most unique was Jerry Williams, a laid back Tennessee good-ole-boy that everyone liked, but his reaction to a particular situation was rarely predictable. His wry backwoods sense of humor often contained an element of surprise that seemed to defy conventional logic and leave the guys both laughing and scratching their heads in amazement.

The trip to the Nationals at Oklahoma City in 1958 had just such an episode. The guys were packed into the '47 Buick sedan with the dragster in tow. The Buick was painted white with red and blue lettering, matching the paint scheme of the full-bodied dragster, which was visible on the open trailer. The rig carried a very professional look for the era.

They were waiting in line at a tollbooth, and the line was not moving. After a few minutes, the guys got out to stretch, and Jerry went up to the head of the line to check out the problem. He quickly found the cause of the bottleneck, a stalled Cadillac sedan. The frustrated male driver was trying to restart the car, while his two female passengers sat in the back seat, and took turns loudly blaming him for the situation, all the while questioning his overall intelligence. Jerry felt sorry for the guy and offered to help. The driver happily slid over, and Jerry got behind the wheel. Reasoning that the car was now flooded, he put the accelerator to the floor and turned the key. The engine cleared within a few seconds and started, to the cheers of the car's original passengers. With this, one of the ladies said, "Why don't you drive for a while, in case this happens again." And Jerry answered simply, "Okay." He shut the car door and drove off.

Meanwhile back at the Buick, the guys were watching from a distance, and gazed at one another dumfounded when the Cadillac drove off. With no explanation, Jerry had driven away in this strange car. They quickly piled into the Buick, got through the tollbooth and gave chase. The Cadillac was nowhere in sight, so they went faster. Soon they were barreling down the highway at nearly 100mph, and still could not catch sight of the Caddy. They slowed to a sane speed, reasoning that Jerry would be waiting at the next tollbooth. After all, there was no place else to go.

After an hour, another tollbooth rose on the horizon. When they got to it, Jerry was standing there waiting for them. He got into the Buick and told them the strange story. One of the guys asked him, "What in the world did you talk about with three complete strangers for a whole hour?"

"Oh, I told them about how I owned this race car and about how all you guys worked for me," came the reply. That was Jerry Williams. You just had to love him!

One Fast Push Truck

In 1964 and '65, Dad often used his 1950 Studebaker shop truck to push start the dragster. He made a special removable wood bumper for the task. At the local tracks like Tri-State at Hamilton, the guys would tow the car over with the '54 Pontiac club car, and Dad would take over the job of push starting with the truck, which had a modified 327 Chevy engine and a lot more horsepower than the stock Pontiac.

Push starting in those days was part of the show. The cars and push trucks would enter the track from the pits at about mid track and start the cars by pushing them toward the starting line. Some tracks required that the cars push down track from the starting line first and turn around at mid track, then push start toward the starting line. In either case, the cars fired up in the opposite direction that they would run, and then turn around behind the starting line to stage. This often required crew members to jump out of the push trucks and physically pull the running cars backwards to line them up properly, since few dragsters had reverse in those days. All this ritual added to the color and the suspense as a great buildup to the run itself. With today's much safer static starting, much of the old fanfare was lost.

With the launch of the dragsters, the push trucks would follow them down the quarter mile, and the fans got another look at some of the unique vehicles that push started dragsters in drag racing's golden era. Dad's truck was not unusual in that many of the push trucks were the result of engine swaps in old pickup trucks or even old hearses and ambulances, some of which were also made into pickups. They often sported a neat paint job as did Dad's truck with nine coats of black lacquer and gold colored scallops. And it was common for these modified push trucks to also race each other down the track, since there were no speed limits on a drag strip. Dad never missed a chance to race the other push vehicle, and the light weight Studebaker truck had an impressive win record in these impromptu races.

One Sunday afternoon at Tri-State Drag Strip, Dad's notoriety was finally recognized. The Pacemaker A/Comp with Darryl Hobbs driving had just beaten the opponent, and Dad was racing the other push truck. The track announcer called the action something like this. "And once again the national record holding Pacemakers come out on top. They are always tough to beat here at Tri-State, and ...Good God, their push truck just went through the clocks at a hundred and three!"

EARNIE'S FAMOUS BURNOUT

The Barnes brothers, Earnie and Harold joined the club about 1962 and were die-hard drag racers from the beginning. They ran a 1961 Corvette in the B/Sports class under the name "Cracklin' Rose" and for a time ran a second car, a B/Dragster under the name "Cracklin' Rose II". Earnie drove both, and Harold, who learned his craft from established wrenches like Dad, Herb Sebastian and Jim Neely, prepared both. Both cars ran well and won often.

The mid 1960s saw the beginning of the burnout, the spinning of the rear tires momentarily before the run to clean and heat the tires and heat the track. Prior to that time, dragster crews would clean the tires by hand with large stiff brushes just before the run, but once the good hardened rear axles were developed, the task could be done by simply spinning the tires. Burnouts would get longer and become part of the show later as match racing funny cars developed the art form, but in 1965 the burnout was still in its infancy.

At the local meets, the tracks normally allowed the racers to perform two short hop burnouts across the line for cars that had reverse gears. Earnie was driving the Corvette one Sunday during his bachelor days, and on this particular Sunday, a brand new girlfriend was watching from the stands. He had told her all about his racing, and he was determined to impress the young lady with his driving. He would make extra long burnouts, and he would wave to her in the stands prior to backing up toward the starting line. The beautiful maroon Corvette was responding nicely from its finely tuned fuel injected engine to its spinning M&H racing slicks. Earnie was on cloud nine, impressing the girl while enjoying his favorite sport. With each burnout she would wave back excitedly, so Earnie knew she was impressed, and he felt the elation that one feels when a plan really comes together.

Long burnout, wave, back up ...long burnout, wave, back up ...it was a great plan, and he could repeat the process with each run of the car. Then it happened. Earnie decided to do an even longer burnout to impress her so much that she'd be telling all her friends back in Middletown. He did the first one, waved and backed up. He took a deep breath as he nailed the throttle for the longest burnout of his illustrious driving career. The Corvette responded with the throaty roar of a finely tuned Chevy V-8, the tires began spinning frantically and the car launched into a beautiful burnout ...backwards!

In his anticipation of the world's greatest burnout, Earnie had left the car in reverse. He nearly wiped out another car approaching from behind, but with lightning quick reflexes, he got the car stopped and reversed its direction so fast that Joey Chitwood himself would envy the move. Earnie didn't look at the stands. He sheepishly staged the car and made a good hard run, vowing never to mix girls and cars again.

Earnie had a long and varied racing career from drag strip to round track. For at least one season, he and Harold ran two cars in two different categories simultaneously at the drags, and a busy Earnie drove both. They won a lot of races over the years, but whenever a group of guys get together and tell drag racing stories, the backward burnout is always the first story Earnie tells.

The Elusive Corvette

Earnie and Harold Barnes began racing their 1961 Corvette in the mid 60s on a limited budget, putting money into performance first and amenities later. They flat towed the car with a tow bar at first until they could afford a trailer. One evening Earnie was driving them home from a meet at Lexington in their Chevy pickup truck, which sported a matching maroon paint job that mirrored the Corvette race car. They were passing through a small town when they heard a thump, and Earnie checked the rear view mirror. The Corvette was still behind them, but the angle of the car behind the truck didn't look right. Then Earnie watched in horror as the Corvette wandered left toward the oncoming traffic lane. The racecar had come loose from the tow truck!

For lack of a better plan, Earnie pulled to the side of the road to avoid contact and slowed down. The Corvette rolled up beside them, and they were proceeding slowly down the road in tandem, two guys in a truck and their unmanned runaway racecar overtaking them.

"What do we do?" yelled Earnie.

"Stop and we'll chase it on foot," came Harold's reply.

With that, Earnie pulled the truck completely off the road, and came to a stop. They jumped out and chased the rolling Corvette down the road. As they ran behind the car, it continued to veer left and proceeded to cut onto the lawns of the adjacent houses. They caught up to the car, grabbed the rear bumper and began dry skiing behind it in an effort to slow its momentum. (Although they were years ahead of their time, dry skiing never really caught on as an organized sport). The car veered farther left until they were completely on grass. They were relieved that it was off of the road, but they had a new problem. It was heading directly for a house with a nice wooden porch on the front. They continued to pull back on the car from behind, some 300 pounds of humanity pulling back 3000 pounds of rolling racecar. There was no use trying to open the car door; the car's roll cage would make it impossible to jump behind the wheel while the car was in motion. The momentum was slowing, but the house was getting closer, and they could now see a maturing couple sitting on the wooden porch enjoying the (so far) quiet evening and watching the approaching car in wide-eyed wonder.

In an effort that can only be described as super human, the two fatiguing siblings rallied to finally bring the car to a complete stop, just inches from the wooden porch. The couple stared in amazement as the two heads popped up from behind the car and Earnie greeted them, "Howdy Folks. Lovely evening."

Hit the Silk

In the mid 1960s NHRA passed a new rule that every car had to have a parachute if the class speed record exceeded 150 mph. The Pacemaker Special ran in the A/Competition class, which had a class record of 151.00 mph by the summer of 1964, the same record which the Pacemaker Special would break at the '64 Nationals. So by mid season in 1964, the guys added a parachute to the car.

The parachute was fun at first, and it was my job to help pack it. But after a while, the job became tedious, and Darryl would use the chute only at tracks where it was really necessary due to limited shutoff area. The chute never failed to deploy properly in competition, and we never had problems with it save for one time when the main shroud line broke and the chute came off the car altogether. On that occasion, Darryl still stopped safely with the car's brakes.

Those were the days of open trailers, and often when the car was being towed, people would drive along beside it on the highway to look the car over. This exercise was conducted much to the displeasure of the driver of the tow car, who was then blocked from any desired lane changes. The people in the cars would often wave or give the "okay" or "thumbs up" sign indicating that they liked what they saw. The guys would politely wave back in appreciation, but also to expedite the end of the encounter so the driver would move on. One evening, towing home from Bluegrass Raceway at Lexington, Kentucky, the tow car pulled across some bumpy railroad tracks, and within a few minutes there was a very animated highway buddy. The guy was waving frantically and blowing his horn. The crew waved back, thinking that the guy was just another race fan, but the guy was persistently waving and pointing at the car. The guys continued to wave back politely, after all a fan was a fan. But this guy was being obnoxious with his adoration. Finally the driver of the tow car noticed the problem in the rear view mirror. The bumpy ride over the railroad tracks had jarred the parachute pin loose, and the chute had deployed as much as the relatively slow highway speed would allow. Cars behind began to honk as the chute was blocking their vision. The crew had to pull over and repack the chute in order to continue. I always told people that we never had a parachute fail to open. In fact we had it open once too often.

The Street Race

Like most car clubs of the era, the Pacemakers promoted safe driving and legal club activities for the members. This was part of the nationwide goal of the car clubs through the NHRA to erase the renegade image of hot rodders. Street racing was highly frowned upon, and if a member received enough traffic tickets, he was subject to expulsion from the club.

By age five I was attending the Pacemaker meetings regularly with Dad, and it was always a special guys night out, often stopping at Frisch's restaurant on South Main afterward for strawberry pie. One night we left the meeting, which at that time was held at the Armco Steel Research Center, and we proceeded toward home behind another club member in his Olds powered Studebaker. We both lived in the same section of Mayfield, a small unincorporated community that was actually part of Middletown. It was late 1955 or early '56, and I was only five at the time, but my memory of the event is quite clear today, more than forty years later. We usually took the '45 Ford truck, but that night we were in the family car, our '51 Olds Rocket 88.

It started out innocently enough. The Studebaker's engine would rev up and suddenly the car would quickly pull out of headlight range, then slow down and fall back. After watching a few of these, Dad responded with his own engine revving. Soon we were taking the long way home along the farm roads that ran along the perimeter of Middletown and around remote sections of the large Armco Steel complex. And we were going awfully fast trying to catch up to the Studebaker.

This scenario illustrates one of the real dangers of street racing, the lack of a standard distance. While drag strips are typically a quarter mile or eighth mile in length, a street race had no such limits. The contest could go on for miles like this example, which was really more like a high-speed chase than a drag race. On the country roads around Middletown a high-speed race could readily encounter slow moving farm equipment crossing the road totally hidden in a dip between hills in the rolling terrain. It was just plain dangerous.

The cars were nearly home, racing along a straight stretch of Lefferson Road at over 100 mph when suddenly every street racer's nightmare appeared. A police car pulled out of a side street behind them and gave chase. Dad saw the car briefly in the headlights as we went flying by, and he watched the rear view mirror closely. The police car was accelerating madly, trying to catch up, but strangely did not use the flashing lights or siren. At this point, all seemed lost. Dad's clean driving record with the club was doomed. He'd have to pay two fines; one for the ticket and second fine to the club. And then there was Mom. He was really going to catch it from Mom. Street racing was bad enough, but with a five-year-old in the car it was too much. Remember, this was long before the days of child restraint seats. Neither one of the cars in the race even had seat belts.

Then an idea struck him. The Studebaker was not stopping, and Dad was certain that he must have seen the police car also. They could run for it. After all, the cop couldn't have gotten a good look at the cars. Not at 100 mph he couldn't. Dad's foot stayed on the floor as the Olds continued to chase the Stude and the home neighborhood closed in.

Soon the Studebaker approached Brentwood Drive, jammed on the brakes and made a moonshiner, tire-squealing right hand turn and hit the throttle again. Dad quickly checked the mirror. The cop was still a good distance behind, so we made an identical Joey Chitwood turn onto Carolina Street, where we lived in the first block. Dad quickly wheeled the car onto our driveway and threw gravel from the spinning tires all the way into the garage. He killed the lights, and lay down in the front seat, pulling me down with him.

"What's wrong?" I asked innocently.

"Be quiet," Dad whispered. "There's a police car after us."

"Why?" I asked.

"We were speeding," he answered frankly.

About that time a spot light lit up the car, its beam circling around the back wall of our garage, producing a strange dancing silhouette of our Olds sedan on the wall.

"Be still!" Dad said.

Soon the light went away, but we stayed there on the front seat for a few minutes, and Dad explained what had happened. He said he'd been racing on the streets, and the policemen don't like that. You'd have to pay a fine if you got caught, and we almost got caught. I began to get scared, but Dad calmed me down.

Dad turned the fiasco into a good lesson for me. He told me that several things could be learned from this. First, you should only drive fast on the drag strip, where it is allowed. Never drive fast on the streets. Second, we were just lucky this time. Someone could have gotten hurt or the police could have given us a big fine to pay. And third (and this seemed to be the most important point, because he repeated it several times), if something like this happens, you are not supposed to tell Mom!

I kept this secret for over forty years, telling the story at Mom and Dad's 50th wedding anniversary on March 15, 1997. Everybody got a big kick out of it, and Mom laughed the loudest of all.

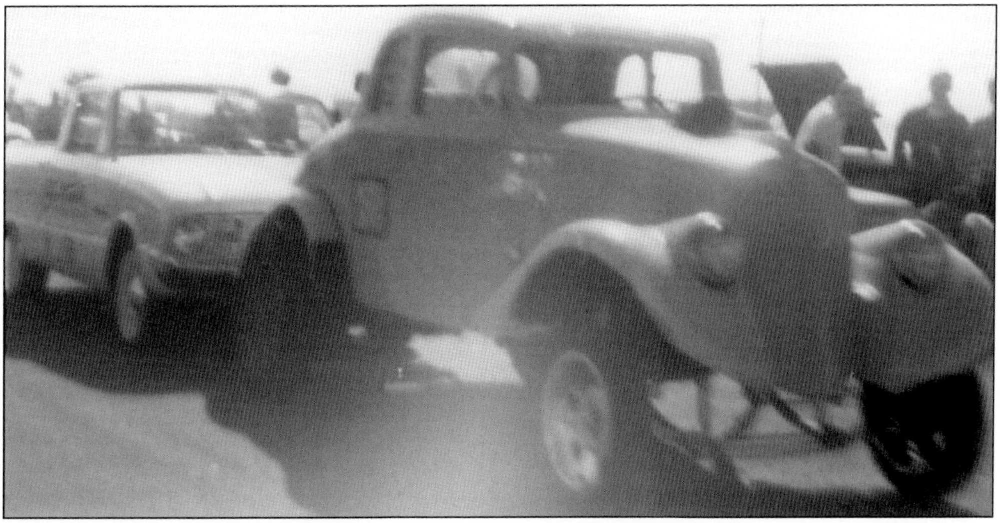

The '33 Willys AA/GS car of Dayton's "Ohio" George Montgomery was nearly unbeatable at the Nationals. This was the final version of the car with a Ford SOHC Hemi engine replacing the Chevy engine. The following year the Willys would be retired in favor of a new Mustang-bodied car. Note the Ford Falcon Ranchero tow car won at the '60 Nationals. (Hobbs collection, 1967.)

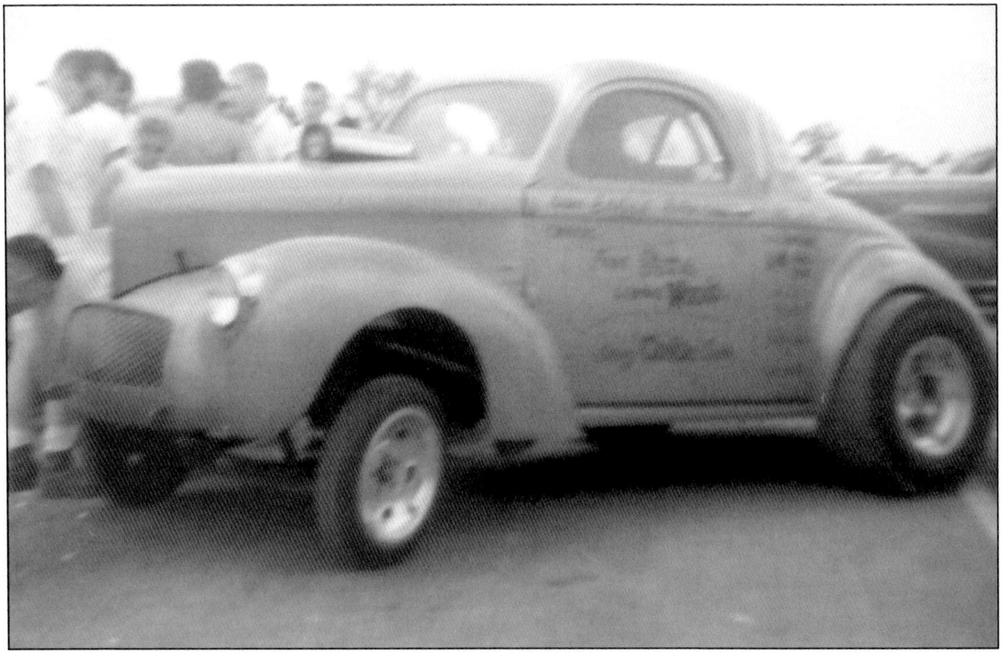
The awesome Stone, Woods and Cook '41 Willys AA/GS coupe from California had switched from Olds to Chrysler engines by the middle of the decade. Cook and Montgomery ran some memorable races at Indy in the '60s. (Hobbs collection, 1967.)

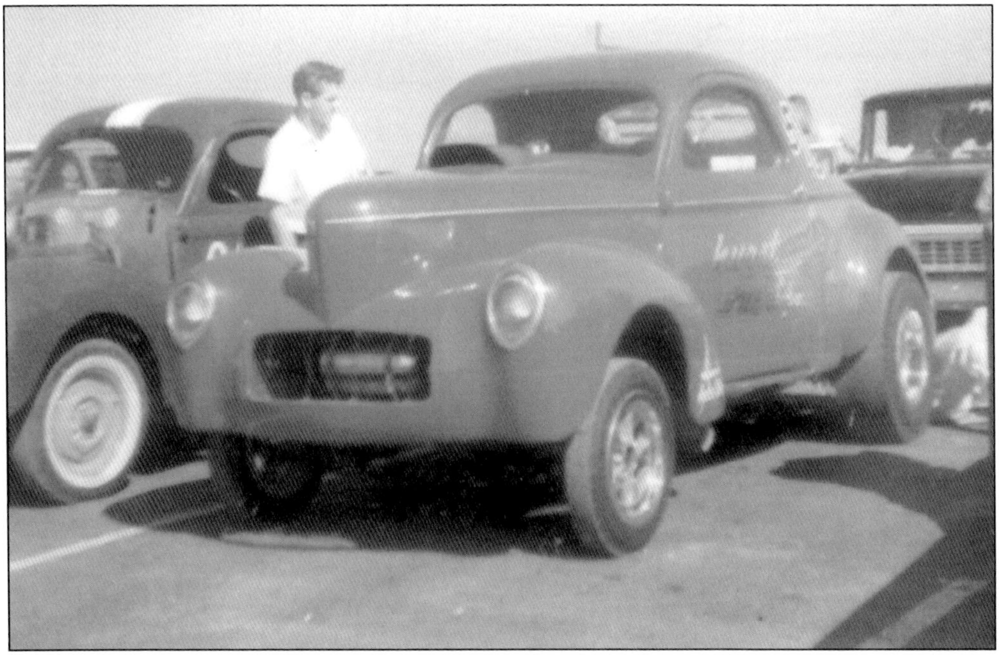
Fred Hurst of Dayton ran this beautiful candy red '41 Willys A/Gasser with an injected Chrysler Hemi engine. Ohio was famous in the '60s for these gas coupes. (Hobbs collection, mid 1960s.)

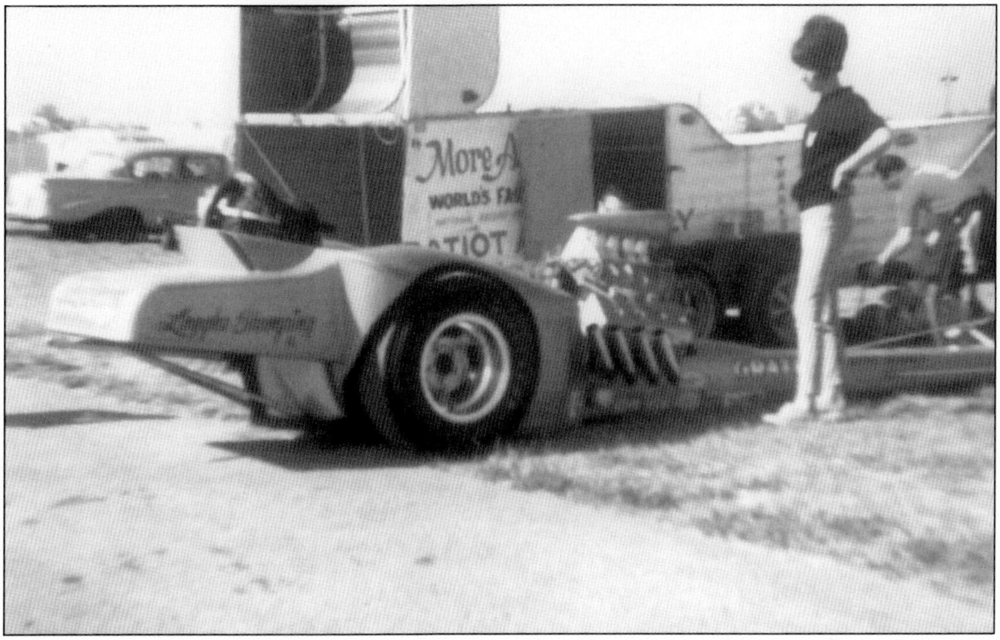

Al Bergler's "More Aggravation" AA/Comp out of Detroit was one of the most beautiful cars we had seen. His enclosed trailer was one of the first in the Midwest. (Hobbs collection, *c.* 1967.)

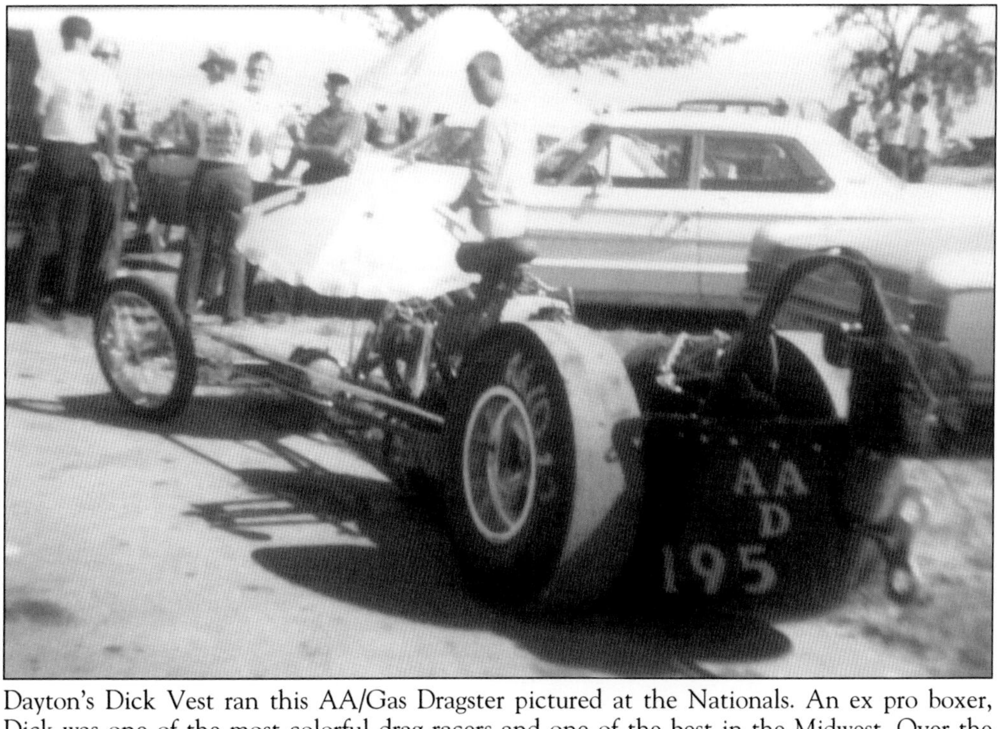

Dayton's Dick Vest ran this AA/Gas Dragster pictured at the Nationals. An ex pro boxer, Dick was one of the most colorful drag racers and one of the best in the Midwest. Over the years, Dick's cars were driven by both himself and Bob Erfman. Note the wind-up key push bar. (Hobbs collection, mid '60s.)

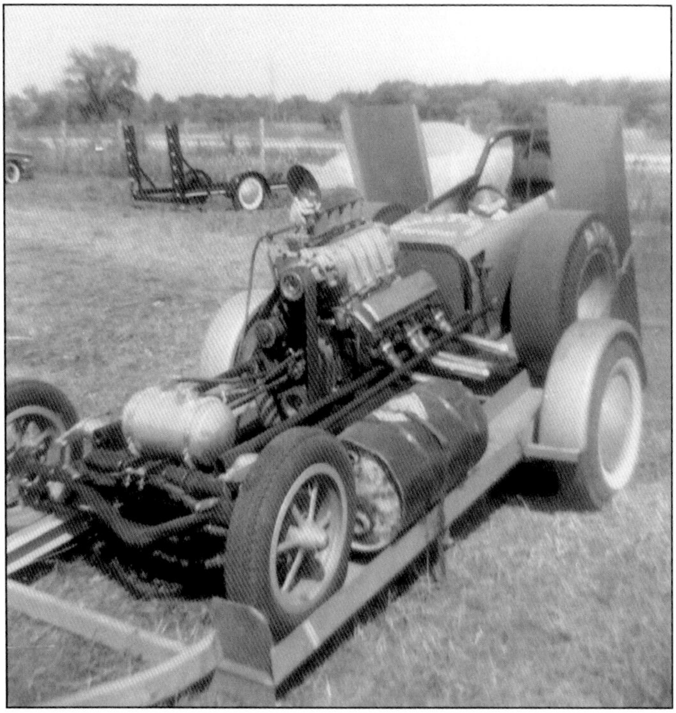

Left: The supercharged Olds powered Bob Erfman and Larry Miller AA/Gas Dragster from Dayton was driven by Erfman. A seasoned and talented driver, Bob later drove for Dick Vest. The single axle open trailers were typical of the day. (Roberson collection, 1960.)

Below: Jim Gouro's "Tweedy Bird" B/Street Roadster from Austin, Texas, was a strong runner at the '58 Nationals with its '50 Cadillac engine. Note that it still has its fenders and taillights. Rules for these cars were similar to those of the gas coupes and sedan classes for closed cars. (Palmer collection, 1958.)

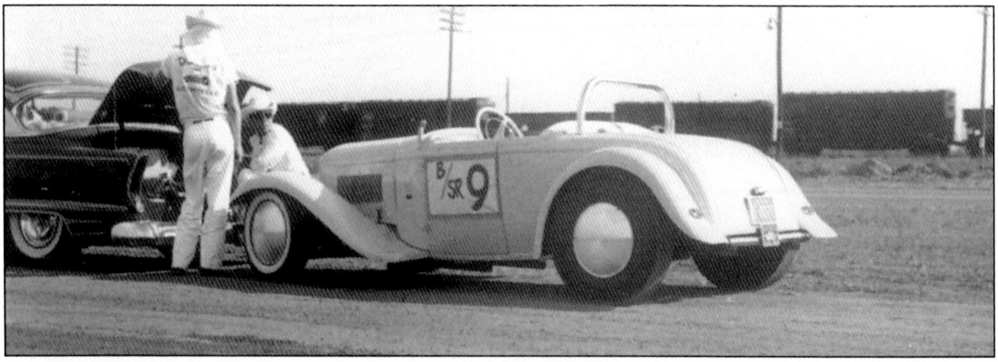

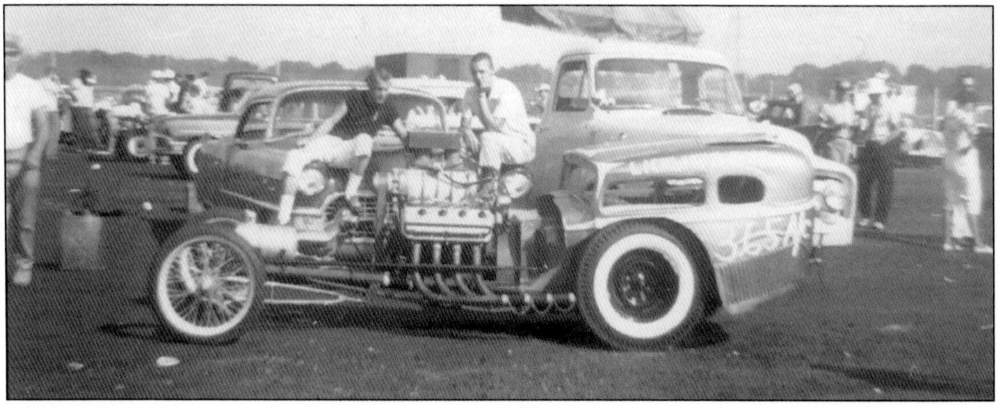

Above: The Lickliter Brothers of Virginia won Middle Eliminator at the '60 Nationals in this A/Competition Coupe with a supercharged Chrysler Hemi engine. (Roberson collection, 1960.)

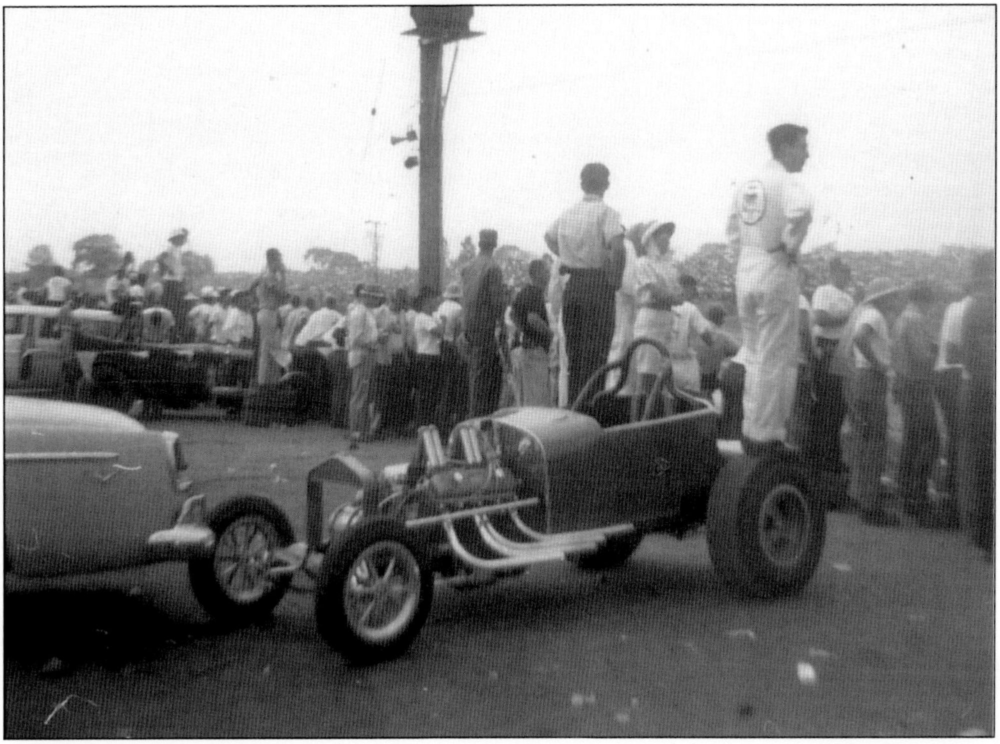

C.J. Kearney of Louisiana won the Best Appearing Car award for his 461 Olds-powered A/ Roadster at the 1960 Nationals. (Roberson collection, 1960.)

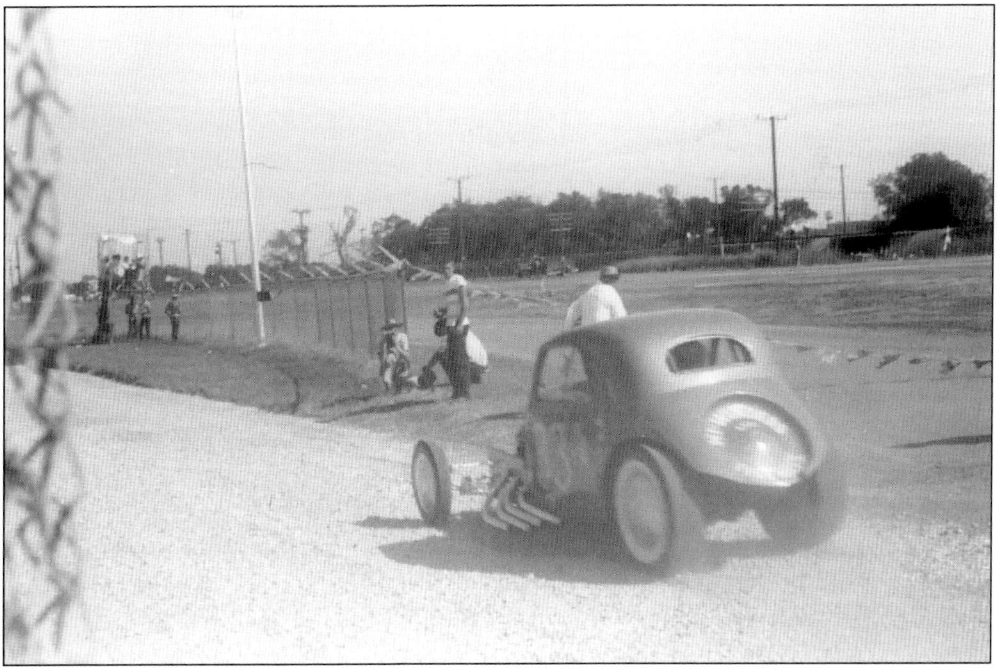

This neat little Fiat bodied altered coupe was entered at the '58 Nationals by the Hi Winders club, and it is typical of the closed altered coupes of the era. (Palmer collection, 1958)

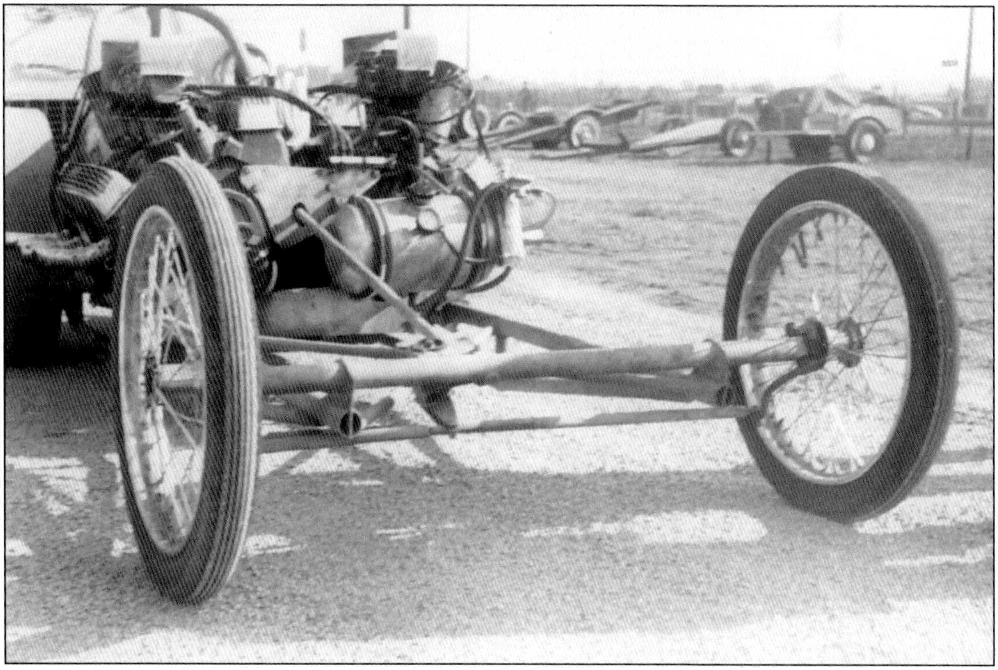

This is the famous "Howard Cams Twin Bear" twin engine car from California at the '58 Nationals, where it was driven by Glen Ward. The car was later driven by California Drag Racing legend Jack Chrisman. (Palmer collection, 1958.)

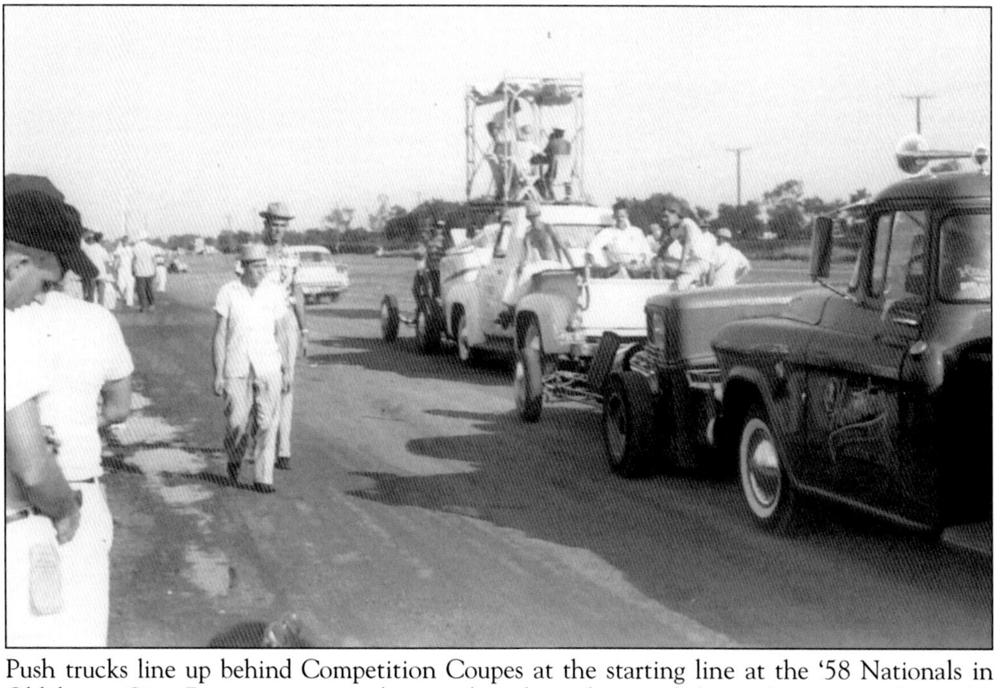

Push trucks line up behind Competition Coupes at the starting line at the '58 Nationals in Oklahoma City. Dragsters were push started in those days, and the push-start ritual was the part of the show. Note the primitive starting line tower and lack of grand stands. (Palmer collection, 1958.)

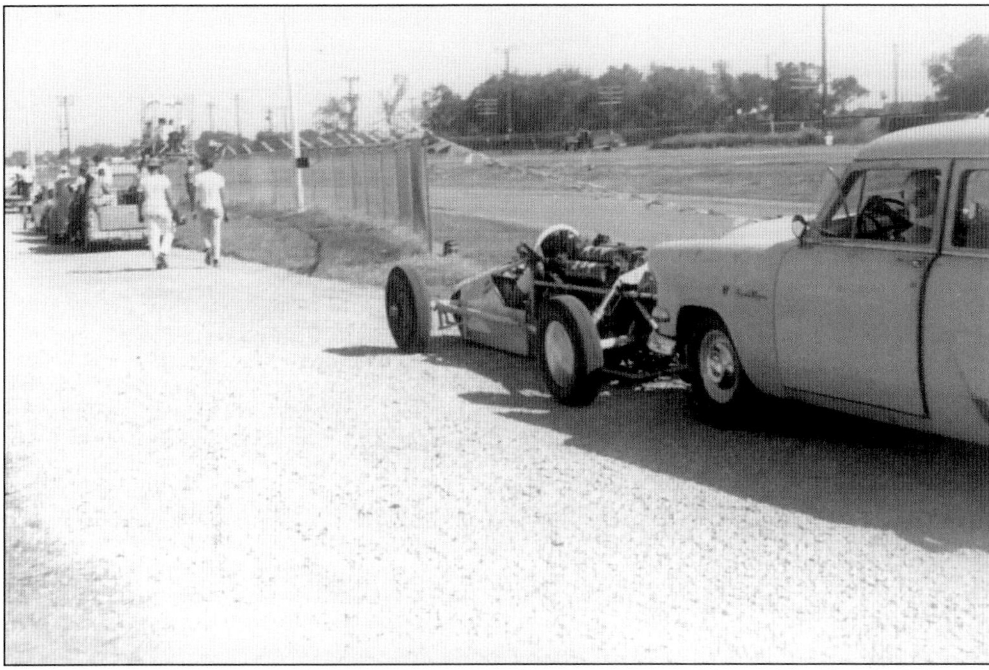

Bob Tennant of Akron ran the "Lone Ranger" A/Dragster powered by a 771 cubic inch Ranger aircraft engine. The 2,100 pound car featured four-wheel drive and was one of several "Green Monster" clones that ran out of the Cam Jammers club. (Palmer collection, 1958.)

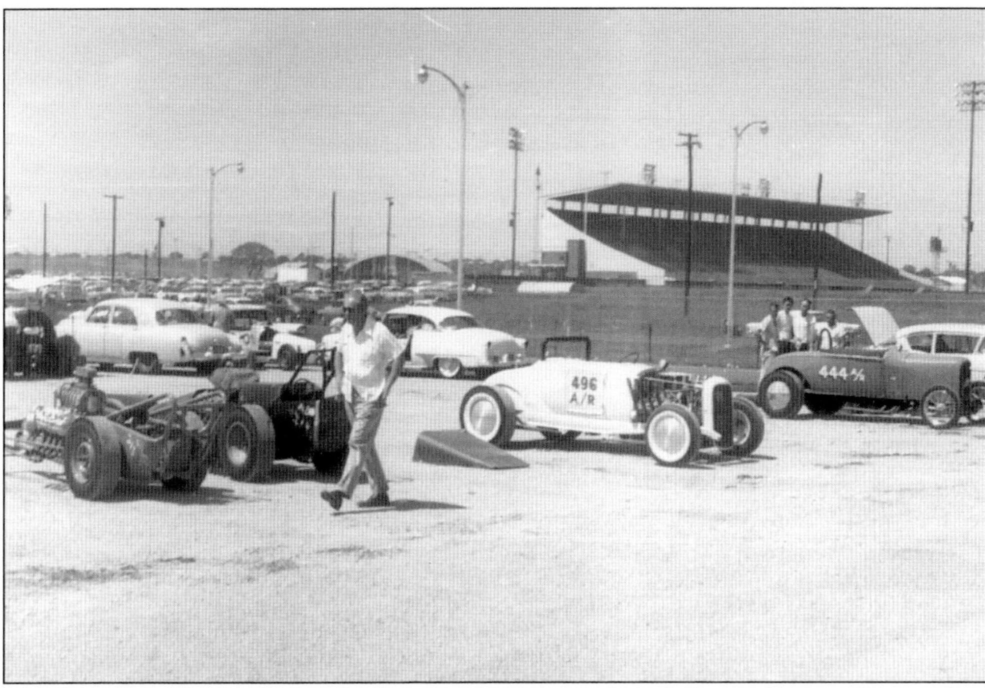

These two open-bodied A/Roadsters at the '58 Nationals still show a heavy influence from the Dry Lakes/Bonneville salt racers of the era. The supercharged dragster at the extreme left belonged to Ted Cyr, who won the event in his older No. 2 car. (Palmer collection, 1958.)

The Pacemaker Roster

The Middletown Pacemakers Hot Rod Club started in 1951 with about two dozen members and ended in 1966 with a similar number. At its peak in the mid '50s the club had about 130 members. A complete list of club members over the 15-year span does not exist, however the list below was compiled in 1994 by Ray Palmer in preparation for the club's first reunion. There is no doubt that some names are missing, and I will gladly add them to a later edition if the missing names are provided. The names appear alphabetically as follows:

Harold Agee
Danny Allen
Bill Angle
Boyd Baker
Earnie Barnes
Harold Barnes
Kenneth Bassford
Dick Beckett
Steve Bennet
Tom Bishop
Dave Booker
Alex Bors
Ray Boyce
Kenneth Bracken
John Buehl
Bill Burton
Luther Colliver
Bob Coughlin
Jack Craft
Herb Dome
Heber "Snip" Dreher
Hoppy Dyas
D.O. Fisher
Dale Foreman
Al Frebis
Tom Frebis
Willard Gill
Sonny Goodman
Waldo Gray
Ron Hackney
Richard Hagin
Kenny Hall
Jack Harrison
Paul Higgleford
Jack Hill
Darryl Hobbs
Paul Hoover
Don Hoskins
Marion Hounshell
George Howard
Bob Hunt
Bob Jay
Don Klamo
Bob Kuhn
Carl Lakes
Cotton Lakes
Winford Lawson
Ballard Long
Bob Long
Robert "Corky" Long
Bill Lovelace
Bob Lykins
Carl Macey
Fred May
Jack McClanahan
Bob McCutchen
Lee McGee
L.G. "Larry" Mead
Harold "Mike" Michael
Kenneth Miller
Dick Miltenberger
Jim Murphy
Jim Neely
Phil Norris
Jack Oaks
Jack Ousley
Ray Palmer Sr.
Ray Palmer Jr.
Jess Patrick
Joe Patrick
Clarence Pence
Gordon Pence
Elliot Perkins
David Rader
Fred Randel
Ron Roberson (Honorary)
Wilbur "Robbie" Roberson
Robert Rossman
Charles Rouster
Jerry Schneider
Paul Scorti
Herb Sebastian
Bill Shockey
Don Scaggs
Alex Slamka
Don Stagge
Jack Stamper
Robert Staton
Bob Styles
Damon "Sully" Sullivan
Tommy Sullivan
Tug Swain
Dave "Skip" Swisher
Jim Tincher Sr.
Jim Tincher
Gene Wells
Jerry Williams
Paul Wilson (Honorary)
Robert Yauch